KAIJUMAX
SEASON THREE
KING of the MONSTAS

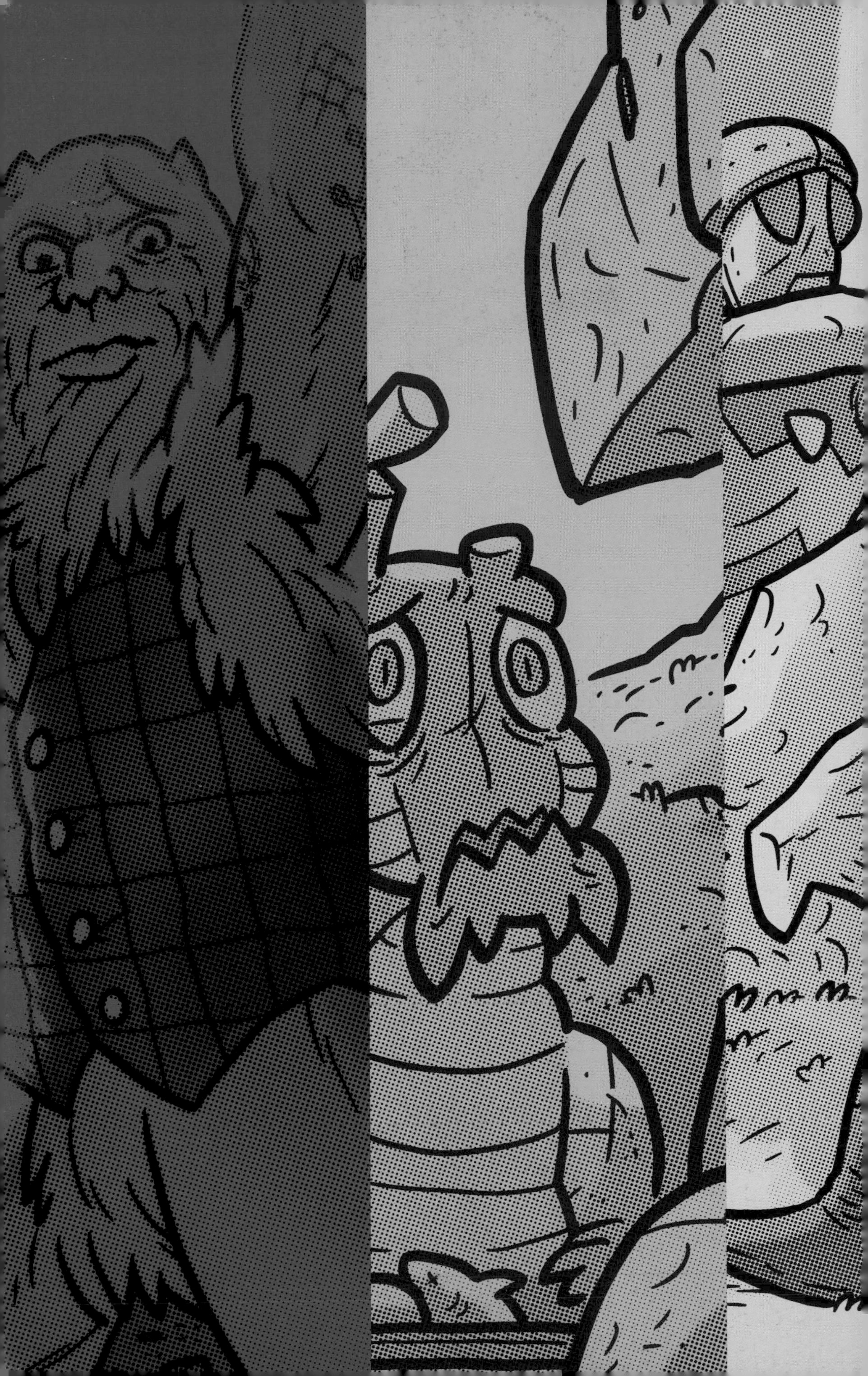

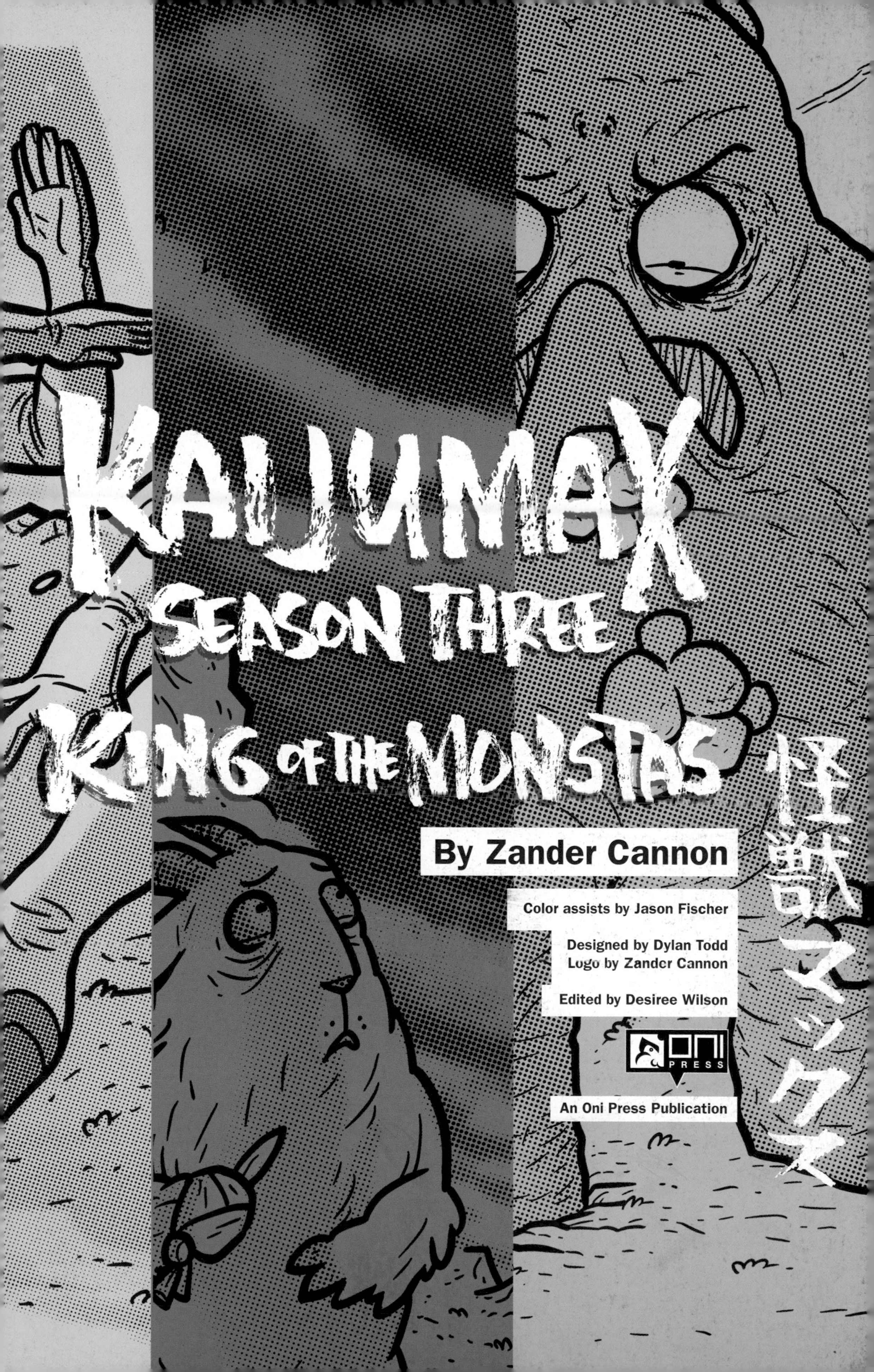

KAIJUMAX
SEASON THREE
KING OF THE MONSTAS

怪獣マックス

By Zander Cannon

Color assists by Jason Fischer

Designed by Dylan Todd
Logo by Zander Cannon

Edited by Desiree Wilson

ONI PRESS

An Oni Press Publication

ON A REMOTE ISLAND IN THE SOUTH PACIFIC LIES KAIJUMAX,

the infamous prison for the world's most terrible monsters. Fiercely divided into gangs, the inmates do their time in a world of shifting alliances, dark moral compromise, and flame breath.

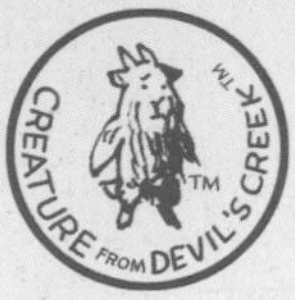
CREATURE FROM DEVIL'S CREEK™
™

The Creature from Devil's Creek has found himself in the unenviable position of being low mon in the Cryptid Brotherhood hierarchy, and he has begun looking desperately for anything to change his fortune.

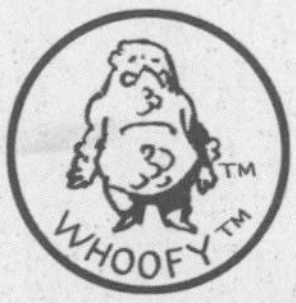
WHOOFY™
™

As the prison emerges from a month-long lockdown after Electrogor and The Green Humongo's well-publicized escape, the J-Pop gang of Japanese kaiju adjusts to a new leader, Whoofy, the woefully unprepared son of legendary monster Ape-Whale.

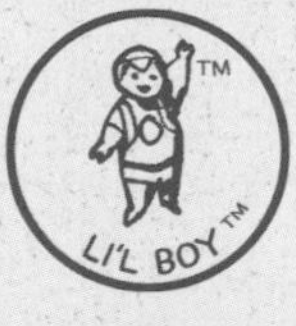
LI'L BOY™
™

Whoofy's sinister consiglieri, the mysterious Li'l Boy, has been whispering advice in his ear all along, but to what end?

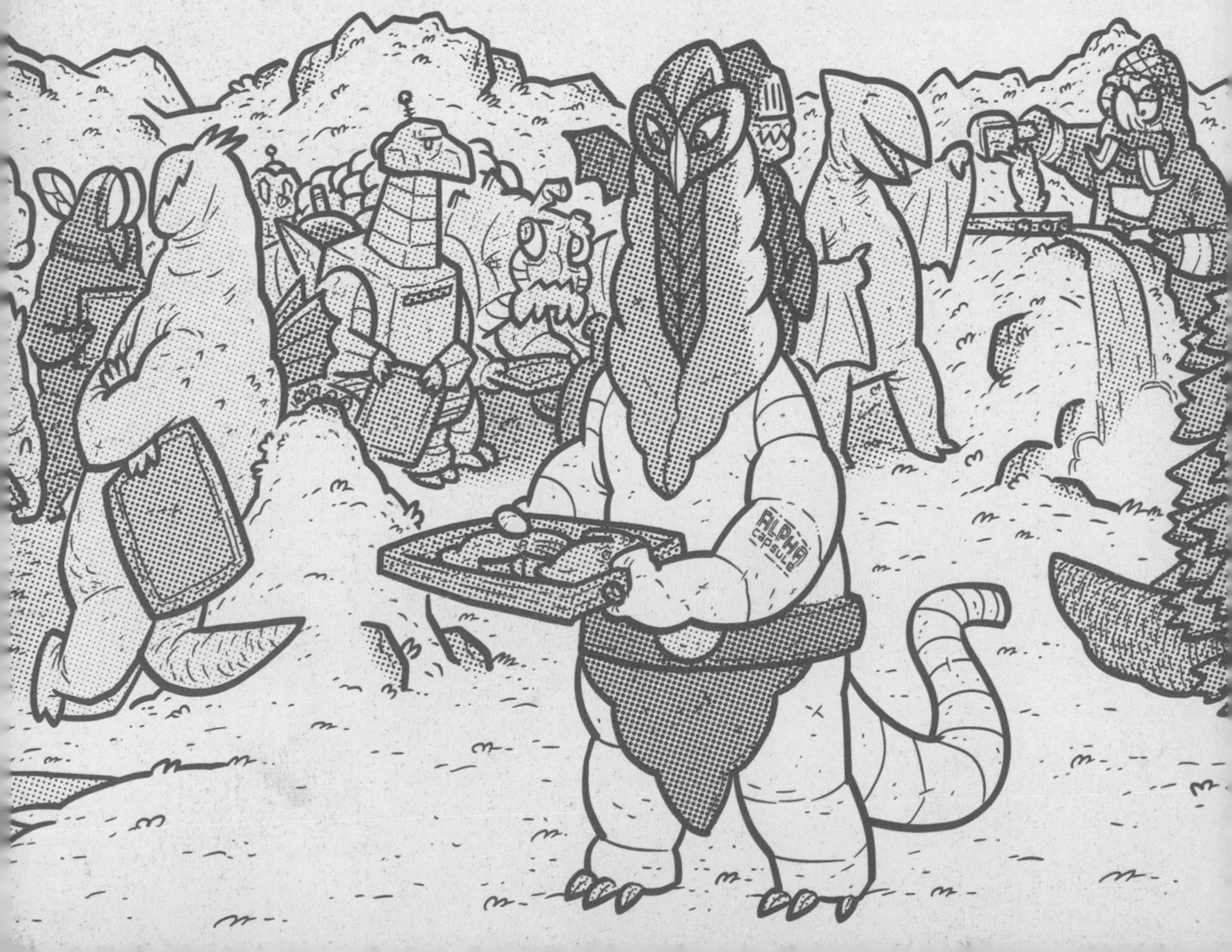
ALPHA capsule

EPISODE 1

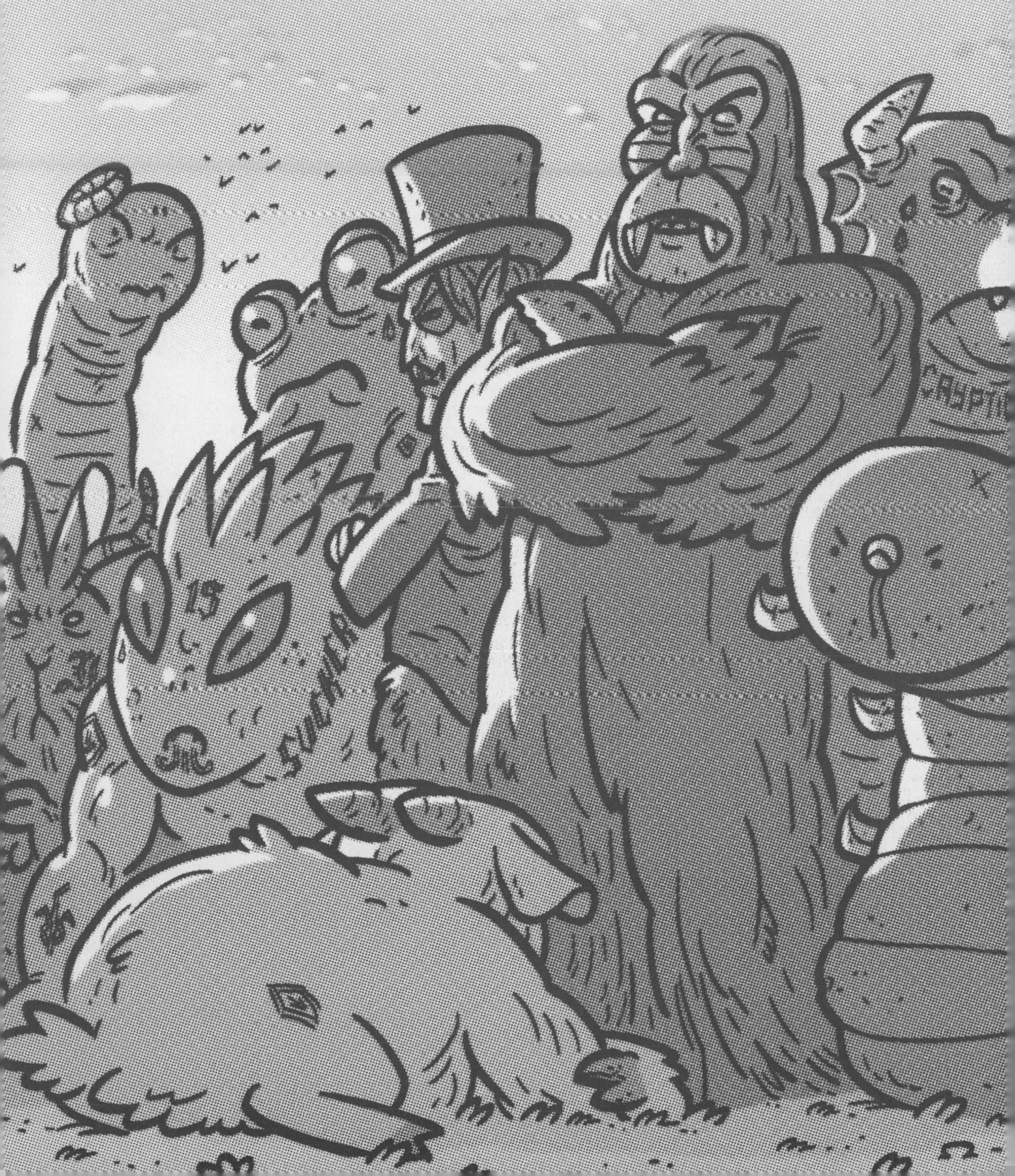

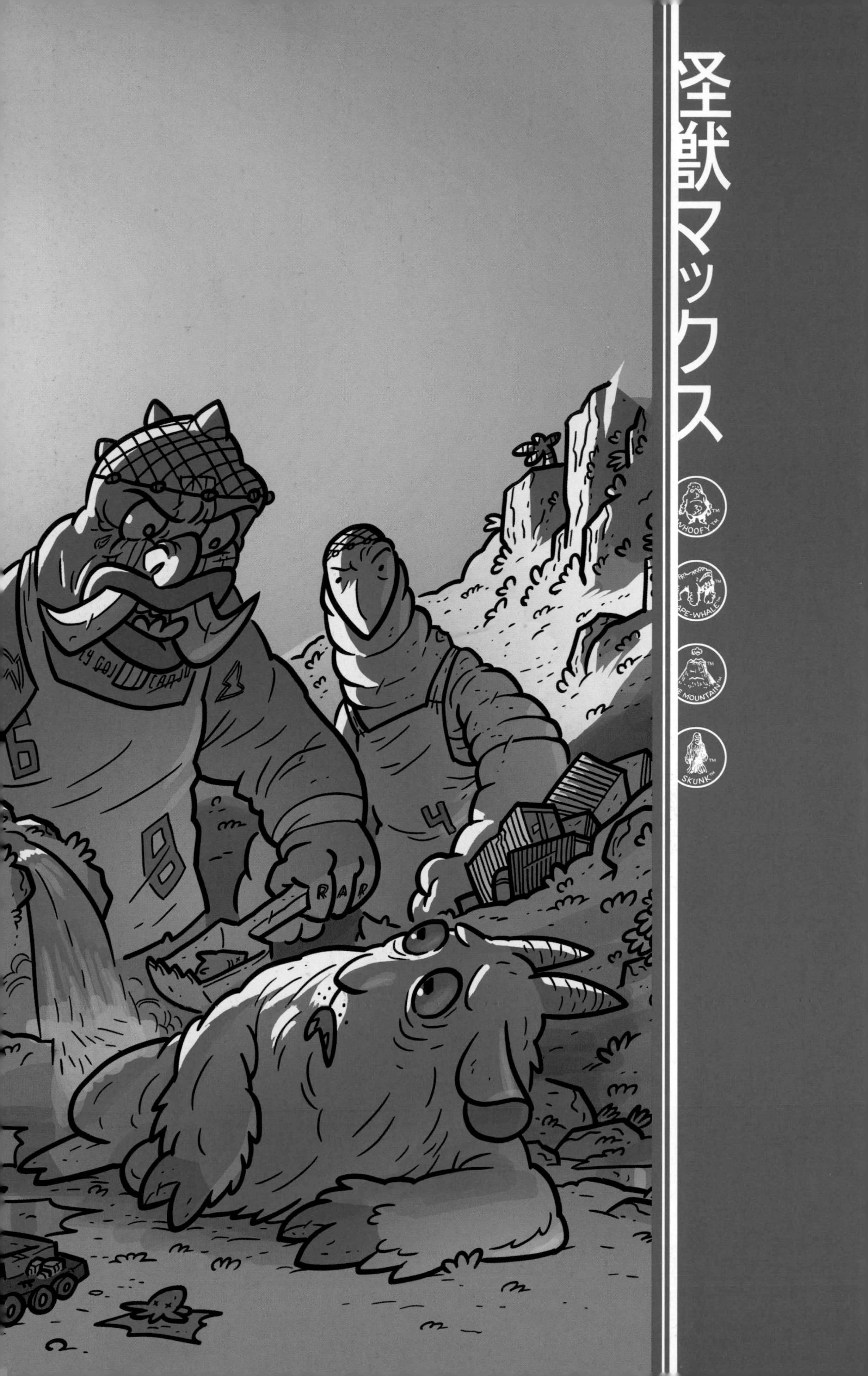
怪獣マックス
WHOOFY™
APE-WHALE™
MOUNTAIN™
SKUNK™
RAR

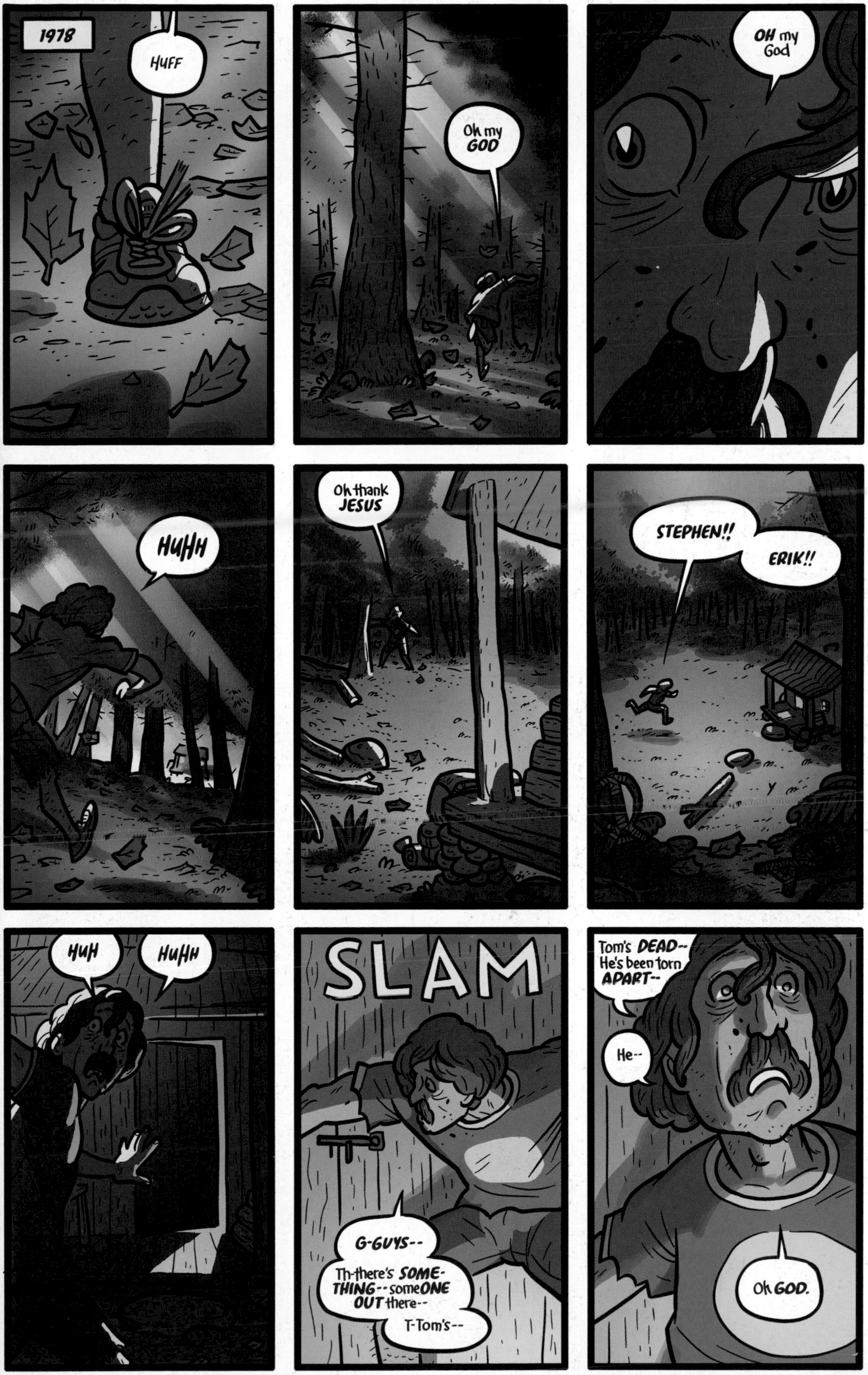

1978
HUFF
Oh my GOD
OH my God
HUHH
Oh thank JESUS
STEPHEN!!
ERIK!!
HUH
HUHH
SLAM
G-GUYS--
Th-there's SOME-THING--someONE OUT there--
T-Tom's--
Tom's DEAD--He's been torn APART--
He--
Oh GOD.

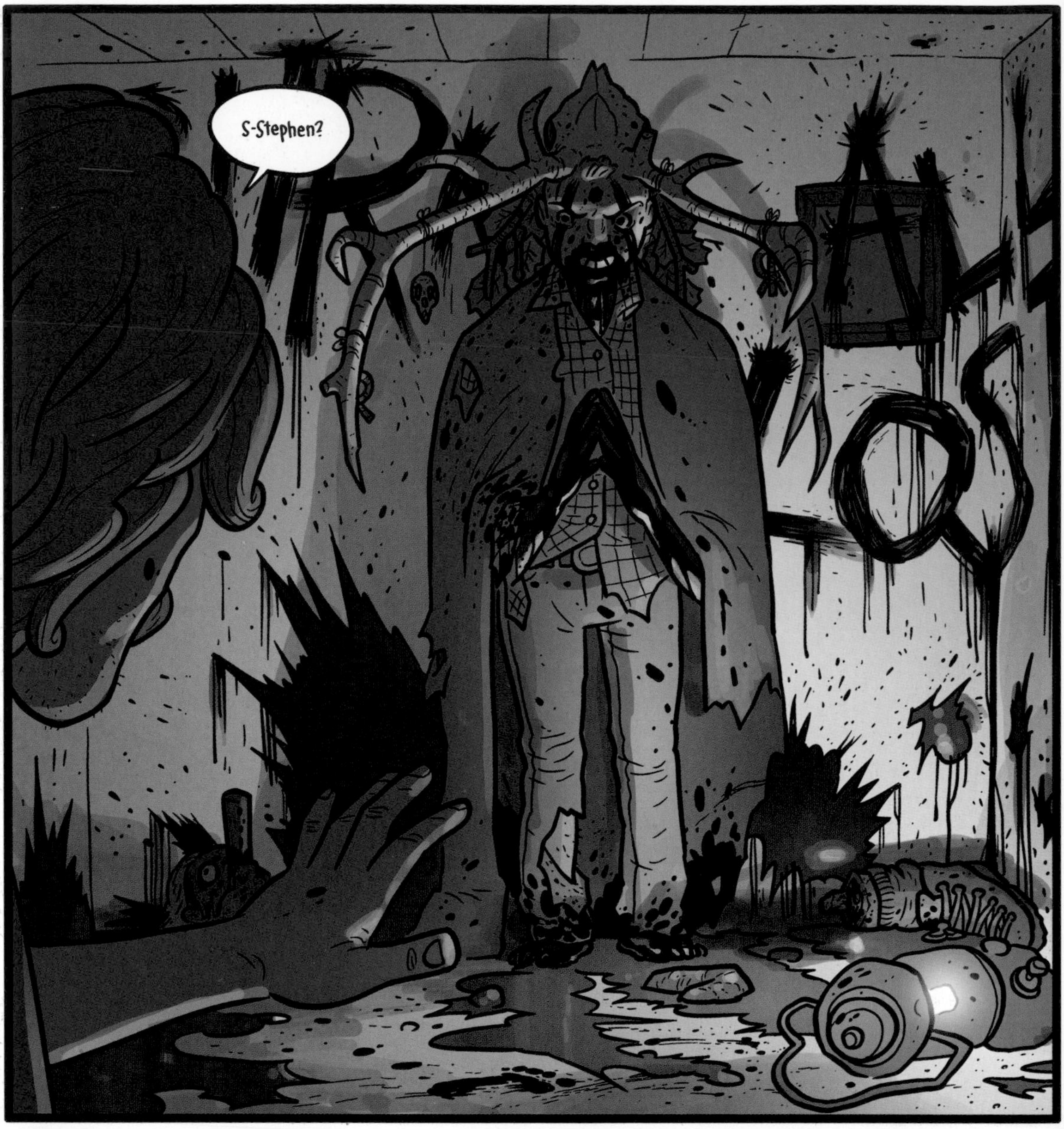
S-Stephen?

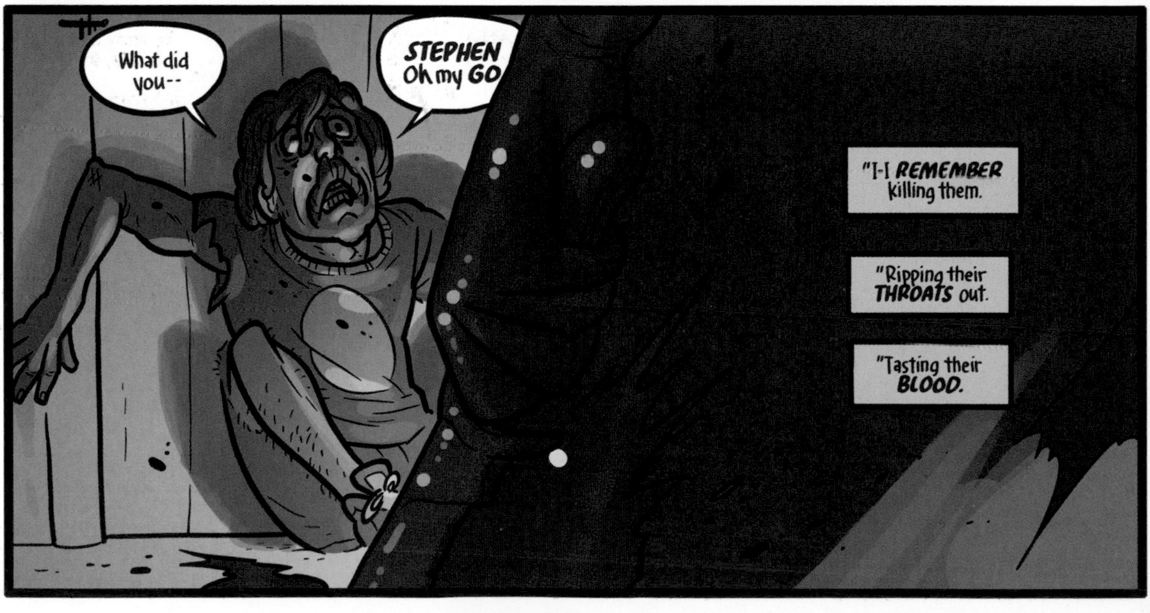
What did you--
STEPHEN Oh my GO
"I-I REMEMBER killing them.
"Ripping their THROATS out.
"Tasting their BLOOD.

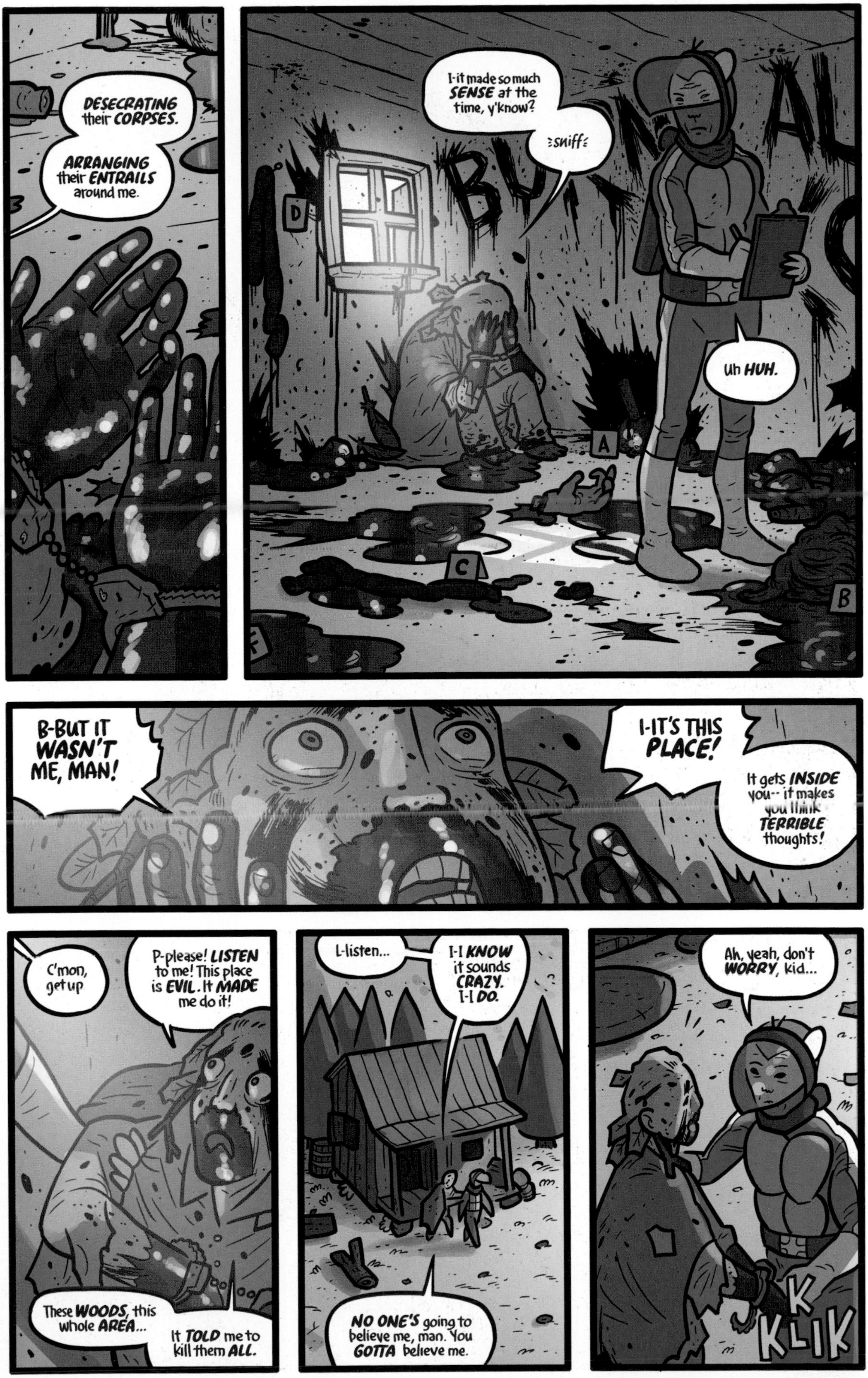
DESECRATING their CORPSES.
ARRANGING their ENTRAILS around me.
I-it made so much SENSE at the time, y'know?
sniff
Uh HUH.
B-BUT IT WASN'T ME, MAN!
I-IT'S THIS PLACE!
It gets INSIDE you-- it makes you think TERRIBLE thoughts!
C'mon, get up
P-please! LISTEN to me! This place is EVIL. It MADE me do it!
These WOODS, this whole AREA...
It TOLD me to kill them ALL.
L-listen...
I-I KNOW it sounds CRAZY. I-I DO.
NO ONE'S going to believe me, man. You GOTTA believe me.
Ah, yeah, don't WORRY, kid...
K KLIK

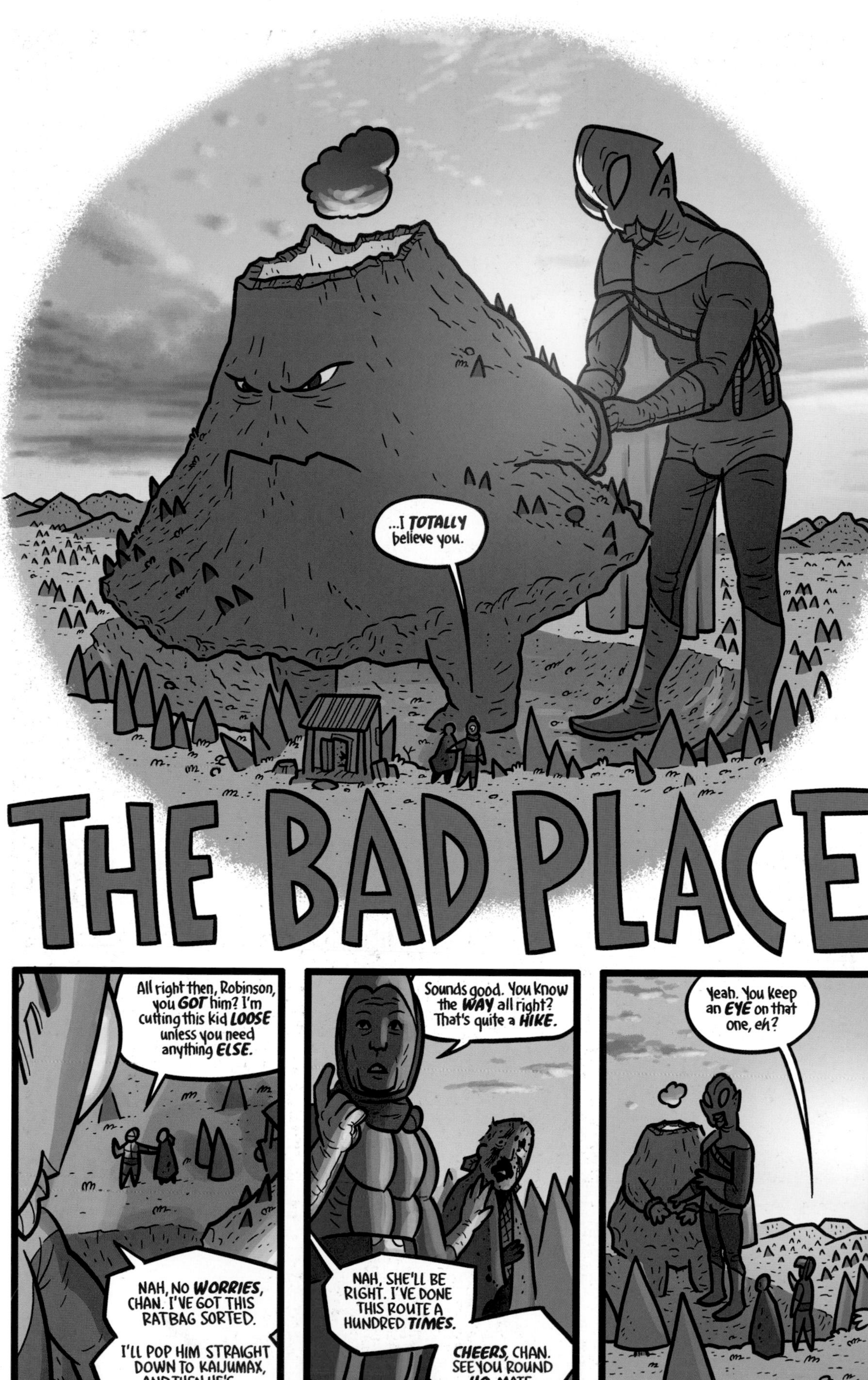
...I TOTALLY believe you.
THE BAD PLACE
All right then, Robinson, you GOT him? I'm cutting this kid LOOSE unless you need anything ELSE.
NAH, NO WORRIES, CHAN. I'VE GOT THIS RATBAG SORTED.
I'LL POP HIM STRAIGHT DOWN TO KAIJUMAX, AND THEN HE'S KIM'S PROBLEM.
Sounds good. You know the WAY all right? That's quite a HIKE.
NAH, SHE'LL BE RIGHT. I'VE DONE THIS ROUTE A HUNDRED TIMES.
CHEERS, CHAN. SEE YOU ROUND HQ, MATE.
Yeah. You keep an EYE on that one, eh?

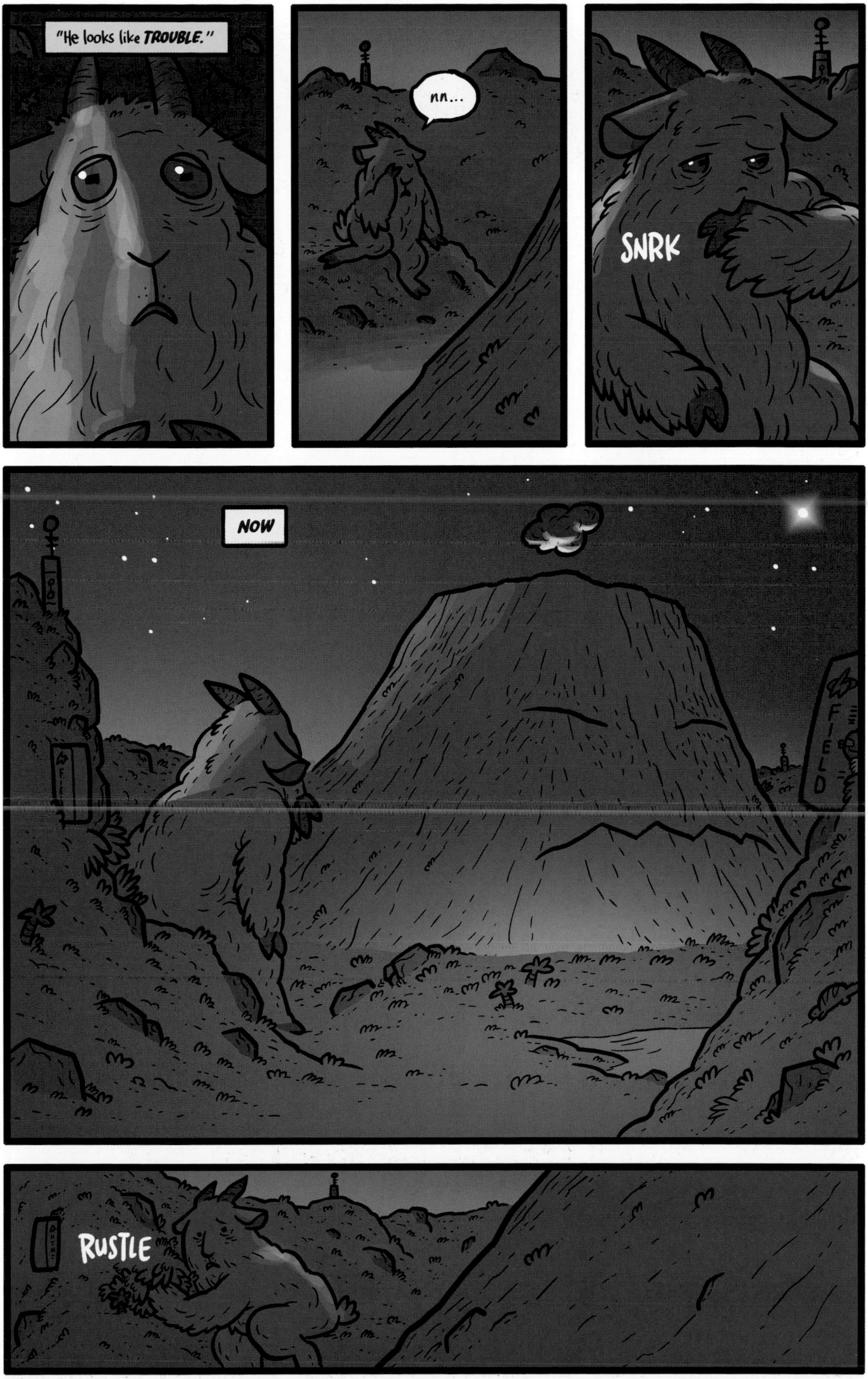
"He looks like TROUBLE."
nn...
SNRK
NOW
FIELD
RUSTLE

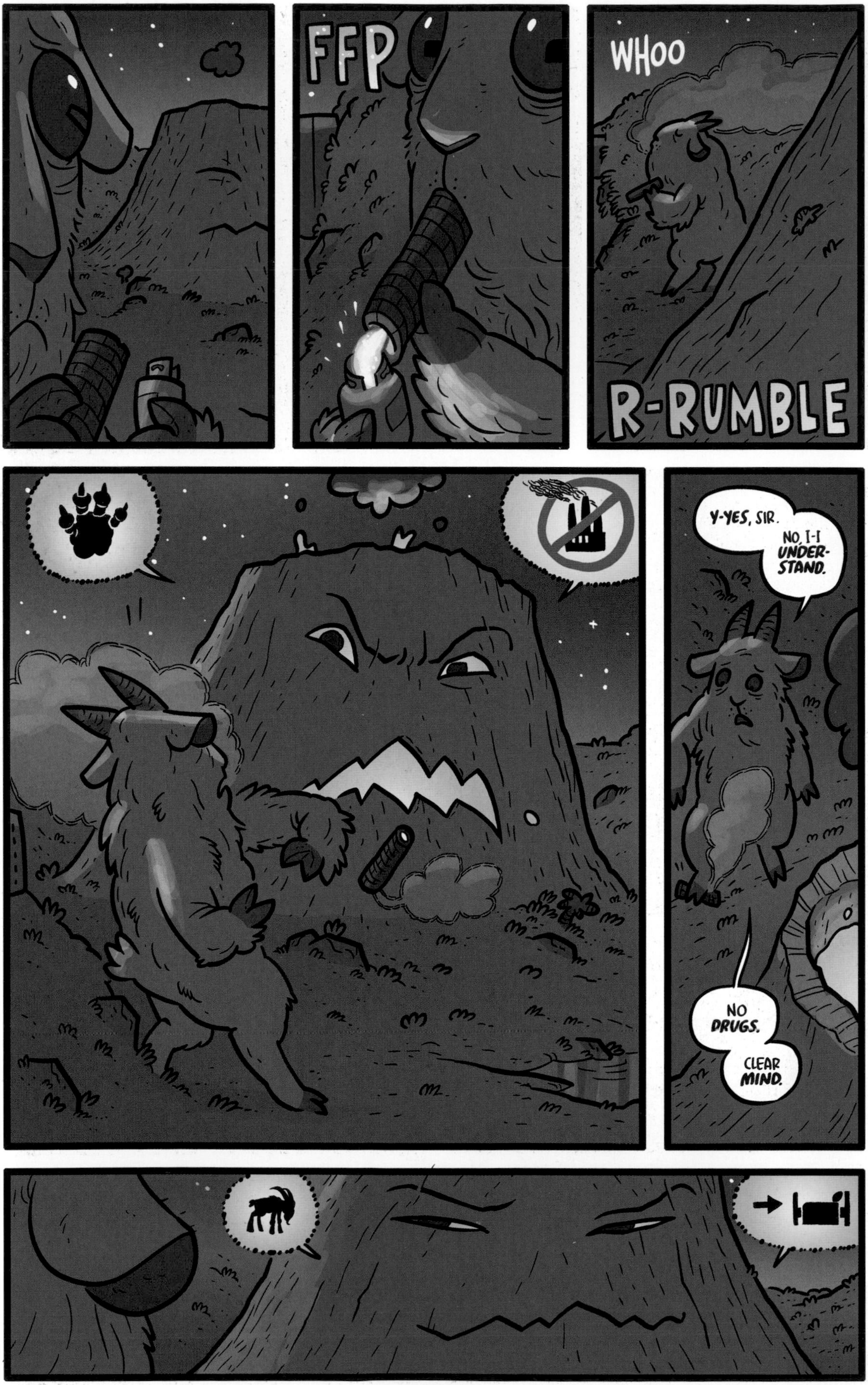
FFP
WHOO
R-RUMBLE
Y-YES, SIR.
NO, I-I UNDERSTAND.
NO DRUGS.
CLEAR MIND.

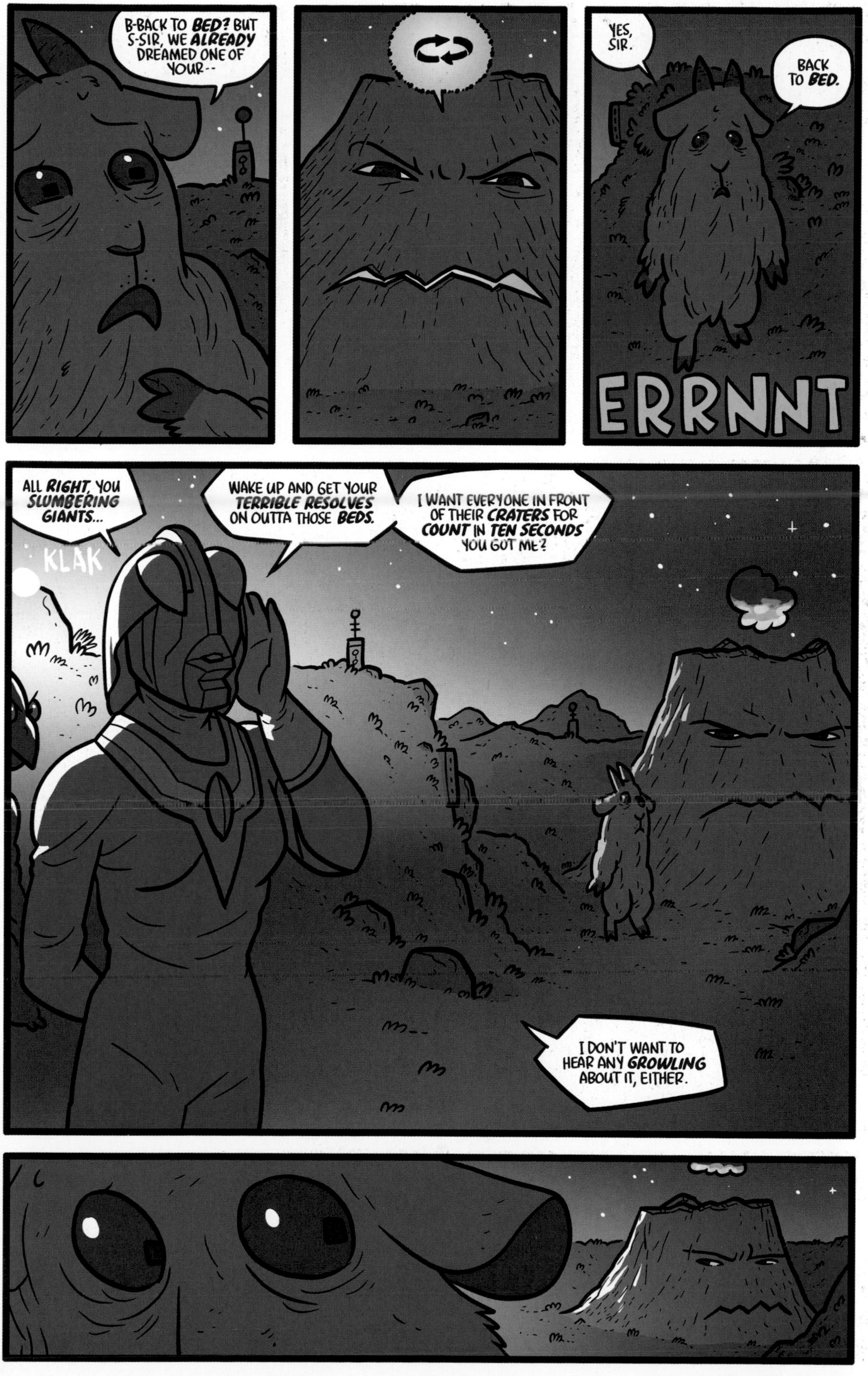
B-BACK TO BED? BUT S-SIR, WE ALREADY DREAMED ONE OF YOUR--
YES, SIR.
BACK TO BED.
ERRNNT
ALL RIGHT, YOU SLUMBERING GIANTS...
KLAK
WAKE UP AND GET YOUR TERRIBLE RESOLVES ON OUTTA THOSE BEDS.
I WANT EVERYONE IN FRONT OF THEIR CRATERS FOR COUNT IN TEN SECONDS YOU GOT ME?
I DON'T WANT TO HEAR ANY GROWLING ABOUT IT, EITHER.

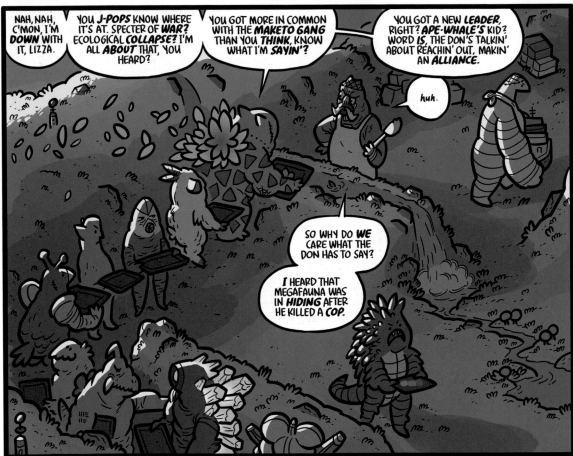

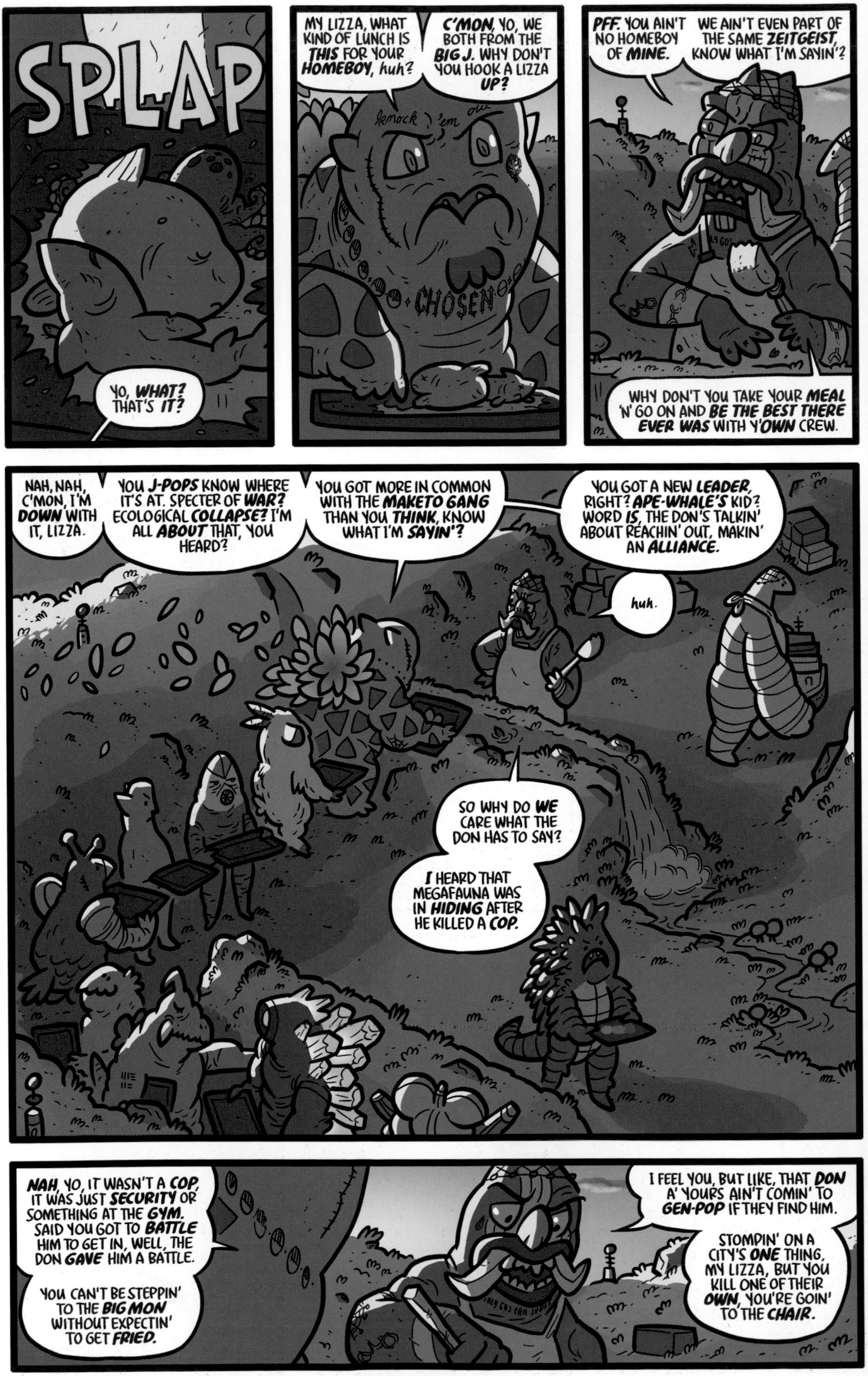

SPLAP

YO, **WHAT?** THAT'S **IT?**

MY LIZZA, WHAT KIND OF LUNCH IS **THIS** FOR YOUR **HOMEBOY**, HUH?

C'MON, YO, WE BOTH FROM THE **BIG J.** WHY DON'T YOU HOOK A LIZZA **UP?**

CHOSEN

PFF. YOU AIN'T NO HOMEBOY OF **MINE.**

WE AIN'T EVEN PART OF THE SAME **ZEITGEIST,** KNOW WHAT I'M SAYIN'?

WHY DON'T YOU TAKE YOUR **MEAL** 'N' GO ON AND **BE THE BEST THERE EVER WAS** WITH Y'**OWN** CREW.

NAH, NAH, C'MON, I'M **DOWN** WITH IT, LIZZA.

YOU **J-POPS** KNOW WHERE IT'S AT. SPECTER OF **WAR?** ECOLOGICAL **COLLAPSE?** I'M ALL **ABOUT** THAT, YOU **HEARD?**

YOU GOT MORE IN COMMON WITH THE **MAKETO** GANG THAN YOU **THINK,** KNOW WHAT I'M **SAYIN'?**

YOU GOT A NEW **LEADER,** RIGHT? **APE-WHALE'S** KID? WORD **IS,** THE DON'S TALKIN' ABOUT REACHIN' OUT, MAKIN' AN **ALLIANCE.**

HUH.

SO WHY DO **WE** CARE WHAT THE DON HAS TO SAY?

I HEARD THAT MEGAFAUNA WAS IN **HIDING** AFTER HE KILLED A **COP.**

NAH, YO, IT WASN'T A **COP,** IT WAS JUST **SECURITY** OR SOMETHING AT THE **GYM.** SAID YOU GOT TO **BATTLE** HIM TO GET IN, WELL, THE DON **GAVE** HIM A BATTLE.

YOU CAN'T BE STEPPIN' TO THE **BIG MON** WITHOUT EXPECTIN' TO GET **FRIED.**

I FEEL YOU, BUT LIKE, THAT **DON** A' YOURS AIN'T COMIN' TO **GEN-POP** IF THEY FIND HIM.

STOMPIN' ON A CITY'S **ONE** THING, MY LIZZA, BUT YOU KILL ONE OF THEIR **OWN,** YOU'RE GOIN' TO THE **CHAIR.**

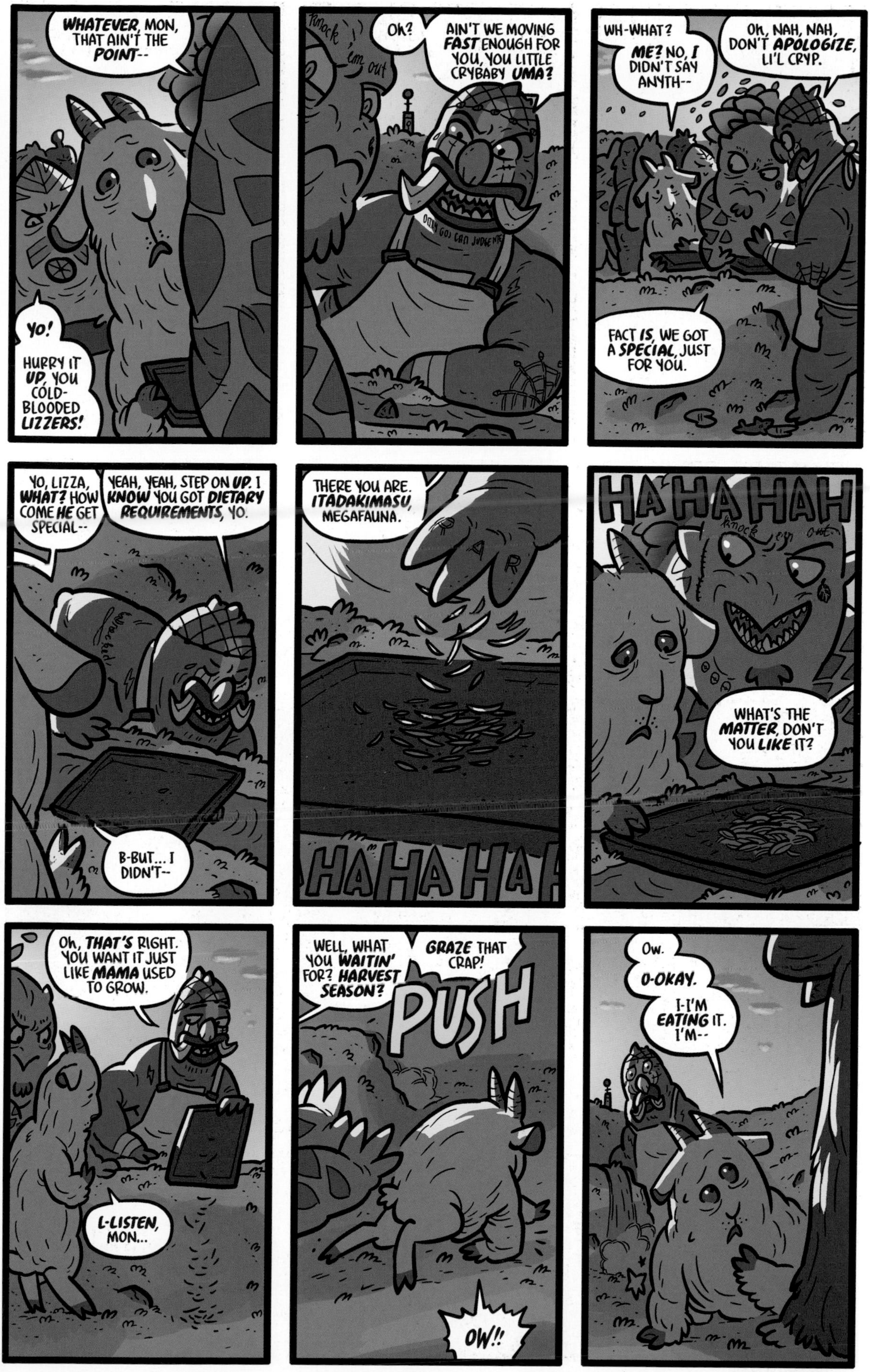
WHATEVER, MON, THAT AIN'T THE POINT--
YO!
HURRY IT UP, YOU COLD-BLOODED LIZZERS!
Oh?
AIN'T WE MOVING FAST ENOUGH FOR YOU, YOU LITTLE CRYBABY UMA?
WH-WHAT?
ME? NO, I DIDN'T SAY ANYTH--
Oh, NAH, NAH, DON'T APOLOGIZE, LI'L CRYP.
FACT IS, WE GOT A SPECIAL, JUST FOR YOU.
YO, LIZZA, WHAT? HOW COME HE GET SPECIAL--
YEAH, YEAH, STEP ON UP. I KNOW YOU GOT DIETARY REQUIREMENTS, YO.
B-BUT... I DIDN'T--
THERE YOU ARE. ITADAKIMASU, MEGAFAUNA.
HAHAHAH
HAHAHAH
WHAT'S THE MATTER, DON'T YOU LIKE IT?
Oh, THAT'S RIGHT. YOU WANT IT JUST LIKE MAMA USED TO GROW.
L-LISTEN, MON...
WELL, WHAT YOU WAITIN' FOR? HARVEST SEASON?
GRAZE THAT CRAP!
PUSH
OW!!
Ow.
O-OKAY.
I-I'M EATING IT. I'M--

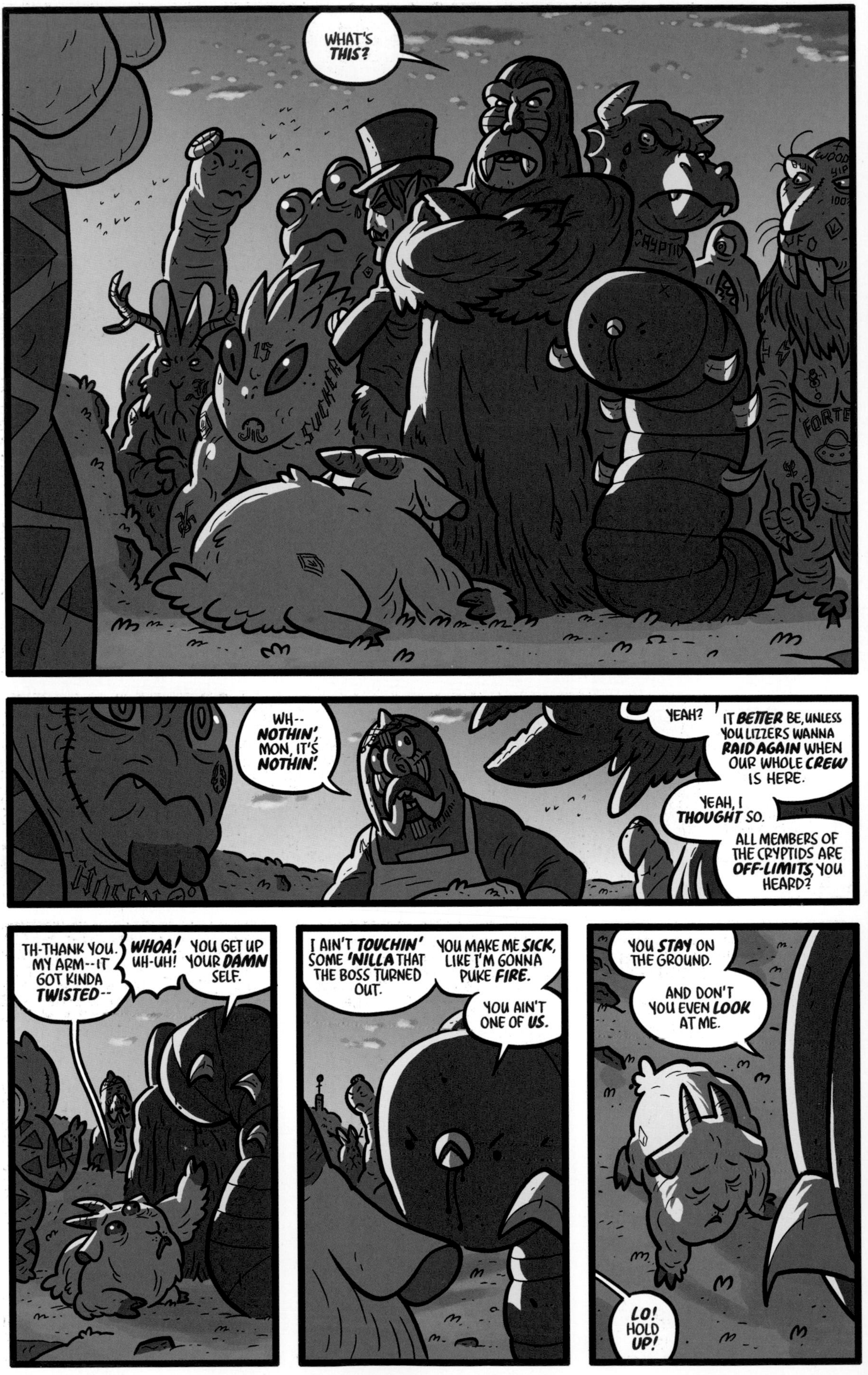

WHAT'S THIS?
WH-- NOTHIN', MON, IT'S NOTHIN'.
YEAH?
IT BETTER BE, UNLESS YOU LIZZERS WANNA RAID AGAIN WHEN OUR WHOLE CREW IS HERE.
YEAH, I THOUGHT SO.
ALL MEMBERS OF THE CRYPTIDS ARE OFF-LIMITS, YOU HEARD?
TH-THANK YOU. MY ARM--IT GOT KINDA TWISTED--
WHOA! UH-UH!
YOU GET UP YOUR DAMN SELF.
I AIN'T TOUCHIN' SOME 'NILLA THAT THE BOSS TURNED OUT.
YOU MAKE ME SICK, LIKE I'M GONNA PUKE FIRE.
YOU AIN'T ONE OF US.
YOU STAY ON THE GROUND.
AND DON'T YOU EVEN LOOK AT ME.
LO! HOLD UP!

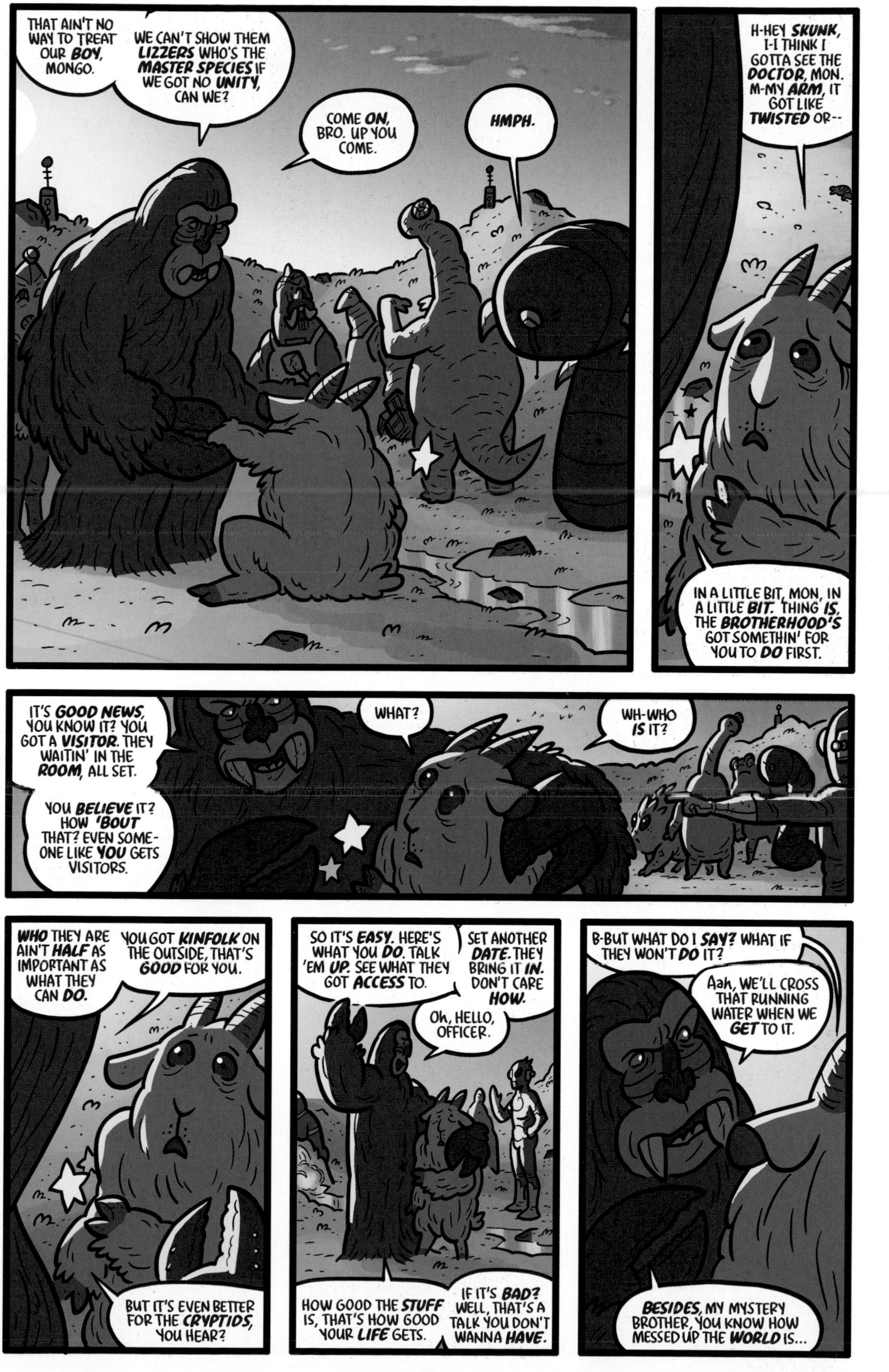
THAT AIN'T NO WAY TO TREAT OUR BOY, MONGO.
WE CAN'T SHOW THEM LIZZERS WHO'S THE MASTER SPECIES IF WE GOT NO UNITY, CAN WE?
COME ON, BRO. UP YOU COME.
HMPH.
H-HEY SKUNK, I-I THINK I GOTTA SEE THE DOCTOR, MON. M-MY ARM, IT GOT LIKE TWISTED OR--
IN A LITTLE BIT, MON, IN A LITTLE BIT. THING IS, THE BROTHERHOOD'S GOT SOMETHIN' FOR YOU TO DO FIRST.
IT'S GOOD NEWS, YOU KNOW IT? YOU GOT A VISITOR. THEY WAITIN' IN THE ROOM, ALL SET.
YOU BELIEVE IT? HOW 'BOUT THAT? EVEN SOME-ONE LIKE YOU GETS VISITORS.
WHAT?
WH-WHO IS IT?
WHO THEY ARE AIN'T HALF AS IMPORTANT AS WHAT THEY CAN DO.
YOU GOT KINFOLK ON THE OUTSIDE, THAT'S GOOD FOR YOU.
BUT IT'S EVEN BETTER FOR THE CRYPTIDS, YOU HEAR?
SO IT'S EASY. HERE'S WHAT YOU DO. TALK 'EM UP. SEE WHAT THEY GOT ACCESS TO.
SET ANOTHER DATE. THEY BRING IT IN. DON'T CARE HOW.
Oh, HELLO, OFFICER.
HOW GOOD THE STUFF IS, THAT'S HOW GOOD YOUR LIFE GETS.
IF IT'S BAD? WELL, THAT'S A TALK YOU DON'T WANNA HAVE.
B-BUT WHAT DO I SAY? WHAT IF THEY WON'T DO IT?
Aah, WE'LL CROSS THAT RUNNING WATER WHEN WE GET TO IT.
BESIDES, MY MYSTERY BROTHER, YOU KNOW HOW MESSED UP THE WORLD IS...

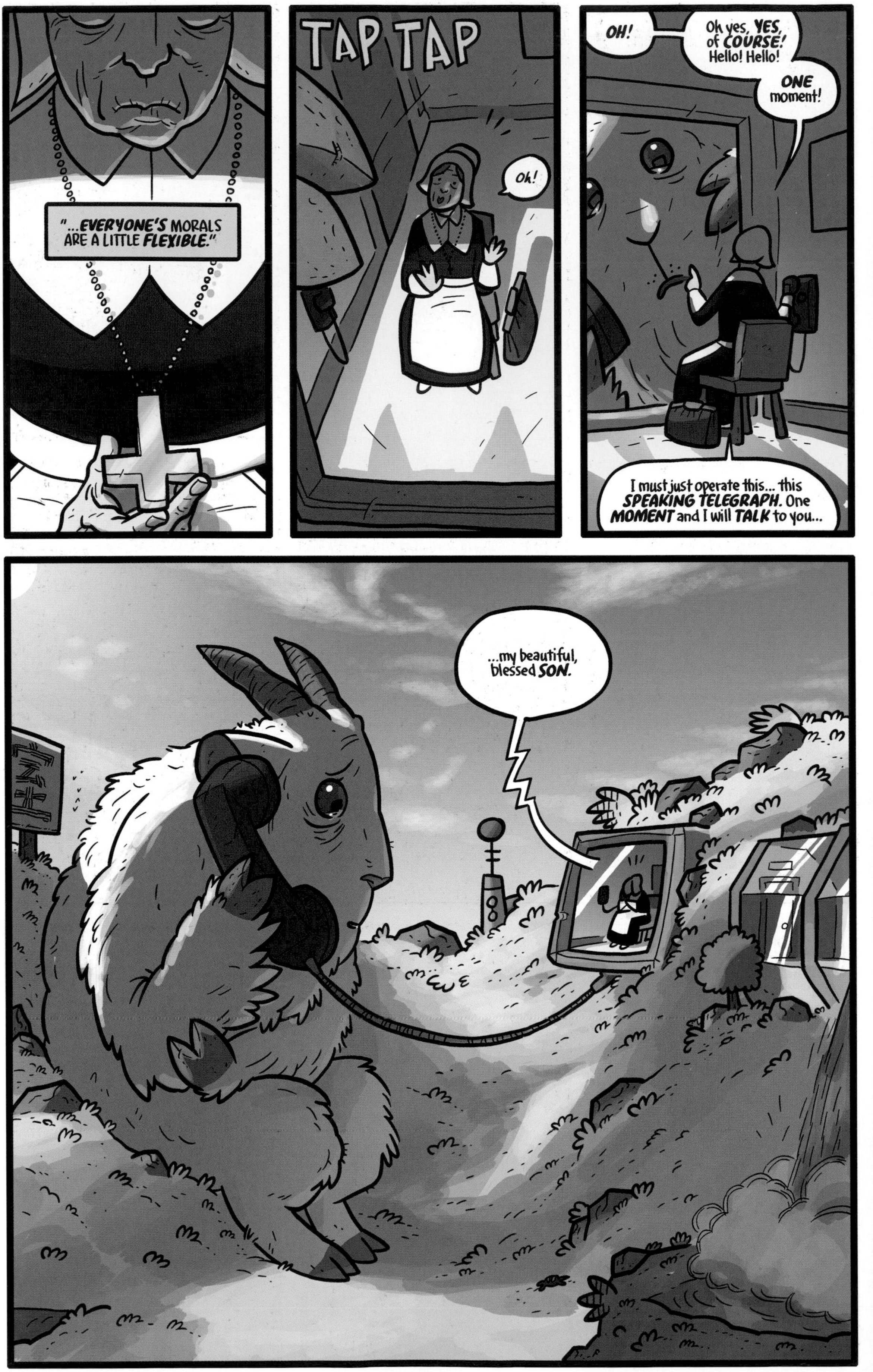
"...EVERYONE'S MORALS ARE A LITTLE FLEXIBLE."
TAP TAP
Oh!
OH!
Oh yes, YES, of COURSE! Hello! Hello!
ONE moment!
I must just operate this... this SPEAKING TELEGRAPH. One MOMENT and I will TALK to you...
...my beautiful, blessed SON.

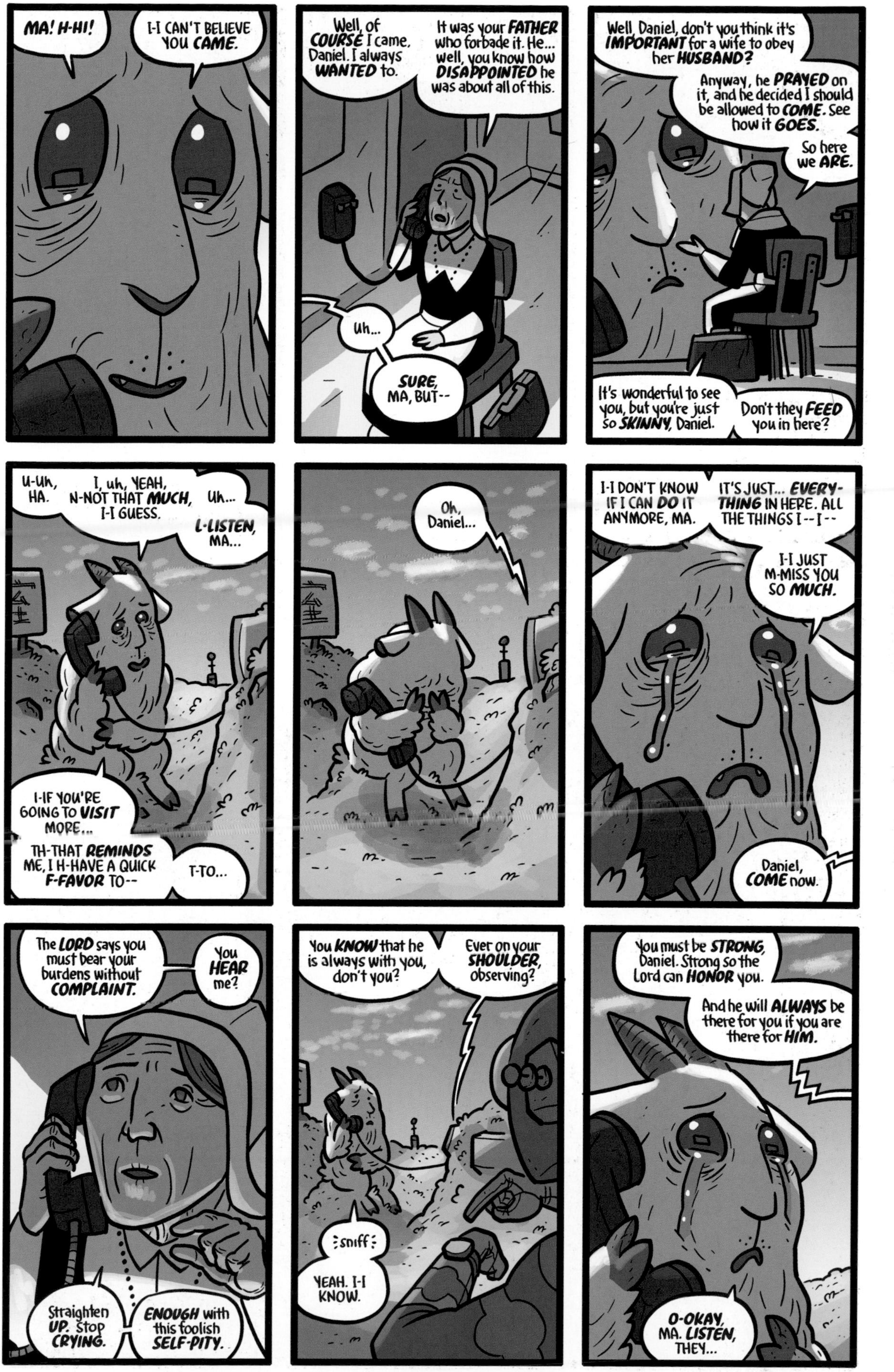
MA! H-HI!
I-I CAN'T BELIEVE YOU CAME.
Well, of COURSE I came, Daniel. I always WANTED to.
It was your FATHER who forbade it. He... well, you know how DISAPPOINTED he was about all of this.
Uh...
SURE, MA, BUT--
Well, Daniel, don't you think it's IMPORTANT for a wife to obey her HUSBAND?
Anyway, he PRAYED on it, and he decided I should be allowed to COME. See how it GOES.
So here we ARE.
It's wonderful to see you, but you're just so SKINNY, Daniel.
Don't they FEED you in here?
U-Uh, HA.
I, uh, YEAH, N-NOT THAT MUCH, I-I GUESS.
Uh...
L-LISTEN, MA...
I-IF YOU'RE GOING TO VISIT MORE...
TH-THAT REMINDS ME, I H-HAVE A QUICK F-FAVOR TO--
T-TO...
Oh, Daniel...
I-I DON'T KNOW IF I CAN DO IT ANYMORE, MA.
IT'S JUST... EVERY-THING IN HERE. ALL THE THINGS I -- I --
I-I JUST M-MISS YOU SO MUCH.
Daniel, COME now.
The LORD says you must bear your burdens without COMPLAINT.
You HEAR me?
Straighten UP. Stop CRYING.
ENOUGH with this foolish SELF-PITY.
You KNOW that he is always with you, don't you?
Ever on your SHOULDER, observing?
sniff
YEAH. I-I KNOW.
You must be STRONG, Daniel. Strong so the Lord can HONOR you.
And he will ALWAYS be there for you if you are there for HIM.
O-OKAY, MA. LISTEN, THEY...

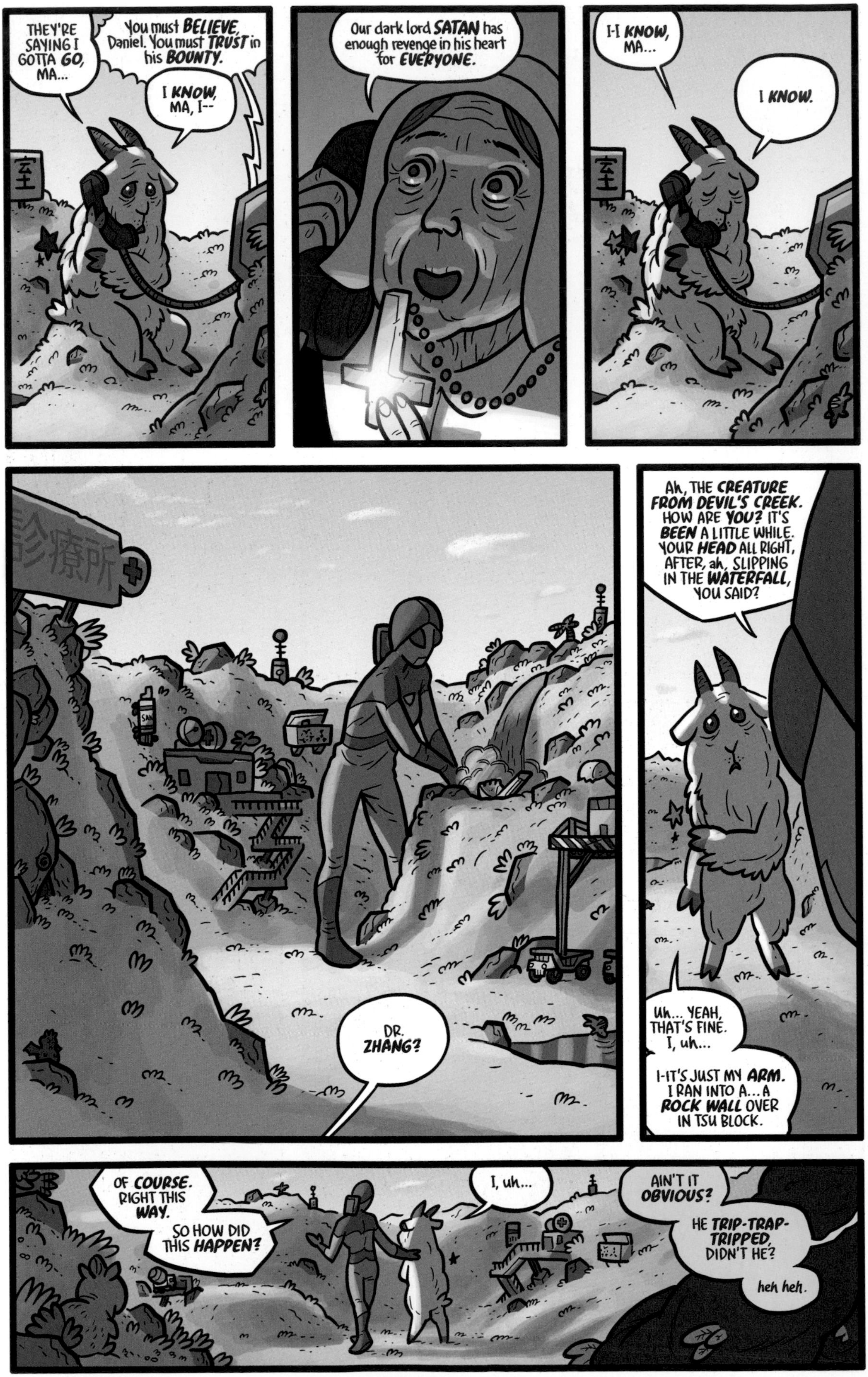
THEY'RE SAYING I GOTTA GO, MA...
You must BELIEVE, Daniel. You must TRUST in his BOUNTY.
I KNOW, MA, I--
Our dark lord SATAN has enough revenge in his heart for EVERYONE.
I-I KNOW, MA...
I KNOW.
診療所
DR. ZHANG?
Ah, THE CREATURE FROM DEVIL'S CREEK. HOW ARE YOU? IT'S BEEN A LITTLE WHILE. YOUR HEAD ALL RIGHT, AFTER, ah, SLIPPING IN THE WATERFALL, YOU SAID?
Uh... YEAH, THAT'S FINE. I, uh...
I-IT'S JUST MY ARM. I RAN INTO A... A ROCK WALL OVER IN TSU BLOCK.
OF COURSE. RIGHT THIS WAY.
SO HOW DID THIS HAPPEN?
I, uh...
AIN'T IT OBVIOUS?
HE TRIP-TRAP-TRIPPED, DIDN'T HE?
heh heh.

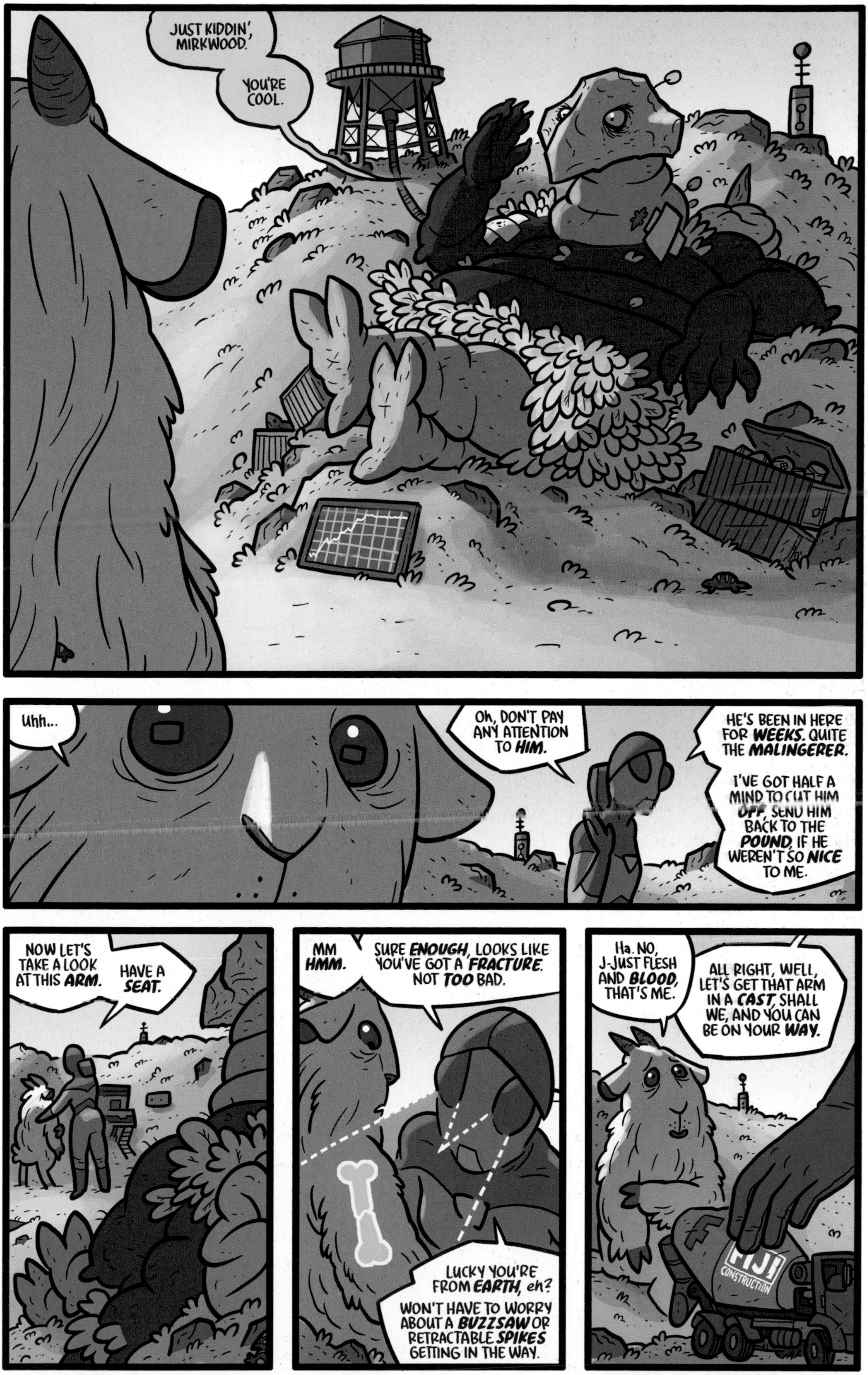
JUST KIDDIN', MIRKWOOD.
YOU'RE COOL.
Uhh...
Oh, DON'T PAY ANY ATTENTION TO HIM.
HE'S BEEN IN HERE FOR WEEKS. QUITE THE MALINGERER.
I'VE GOT HALF A MIND TO CUT HIM OFF, SEND HIM BACK TO THE POUND, IF HE WEREN'T SO NICE TO ME.
NOW LET'S TAKE A LOOK AT THIS ARM.
HAVE A SEAT.
MM HMM.
SURE ENOUGH, LOOKS LIKE YOU'VE GOT A FRACTURE. NOT TOO BAD.
LUCKY YOU'RE FROM EARTH, eh?
WON'T HAVE TO WORRY ABOUT A BUZZSAW OR RETRACTABLE SPIKES GETTING IN THE WAY.
Ha. NO, J-JUST FLESH AND BLOOD, THAT'S ME.
ALL RIGHT, WELL, LET'S GET THAT ARM IN A CAST, SHALL WE, AND YOU CAN BE ON YOUR WAY.
FIJI CONSTRUCTION

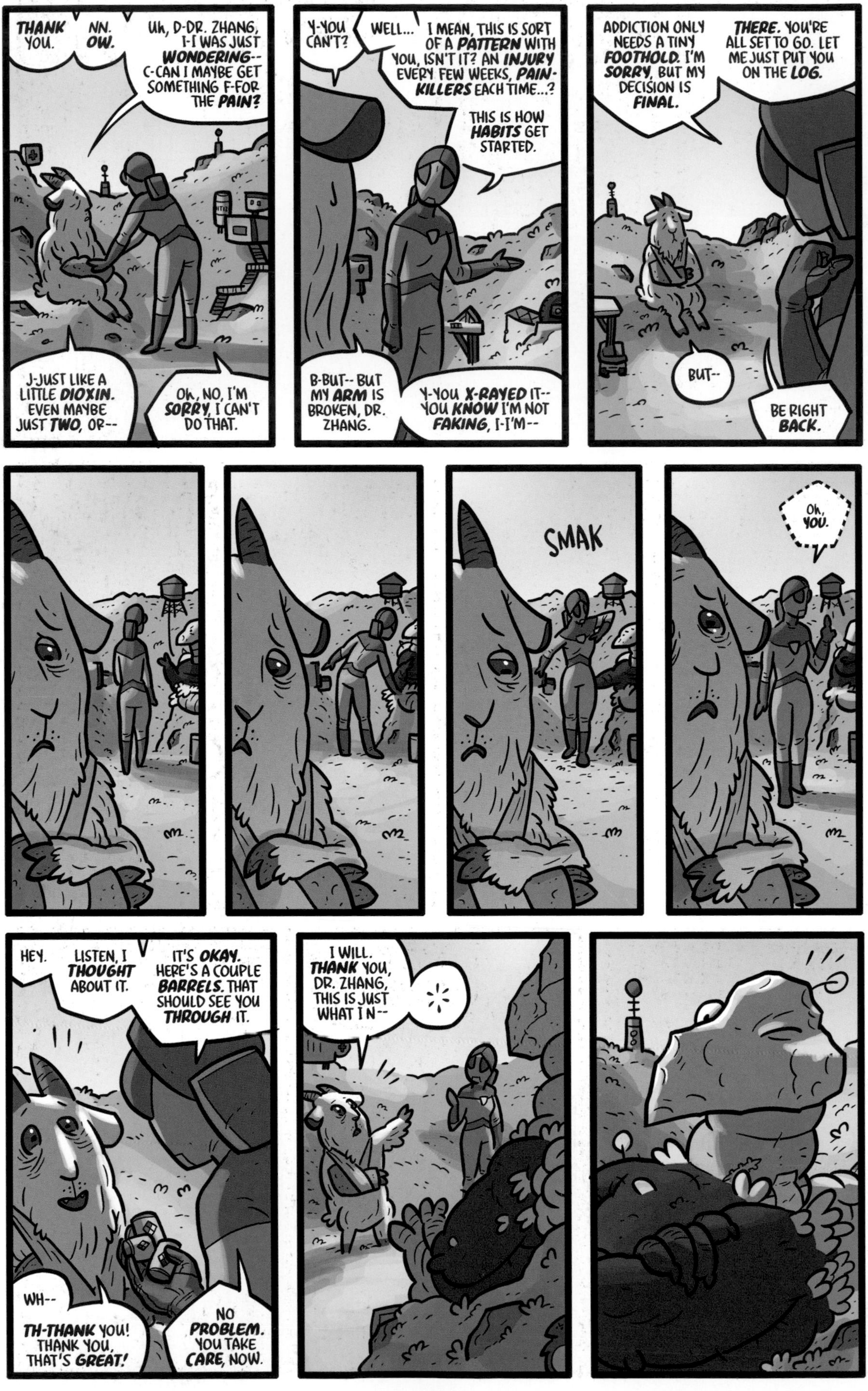

THANK YOU.
NN. OW.
Uh, D-DR. ZHANG, I-I WAS JUST WONDERING-- C-CAN I MAYBE GET SOMETHING F-FOR THE PAIN?
J-JUST LIKE A LITTLE DIOXIN. EVEN MAYBE JUST TWO, OR--
Oh, NO, I'M SORRY, I CAN'T DO THAT.
Y-YOU CAN'T?
WELL...
I MEAN, THIS IS SORT OF A PATTERN WITH YOU, ISN'T IT? AN INJURY EVERY FEW WEEKS, PAIN-KILLERS EACH TIME...?
THIS IS HOW HABITS GET STARTED.
B-BUT-- BUT MY ARM IS BROKEN, DR. ZHANG.
Y-YOU X-RAYED IT-- YOU KNOW I'M NOT FAKING, I-I'M--
ADDICTION ONLY NEEDS A TINY FOOTHOLD. I'M SORRY, BUT MY DECISION IS FINAL.
THERE. YOU'RE ALL SET TO GO. LET ME JUST PUT YOU ON THE LOG.
BUT--
BE RIGHT BACK.
SMAK
Oh, YOU.
HEY.
LISTEN, I THOUGHT ABOUT IT.
IT'S OKAY. HERE'S A COUPLE BARRELS. THAT SHOULD SEE YOU THROUGH IT.
WH--
TH-THANK YOU! THANK YOU, THAT'S GREAT!
NO PROBLEM. YOU TAKE CARE, NOW.
I WILL. THANK YOU, DR. ZHANG, THIS IS JUST WHAT I N--

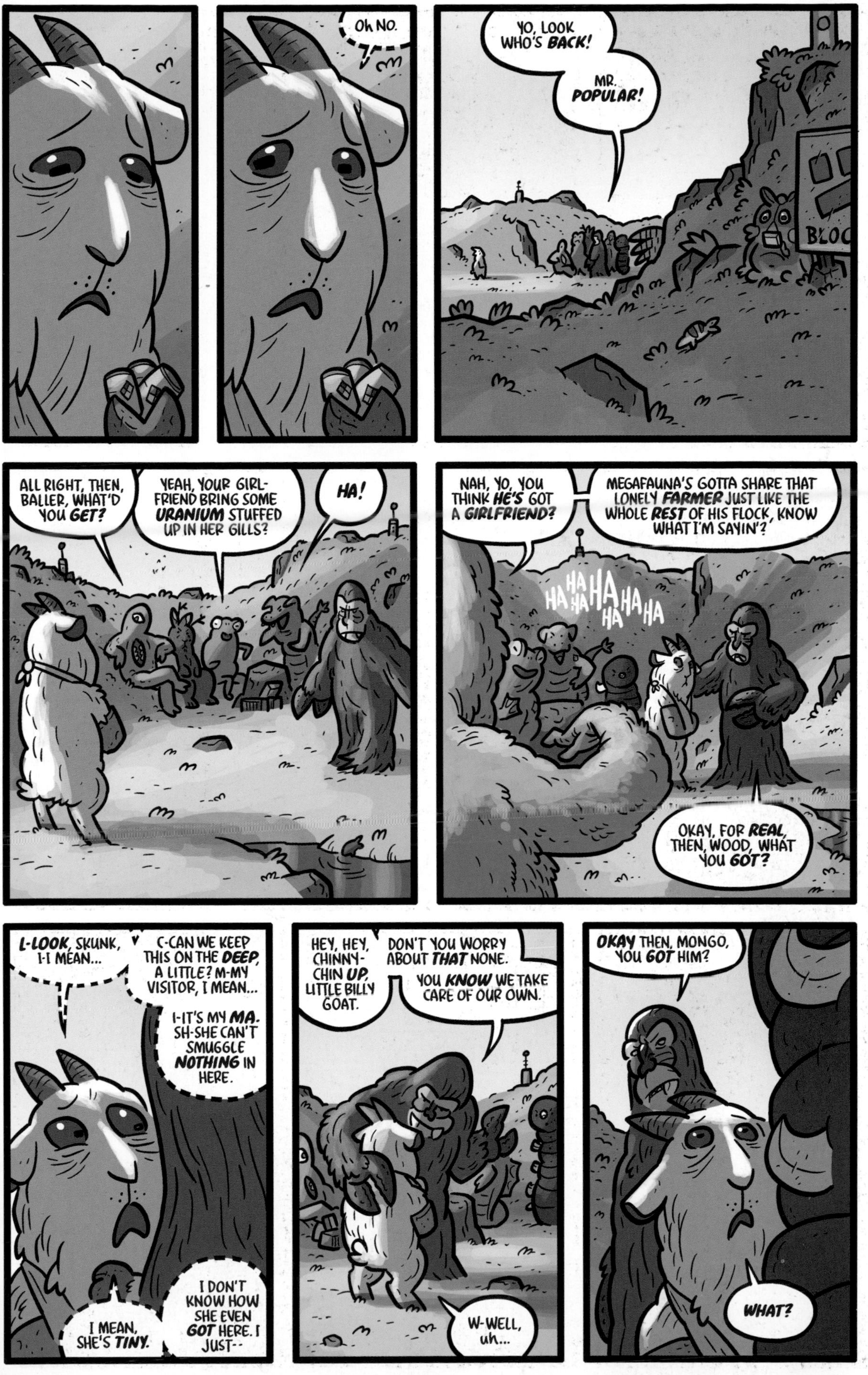

Oh NO.
YO, LOOK WHO'S **BACK!**
MR. **POPULAR!**
BLOC
ALL RIGHT, THEN, BALLER, WHAT'D YOU **GET?**
YEAH, YOUR GIRL-FRIEND BRING SOME **URANIUM** STUFFED UP IN HER GILLS?
HA!
NAH, YO, YOU THINK **HE'S** GOT A **GIRLFRIEND?**
MEGAFAUNA'S GOTTA SHARE THAT LONELY **FARMER** JUST LIKE THE WHOLE **REST** OF HIS FLOCK, KNOW WHAT I'M SAYIN'?
HA HA HA HA HA HA HA HA
OKAY, FOR **REAL**, THEN, WOOD, WHAT YOU **GOT?**
L-LOOK, SKUNK, I-I MEAN...
C-CAN WE KEEP THIS ON THE **DEEP**, A LITTLE? M-MY VISITOR, I MEAN...
I-IT'S MY **MA**. SH-SHE CAN'T SMUGGLE **NOTHING** IN HERE.
I MEAN, SHE'S **TINY**.
I DON'T KNOW HOW SHE EVEN **GOT** HERE. I JUST--
HEY, HEY, CHINNY-CHIN **UP**, LITTLE BILLY GOAT.
DON'T YOU WORRY ABOUT **THAT** NONE.
YOU **KNOW** WE TAKE CARE OF OUR OWN.
W-WELL, uh...
OKAY THEN, MONGO, YOU **GOT** HIM?
WHAT?

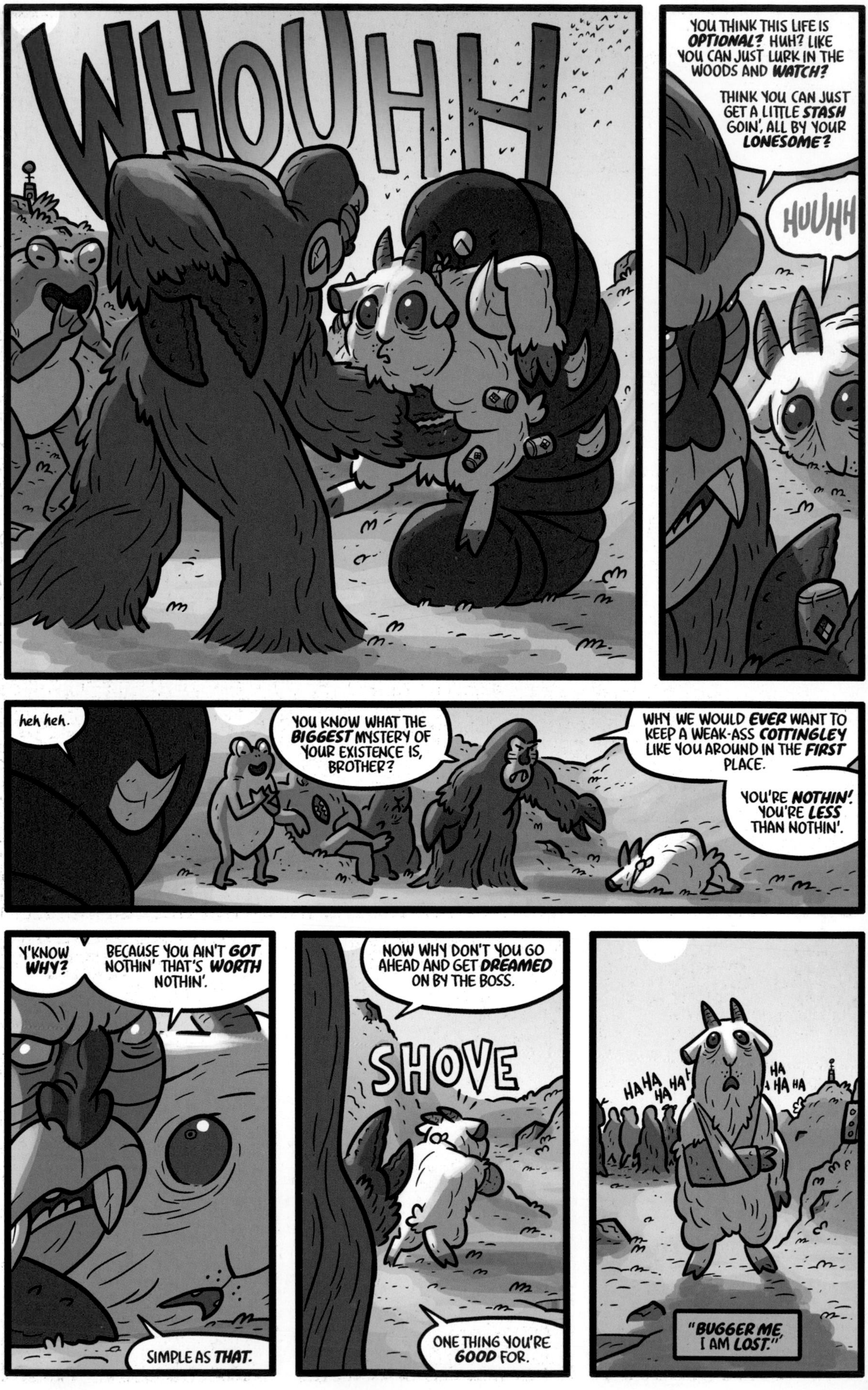
WHOUHH
YOU THINK THIS LIFE IS OPTIONAL? HUH? LIKE YOU CAN JUST LURK IN THE WOODS AND WATCH?
THINK YOU CAN JUST GET A LITTLE STASH GOIN', ALL BY YOUR LONESOME?
HUUHH
heh heh.
YOU KNOW WHAT THE BIGGEST MYSTERY OF YOUR EXISTENCE IS, BROTHER?
WHY WE WOULD EVER WANT TO KEEP A WEAK-ASS COTTINGLEY LIKE YOU AROUND IN THE FIRST PLACE.
YOU'RE NOTHIN'. YOU'RE LESS THAN NOTHIN'.
Y'KNOW WHY?
BECAUSE YOU AIN'T GOT NOTHIN' THAT'S WORTH NOTHIN'.
SIMPLE AS THAT.
NOW WHY DON'T YOU GO AHEAD AND GET DREAMED ON BY THE BOSS.
SHOVE
ONE THING YOU'RE GOOD FOR.
HA HA HA HA!
HA HA HA
"BUGGER ME, I AM LOST."

BLOODY *MONSTER GRAVEYARD,* ISN'T THIS A *CAESAR'S BREAKFAST.*

WAUKENABO LAKE? WHERE IS TH-- *MINNESOTA?!* THAT'S NOT EVEN ON THE BLOODY *WAY.*

HOW IN THE *NEBULA OF THE ETERNAL SUNRISE* DID I GET SO TURNED *AROUND?*

RIGHTO, WE'RE RESTING *HERE. PARK IT,* YOU HALF-ARSED WANNABE *ULURU.*

I HAVE TO SORT OUT THIS BLOODY *MAP.*

ETERNAL LIGHT OF THE BLEEDING *UNIVERSE,* THIS IS DOING MY *HEAD* IN.

CAN'T *THINK* STRAIGHT, AND THIS DAMN THING'S SENDING ME OUT TO THE MIDDLE OF *WOOP WOOP*--

?

TAP TAP

BLOOP

Hmm?

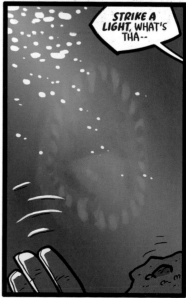

STRIKE A LIGHT, WHAT'S THA--

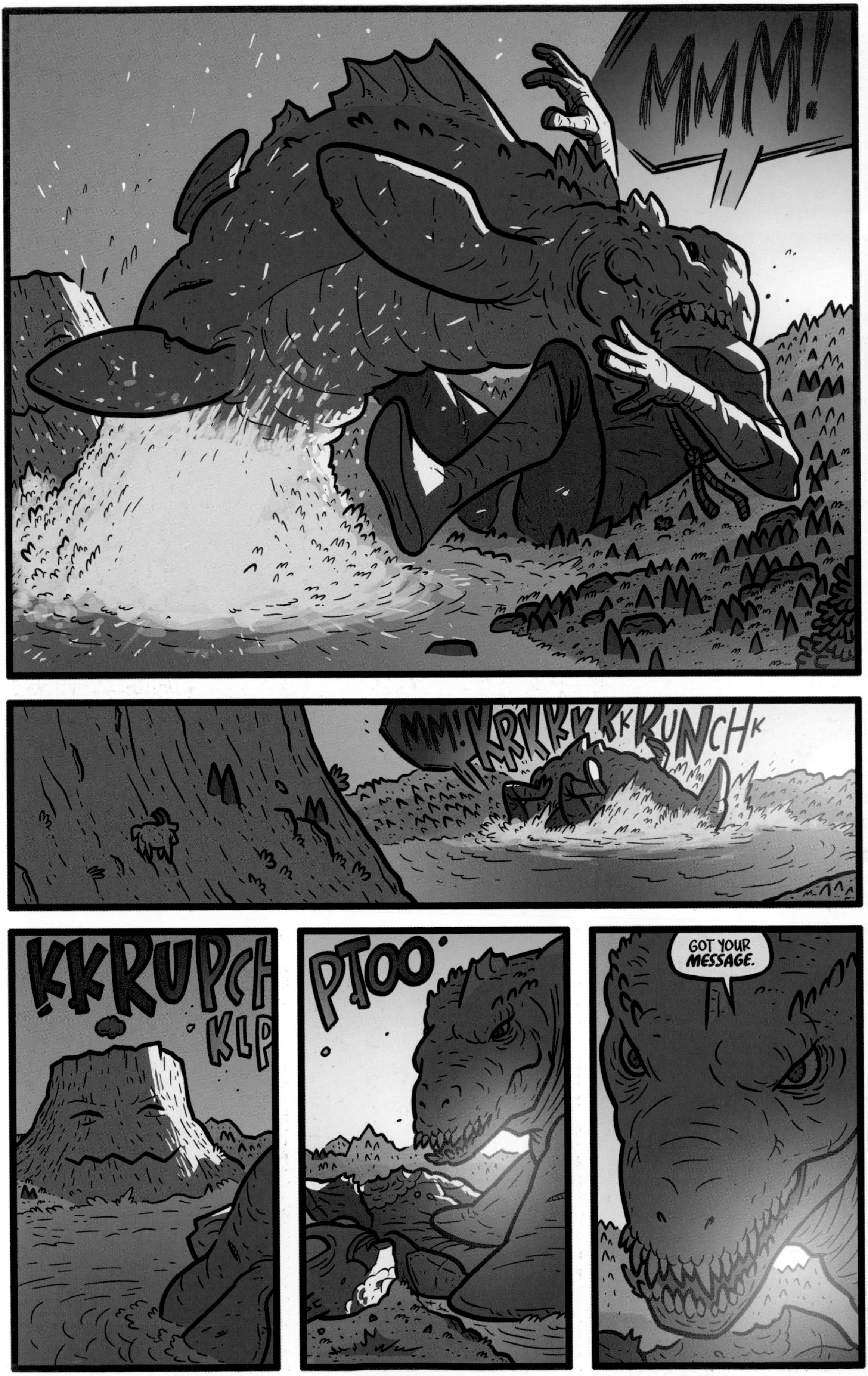
MMM!
MM! KRKKRKKKRUNCH K
KKRUPCH
KLP
PTOO
GOT YOUR MESSAGE.

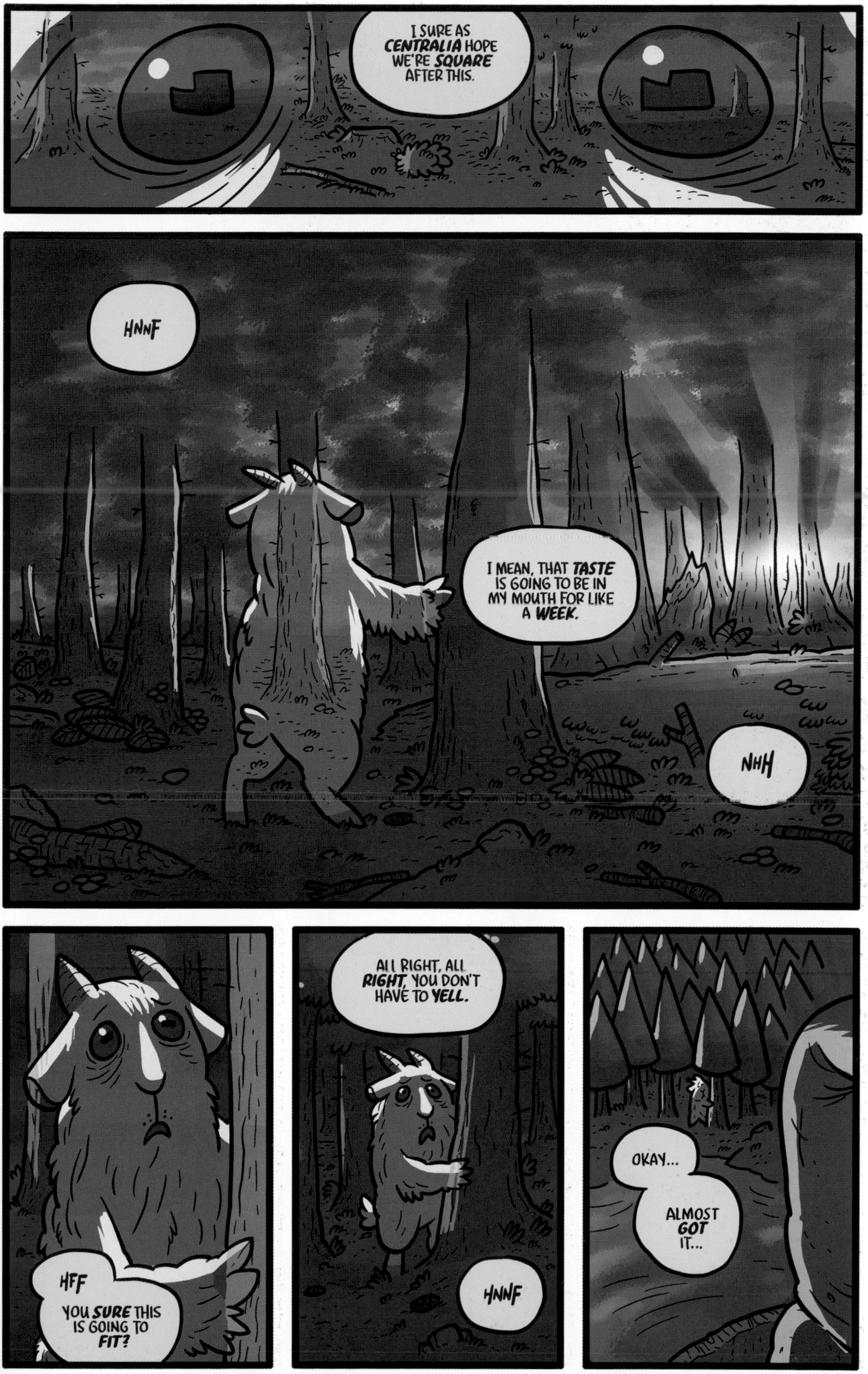
I SURE AS CENTRALIA HOPE WE'RE SQUARE AFTER THIS.
HNNF
I MEAN, THAT TASTE IS GOING TO BE IN MY MOUTH FOR LIKE A WEEK.
NHH
HFF
YOU SURE THIS IS GOING TO FIT?
ALL RIGHT, ALL RIGHT, YOU DON'T HAVE TO YELL.
HNNF
OKAY...
ALMOST GOT IT...

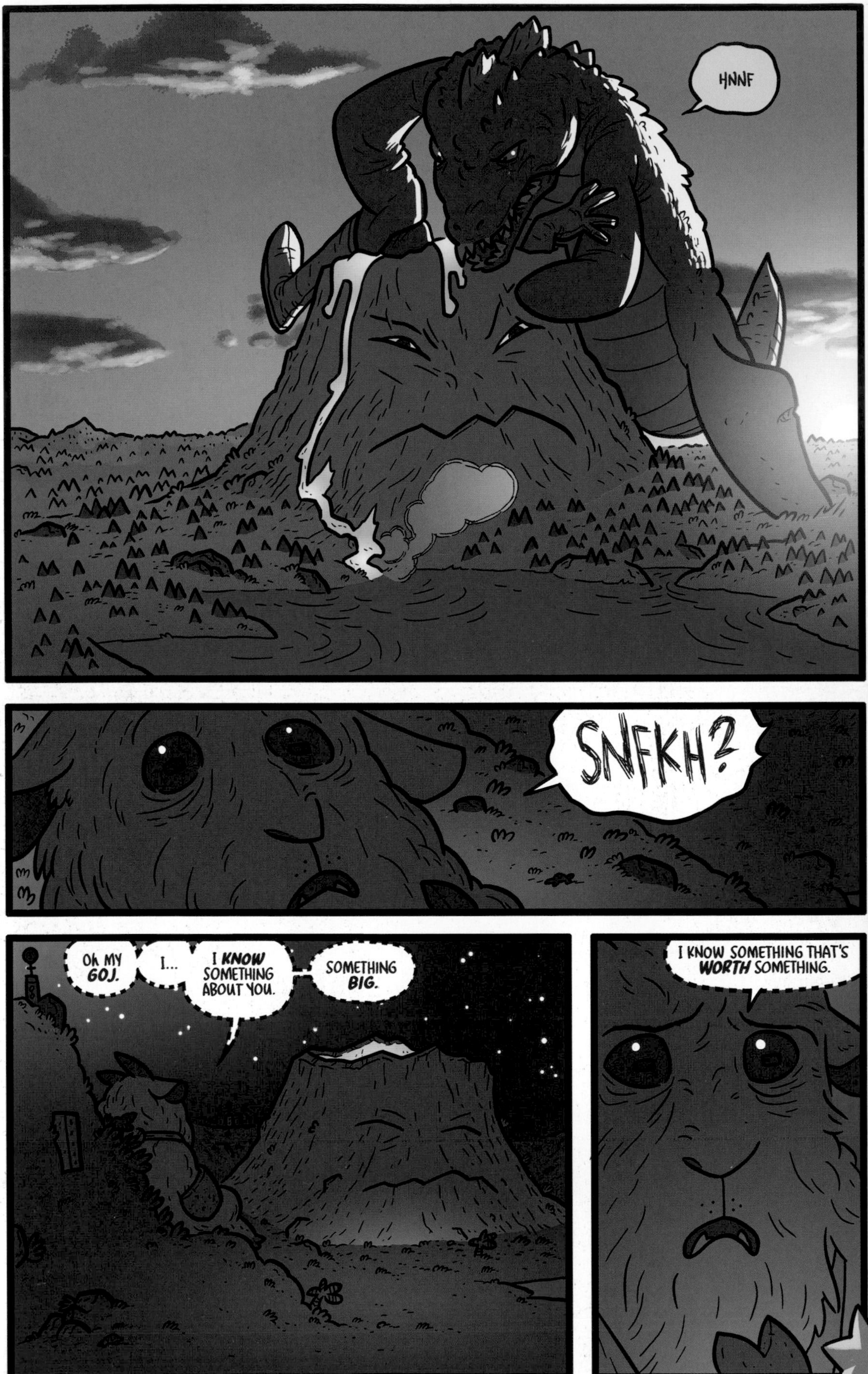
HNNF
SNFKH?
Oh MY *GOJ*.
I...
I *KNOW* SOMETHING ABOUT YOU.
SOMETHING *BIG*.
I KNOW SOMETHING THAT'S *WORTH* SOMETHING.

EPISODE 2

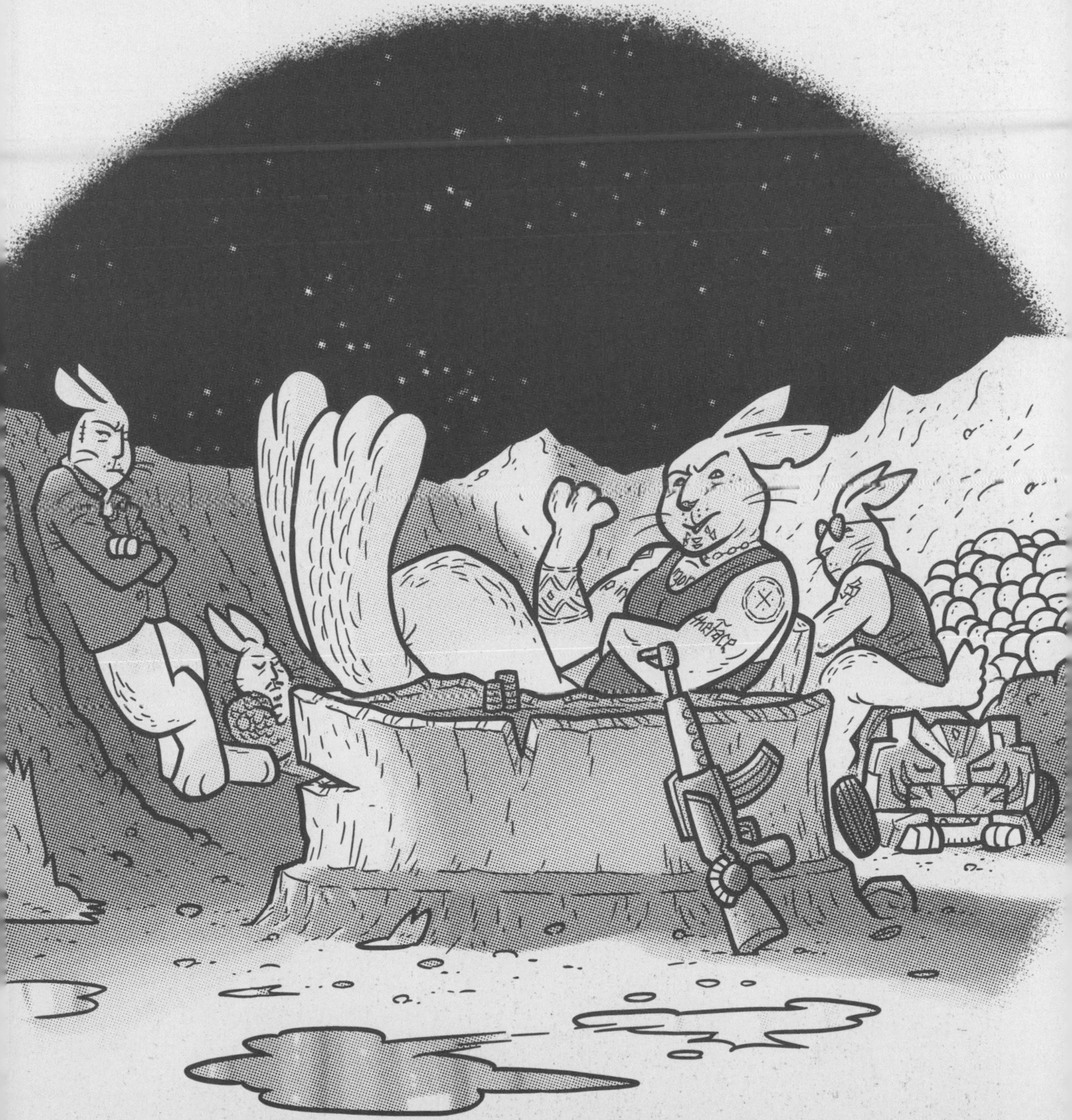

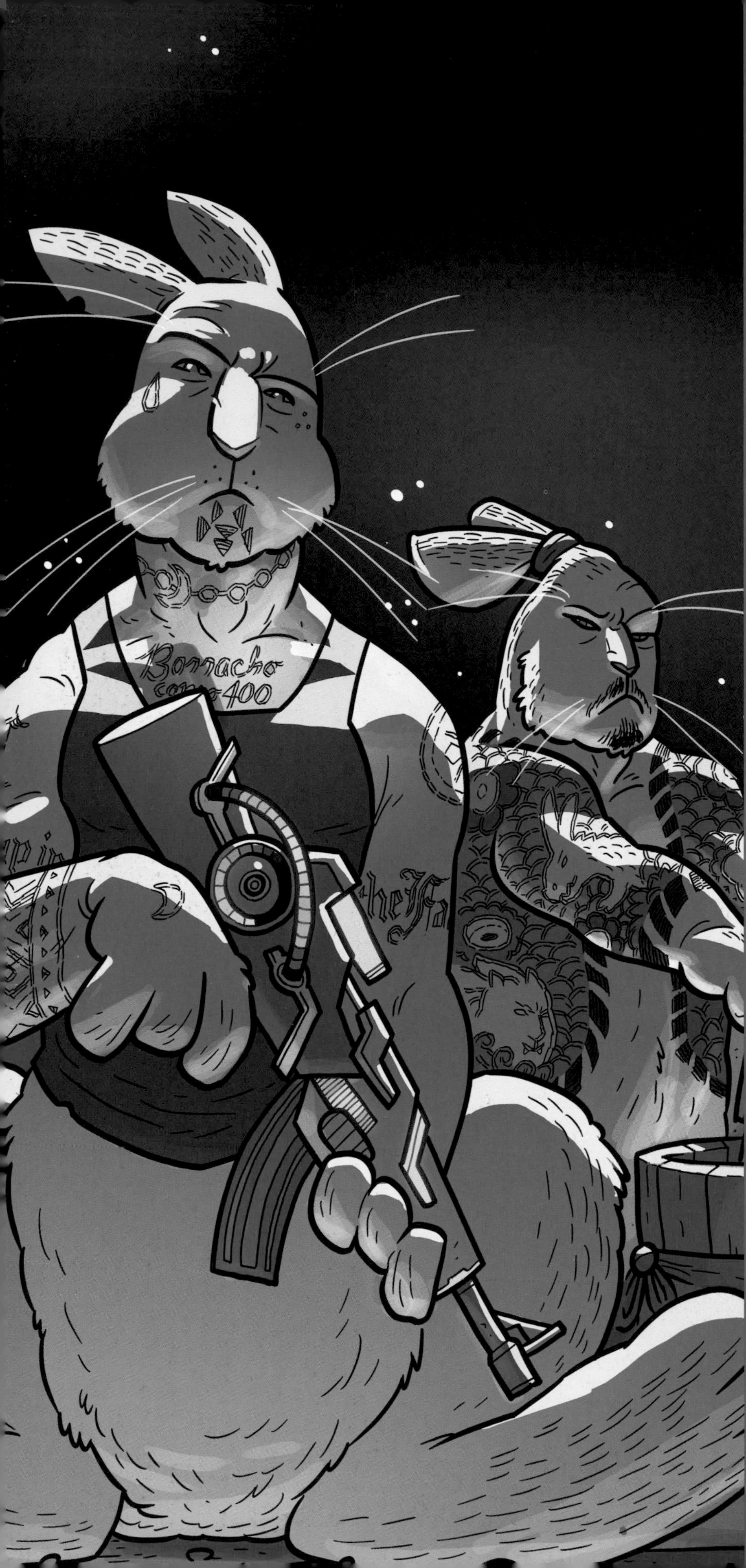
Borracho
400

圣獣マックス

WHOOFY™

APE-WHALE™

MOUNTAIN™

SKUNK™

≈giggle≈

Oh my GOJ, BABE, this is CRAZY.

I CAN'T BELIEVE I'M DOING THIS.

LIKE... MY HEART IS POUNDING! ARE YOU SURE THEY'RE EXPECTING ME?

YEAH, 'COURSE THEY ARE. WHY?

I DUNNO. I JUST--

THIS IS ALL SO NEW TO ME.

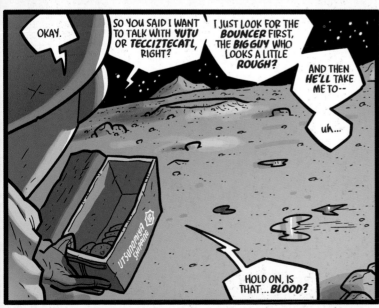

OKAY.

SO YOU SAID I WANT TO TALK WITH YUTU OR TECCIZTECATL, RIGHT?

I JUST LOOK FOR THE BOUNCER FIRST, THE BIG GUY WHO LOOKS A LITTLE ROUGH?

AND THEN HE'LL TAKE ME TO--

uh...

HOLD ON, IS THAT...BLOOD?

Uh, BABE, I... I THINK SOME-THING WENT DOWN HERE.

LIKE, SOME-THING PRETTY SERIOUS.

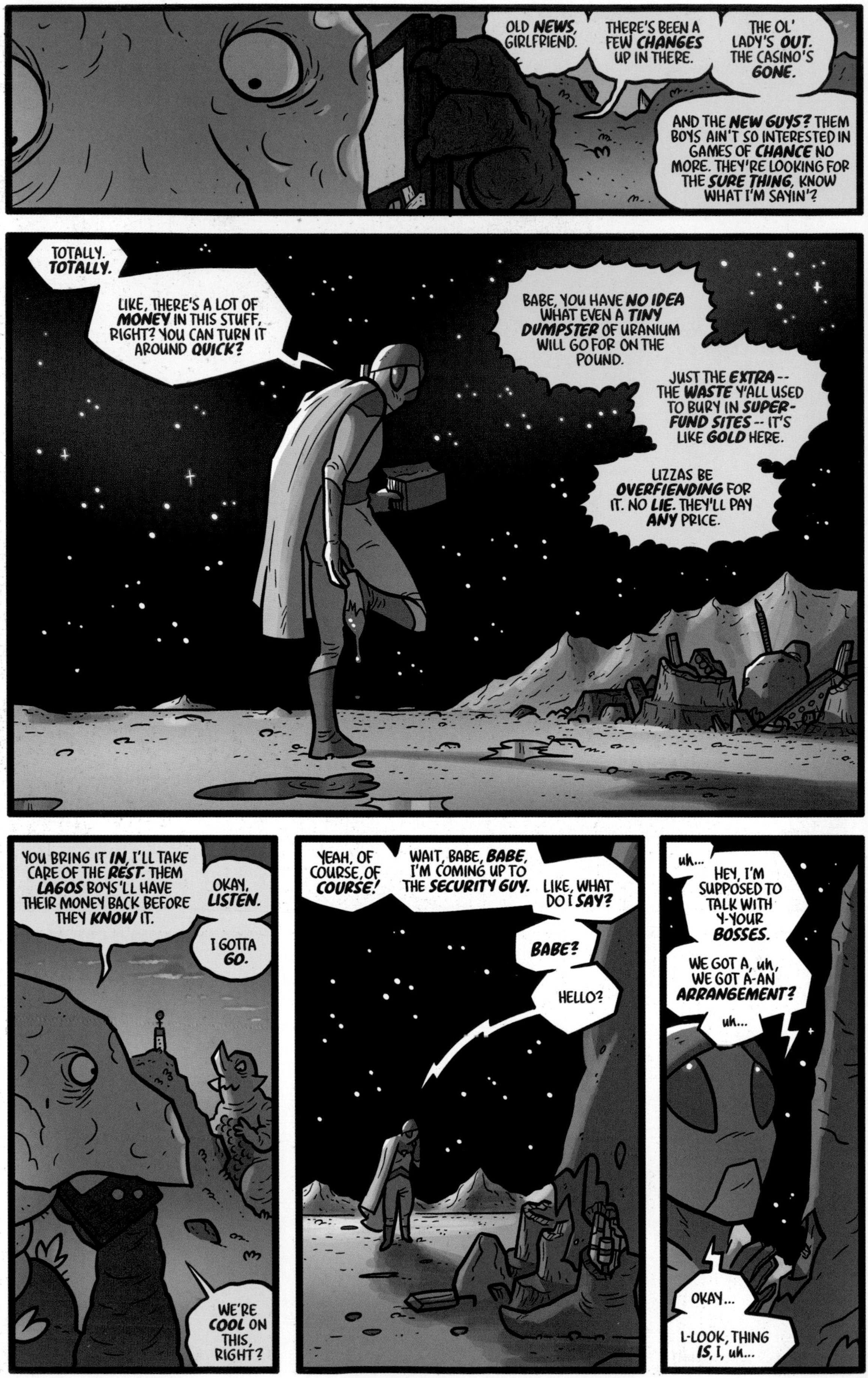
OLD NEWS, GIRLFRIEND.
THERE'S BEEN A FEW CHANGES UP IN THERE.
THE OL' LADY'S OUT. THE CASINO'S GONE.
AND THE NEW GUYS? THEM BOYS AIN'T SO INTERESTED IN GAMES OF CHANCE NO MORE. THEY'RE LOOKING FOR THE SURE THING, KNOW WHAT I'M SAYIN'?
TOTALLY. TOTALLY.
LIKE, THERE'S A LOT OF MONEY IN THIS STUFF, RIGHT? YOU CAN TURN IT AROUND QUICK?
BABE, YOU HAVE NO IDEA WHAT EVEN A TINY DUMPSTER OF URANIUM WILL GO FOR ON THE POUND.
JUST THE EXTRA -- THE WASTE Y'ALL USED TO BURY IN SUPER-FUND SITES -- IT'S LIKE GOLD HERE.
LIZZAS BE OVERFIENDING FOR IT. NO LIE. THEY'LL PAY ANY PRICE.
YOU BRING IT IN, I'LL TAKE CARE OF THE REST. THEM LAGOS BOYS'LL HAVE THEIR MONEY BACK BEFORE THEY KNOW IT.
OKAY, LISTEN.
I GOTTA GO.
WE'RE COOL ON THIS, RIGHT?
YEAH, OF COURSE, OF COURSE!
WAIT, BABE, BABE, I'M COMING UP TO THE SECURITY GUY.
LIKE, WHAT DO I SAY?
BABE?
HELLO?
uh...
HEY, I'M SUPPOSED TO TALK WITH Y-YOUR BOSSES.
WE GOT A, uh, WE GOT A-AN ARRANGEMENT?
uh...
OKAY...
L-LOOK, THING IS, I, uh...

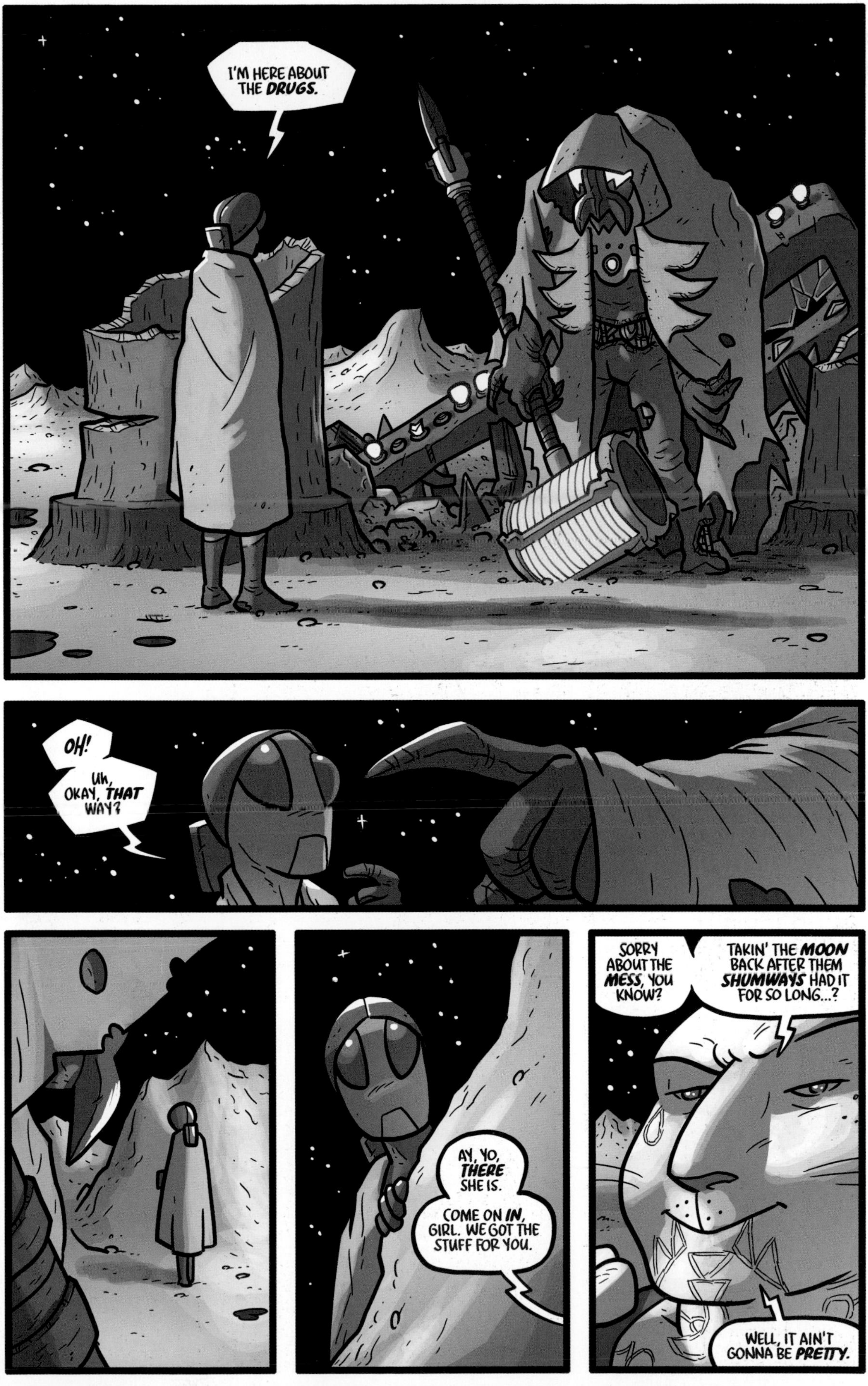
I'M HERE ABOUT THE DRUGS.
OH!
Uh, OKAY, THAT WAY?
AY, YO, THERE SHE IS.
COME ON IN, GIRL. WE GOT THE STUFF FOR YOU.
SORRY ABOUT THE MESS, YOU KNOW?
TAKIN' THE MOON BACK AFTER THEM SHUMWAYS HAD IT FOR SO LONG...?
WELL, IT AIN'T GONNA BE PRETTY.

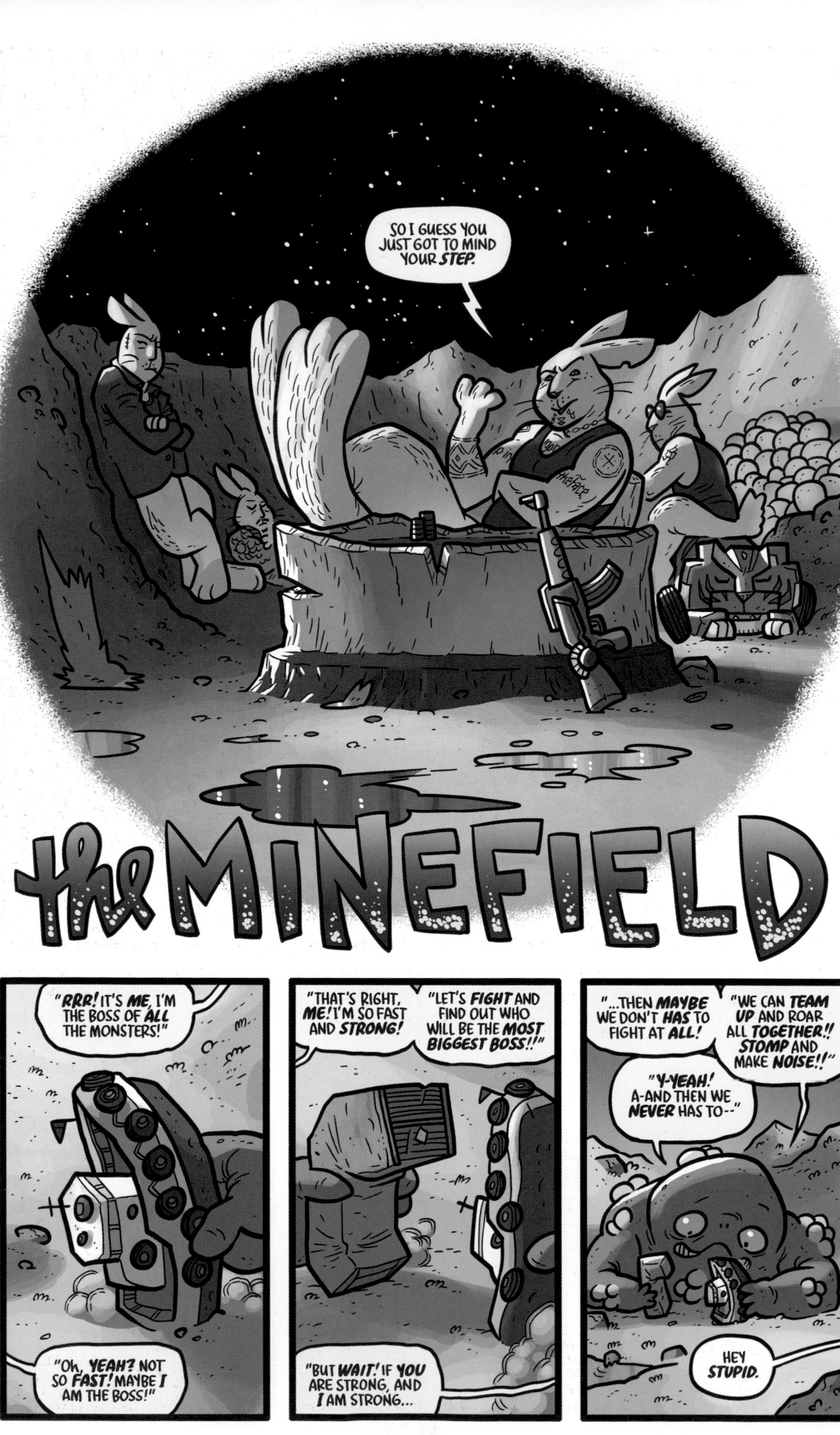
SO I GUESS YOU JUST GOT TO MIND YOUR STEP.
the MINEFIELD
"RRR! IT'S ME, I'M THE BOSS OF ALL THE MONSTERS!"
"Oh, YEAH? NOT SO FAST! MAYBE I AM THE BOSS!"
"THAT'S RIGHT, ME! I'M SO FAST AND STRONG!
"LET'S FIGHT AND FIND OUT WHO WILL BE THE MOST BIGGEST BOSS!!"
"BUT WAIT! IF YOU ARE STRONG, AND I AM STRONG...
"...THEN MAYBE WE DON'T HAS TO FIGHT AT ALL!
"WE CAN TEAM UP AND ROAR ALL TOGETHER!! STOMP AND MAKE NOISE!!"
"Y-YEAH! A-AND THEN WE NEVER HAS TO--"
HEY STUPID.

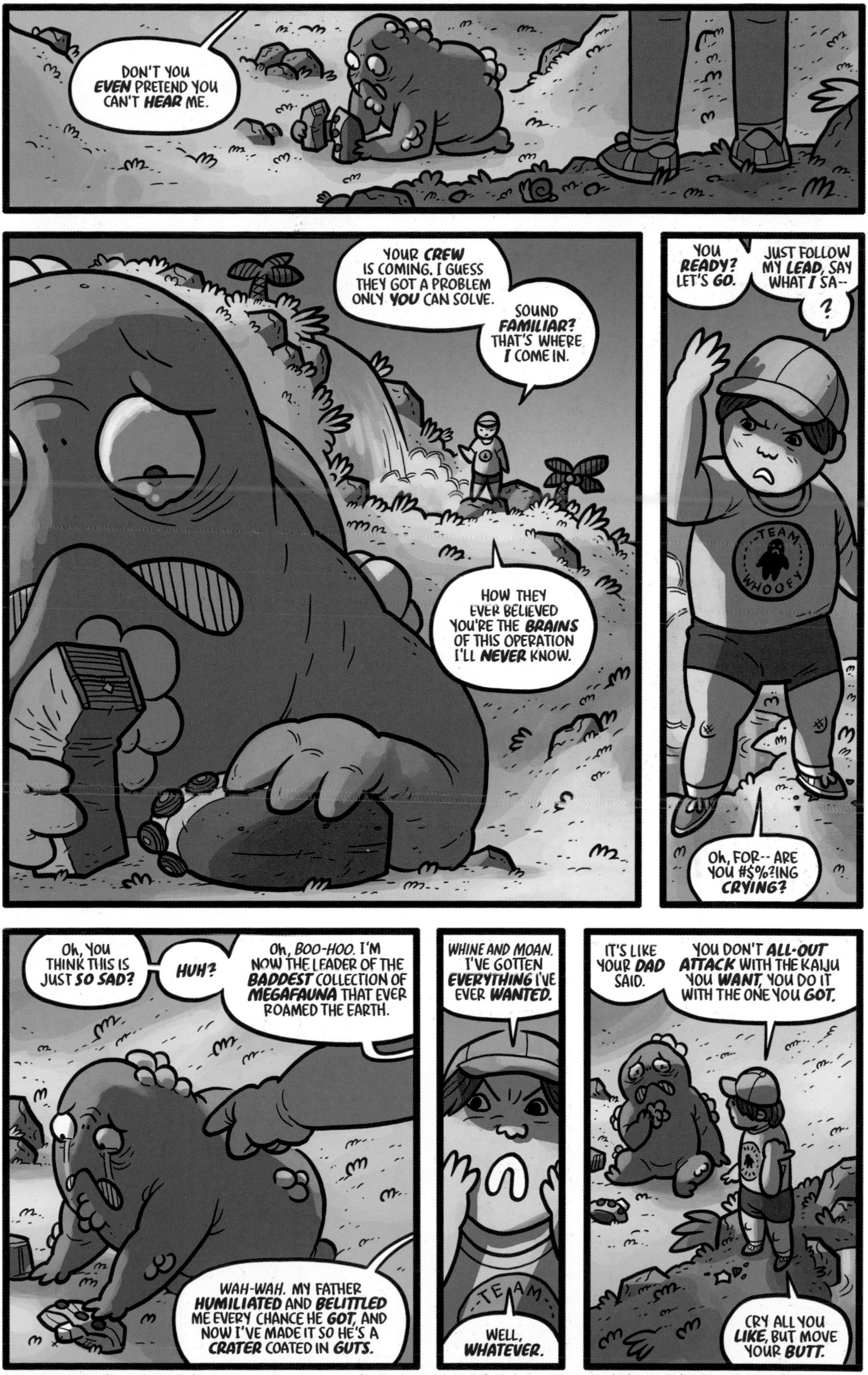
DON'T YOU EVEN PRETEND YOU CAN'T HEAR ME.
YOUR CREW IS COMING. I GUESS THEY GOT A PROBLEM ONLY YOU CAN SOLVE.
SOUND FAMILIAR? THAT'S WHERE I COME IN.
HOW THEY EVER BELIEVED YOU'RE THE BRAINS OF THIS OPERATION I'LL NEVER KNOW.
YOU READY? LET'S GO.
JUST FOLLOW MY LEAD, SAY WHAT I SA--
?
Oh, FOR-- ARE YOU #$%?ING CRYING?
Oh, YOU THINK THIS IS JUST SO SAD?
HUH?
Oh, BOO-HOO. I'M NOW THE LEADER OF THE BADDEST COLLECTION OF MEGAFAUNA THAT EVER ROAMED THE EARTH.
WAH-WAH. MY FATHER HUMILIATED AND BELITTLED ME EVERY CHANCE HE GOT, AND NOW I'VE MADE IT SO HE'S A CRATER COATED IN GUTS.
WHINE AND MOAN. I'VE GOTTEN EVERYTHING I'VE EVER WANTED.
TEAM
WELL, WHATEVER.
IT'S LIKE YOUR DAD SAID.
YOU DON'T ALL-OUT ATTACK WITH THE KAIJU YOU WANT, YOU DO IT WITH THE ONE YOU GOT.
CRY ALL YOU LIKE, BUT MOVE YOUR BUTT.

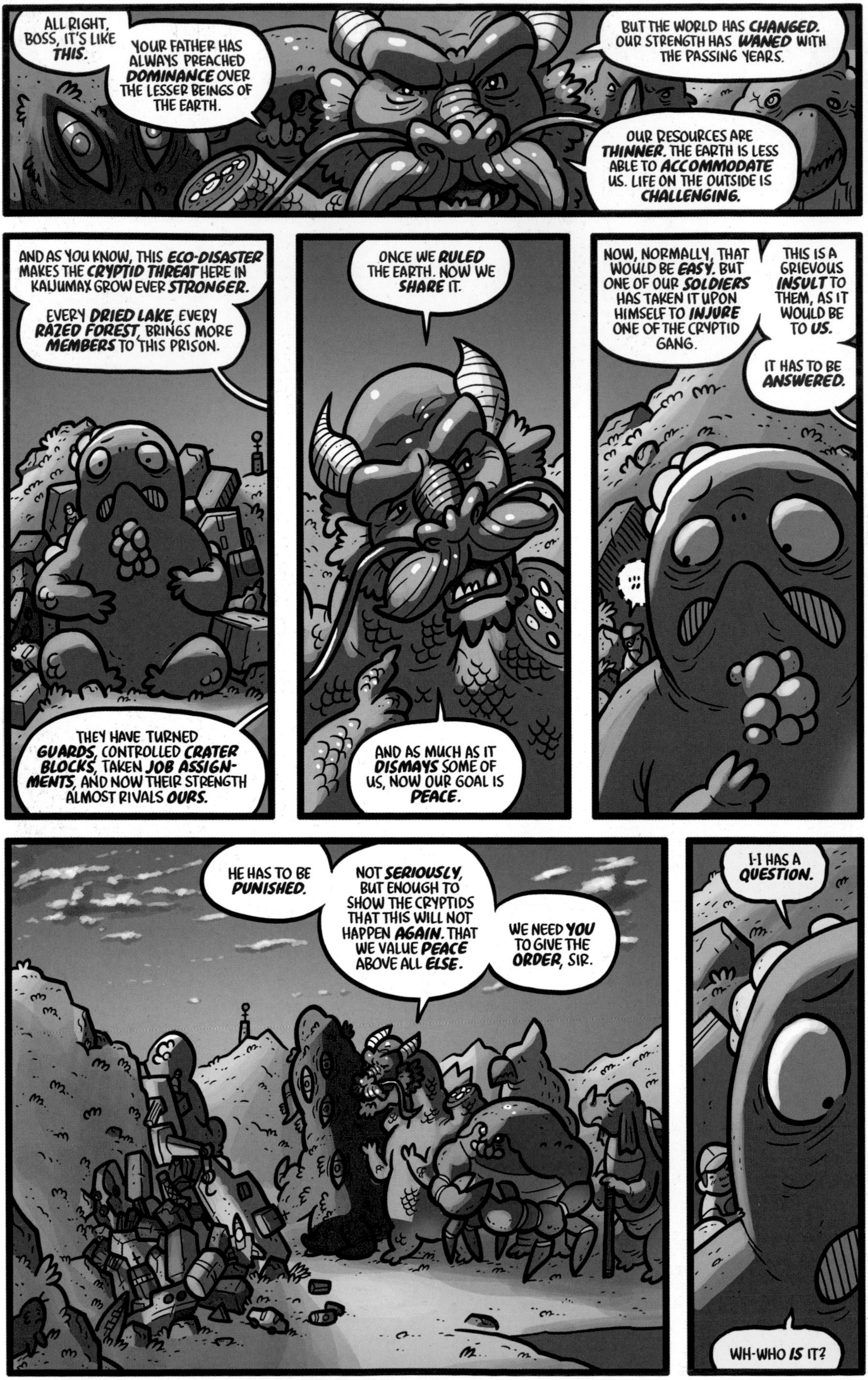
ALL RIGHT, BOSS, IT'S LIKE THIS.
YOUR FATHER HAS ALWAYS PREACHED DOMINANCE OVER THE LESSER BEINGS OF THE EARTH.
BUT THE WORLD HAS CHANGED. OUR STRENGTH HAS WANED WITH THE PASSING YEARS.
OUR RESOURCES ARE THINNER. THE EARTH IS LESS ABLE TO ACCOMMODATE US. LIFE ON THE OUTSIDE IS CHALLENGING.
AND AS YOU KNOW, THIS ECO-DISASTER MAKES THE CRYPTID THREAT HERE IN KAIJUMAX GROW EVER STRONGER.
EVERY DRIED LAKE, EVERY RAZED FOREST, BRINGS MORE MEMBERS TO THIS PRISON.
THEY HAVE TURNED GUARDS, CONTROLLED CRATER BLOCKS, TAKEN JOB ASSIGNMENTS, AND NOW THEIR STRENGTH ALMOST RIVALS OURS.
ONCE WE RULED THE EARTH. NOW WE SHARE IT.
AND AS MUCH AS IT DISMAYS SOME OF US, NOW OUR GOAL IS PEACE.
NOW, NORMALLY, THAT WOULD BE EASY. BUT ONE OF OUR SOLDIERS HAS TAKEN IT UPON HIMSELF TO INJURE ONE OF THE CRYPTID GANG.
THIS IS A GRIEVOUS INSULT TO THEM, AS IT WOULD BE TO US.
IT HAS TO BE ANSWERED.
...
HE HAS TO BE PUNISHED.
NOT SERIOUSLY, BUT ENOUGH TO SHOW THE CRYPTIDS THAT THIS WILL NOT HAPPEN AGAIN. THAT WE VALUE PEACE ABOVE ALL ELSE.
WE NEED YOU TO GIVE THE ORDER, SIR.
I-I HAS A QUESTION.
WH-WHO IS IT?

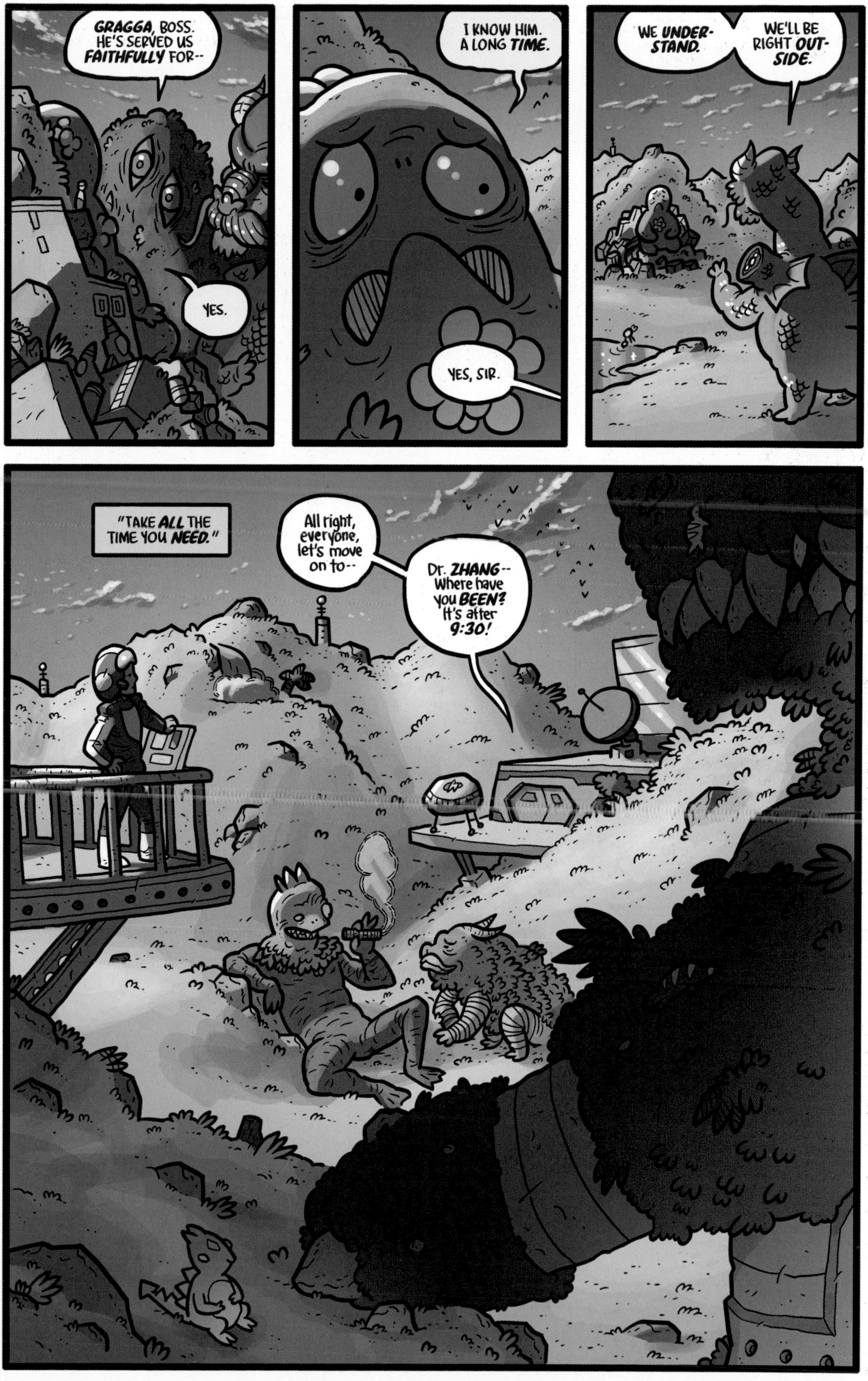
GRAGGA, BOSS. HE'S SERVED US FAITHFULLY FOR--
YES.
I KNOW HIM. A LONG TIME.
YES, SIR.
WE UNDER-STAND.
WE'LL BE RIGHT OUT-SIDE.
"TAKE ALL THE TIME YOU NEED."
All right, everyone, let's move on to--
Dr. ZHANG-- Where have you BEEN? It's after 9:30!

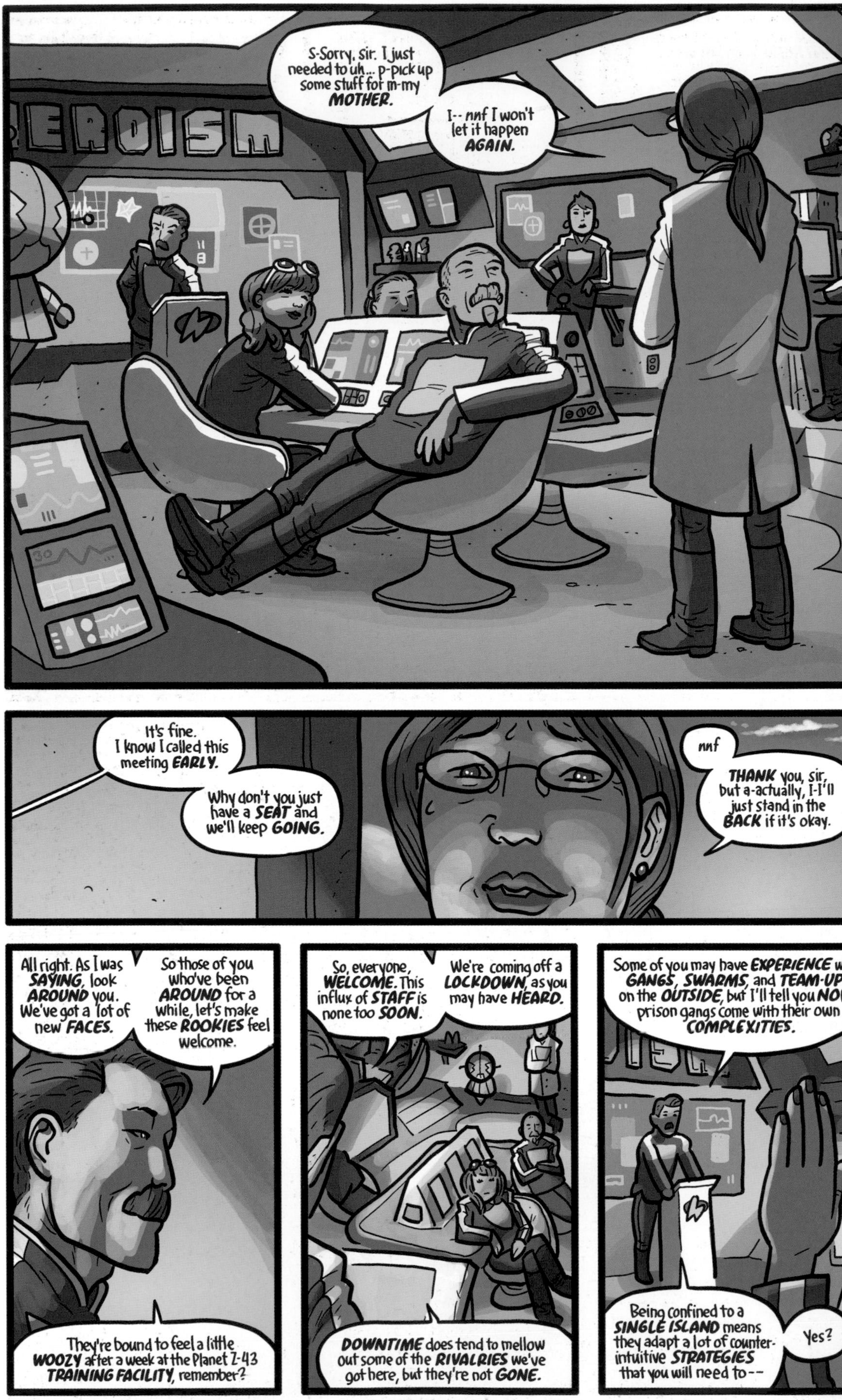
EROISM
S-Sorry, sir. I just needed to uh... p-pick up some stuff for m-my MOTHER.
I-- nnf I won't let it happen AGAIN.
It's fine. I know I called this meeting EARLY.
Why don't you just have a SEAT and we'll keep GOING.
nnf
THANK you, sir, but a-actually, I-I'll just stand in the BACK if it's okay.
All right. As I was SAYING, look AROUND you. We've got a lot of new FACES.
So those of you who've been AROUND for a while, let's make these ROOKIES feel welcome.
They're bound to feel a little WOOZY after a week at the Planet Z-43 TRAINING FACILITY, remember?
So, everyone, WELCOME. This influx of STAFF is none too SOON.
We're coming off a LOCKDOWN, as you may have HEARD.
DOWNTIME does tend to mellow out some of the RIVALRIES we've got here, but they're not GONE.
Some of you may have EXPERIENCE with GANGS, SWARMS, and TEAM-UPS on the OUTSIDE, but I'll tell you NOW: prison gangs come with their own COMPLEXITIES.
Being confined to a SINGLE ISLAND means they adapt a lot of counter-intuitive STRATEGIES that you will need to--
Yes?

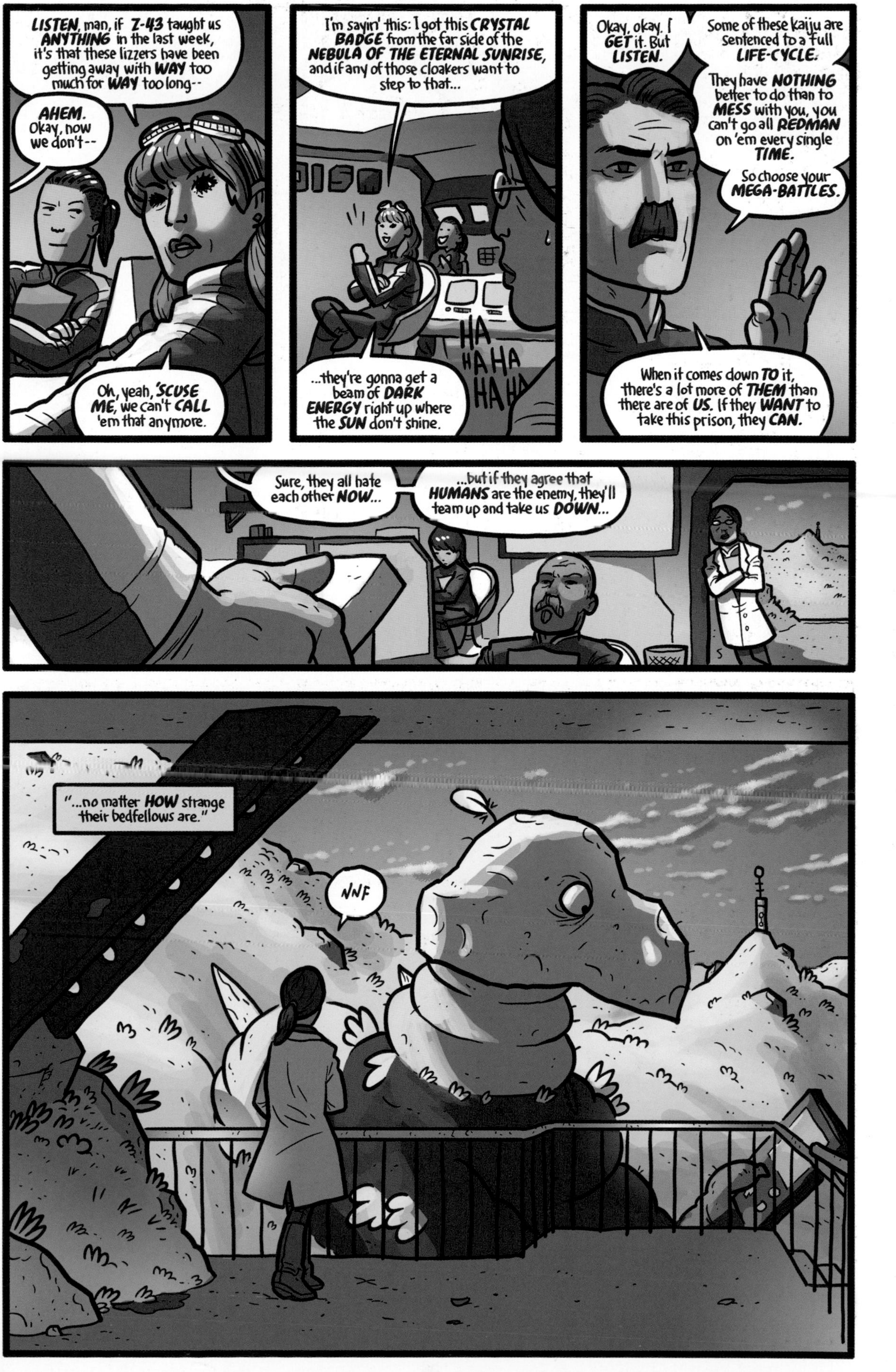
LISTEN, man, if Z-43 taught us ANYTHING in the last week, it's that these lizzers have been getting away with WAY too much for WAY too long--
AHEM. Okay, now we don't--
Oh, yeah, 'SCUSE ME, we can't CALL 'em that anymore.
I'm sayin' this: I got this CRYSTAL BADGE from the far side of the NEBULA OF THE ETERNAL SUNRISE, and if any of those cloakers want to step to that...
...they're gonna get a beam of DARK ENERGY right up where the SUN don't shine.
HA HA HA HA HA HA
Okay, okay. I GET it. But LISTEN.
Some of these kaiju are sentenced to a full LIFE-CYCLE.
They have NOTHING better to do than to MESS with you, you can't go all REDMAN on 'em every single TIME.
So choose your MEGA-BATTLES.
When it comes down TO it, there's a lot more of THEM than there are of US. If they WANT to take this prison, they CAN.
Sure, they all hate each other NOW...
...but if they agree that HUMANS are the enemy, they'll team up and take us DOWN...
"...no matter HOW strange their bedfellows are."
NNF

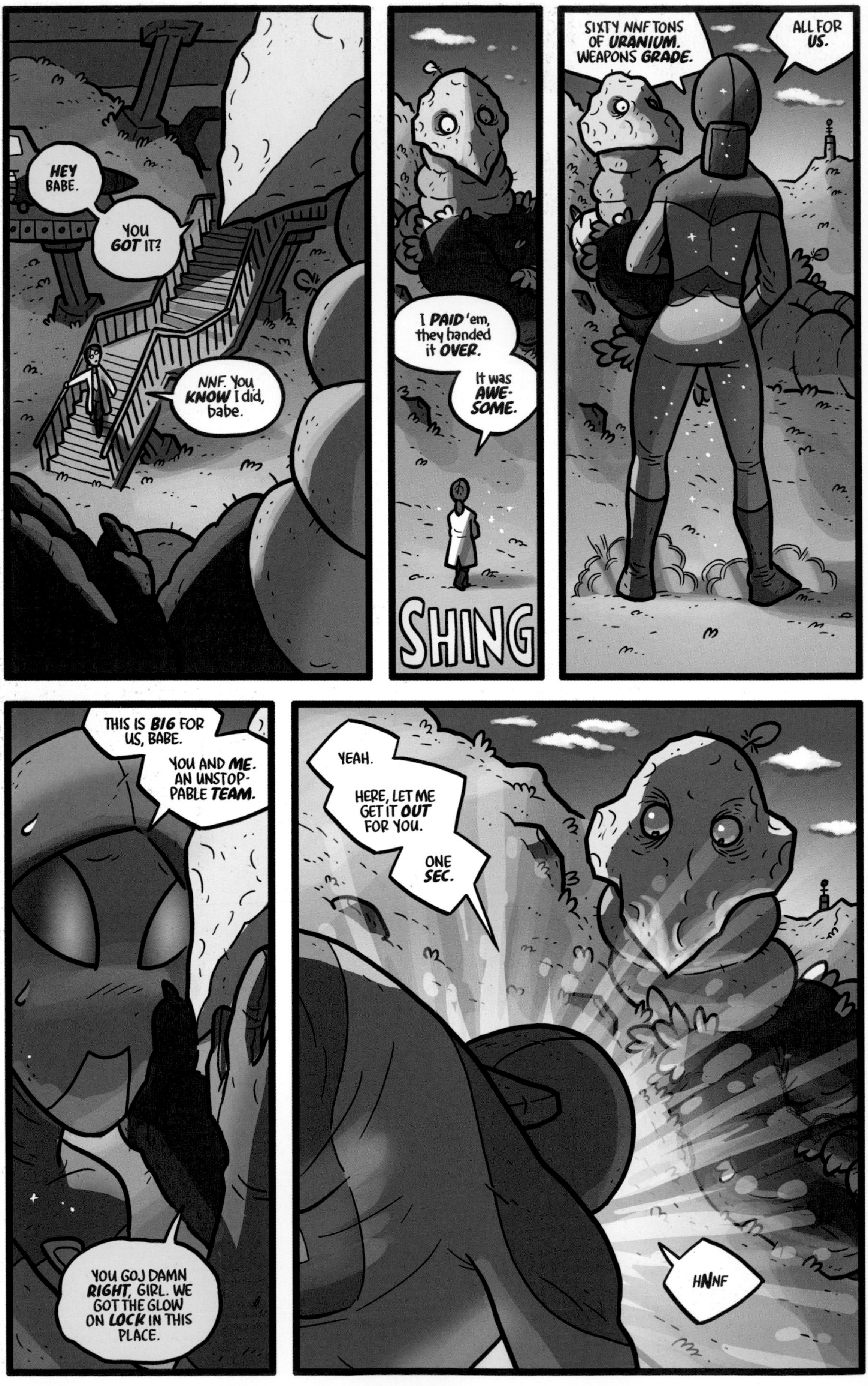
HEY BABE.
YOU GOT IT?
NNF. YOU KNOW I did, babe.
I PAID 'em, they handed it OVER.
It was AWE-SOME.
SHING
SIXTY NNF TONS OF URANIUM. WEAPONS GRADE.
ALL FOR US.
THIS IS BIG FOR US, BABE.
YOU AND ME. AN UNSTOP-PABLE TEAM.
YOU GOJ DAMN RIGHT, GIRL. WE GOT THE GLOW ON LOCK IN THIS PLACE.
YEAH.
HERE, LET ME GET IT OUT FOR YOU.
ONE SEC.
HNNF

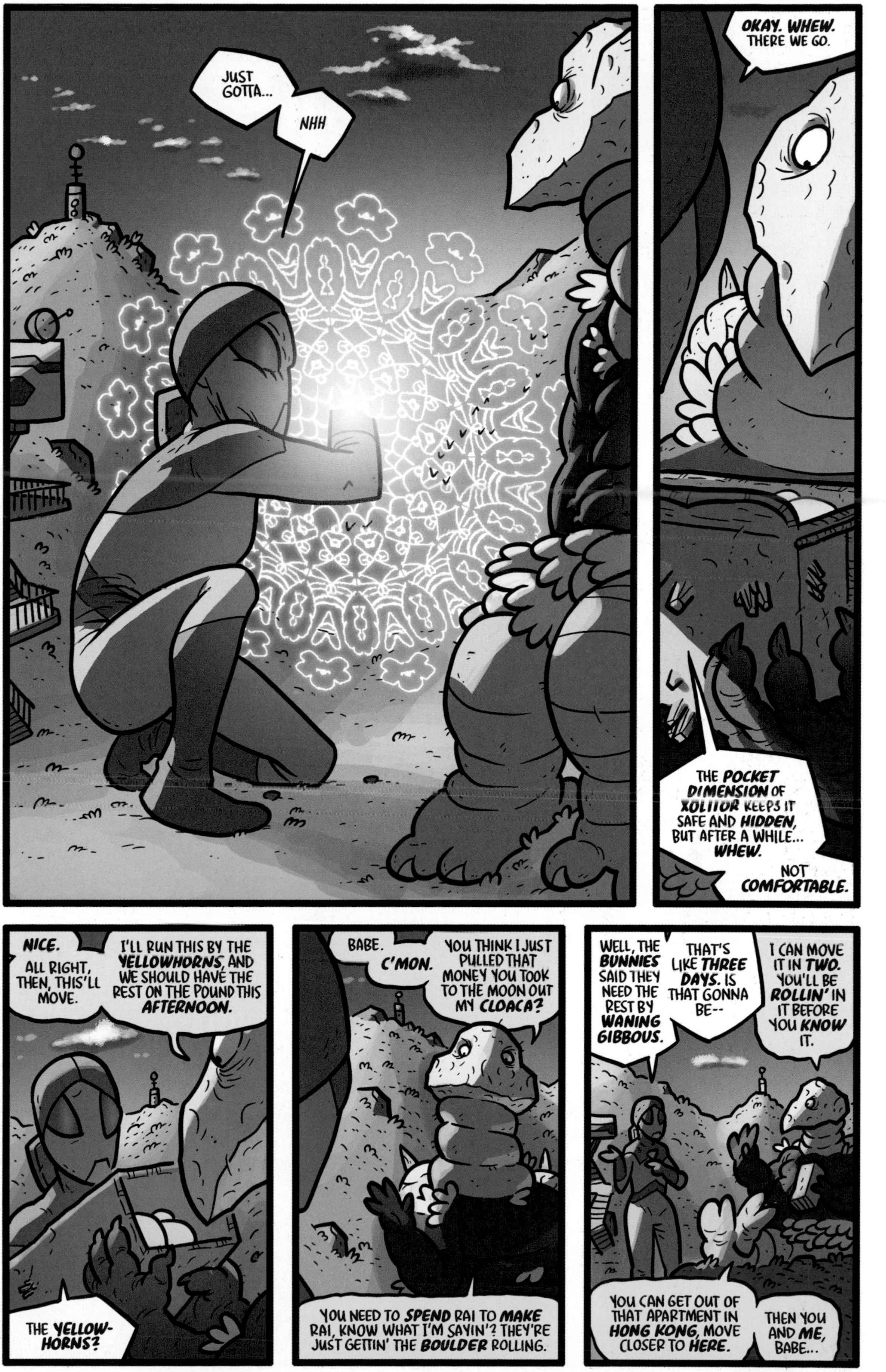
JUST GOTTA...
NHH
OKAY. WHEW. THERE WE GO.
THE POCKET DIMENSION OF XOLITOR KEEPS IT SAFE AND HIDDEN, BUT AFTER A WHILE... WHEW.
NOT COMFORTABLE.
NICE. ALL RIGHT, THEN, THIS'LL MOVE.
I'LL RUN THIS BY THE YELLOWHORNS, AND WE SHOULD HAVE THE REST ON THE POUND THIS AFTERNOON.
THE YELLOW-HORNS?
BABE. C'MON.
YOU THINK I JUST PULLED THAT MONEY YOU TOOK TO THE MOON OUT MY CLOACA?
YOU NEED TO SPEND RAI TO MAKE RAI, KNOW WHAT I'M SAYIN'? THEY'RE JUST GETTIN' THE BOULDER ROLLING.
WELL, THE BUNNIES SAID THEY NEED THE REST BY WANING GIBBOUS.
THAT'S LIKE THREE DAYS. IS THAT GONNA BE--
I CAN MOVE IT IN TWO. YOU'LL BE ROLLIN' IN IT BEFORE YOU KNOW IT.
YOU CAN GET OUT OF THAT APARTMENT IN HONG KONG, MOVE CLOSER TO HERE.
THEN YOU AND ME, BABE...

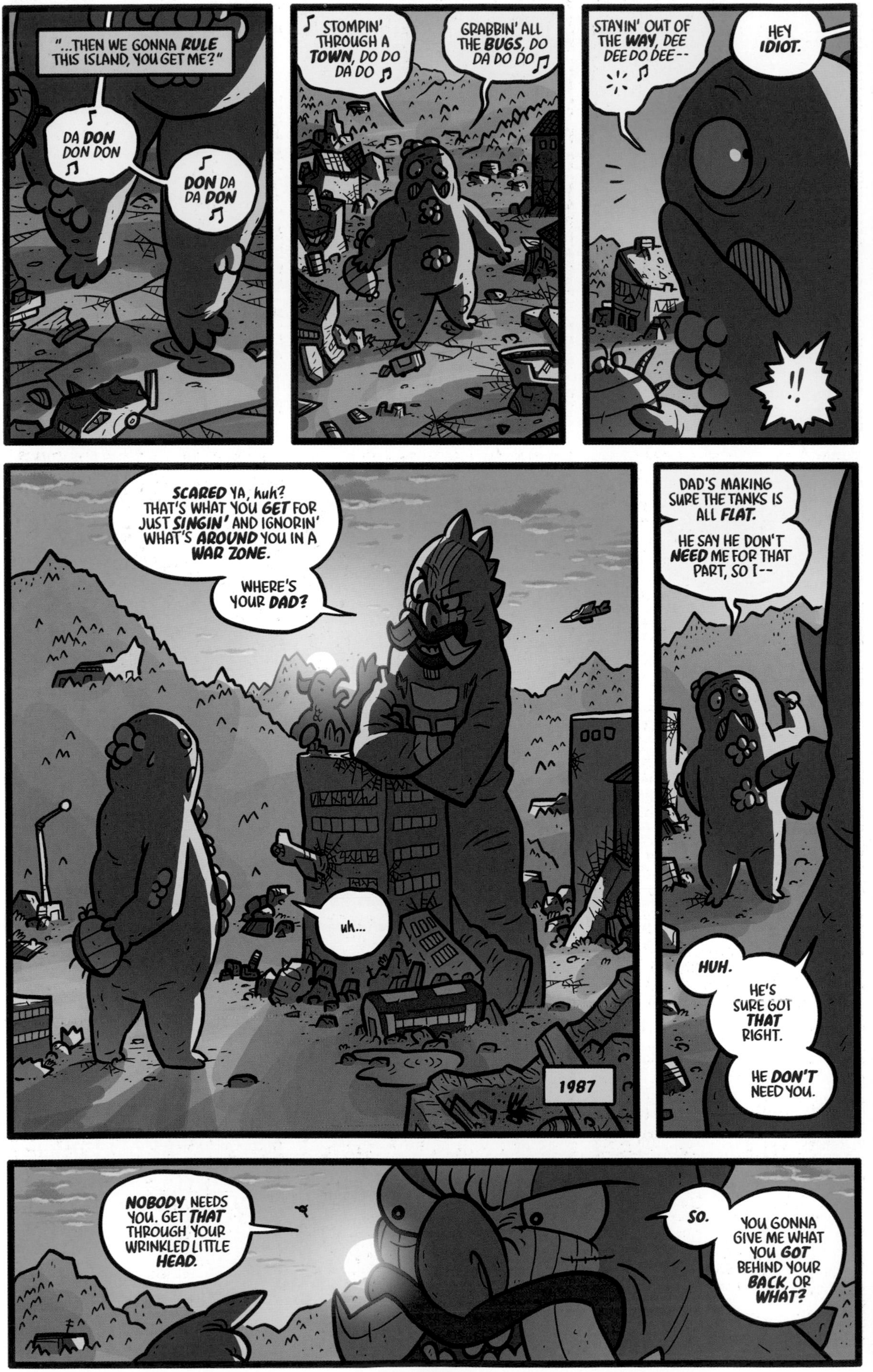
"...THEN WE GONNA RULE THIS ISLAND, YOU GET ME?"
DA DON DON DON
DON DA DA DON
STOMPIN' THROUGH A TOWN, DO DO DA DO
GRABBIN' ALL THE BUGS, DO DA DO DO
STAYIN' OUT OF THE WAY, DEE DEE DO DEE--
HEY IDIOT.
!!
SCARED YA, huh? THAT'S WHAT YOU GET FOR JUST SINGIN' AND IGNORIN' WHAT'S AROUND YOU IN A WAR ZONE.
WHERE'S YOUR DAD?
uh...
1987
DAD'S MAKING SURE THE TANKS IS ALL FLAT.
HE SAY HE DON'T NEED ME FOR THAT PART, SO I--
HUH.
HE'S SURE GOT THAT RIGHT.
HE DON'T NEED YOU.
NOBODY NEEDS YOU. GET THAT THROUGH YOUR WRINKLED LITTLE HEAD.
SO.
YOU GONNA GIVE ME WHAT YOU GOT BEHIND YOUR BACK, OR WHAT?

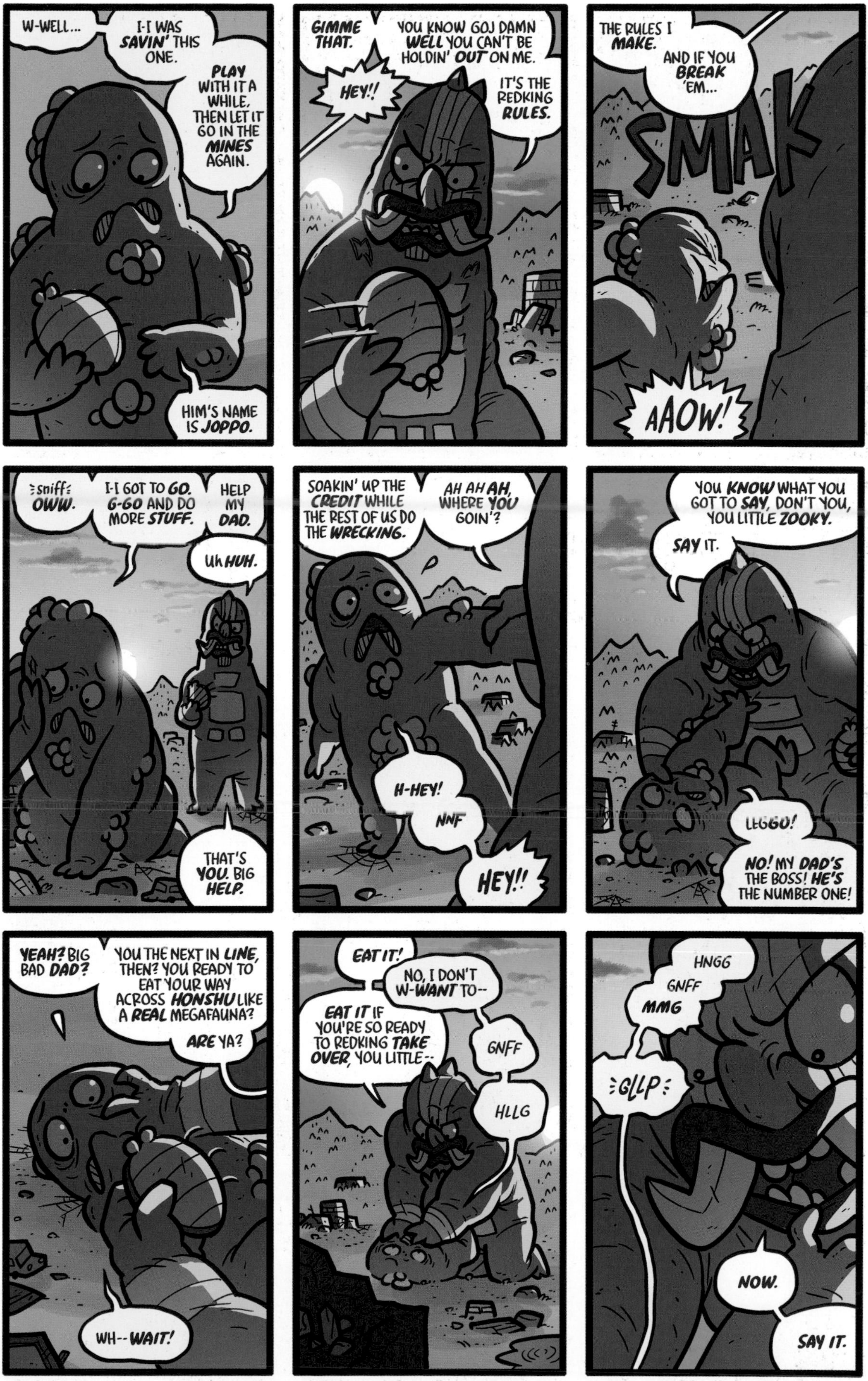

W-WELL...
I-I WAS SAVIN' THIS ONE.
PLAY WITH IT A WHILE, THEN LET IT GO IN THE MINES AGAIN.
HIM'S NAME IS JOPPO.
GIMME THAT.
YOU KNOW GOJ DAMN WELL YOU CAN'T BE HOLDIN' OUT ON ME.
HEY!!
IT'S THE REDKING RULES.
THE RULES I MAKE.
AND IF YOU BREAK 'EM...
SMAK
AAOW!
sniff OWW.
I-I GOT TO GO. G-GO AND DO MORE STUFF.
HELP MY DAD.
Uh HUH.
THAT'S YOU. BIG HELP.
SOAKIN' UP THE CREDIT WHILE THE REST OF US DO THE WRECKING.
AH AH AH, WHERE YOU GOIN'?
H-HEY!
NNF
HEY!!
YOU KNOW WHAT YOU GOT TO SAY, DON'T YOU, YOU LITTLE ZOOKY.
SAY IT.
LEGGO!
NO! MY DAD'S THE BOSS! HE'S THE NUMBER ONE!
YEAH? BIG BAD DAD?
YOU THE NEXT IN LINE, THEN? YOU READY TO EAT YOUR WAY ACROSS HONSHU LIKE A REAL MEGAFAUNA?
ARE YA?
WH--WAIT!
EAT IT!
NO, I DON'T W-WANT TO--
EAT IT IF YOU'RE SO READY TO REDKING TAKE OVER, YOU LITTLE--
GNFF
HLLG
HNGG
GNFF
MMG
GLLP
NOW.
SAY IT.

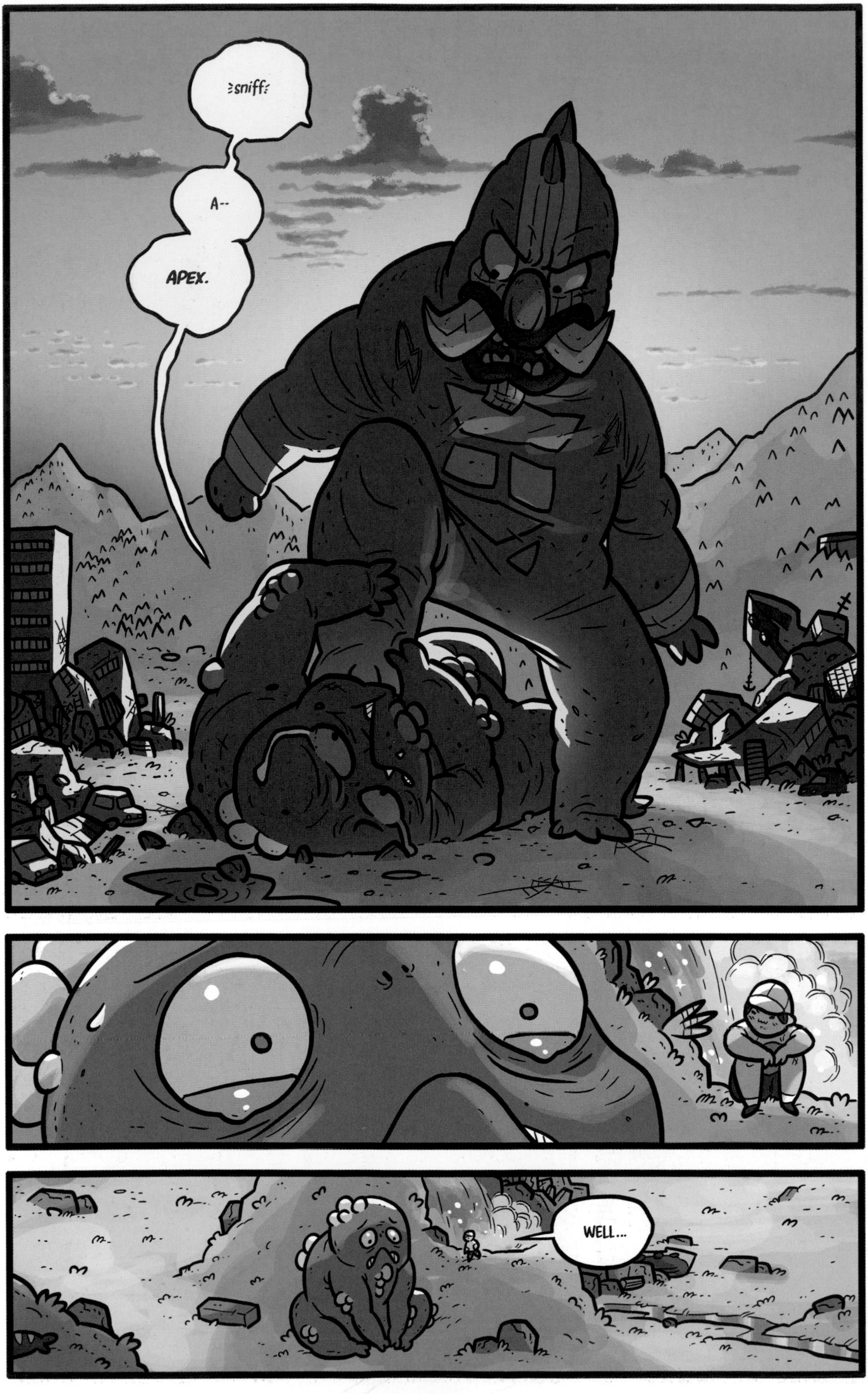
≈sniff≈
A--
APEX.
WELL...

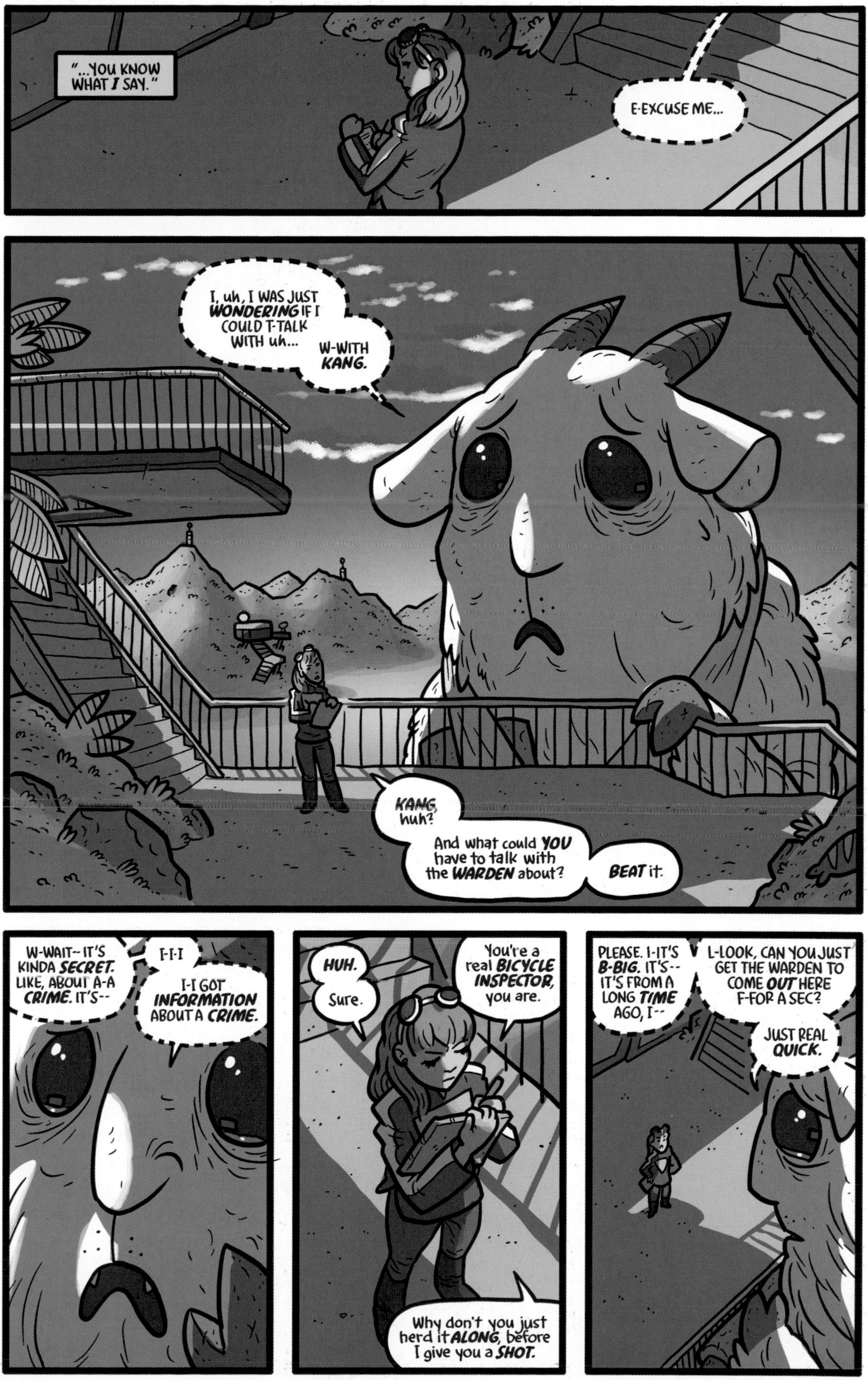
"...YOU KNOW WHAT I SAY."
E-EXCUSE ME...
I, uh, I WAS JUST WONDERING IF I COULD T-TALK WITH uh...
W-WITH KANG.
KANG, huh?
And what could YOU have to talk with the WARDEN about?
BEAT it.
W-WAIT-- IT'S KINDA SECRET. LIKE, ABOUT A-A CRIME. IT'S--
I-I-I
I-I GOT INFORMATION ABOUT A CRIME.
HUH.
Sure.
You're a real BICYCLE INSPECTOR, you are.
Why don't you just herd it ALONG, before I give you a SHOT.
PLEASE. I-IT'S B-BIG. IT'S-- IT'S FROM A LONG TIME AGO, I--
L-LOOK, CAN YOU JUST GET THE WARDEN TO COME OUT HERE F-FOR A SEC?
JUST REAL QUICK.

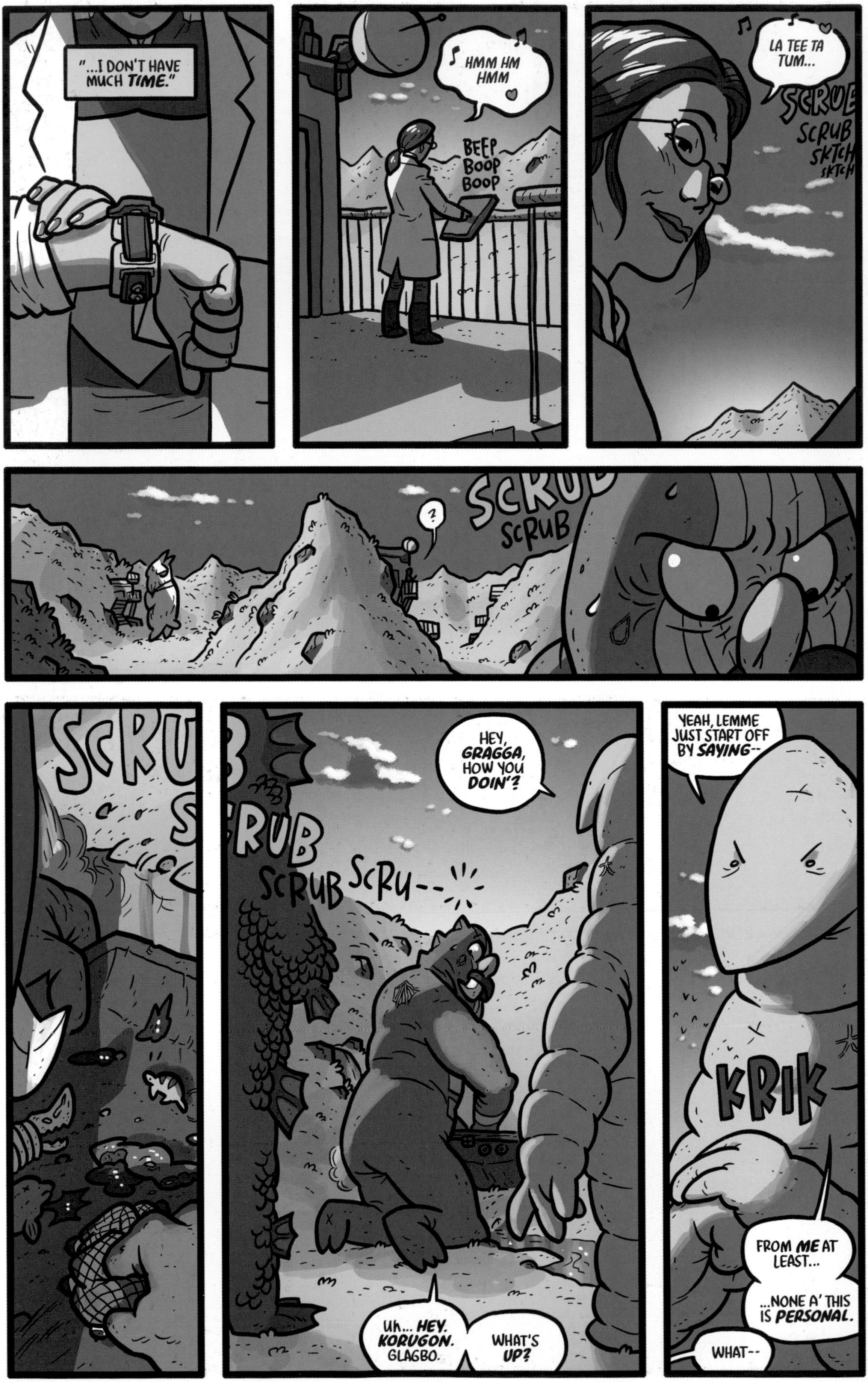
"...I DON'T HAVE MUCH TIME."
HMM HM HMM
BEEP BOOP BOOP
LA TEE TA TUM...
SCRUB
SCRUB
SKTCH
SKTCH
?
SCRUB
SCRUB
SCRUB
SCRUB
SCRUB
SCRUB
SCRU--
HEY, GRAGGA, HOW YOU DOIN'?
Uh... HEY. KORUGON. GLAGBO.
WHAT'S UP?
YEAH, LEMME JUST START OFF BY SAYING--
KRIK
FROM ME AT LEAST...
...NONE A' THIS IS PERSONAL.
WHAT--

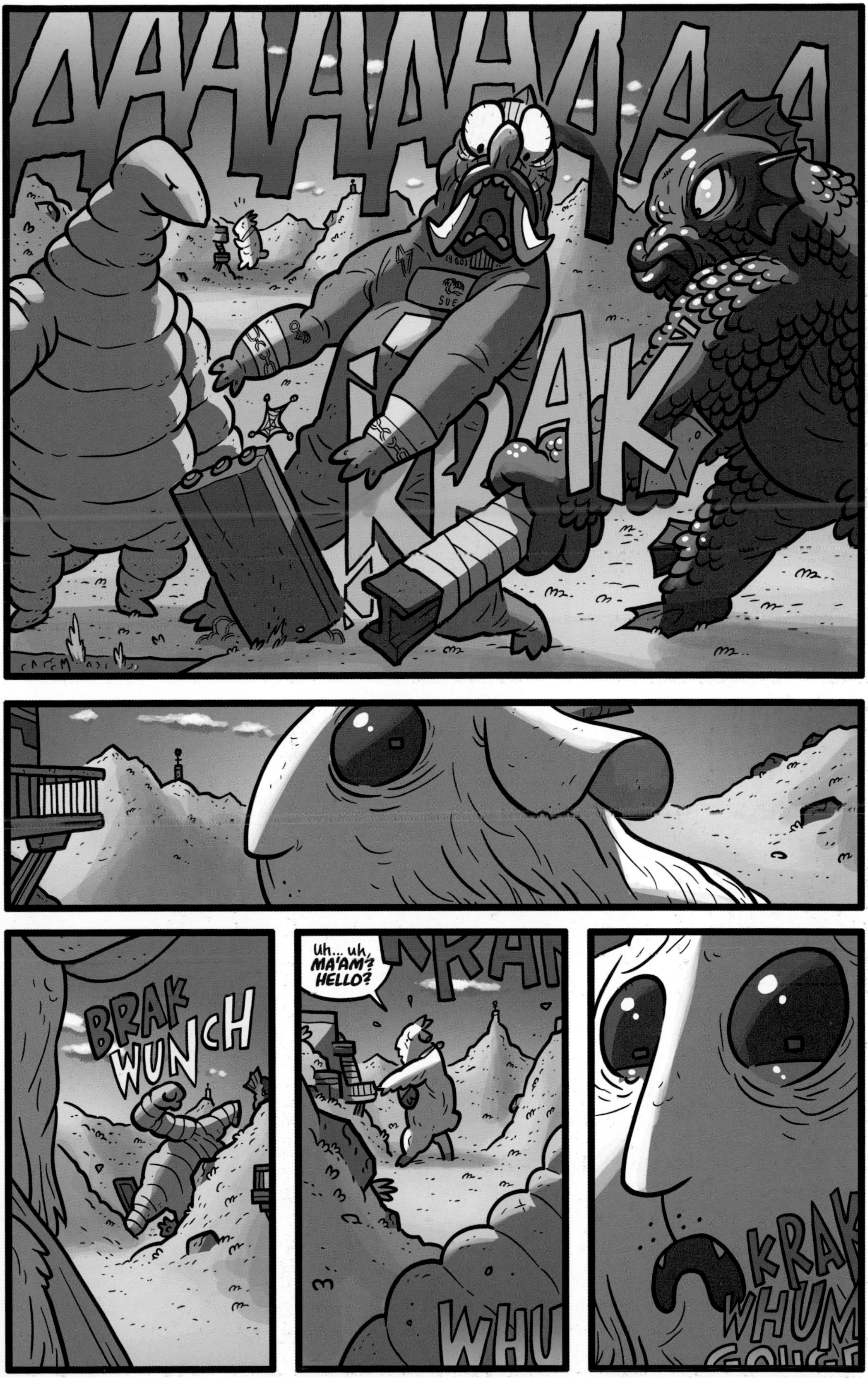
AAAAAAAAAAA
SUE
KRAK
BRAK
WUNCH
Uh... uh, MA'AM? HELLO?
KRAK
WHU
KRAK
WHUM

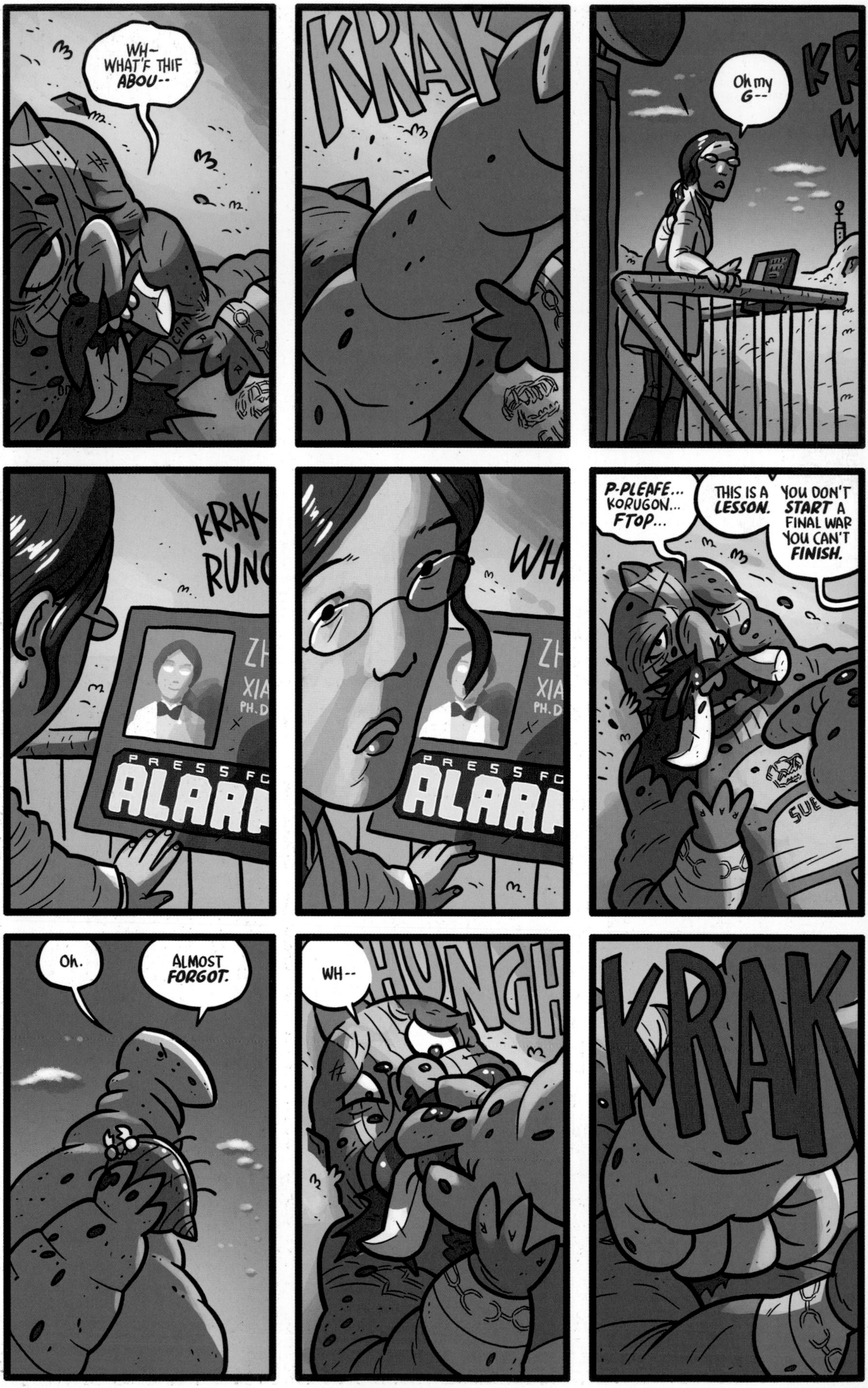
WH- WHAT'F THIF ABOU--
KRAK
Oh my G--
KRAK
RUNC
ZH
XIA
PH.D
PRESS FO
ALAR
WH
P-PLEAFE... KORUGON... FTOP...
THIS IS A LESSON.
YOU DON'T START A FINAL WAR YOU CAN'T FINISH.
SUE
Oh.
ALMOST FORGOT.
WH--
HUNGH
KRAK

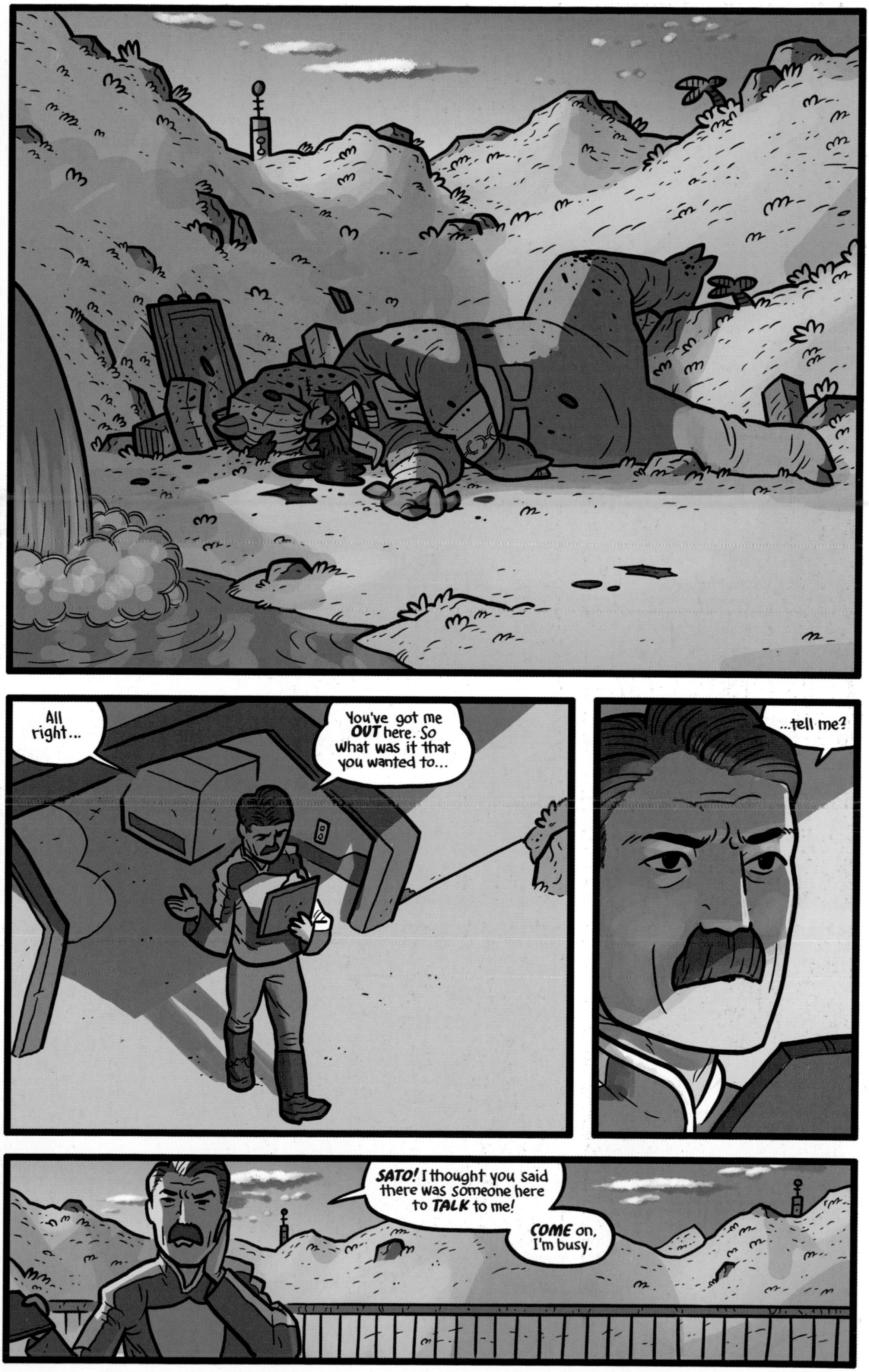
All right...
You've got me OUT here. So what was it that you wanted to...
...tell me?
SATO! I thought you said there was someone here to TALK to me!
COME on, I'm busy.

"I've got NO time for FOOLISHNESS."

ZONN!

LISTEN, WE NEED TO GET THAT MONEY, AND WE NEED TO GET IT NOW.

HMH?

EVEN JUST A BIT, Y-YOU KNOW, TO SHOW SOME GOOD FAITH BEFORE YOU GET THE REST.

PFF! C'MON, BABE.

WHAT'S A BIG DEAL ALL A SUDDEN?

NOTHING'S THE BIG DEAL, IT'S JUST...

...I-IT'S JUST WE JUST NEED TO STAY ON TOP OF THIS STUFF IF--

WAIT A SEC-- HAVE YOU EVEN MOVED?

MOVED? WHY?

THERE'S NO NEED, BABE. YELLOWHORNS SENT SOMEONE BY TO COLLECT.

THE MONEY I BORROWED FOR THIS, PLUS WHAT I OWED THEM FROM BEFORE.

IS COOL. THEY JUST TOOK SOME OF THE URANIUM AS PAYMENT AND WE'RE SQUARE.

WHAT?!

SQUARE WITH THEM, BUT WHAT ABOUT THE FRIGGIN' BUNNIES ON THE MOON?

HUH?

THEY'RE GONNA NEED THEIR MONEY BACK IN LESS THAN--

??!

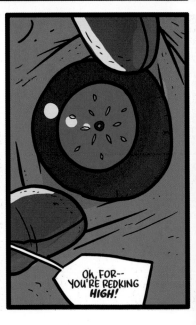

OH, FOR-- YOU'RE REDKING HIGH!

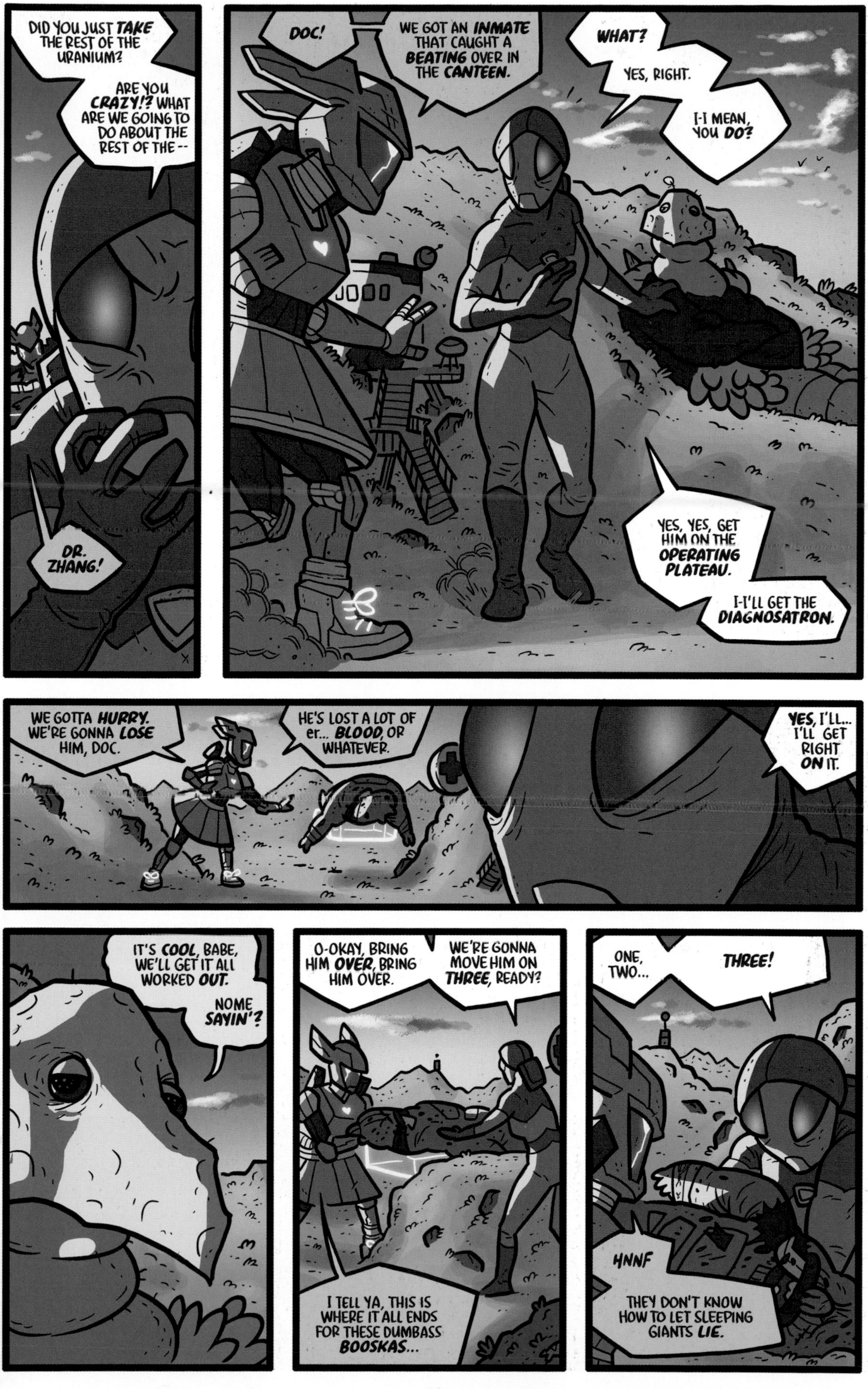
DID YOU JUST TAKE THE REST OF THE URANIUM?
ARE YOU CRAZY!? WHAT ARE WE GOING TO DO ABOUT THE REST OF THE--
DR. ZHANG!
DOC!
WE GOT AN INMATE THAT CAUGHT A BEATING OVER IN THE CANTEEN.
WHAT?
YES, RIGHT.
I-I MEAN, YOU DO?
YES, YES, GET HIM ON THE OPERATING PLATEAU.
I-I'LL GET THE DIAGNOSATRON.
WE GOTTA HURRY. WE'RE GONNA LOSE HIM, DOC.
HE'S LOST A LOT OF er... BLOOD, OR WHATEVER.
YES, I'LL... I'LL GET RIGHT ON IT.
IT'S COOL, BABE, WE'LL GET IT ALL WORKED OUT.
NOME SAYIN'?
O-OKAY, BRING HIM OVER, BRING HIM OVER.
WE'RE GONNA MOVE HIM ON THREE, READY?
I TELL YA, THIS IS WHERE IT ALL ENDS FOR THESE DUMBASS BOOSKAS...
ONE, TWO...
THREE!
HNNF
THEY DON'T KNOW HOW TO LET SLEEPING GIANTS LIE.

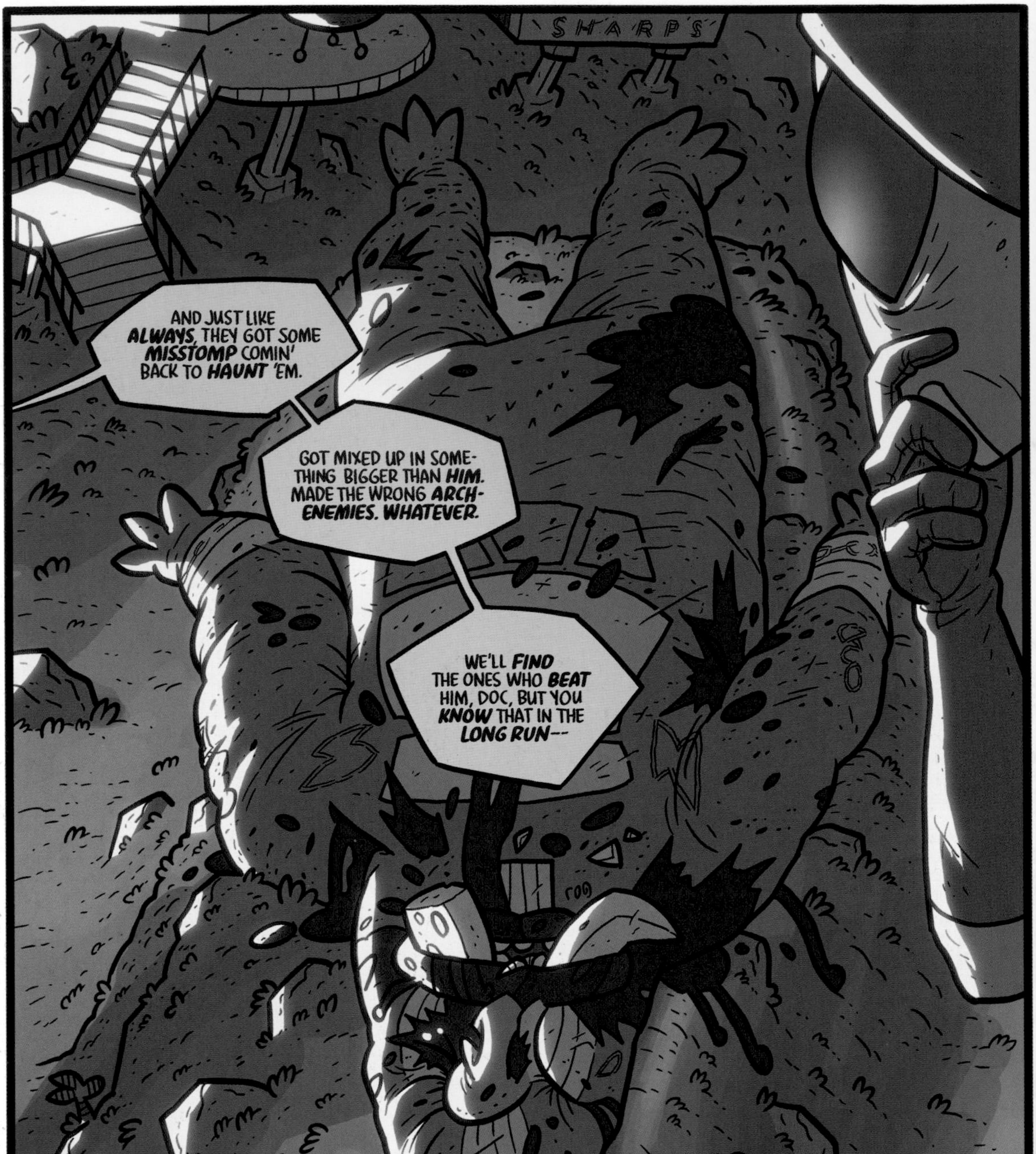
SHARPS
AND JUST LIKE **ALWAYS**, THEY GOT SOME **MISSTOMP** COMIN' BACK TO **HAUNT** 'EM.
GOT MIXED UP IN SOMETHING BIGGER THAN **HIM**. MADE THE WRONG **ARCHENEMIES. WHATEVER.**
WE'LL **FIND** THE ONES WHO **BEAT** HIM, DOC, BUT YOU **KNOW** THAT IN THE **LONG RUN**--

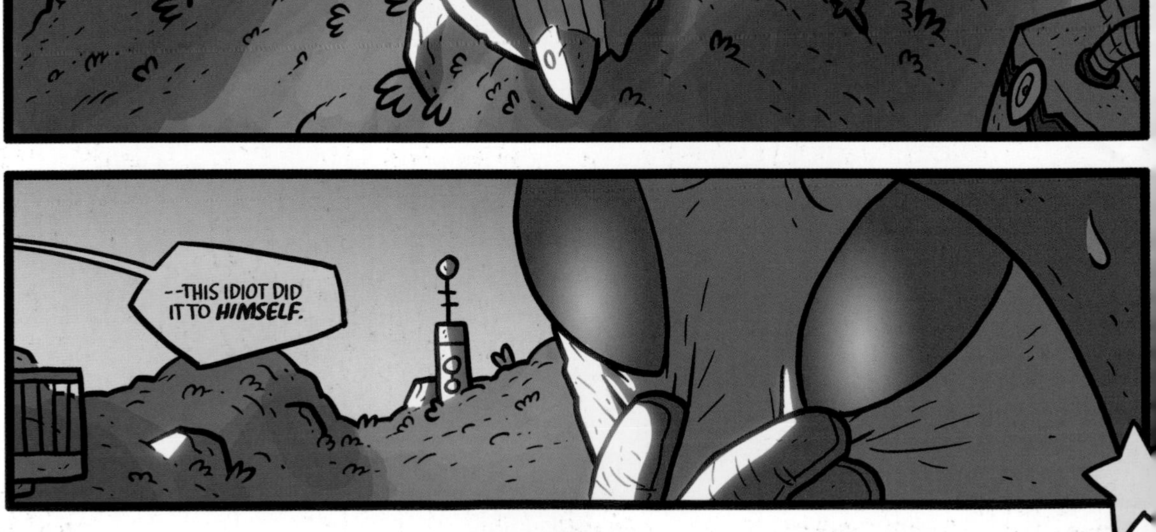
--THIS IDIOT DID IT TO **HIMSELF.**

EPISODE 3

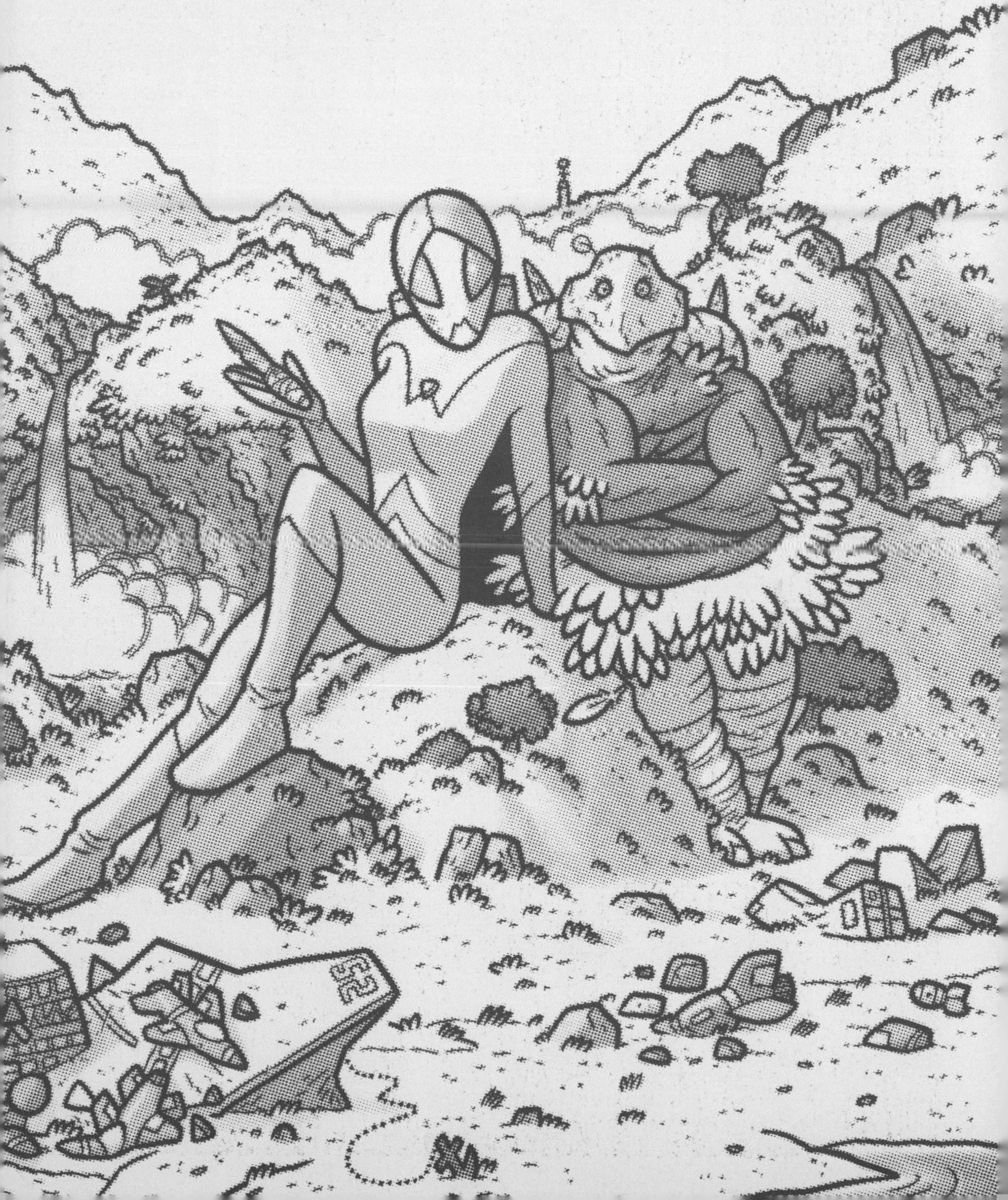

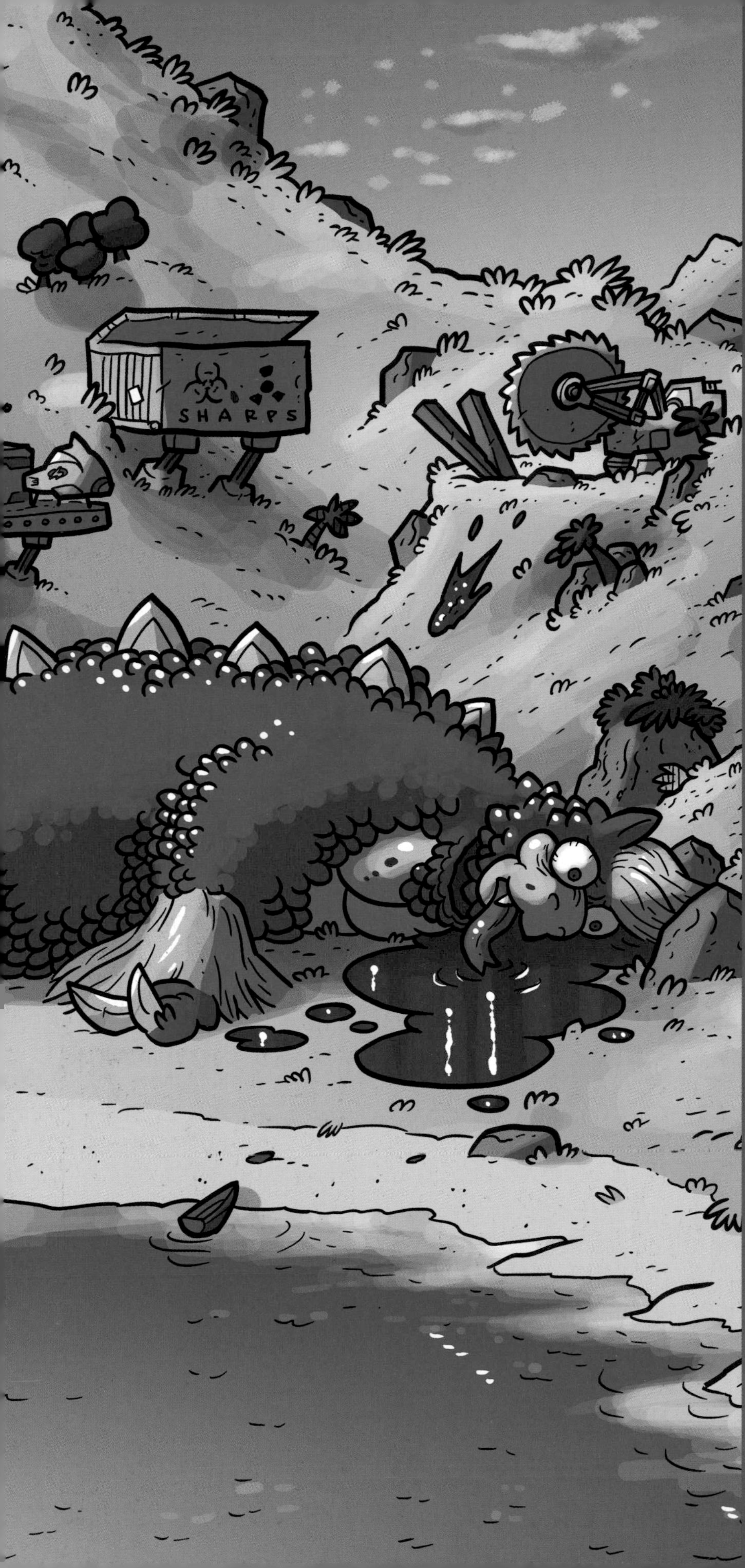
SHARPS

怪獣マックス

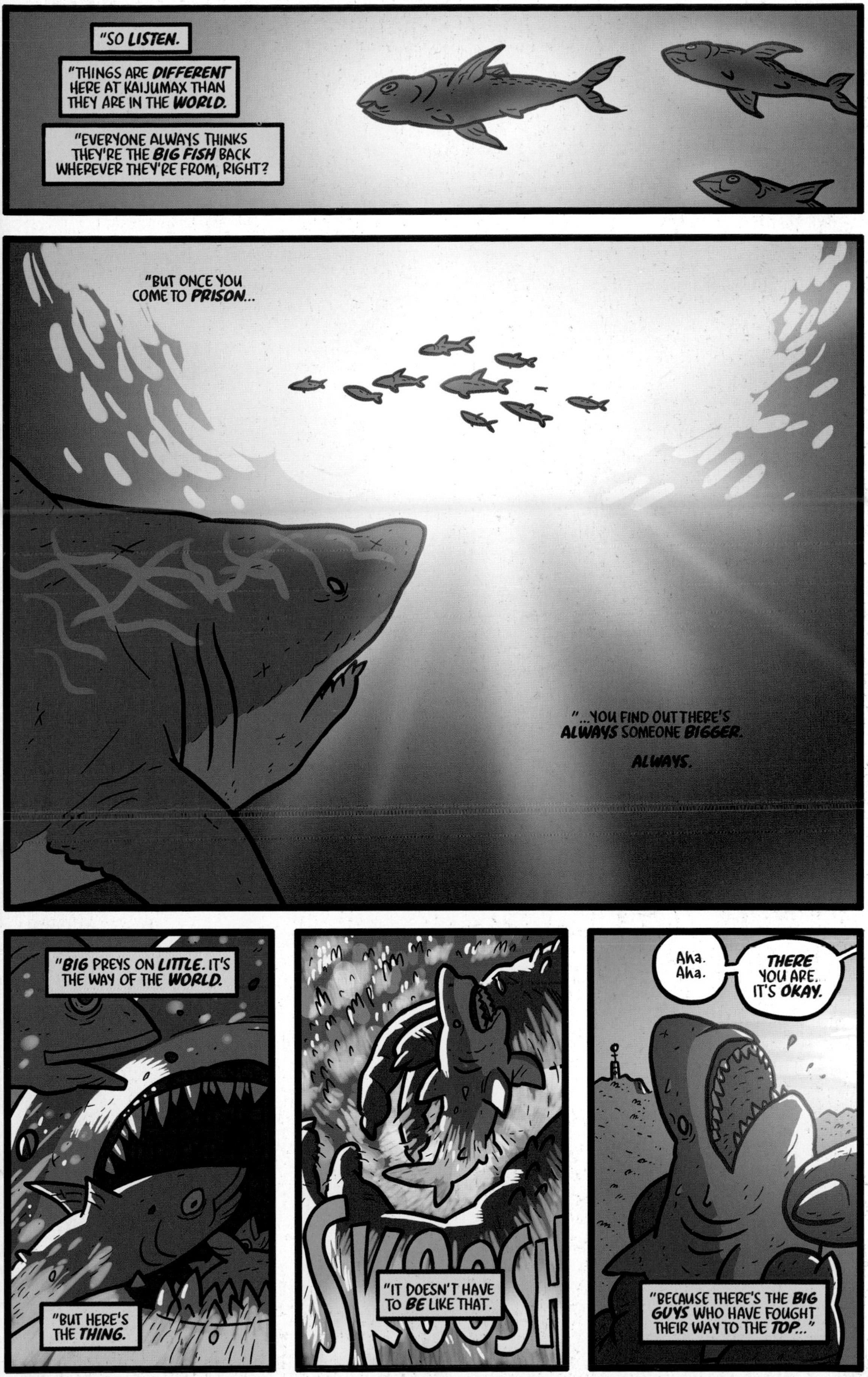
"SO LISTEN.
"THINGS ARE DIFFERENT HERE AT KAIJUMAX THAN THEY ARE IN THE WORLD.
"EVERYONE ALWAYS THINKS THEY'RE THE BIG FISH BACK WHEREVER THEY'RE FROM, RIGHT?
"BUT ONCE YOU COME TO PRISON...
"...YOU FIND OUT THERE'S ALWAYS SOMEONE BIGGER.
ALWAYS.
"BIG PREYS ON LITTLE. IT'S THE WAY OF THE WORLD.
"BUT HERE'S THE THING.
SKOOSH
"IT DOESN'T HAVE TO BE LIKE THAT.
Aha. Aha.
THERE YOU ARE. IT'S OKAY.
"BECAUSE THERE'S THE BIG GUYS WHO HAVE FOUGHT THEIR WAY TO THE TOP..."

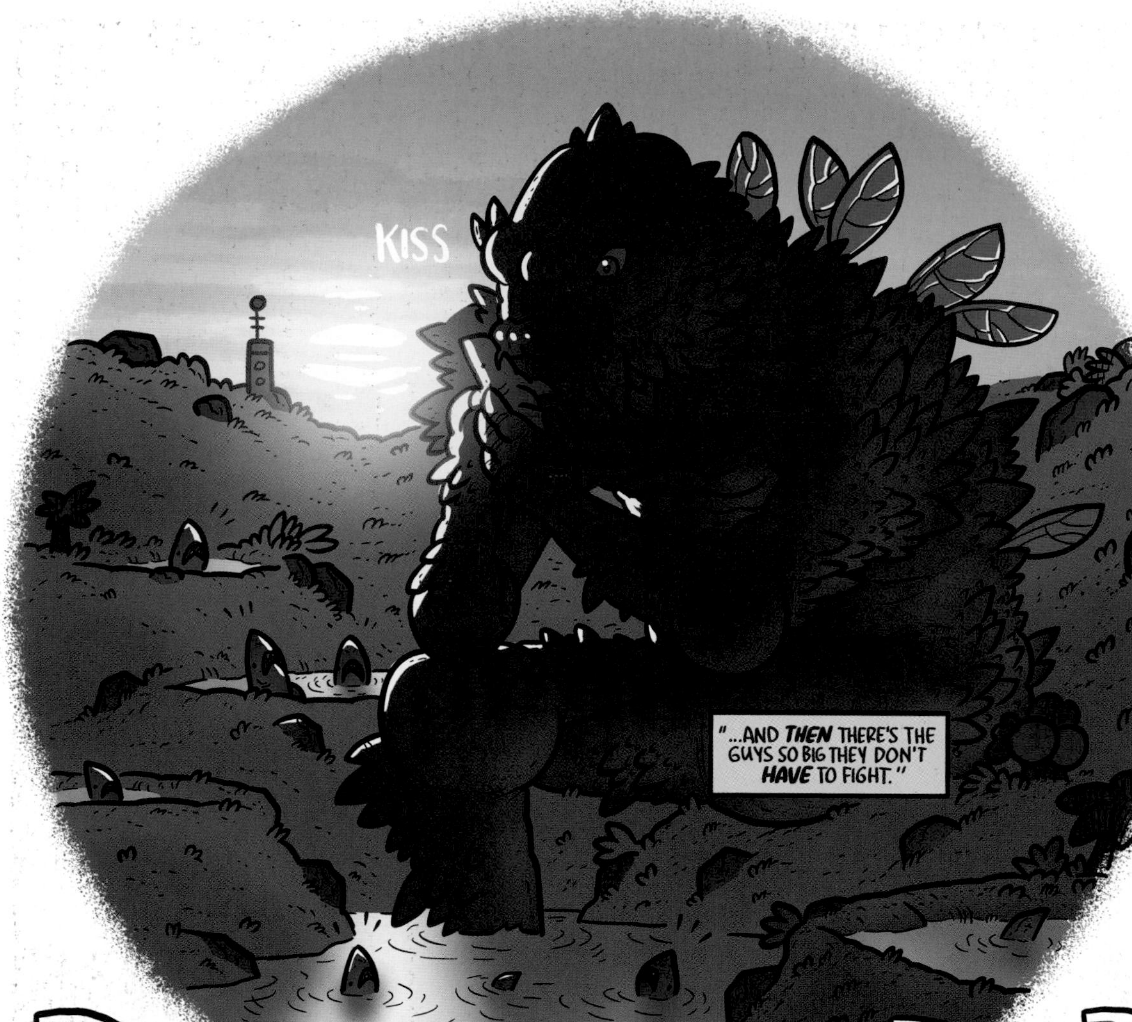
KISS
"...AND THEN THERE'S THE GUYS SO BIG THEY DON'T HAVE TO FIGHT."

ROCK SOLID REP

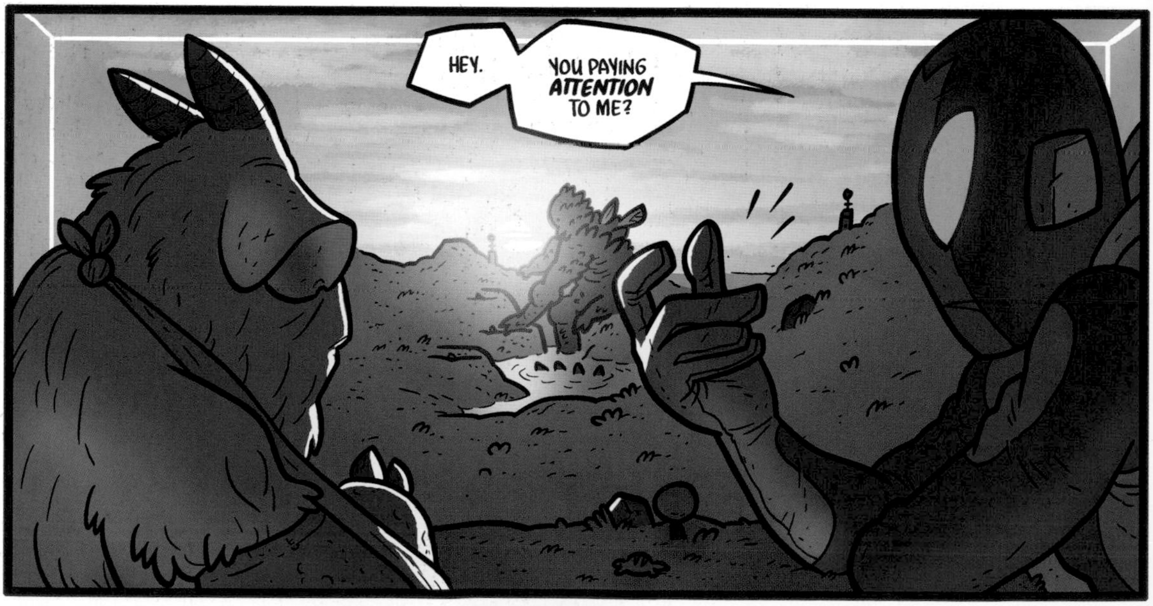
HEY.
YOU PAYING ATTENTION TO ME?

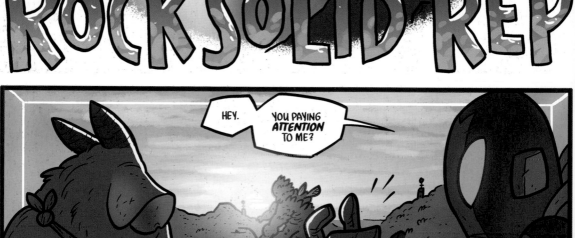

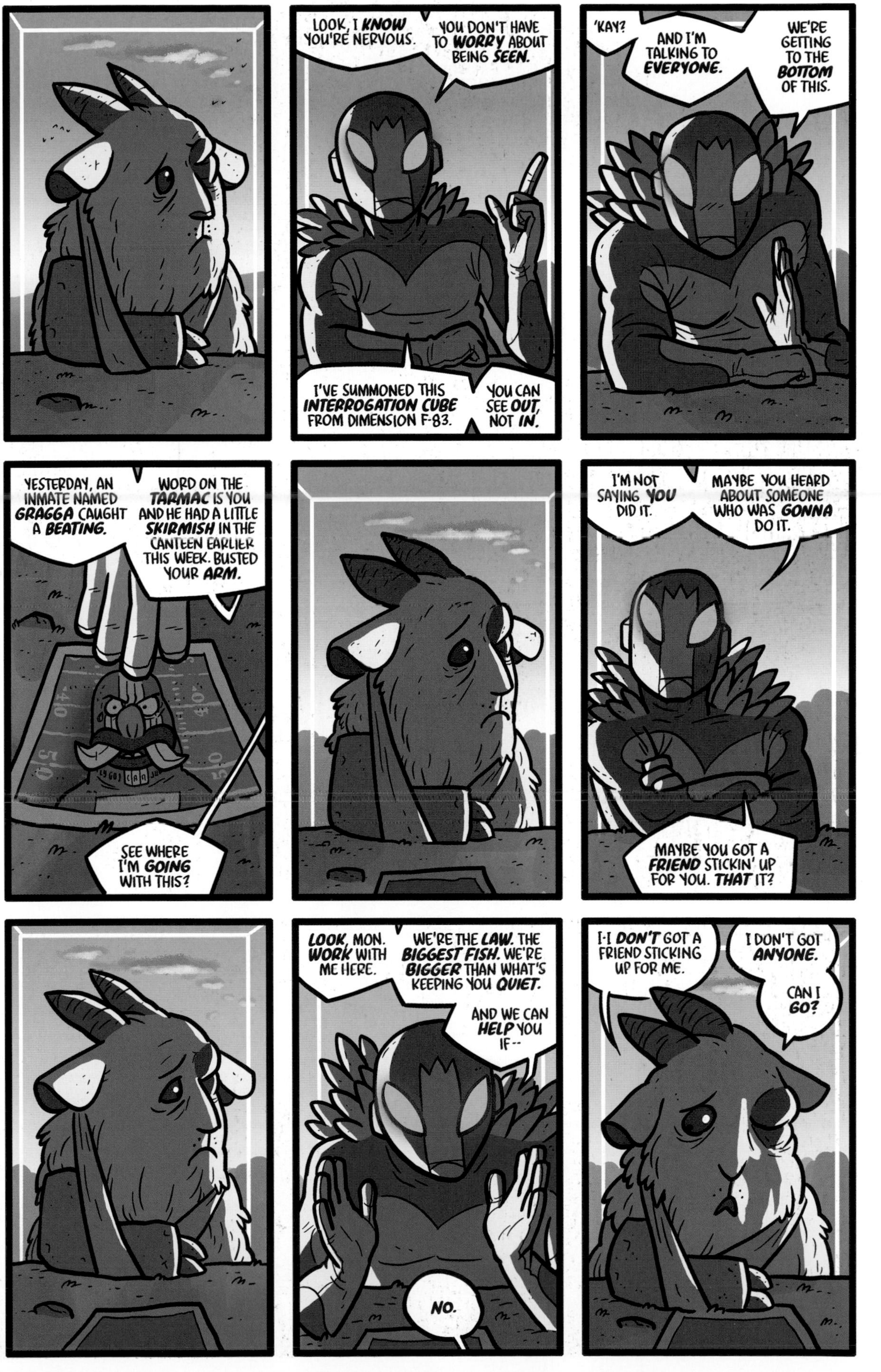
LOOK, I KNOW YOU'RE NERVOUS.
YOU DON'T HAVE TO WORRY ABOUT BEING SEEN.
I'VE SUMMONED THIS INTERROGATION CUBE FROM DIMENSION F-83.
YOU CAN SEE OUT, NOT IN.
'KAY?
AND I'M TALKING TO EVERYONE.
WE'RE GETTING TO THE BOTTOM OF THIS.
YESTERDAY, AN INMATE NAMED GRAGGA CAUGHT A BEATING.
WORD ON THE TARMAC IS YOU AND HE HAD A LITTLE SKIRMISH IN THE CANTEEN EARLIER THIS WEEK. BUSTED YOUR ARM.
SEE WHERE I'M GOING WITH THIS?
I'M NOT SAYING YOU DID IT.
MAYBE YOU HEARD ABOUT SOMEONE WHO WAS GONNA DO IT.
MAYBE YOU GOT A FRIEND STICKIN' UP FOR YOU. THAT IT?
LOOK, MON. WORK WITH ME HERE.
WE'RE THE LAW. THE BIGGEST FISH. WE'RE BIGGER THAN WHAT'S KEEPING YOU QUIET.
AND WE CAN HELP YOU IF--
NO.
I-I DON'T GOT A FRIEND STICKING UP FOR ME.
I DON'T GOT ANYONE.
CAN I GO?

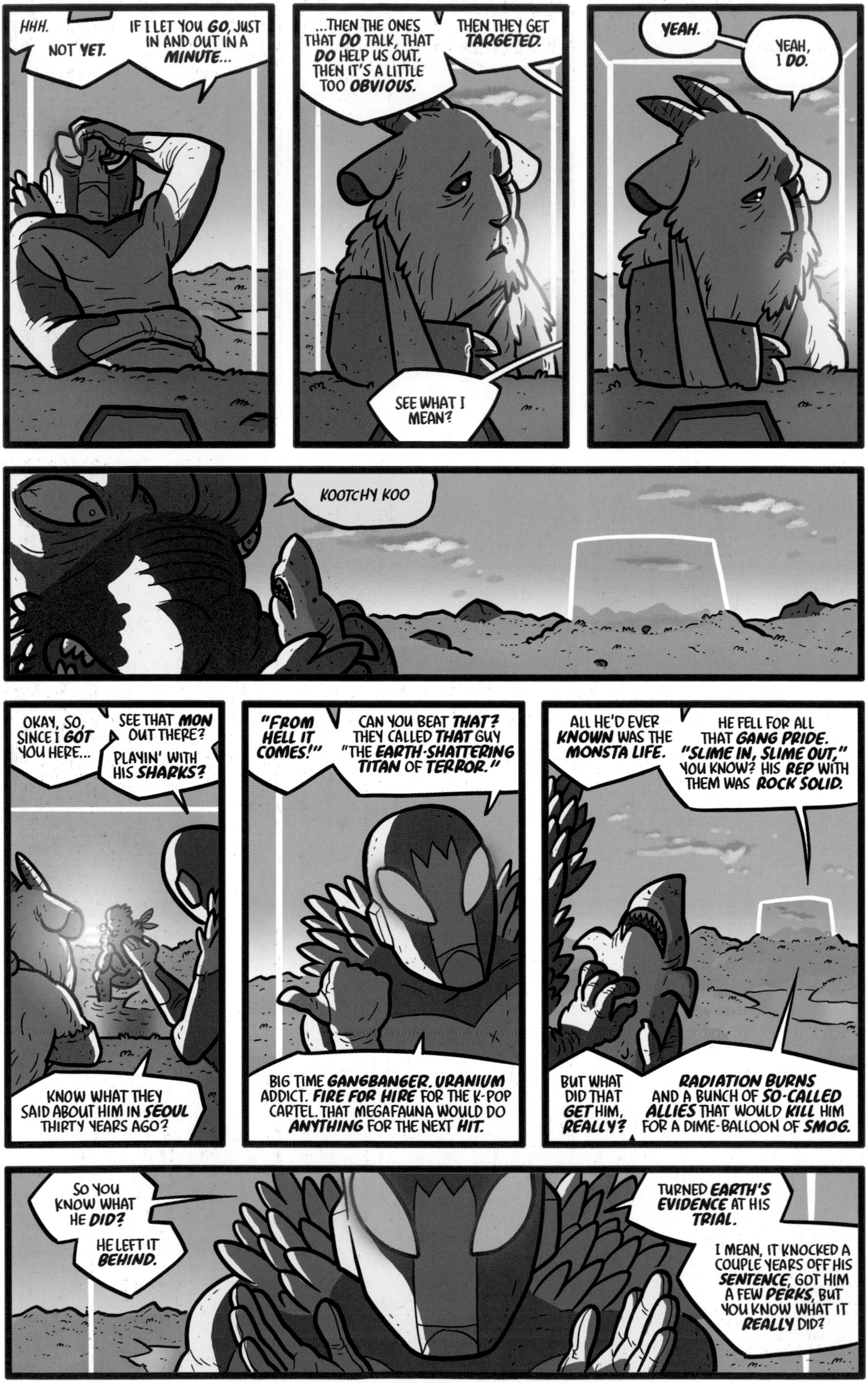
HHH.
NOT YET.
IF I LET YOU GO, JUST IN AND OUT IN A MINUTE...
...THEN THE ONES THAT DO TALK, THAT DO HELP US OUT, THEN IT'S A LITTLE TOO OBVIOUS.
THEN THEY GET TARGETED.
SEE WHAT I MEAN?
YEAH.
YEAH, I DO.
KOOTCHY KOO
OKAY, SO, SINCE I GOT YOU HERE...
SEE THAT MON OUT THERE?
PLAYIN' WITH HIS SHARKS?
KNOW WHAT THEY SAID ABOUT HIM IN SEOUL THIRTY YEARS AGO?
"FROM HELL IT COMES!"
CAN YOU BEAT THAT? THEY CALLED THAT GUY "THE EARTH-SHATTERING TITAN OF TERROR."
BIG TIME GANGBANGER. URANIUM ADDICT. FIRE FOR HIRE FOR THE K-POP CARTEL. THAT MEGAFAUNA WOULD DO ANYTHING FOR THE NEXT HIT.
ALL HE'D EVER KNOWN WAS THE MONSTA LIFE.
HE FELL FOR ALL THAT GANG PRIDE. "SLIME IN, SLIME OUT," YOU KNOW? HIS REP WITH THEM WAS ROCK SOLID.
BUT WHAT DID THAT GET HIM, REALLY?
RADIATION BURNS AND A BUNCH OF SO-CALLED ALLIES THAT WOULD KILL HIM FOR A DIME-BALLOON OF SMOG.
SO YOU KNOW WHAT HE DID?
HE LEFT IT BEHIND.
TURNED EARTH'S EVIDENCE AT HIS TRIAL.
I MEAN, IT KNOCKED A COUPLE YEARS OFF HIS SENTENCE, GOT HIM A FEW PERKS, BUT YOU KNOW WHAT IT REALLY DID?

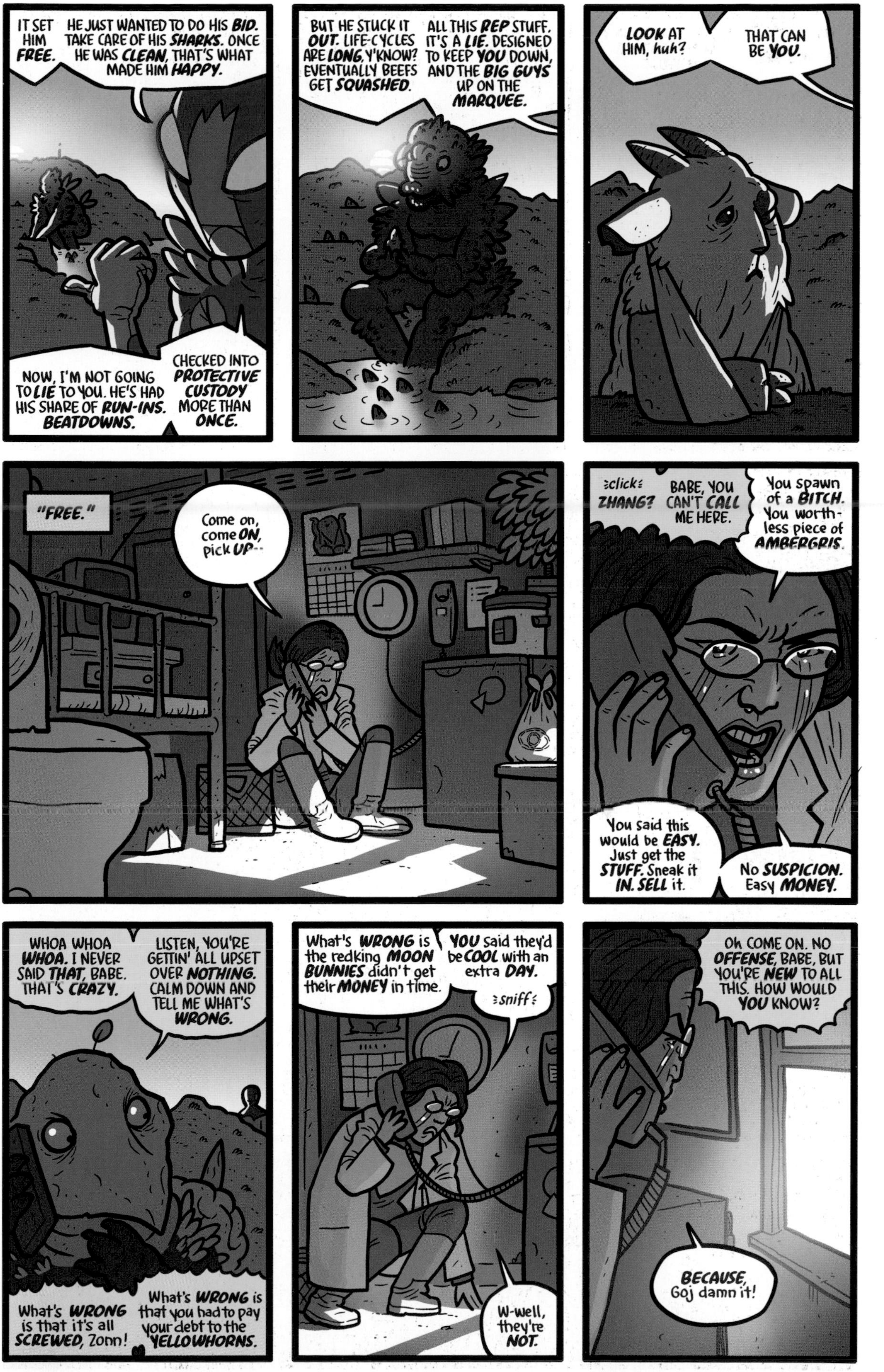

IT SET HIM FREE.
HE JUST WANTED TO DO HIS BID. TAKE CARE OF HIS SHARKS. ONCE HE WAS CLEAN, THAT'S WHAT MADE HIM HAPPY.
NOW, I'M NOT GOING TO LIE TO YOU. HE'S HAD HIS SHARE OF RUN-INS. BEATDOWNS.
CHECKED INTO PROTECTIVE CUSTODY MORE THAN ONCE.
BUT HE STUCK IT OUT. LIFE-CYCLES ARE LONG, Y'KNOW? EVENTUALLY BEEFS GET SQUASHED.
ALL THIS REP STUFF. IT'S A LIE. DESIGNED TO KEEP YOU DOWN, AND THE BIG GUYS UP ON THE MARQUEE.
LOOK AT HIM, huh?
THAT CAN BE YOU.
"FREE."
Come on, come ON, pick UP--
≥click≤ ZHANG?
BABE, YOU CAN'T CALL ME HERE.
You spawn of a BITCH. You worthless piece of AMBERGRIS.
You said this would be EASY. Just get the STUFF. Sneak it IN. SELL it.
No SUSPICION. Easy MONEY.
WHOA WHOA WHOA. I NEVER SAID THAT, BABE. THAT'S CRAZY.
LISTEN, YOU'RE GETTIN' ALL UPSET OVER NOTHING. CALM DOWN AND TELL ME WHAT'S WRONG.
What's WRONG is that it's all SCREWED, Zonn!
What's WRONG is that you had to pay your debt to the YELLOWHORNS.
What's WRONG is the redking MOON BUNNIES didn't get their MONEY in time.
YOU said they'd be COOL with an extra DAY.
≥sniff≤
W-well, they're NOT.
Oh COME ON. NO OFFENSE, BABE, BUT YOU'RE NEW TO ALL THIS. HOW WOULD YOU KNOW?
BECAUSE, Goj damn it!

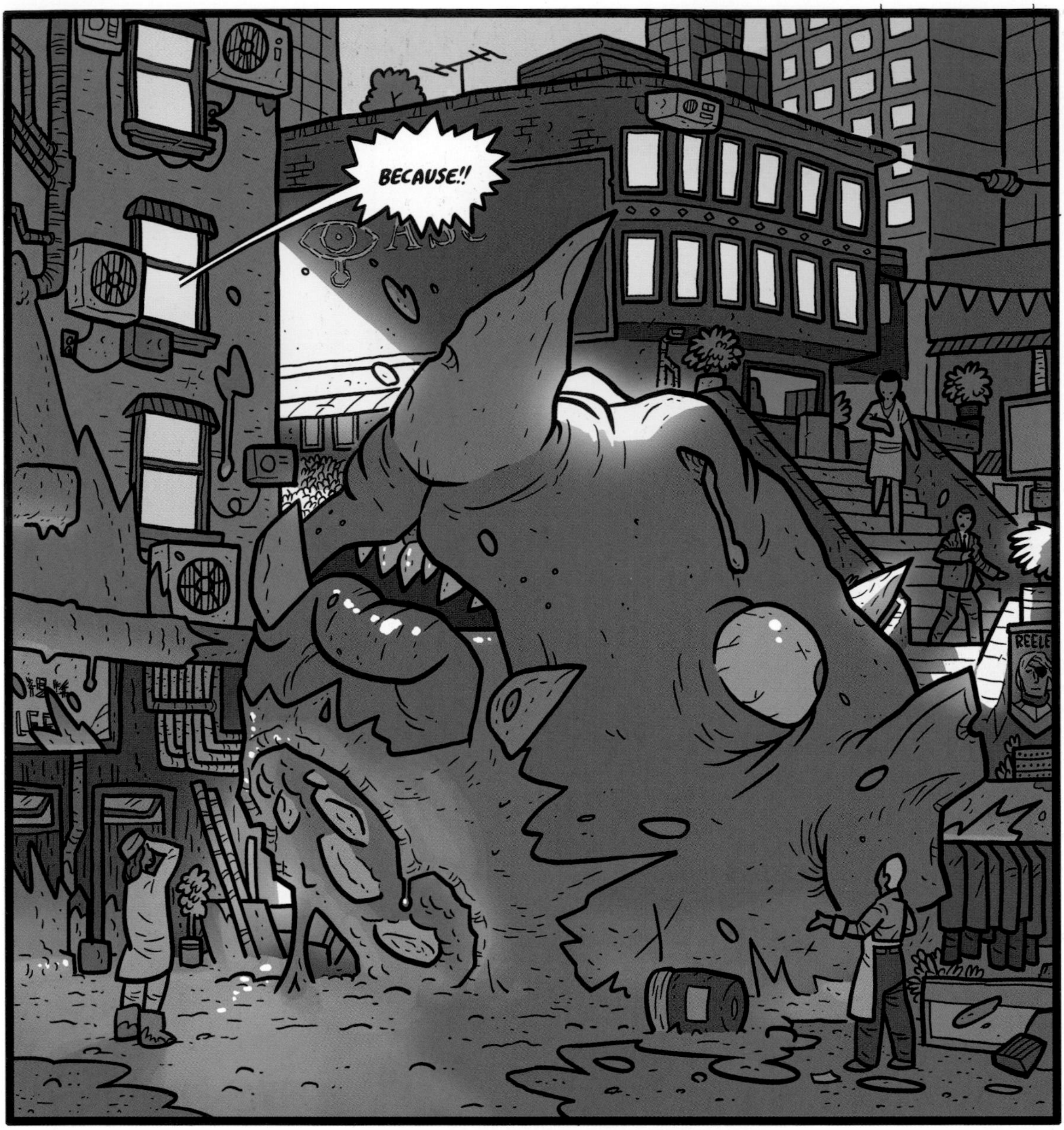
BECAUSE!!

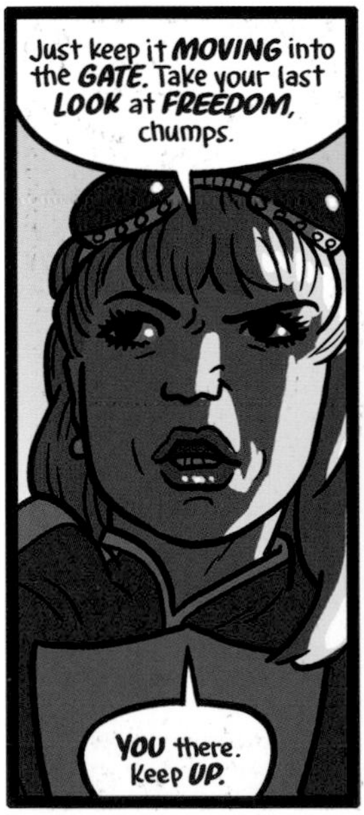
Just keep it MOVING into the GATE. Take your last LOOK at FREEDOM, chumps.
YOU there. Keep UP.

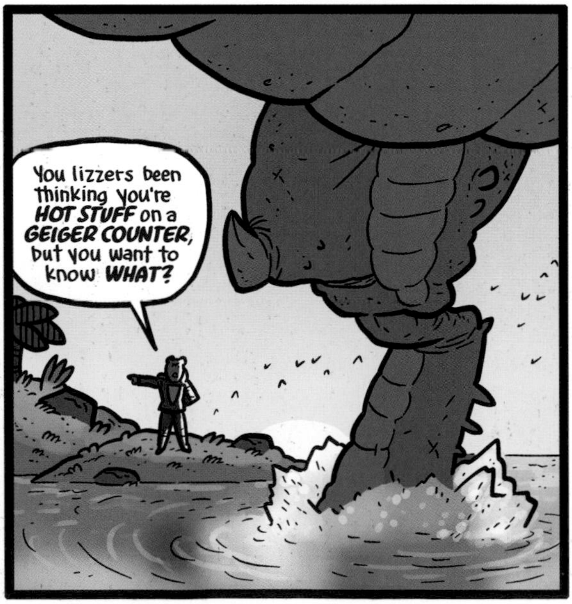
You lizzers been thinking you're HOT STUFF on a GEIGER COUNTER, but you want to know WHAT?

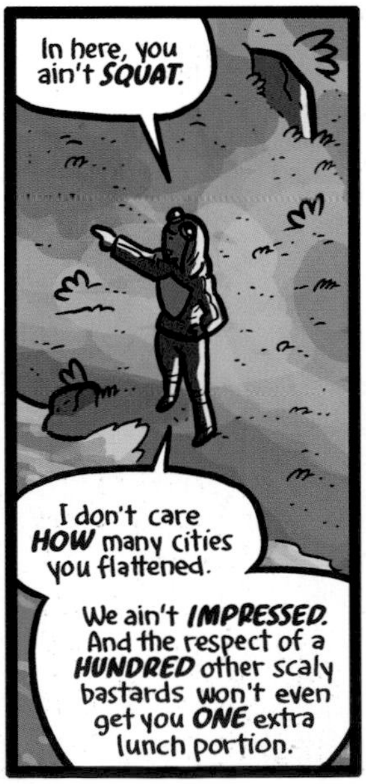
In here, you ain't SQUAT.
I don't care HOW many cities you flattened.
We ain't IMPRESSED. And the respect of a HUNDRED other scaly bastards won't even get you ONE extra lunch portion.

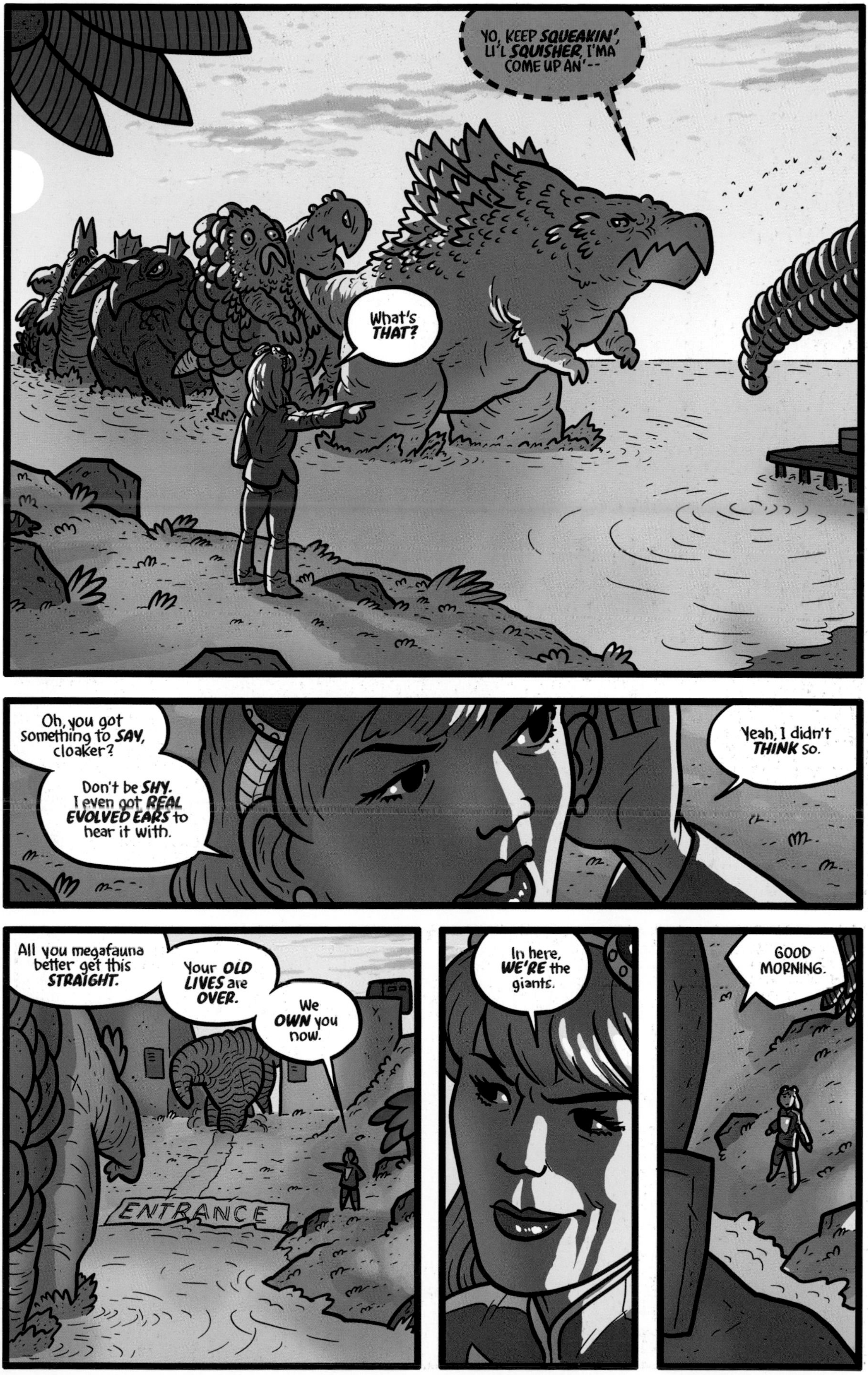
YO, KEEP SQUEAKIN', LI'L SQUISHER, I'MA COME UP AN'--
What's THAT?
Oh, you got something to SAY, cloaker?
Don't be SHY. I even got REAL EVOLVED EARS to hear it with.
Yeah, I didn't THINK so.
All you megafauna better get this STRAIGHT.
Your OLD LIVES are OVER.
We OWN you now.
ENTRANCE
In here, WE'RE the giants.
GOOD MORNING.

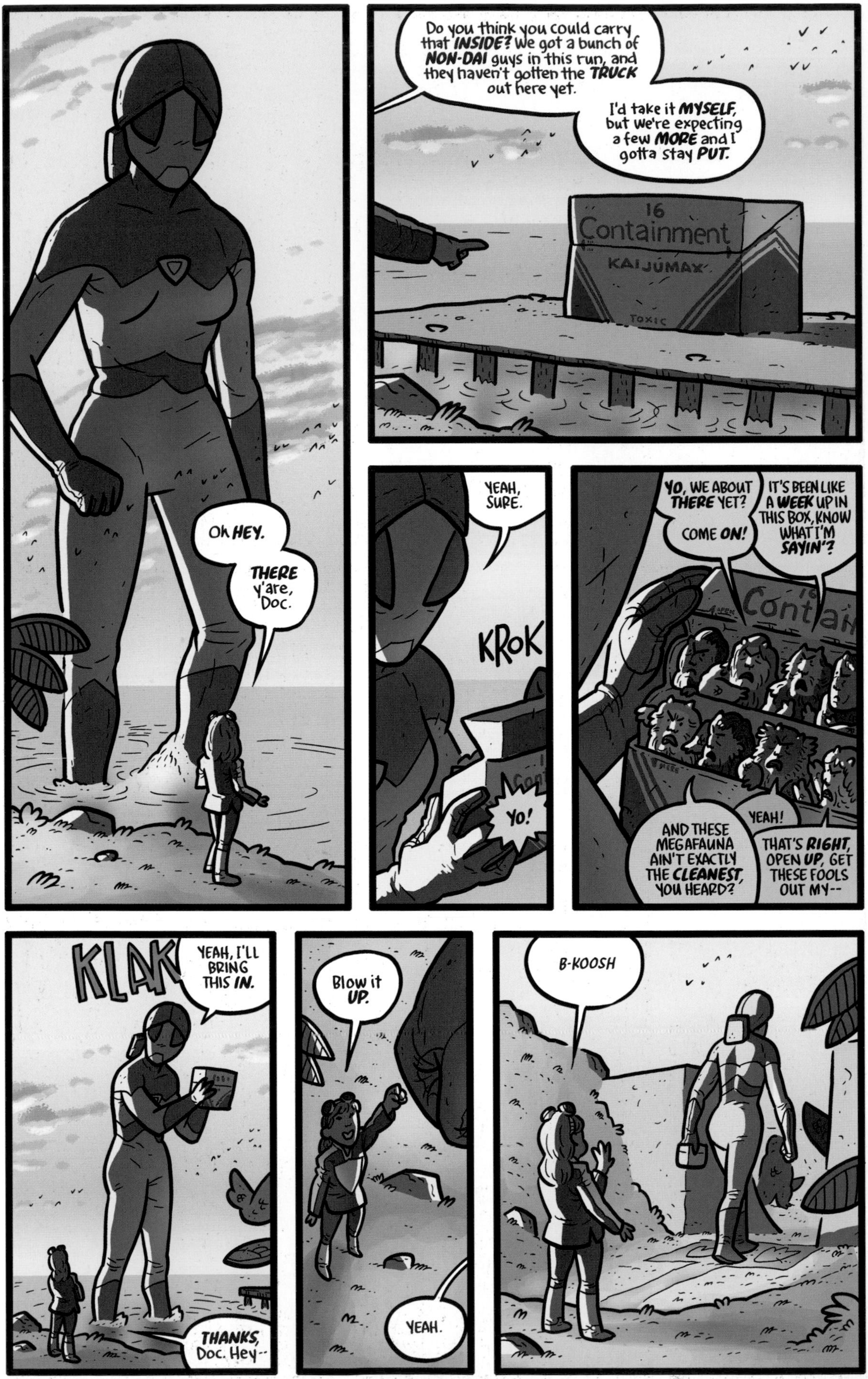
Oh HEY.
THERE y'are, Doc.
Do you think you could carry that INSIDE? We got a bunch of NON-DAI guys in this run, and they haven't gotten the TRUCK out here yet.
I'd take it MYSELF, but we're expecting a few MORE and I gotta stay PUT.
16 Containment
KAIJÚMAX
TOXIC
YEAH, SURE.
KROK
YO!
YO, WE ABOUT THERE YET?
COME ON!
IT'S BEEN LIKE A WEEK UP IN THIS BOX, KNOW WHAT I'M SAYIN'?
AND THESE MEGAFAUNA AIN'T EXACTLY THE CLEANEST, YOU HEARD?
YEAH!
THAT'S RIGHT, OPEN UP, GET THESE FOOLS OUT MY--
KLAK
YEAH, I'LL BRING THIS IN.
THANKS, Doc. Hey--
Blow it UP.
YEAH.
B-KOOSH

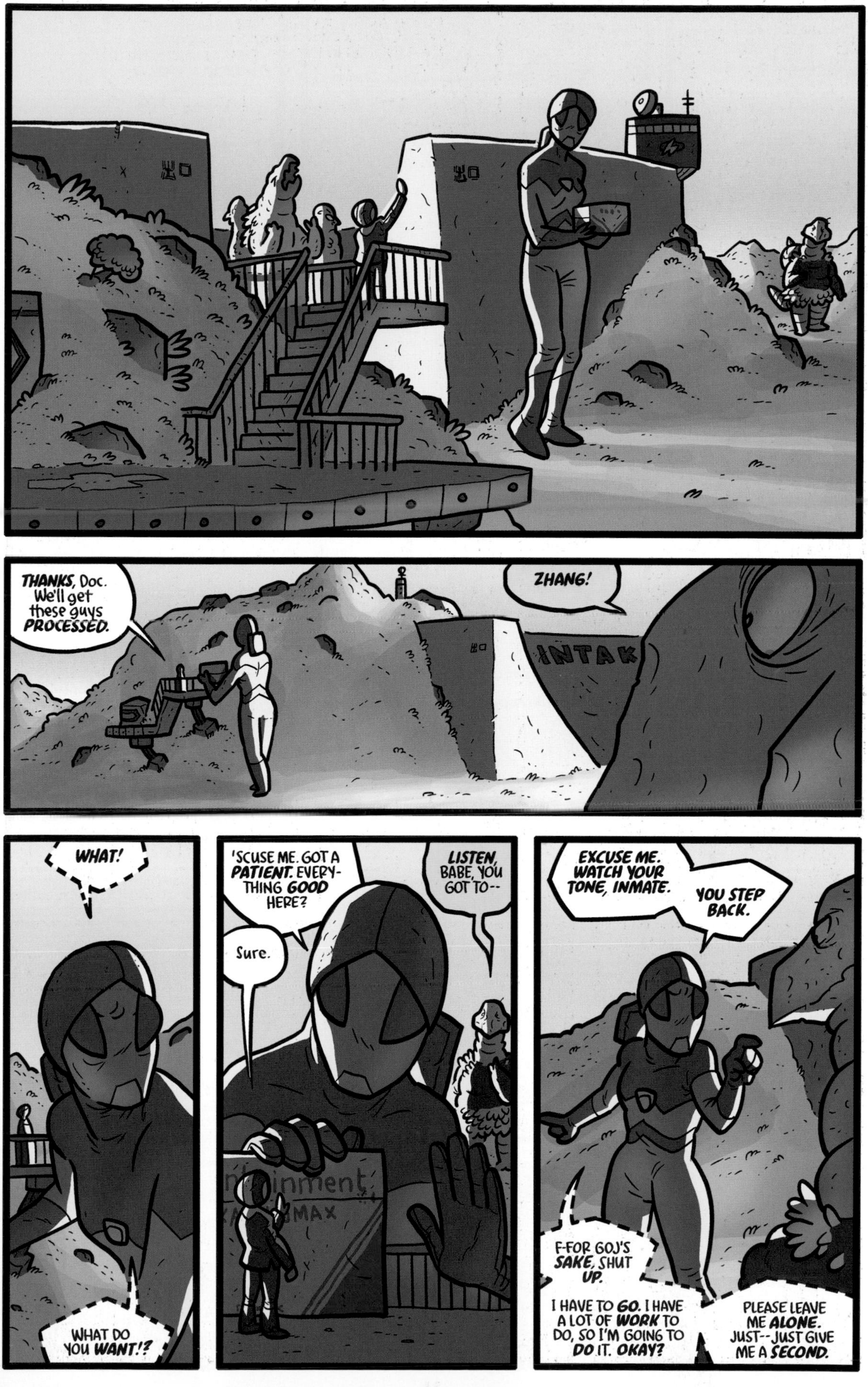
THANKS, Doc. We'll get these guys PROCESSED.
ZHANG!
INTAK
WHAT!
WHAT DO YOU WANT!?
'SCUSE ME. GOT A PATIENT. EVERY-THING GOOD HERE?
Sure.
LISTEN, BABE, YOU GOT TO--
EXCUSE ME. WATCH YOUR TONE, INMATE.
YOU STEP BACK.
F-FOR GOJ'S SAKE, SHUT UP.
I HAVE TO GO. I HAVE A LOT OF WORK TO DO, SO I'M GOING TO DO IT. OKAY?
PLEASE LEAVE ME ALONE. JUST--JUST GIVE ME A SECOND.

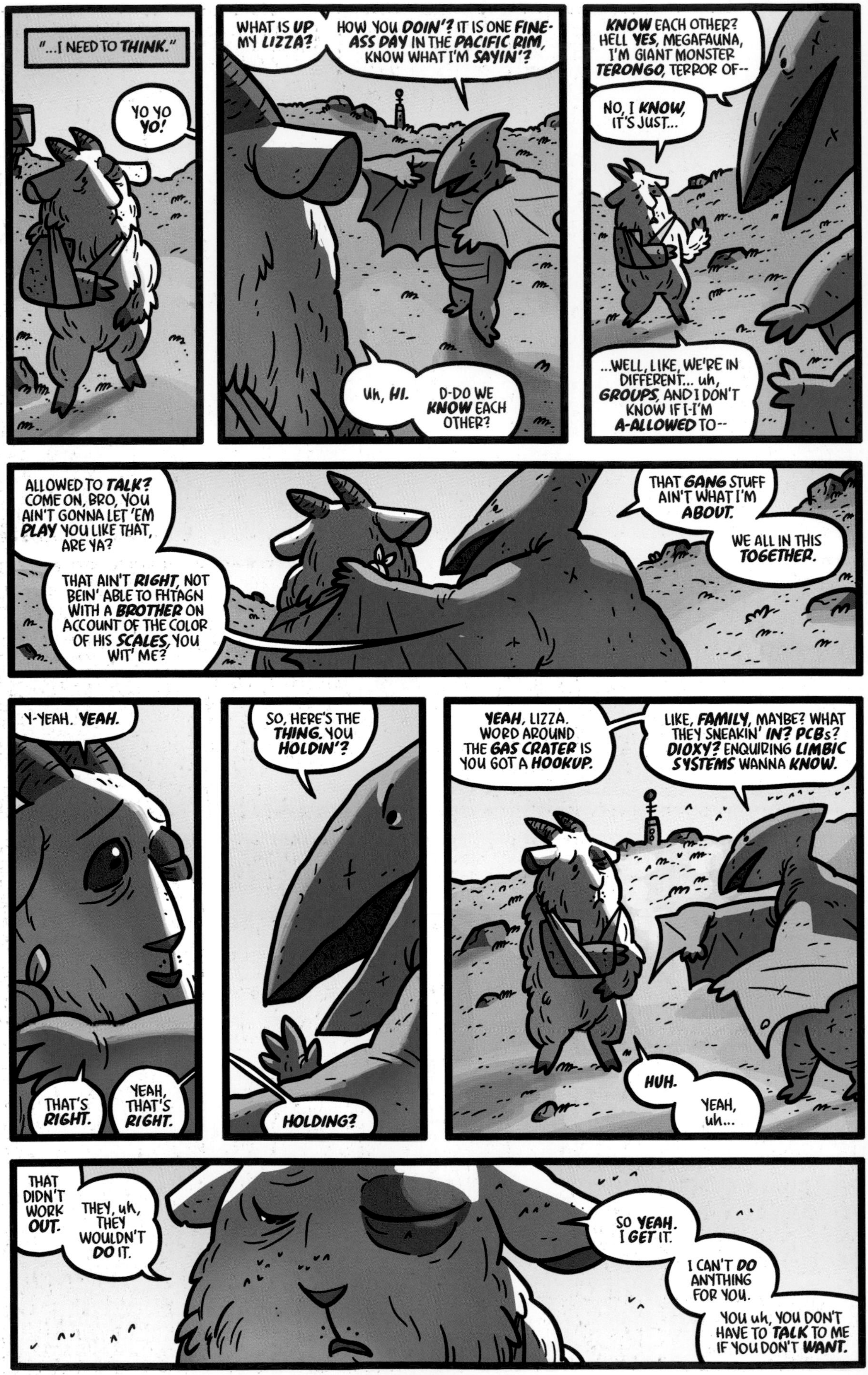
"...I NEED TO THINK."
YO YO YO!
WHAT IS UP MY LIZZA?
HOW YOU DOIN'? IT IS ONE FINE-ASS DAY IN THE PACIFIC RIM, KNOW WHAT I'M SAYIN'?
Uh, HI.
D-DO WE KNOW EACH OTHER?
KNOW EACH OTHER? HELL YES, MEGAFAUNA, I'M GIANT MONSTER TERONGO, TERROR OF--
NO, I KNOW, IT'S JUST...
...WELL, LIKE, WE'RE IN DIFFERENT... uh, GROUPS, AND I DON'T KNOW IF I-I'M A-ALLOWED TO--
ALLOWED TO TALK? COME ON, BRO, YOU AIN'T GONNA LET 'EM PLAY YOU LIKE THAT, ARE YA?
THAT AIN'T RIGHT, NOT BEIN' ABLE TO FHTAGN WITH A BROTHER ON ACCOUNT OF THE COLOR OF HIS SCALES, YOU WIT' ME?
THAT GANG STUFF AIN'T WHAT I'M ABOUT.
WE ALL IN THIS TOGETHER.
Y-YEAH. YEAH.
THAT'S RIGHT.
YEAH, THAT'S RIGHT.
SO, HERE'S THE THING. YOU HOLDIN'?
HOLDING?
YEAH, LIZZA. WORD AROUND THE GAS CRATER IS YOU GOT A HOOKUP.
LIKE, FAMILY, MAYBE? WHAT THEY SNEAKIN' IN? PCBs? DIOXY? ENQUIRING LIMBIC SYSTEMS WANNA KNOW.
HUH.
YEAH, uh...
THAT DIDN'T WORK OUT.
THEY, uh, THEY WOULDN'T DO IT.
SO YEAH. I GET IT.
I CAN'T DO ANYTHING FOR YOU.
YOU uh, YOU DON'T HAVE TO TALK TO ME IF YOU DON'T WANT.

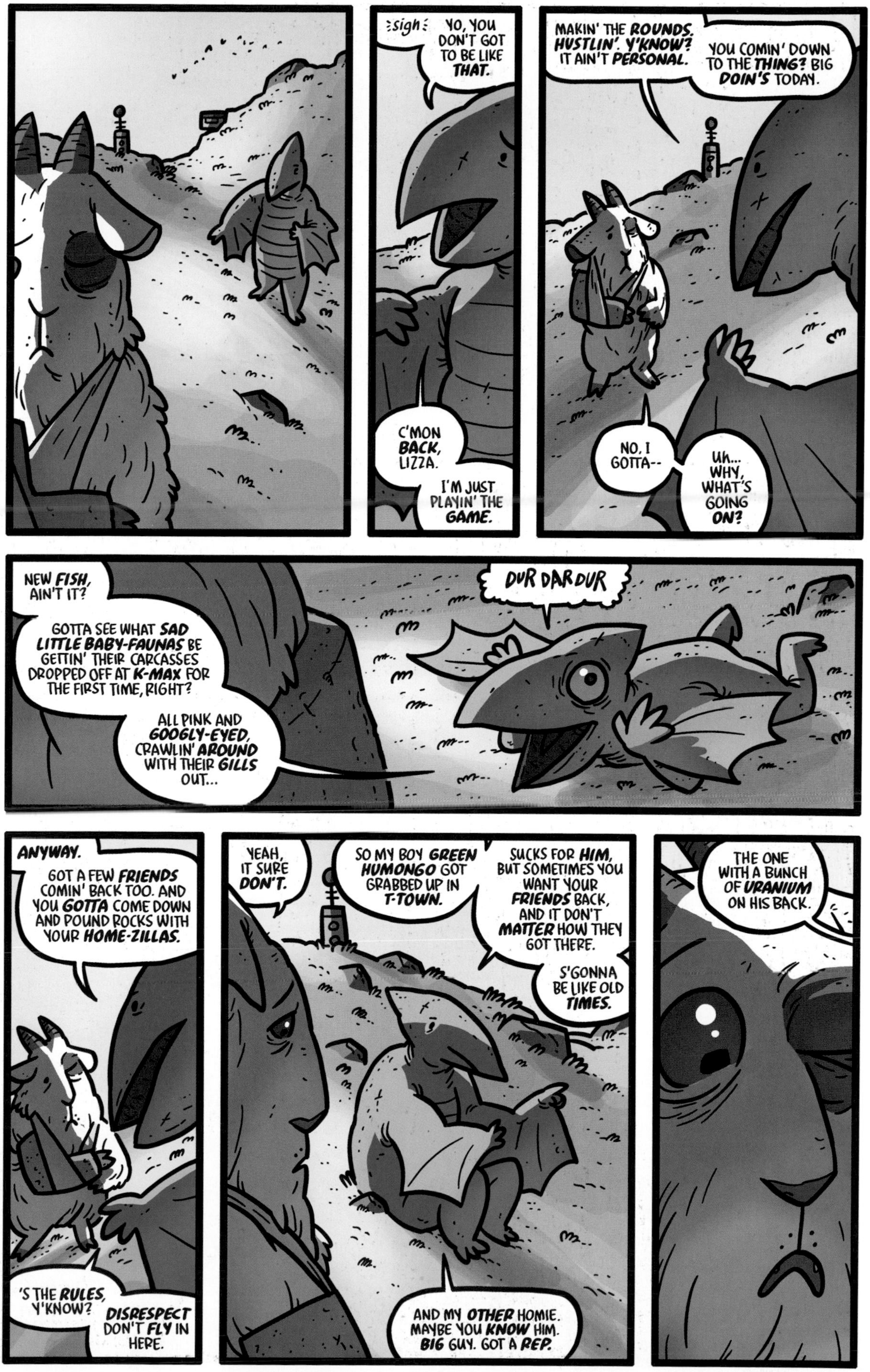

sigh
YO, YOU DON'T GOT TO BE LIKE THAT.
C'MON BACK, LIZZA.
I'M JUST PLAYIN' THE GAME.
MAKIN' THE ROUNDS. HUSTLIN'. Y'KNOW? IT AIN'T PERSONAL.
YOU COMIN' DOWN TO THE THING? BIG DOIN'S TODAY.
NO, I GOTTA--
Uh... WHY, WHAT'S GOING ON?
NEW FISH, AIN'T IT?
GOTTA SEE WHAT SAD LITTLE BABY-FAUNAS BE GETTIN' THEIR CARCASSES DROPPED OFF AT K-MAX FOR THE FIRST TIME, RIGHT?
ALL PINK AND GOOGLY-EYED, CRAWLIN' AROUND WITH THEIR GILLS OUT...
DUR DAR DUR
ANYWAY.
GOT A FEW FRIENDS COMIN' BACK TOO. AND YOU GOTTA COME DOWN AND POUND ROCKS WITH YOUR HOME-ZILLAS.
'S THE RULES, Y'KNOW?
DISRESPECT DON'T FLY IN HERE.
YEAH, IT SURE DON'T.
SO MY BOY GREEN HUMONGO GOT GRABBED UP IN T-TOWN.
SUCKS FOR HIM, BUT SOMETIMES YOU WANT YOUR FRIENDS BACK, AND IT DON'T MATTER HOW THEY GOT THERE.
S'GONNA BE LIKE OLD TIMES.
AND MY OTHER HOMIE. MAYBE YOU KNOW HIM. BIG GUY. GOT A REP.
THE ONE WITH A BUNCH OF URANIUM ON HIS BACK.

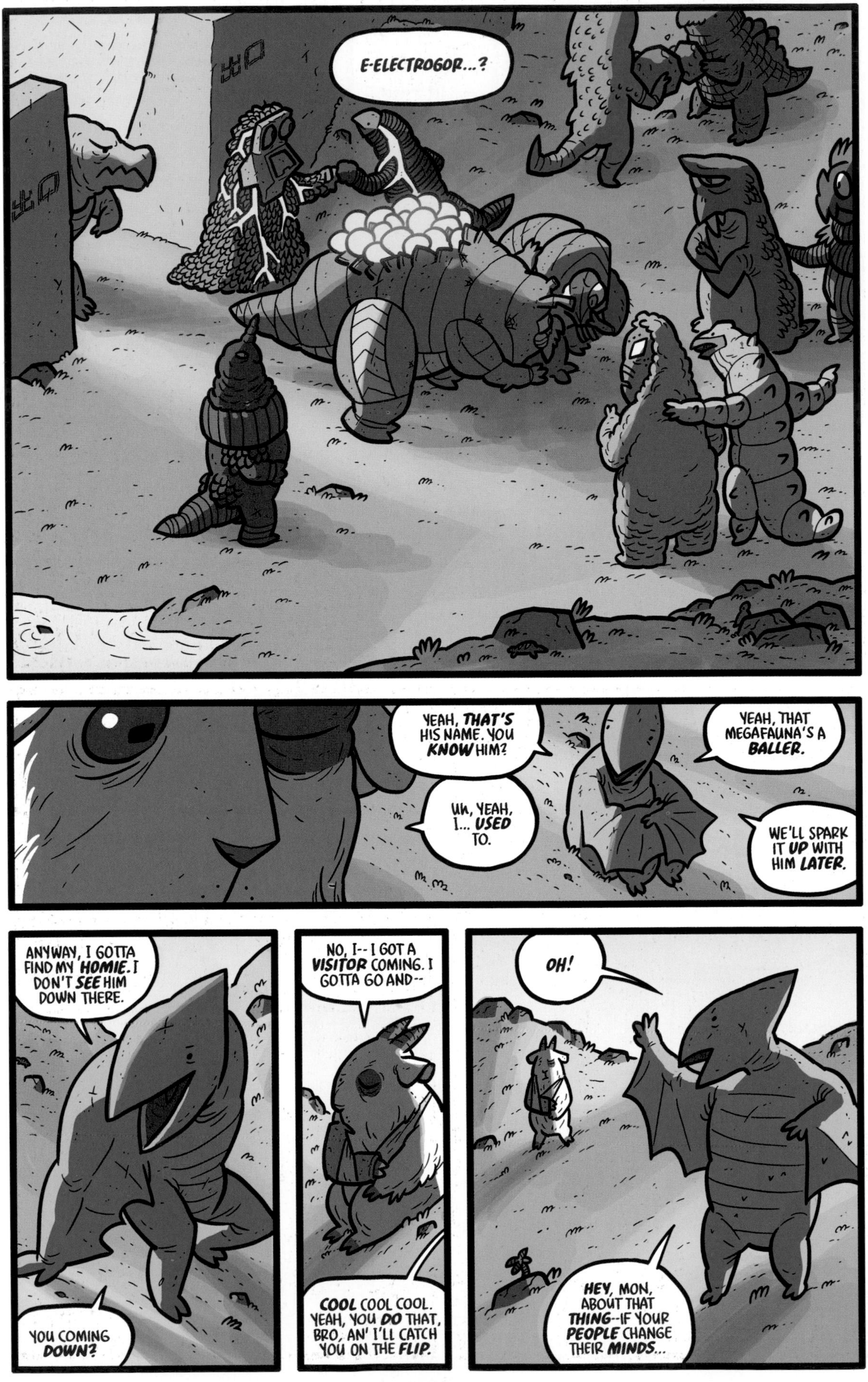
E-ELECTROGOR...?
YEAH, THAT'S HIS NAME. YOU KNOW HIM?
Uh, YEAH, I... USED TO.
YEAH, THAT MEGAFAUNA'S A BALLER.
WE'LL SPARK IT UP WITH HIM LATER.
ANYWAY, I GOTTA FIND MY HOMIE. I DON'T SEE HIM DOWN THERE.
YOU COMING DOWN?
NO, I-- I GOT A VISITOR COMING. I GOTTA GO AND--
COOL COOL COOL. YEAH, YOU DO THAT, BRO, AN' I'LL CATCH YOU ON THE FLIP.
OH!
HEY, MON, ABOUT THAT THING--IF YOUR PEOPLE CHANGE THEIR MINDS...

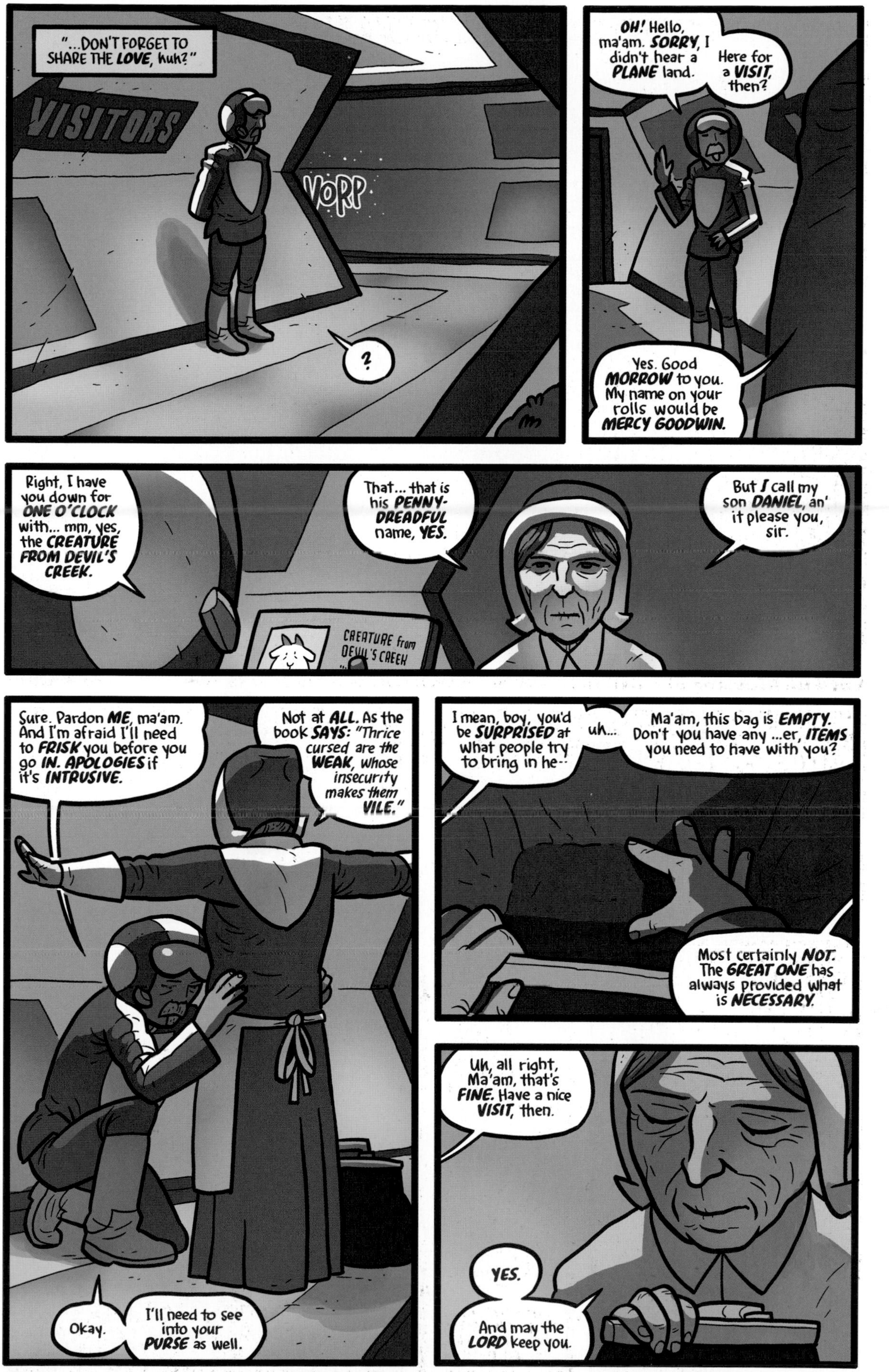
"...DON'T FORGET TO SHARE THE LOVE, huh?"
VISITORS
VORP
?
OH! Hello, ma'am. SORRY, I didn't hear a PLANE land.
Here for a VISIT, then?
Yes. Good MORROW to you. My name on your rolls would be MERCY GOODWIN.
Right, I have you down for ONE O'CLOCK with... mm, yes, the CREATURE FROM DEVIL'S CREEK.
That... that is his PENNY-DREADFUL name, YES.
But I call my son DANIEL, an' it please you, sir.
CREATURE from DEVIL'S CREEK
Sure. Pardon ME, ma'am. And I'm afraid I'll need to FRISK you before you go IN. APOLOGIES if it's INTRUSIVE.
Not at ALL. As the book SAYS: "Thrice cursed are the WEAK, whose insecurity makes them VILE."
Okay.
I'll need to see into your PURSE as well.
I mean, boy, you'd be SURPRISED at what people try to bring in he--
uh...
Ma'am, this bag is EMPTY. Don't you have any ...er, ITEMS you need to have with you?
Most certainly NOT. The GREAT ONE has always provided what is NECESSARY.
Uh, all right, Ma'am, that's FINE. Have a nice VISIT, then.
YES.
And may the LORD keep you.

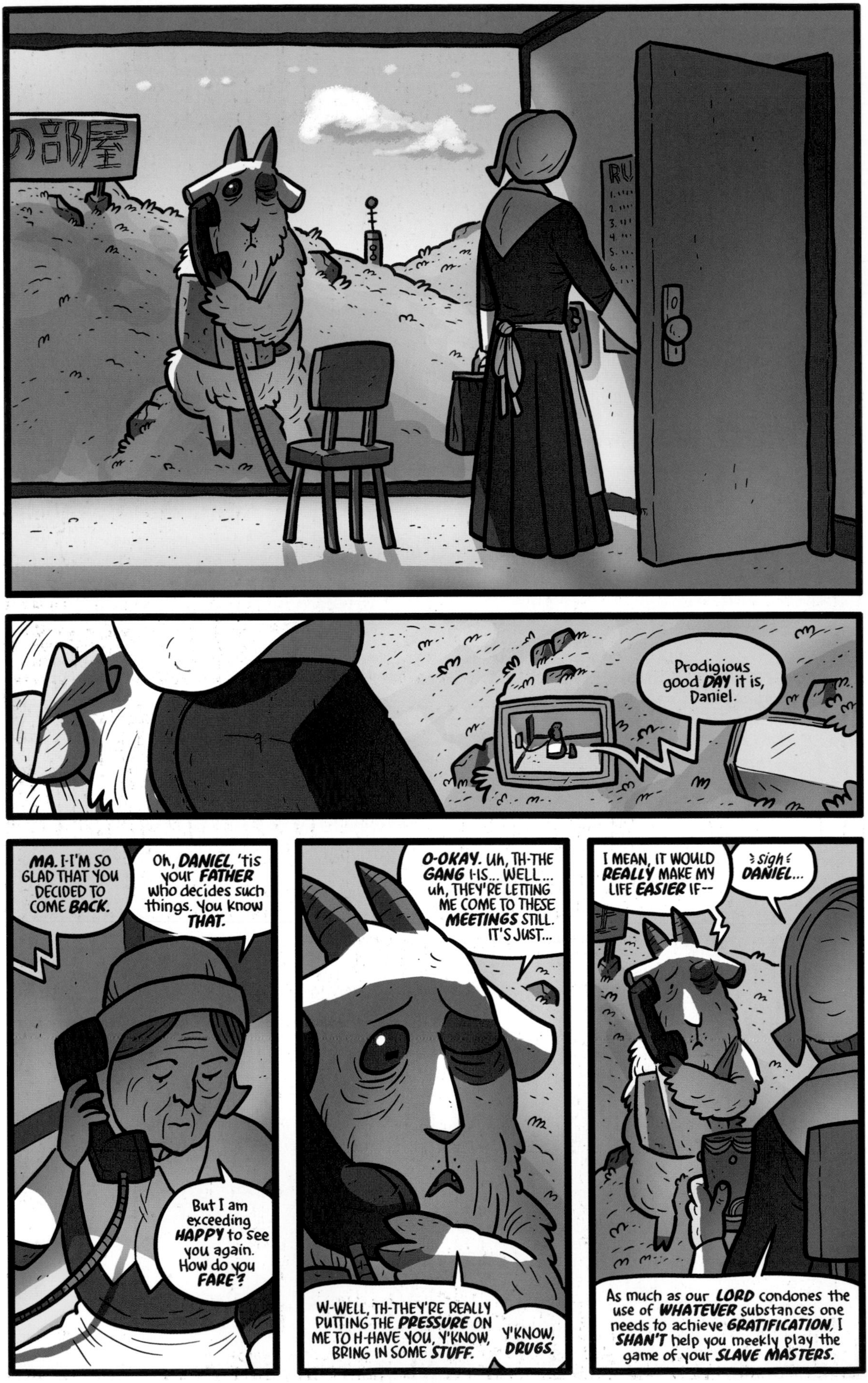
の部屋
Prodigious good DAY it is, Daniel.
MA. I-I'M SO GLAD THAT YOU DECIDED TO COME BACK.
Oh, DANIEL, 'tis your FATHER who decides such things. You know THAT.
But I am exceeding HAPPY to see you again. How do you FARE?
O-OKAY. Uh, TH-THE GANG I-IS... WELL... uh, THEY'RE LETTING ME COME TO THESE MEETINGS STILL. IT'S JUST...
W-WELL, TH-THEY'RE REALLY PUTTING THE PRESSURE ON ME TO H-HAVE YOU, Y'KNOW, BRING IN SOME STUFF.
Y'KNOW, DRUGS.
I MEAN, IT WOULD REALLY MAKE MY LIFE EASIER IF--
sigh
DANIEL...
As much as our LORD condones the use of WHATEVER substances one needs to achieve GRATIFICATION, I SHAN'T help you meekly play the game of your SLAVE MASTERS.

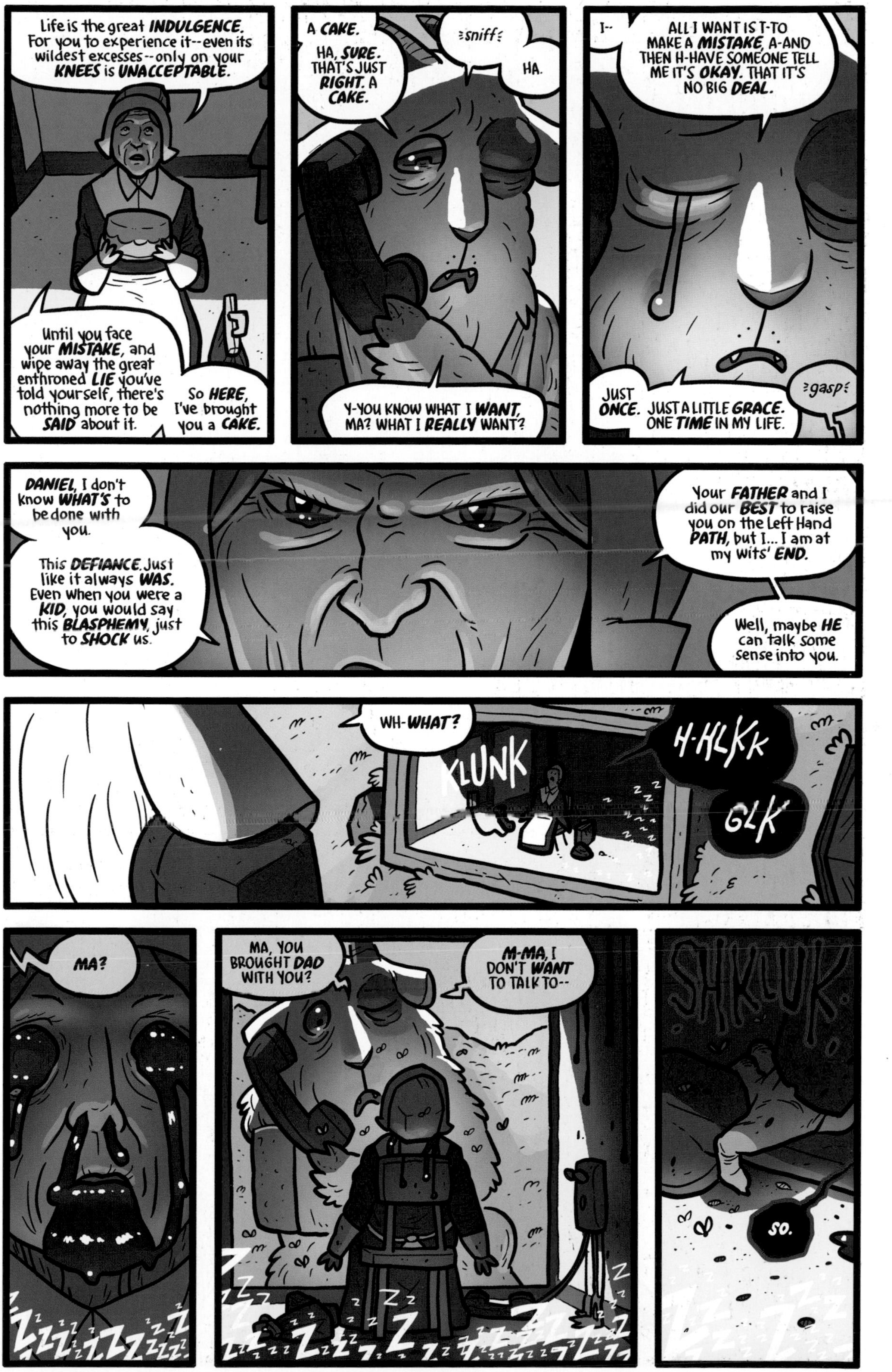
Life is the great INDULGENCE. For you to experience it--even its wildest excesses--only on your KNEES is UNACCEPTABLE.
Until you face your MISTAKE, and wipe away the great enthroned LIE you've told yourself, there's nothing more to be SAID about it.
So HERE, I've brought you a CAKE.
A CAKE.
HA, SURE. THAT'S JUST RIGHT. A CAKE.
sniff
HA.
Y-YOU KNOW WHAT I WANT, MA? WHAT I REALLY WANT?
I--
ALL I WANT IS T-TO MAKE A MISTAKE, A-AND THEN H-HAVE SOMEONE TELL ME IT'S OKAY. THAT IT'S NO BIG DEAL.
JUST ONCE.
JUST A LITTLE GRACE. ONE TIME IN MY LIFE.
gasp
DANIEL, I don't know WHAT'S to be done with you.
This DEFIANCE. Just like it always WAS. Even when you were a KID, you would say this BLASPHEMY, just to SHOCK us.
Your FATHER and I did our BEST to raise you on the Left Hand PATH, but I... I am at my wits' END.
Well, maybe HE can talk some sense into you.
WH-WHAT?
KLUNK
H-HLKK
GLK
MA?
MA, YOU BROUGHT DAD WITH YOU?
M-MA, I DON'T WANT TO TALK TO--
SHKLUK
SO.

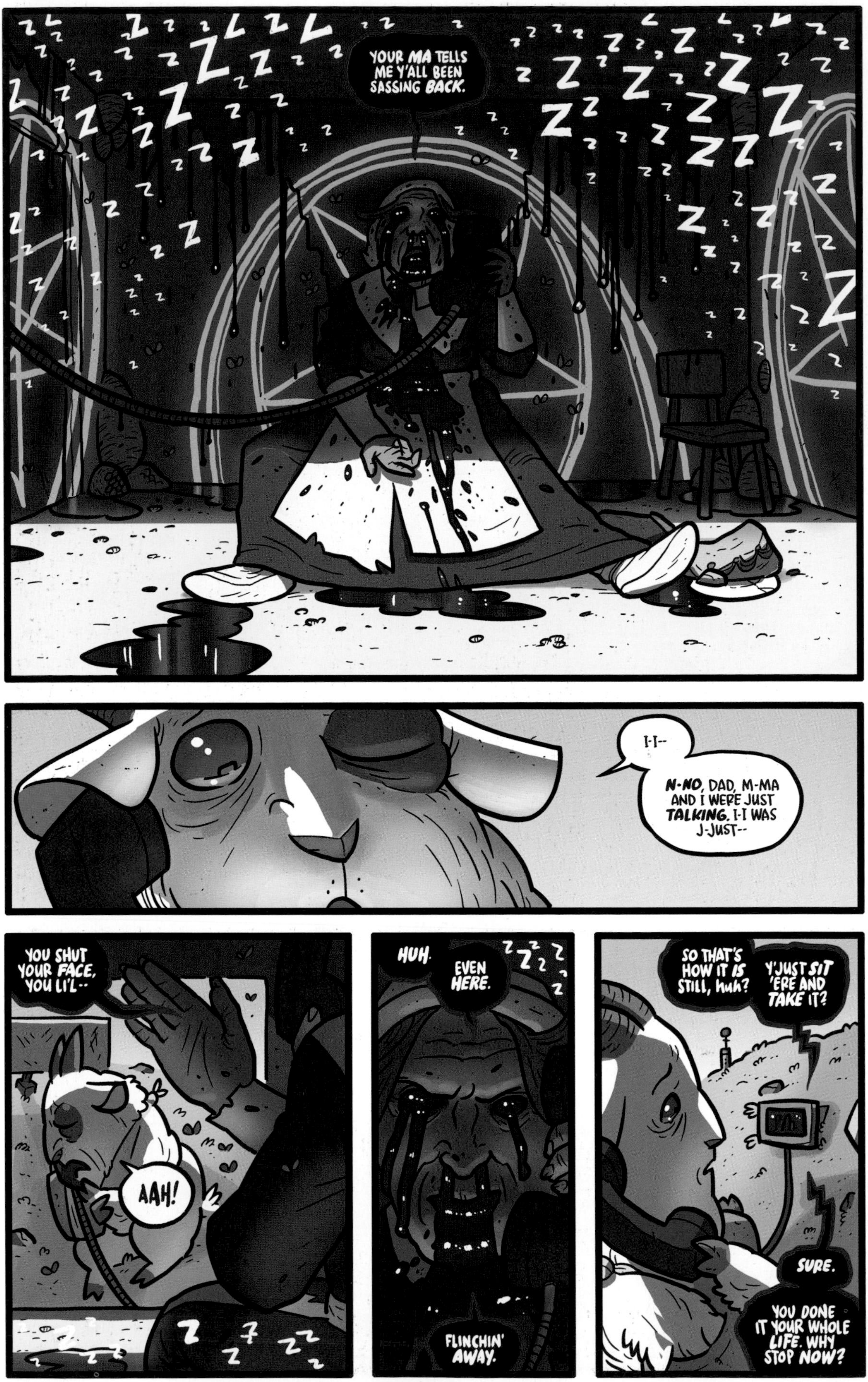
YOUR MA TELLS ME Y'ALL BEEN SASSING BACK.
I-I--
N-NO, DAD, M-MA AND I WERE JUST TALKING. I-I WAS J-JUST--
YOU SHUT YOUR FACE, YOU LI'L--
AAH!
HUH.
EVEN HERE.
FLINCHIN' AWAY.
SO THAT'S HOW IT IS STILL, huh?
Y'JUST SIT 'ERE AND TAKE IT?
SURE.
YOU DONE IT YOUR WHOLE LIFE. WHY STOP NOW?

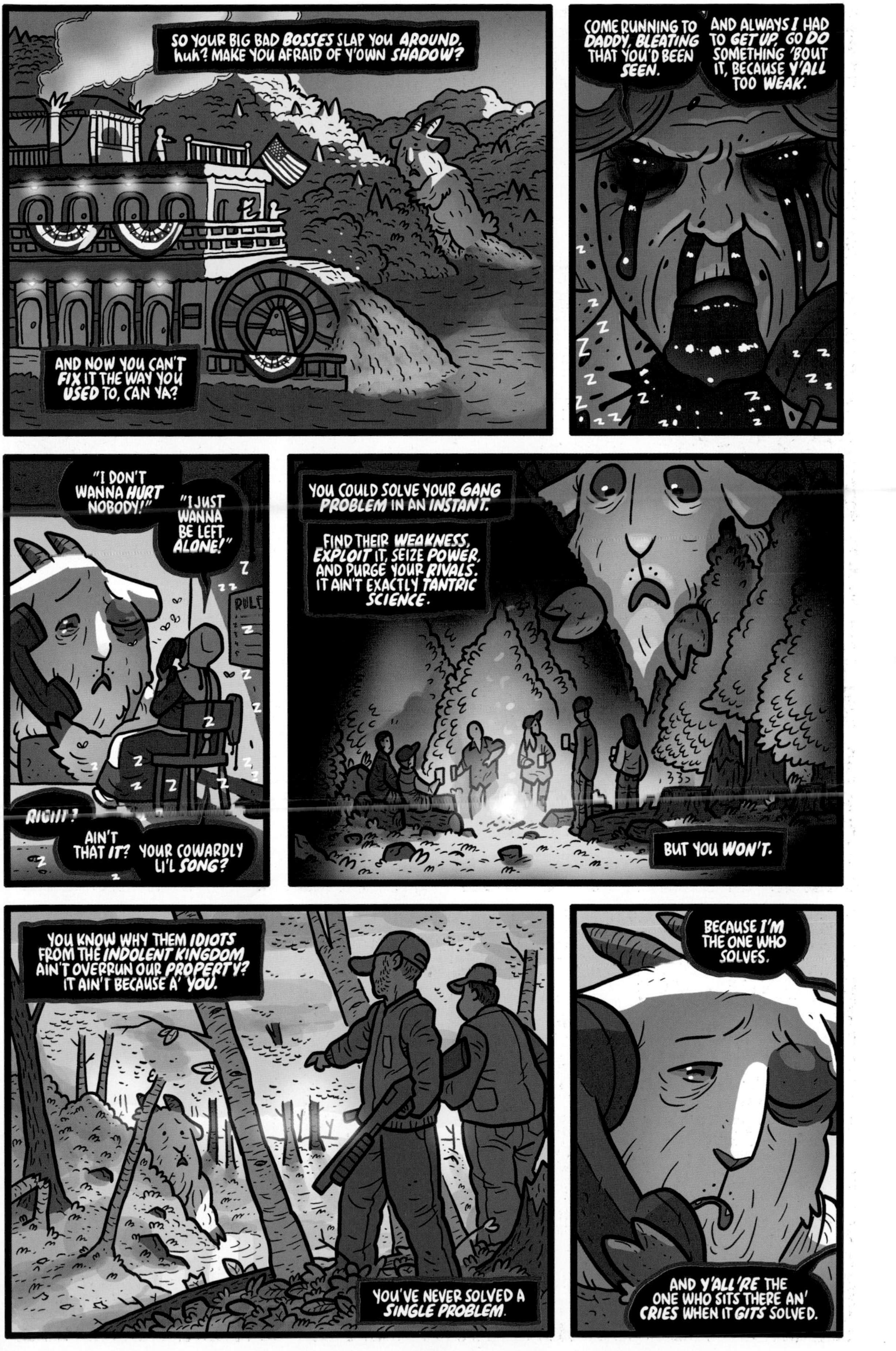
SO YOUR BIG BAD BOSSES SLAP YOU AROUND, huh? MAKE YOU AFRAID OF Y'OWN SHADOW?
AND NOW YOU CAN'T FIX IT THE WAY YOU USED TO, CAN YA?
COME RUNNING TO DADDY, BLEATING THAT YOU'D BEEN SEEN.
AND ALWAYS I HAD TO GET UP, GO DO SOMETHING 'BOUT IT, BECAUSE Y'ALL TOO WEAK.
"I DON'T WANNA HURT NOBODY!"
"I JUST WANNA BE LEFT ALONE!"
RIGHT?
AIN'T THAT IT?
YOUR COWARDLY LI'L SONG?
YOU COULD SOLVE YOUR GANG PROBLEM IN AN INSTANT.
FIND THEIR WEAKNESS, EXPLOIT IT, SEIZE POWER, AND PURGE YOUR RIVALS. IT AIN'T EXACTLY TANTRIC SCIENCE.
BUT YOU WON'T.
YOU KNOW WHY THEM IDIOTS FROM THE INDOLENT KINGDOM AIN'T OVERRUN OUR PROPERTY? IT AIN'T BECAUSE A' YOU.
YOU'VE NEVER SOLVED A SINGLE PROBLEM.
BECAUSE I'M THE ONE WHO SOLVES.
AND Y'ALL'RE THE ONE WHO SITS THERE AN' CRIES WHEN IT GITS SOLVED.

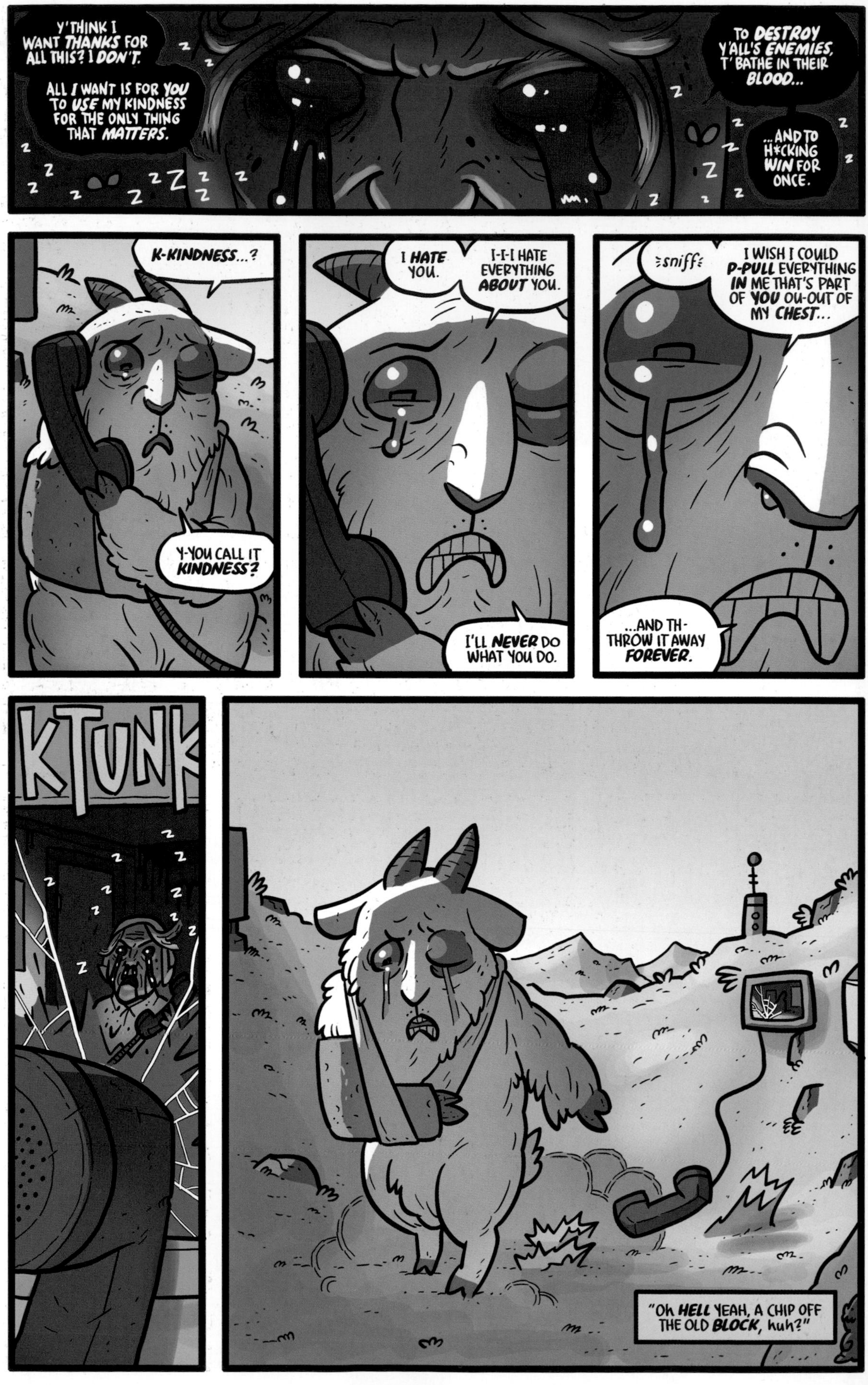

Y'THINK I WANT THANKS FOR ALL THIS? I DON'T.
ALL I WANT IS FOR YOU TO USE MY KINDNESS FOR THE ONLY THING THAT MATTERS.
TO DESTROY Y'ALL'S ENEMIES, T' BATHE IN THEIR BLOOD...
...AND TO H*CKING WIN FOR ONCE.
K-KINDNESS...?
Y-YOU CALL IT KINDNESS?
I HATE YOU.
I-I-I HATE EVERYTHING ABOUT YOU.
I'LL NEVER DO WHAT YOU DO.
sniff
I WISH I COULD P-PULL EVERYTHING IN ME THAT'S PART OF YOU OU-OUT OF MY CHEST...
...AND TH-THROW IT AWAY FOREVER.
KTUNK
"Oh HELL YEAH, A CHIP OFF THE OLD BLOCK, huh?"

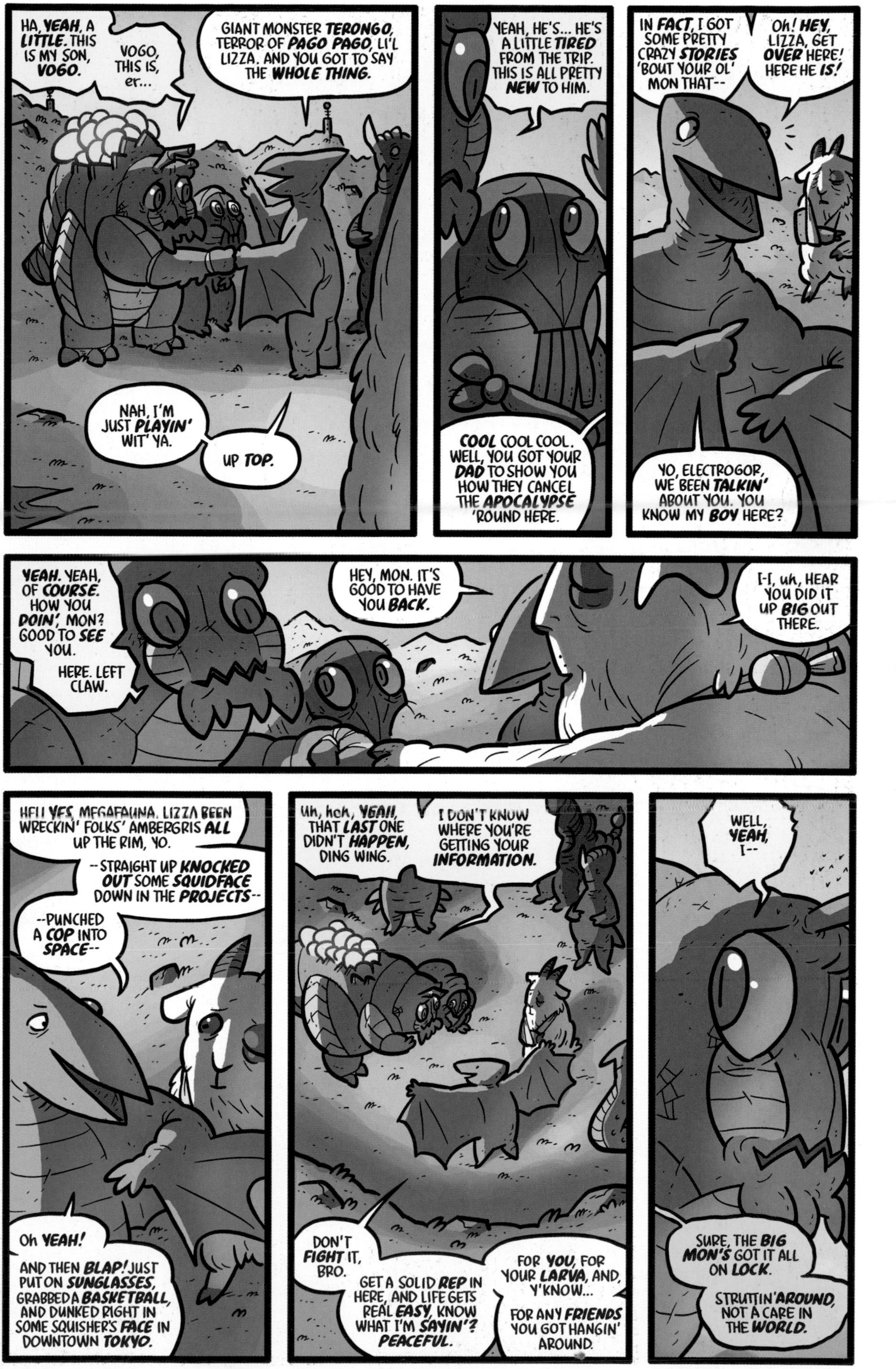
HA, YEAH, A LITTLE. THIS IS MY SON, VOGO.
VOGO, THIS IS, er...
GIANT MONSTER TERONGO, TERROR OF PAGO PAGO, LI'L LIZZA. AND YOU GOT TO SAY THE WHOLE THING.
NAH, I'M JUST PLAYIN' WIT' YA.
UP TOP.
YEAH, HE'S... HE'S A LITTLE TIRED FROM THE TRIP. THIS IS ALL PRETTY NEW TO HIM.
COOL COOL COOL. WELL, YOU GOT YOUR DAD TO SHOW YOU HOW THEY CANCEL THE APOCALYPSE 'ROUND HERE.
IN FACT, I GOT SOME PRETTY CRAZY STORIES 'BOUT YOUR OL' MON THAT--
Oh! HEY, LIZZA, GET OVER HERE! HERE HE IS!
YO, ELECTROGOR, WE BEEN TALKIN' ABOUT YOU. YOU KNOW MY BOY HERE?
YEAH. YEAH, OF COURSE. HOW YOU DOIN', MON? GOOD TO SEE YOU.
HERE. LEFT CLAW.
HEY, MON. IT'S GOOD TO HAVE YOU BACK.
I-I, uh, HEAR YOU DID IT UP BIG OUT THERE.
HELL YES, MEGAFAUNA. LIZZA BEEN WRECKIN' FOLKS' AMBERGRIS ALL UP THE RIM, YO.
--STRAIGHT UP KNOCKED OUT SOME SQUIDFACE DOWN IN THE PROJECTS--
--PUNCHED A COP INTO SPACE--
Oh YEAH!
AND THEN BLAP! JUST PUT ON SUNGLASSES, GRABBED A BASKETBALL, AND DUNKED RIGHT IN SOME SQUISHER'S FACE IN DOWNTOWN TOKYO.
uh, heh, YEAH, THAT LAST ONE DIDN'T HAPPEN, DING WING.
I DON'T KNOW WHERE YOU'RE GETTING YOUR INFORMATION.
DON'T FIGHT IT, BRO.
GET A SOLID REP IN HERE, AND LIFE GETS REAL EASY, KNOW WHAT I'M SAYIN'? PEACEFUL.
FOR YOU, FOR YOUR LARVA, AND, Y'KNOW...
FOR ANY FRIENDS YOU GOT HANGIN' AROUND.
WELL, YEAH, I--
SURE, THE BIG MON'S GOT IT ALL ON LOCK.
STRUTTIN' AROUND, NOT A CARE IN THE WORLD.

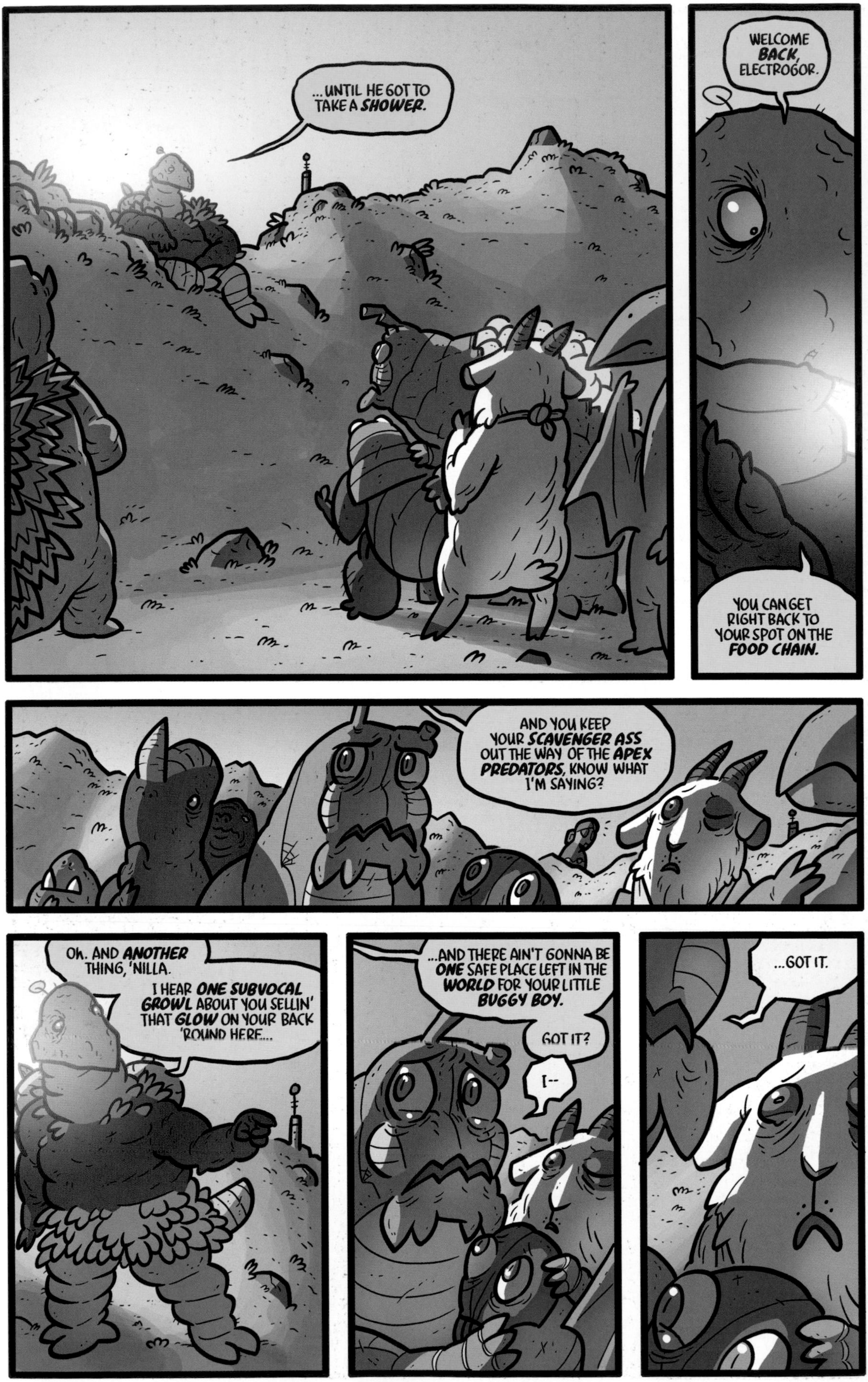
...UNTIL HE GOT TO TAKE A SHOWER.
WELCOME BACK, ELECTROGOR.
YOU CAN GET RIGHT BACK TO YOUR SPOT ON THE FOOD CHAIN.
AND YOU KEEP YOUR SCAVENGER ASS OUT THE WAY OF THE APEX PREDATORS, KNOW WHAT I'M SAYING?
Oh. AND ANOTHER THING, 'NILLA.
I HEAR ONE SUBVOCAL GROWL ABOUT YOU SELLIN' THAT GLOW ON YOUR BACK 'ROUND HERE...
...AND THERE AIN'T GONNA BE ONE SAFE PLACE LEFT IN THE WORLD FOR YOUR LITTLE BUGGY BOY.
GOT IT?
I--
...GOT IT.

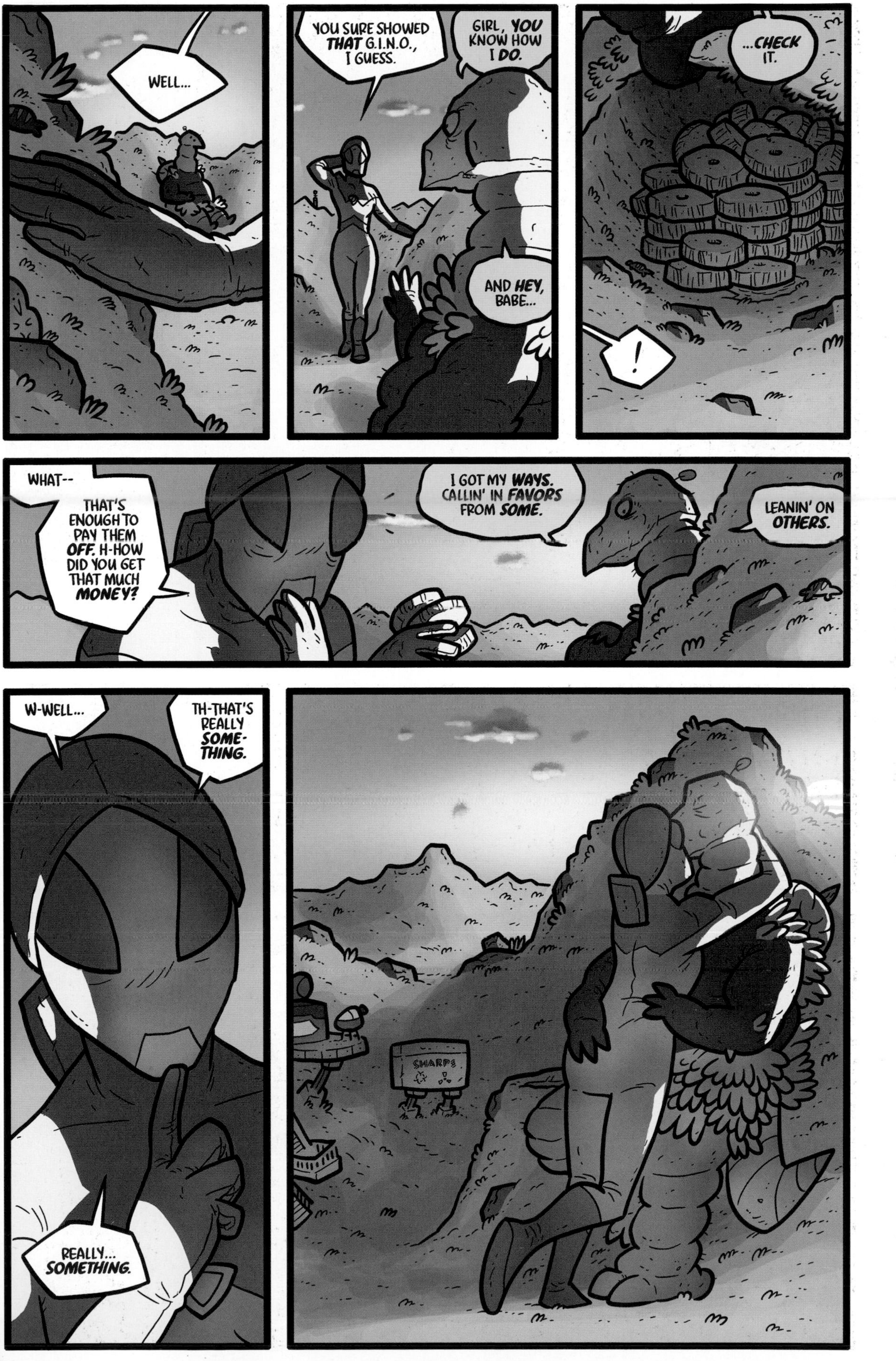
WELL...
YOU SURE SHOWED **THAT** G.I.N.O., I GUESS.
GIRL, **YOU** KNOW HOW I **DO**.
AND **HEY**, BABE...
...**CHECK** IT.
!
WHAT--
THAT'S ENOUGH TO PAY THEM **OFF**. H-HOW DID YOU GET THAT MUCH **MONEY?**
I GOT MY **WAYS**. CALLIN' IN **FAVORS** FROM **SOME**.
LEANIN' ON **OTHERS**.
W-WELL...
TH-THAT'S REALLY **SOME-THING.**
REALLY... **SOMETHING.**
SHARPS

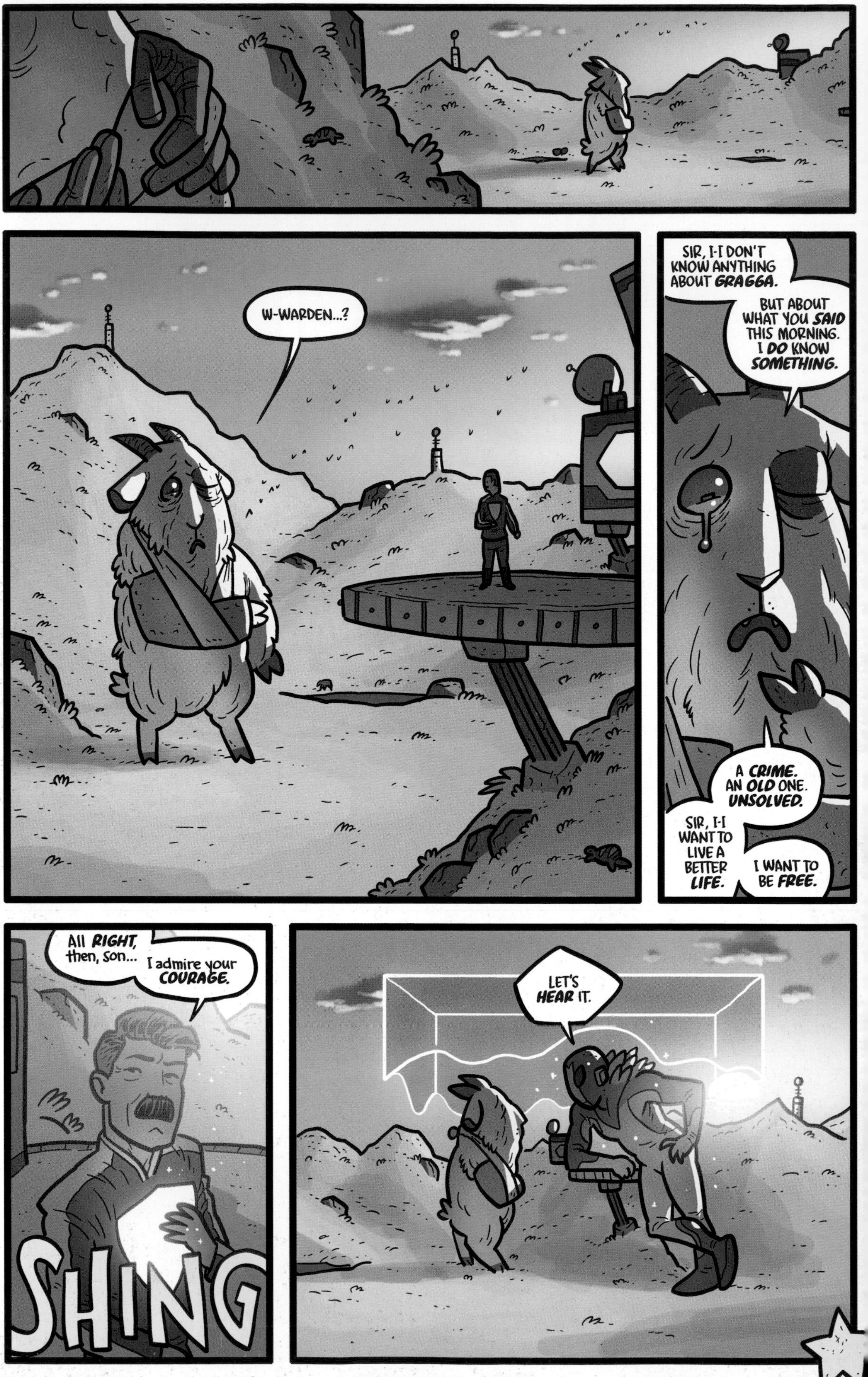
W-WARDEN...?
SIR, I-I DON'T KNOW ANYTHING ABOUT GRAGGA.
BUT ABOUT WHAT YOU SAID THIS MORNING. I DO KNOW SOMETHING.
A CRIME. AN OLD ONE. UNSOLVED.
SIR, I-I WANT TO LIVE A BETTER LIFE.
I WANT TO BE FREE.
All RIGHT, then, son...
I admire your COURAGE.
SHING
LET'S HEAR IT.

EPISODE 4

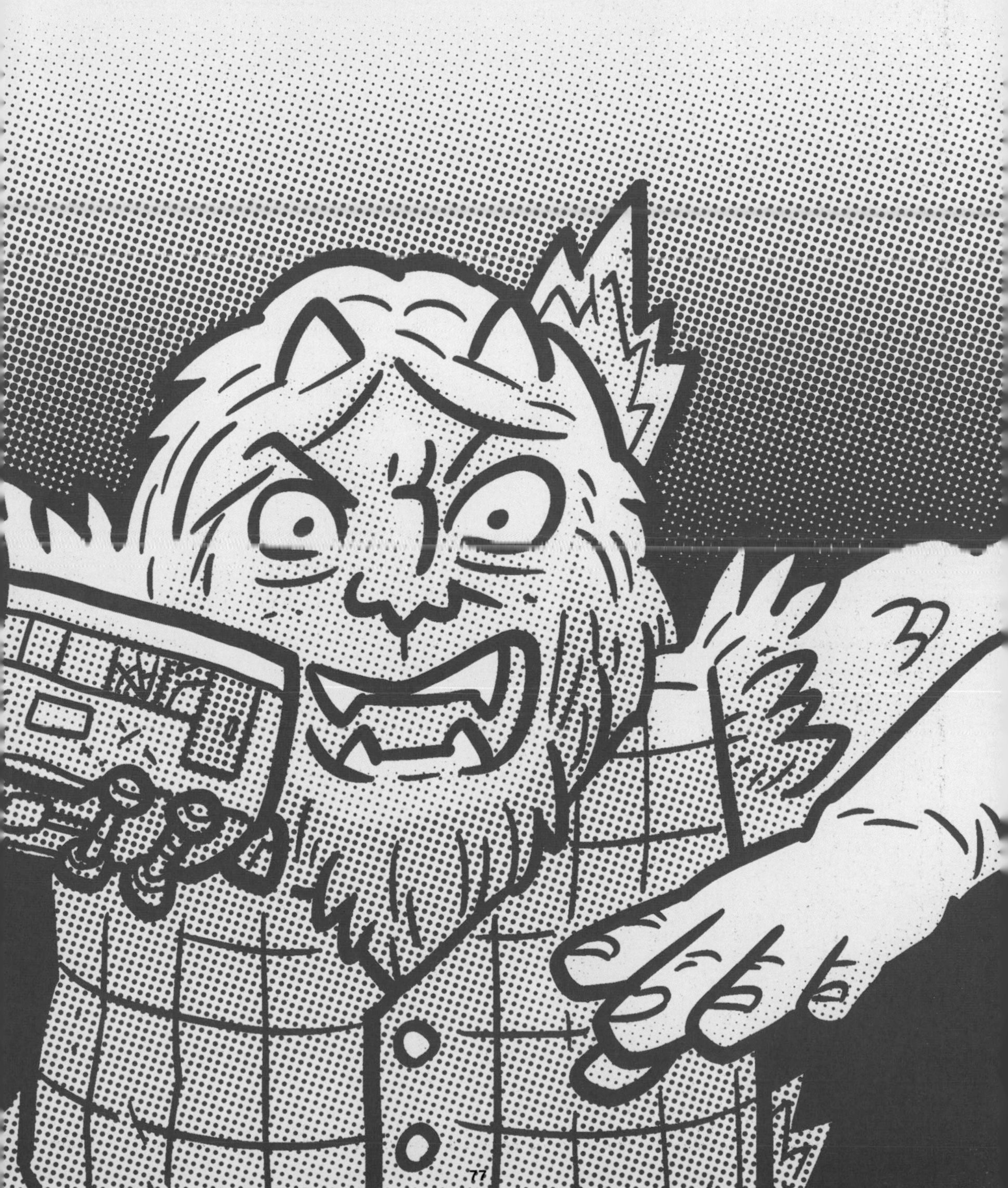

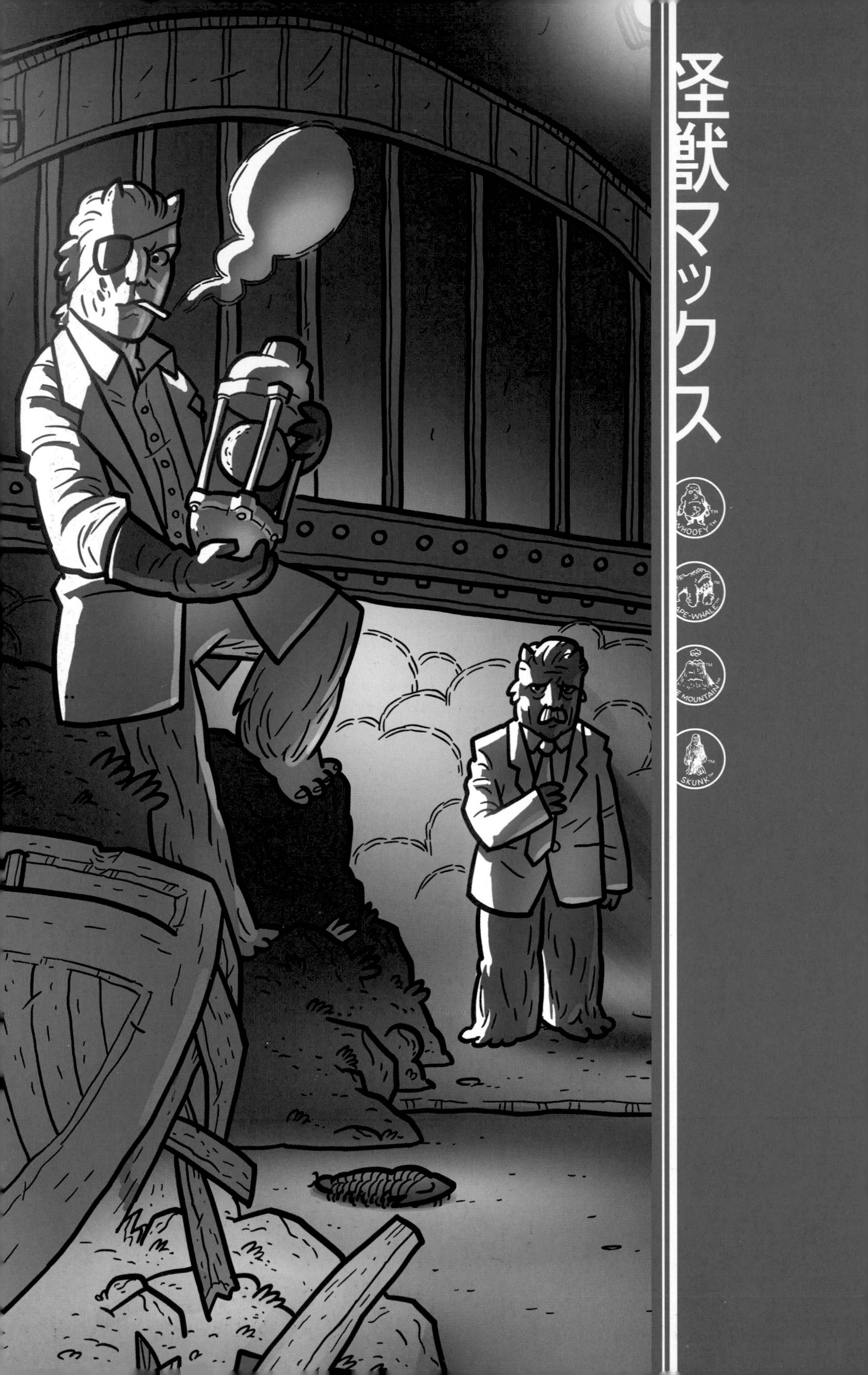

怪獣マックス
WHOOFY™
APE-WHALE™
MOUNTAIN™
SKUNK™

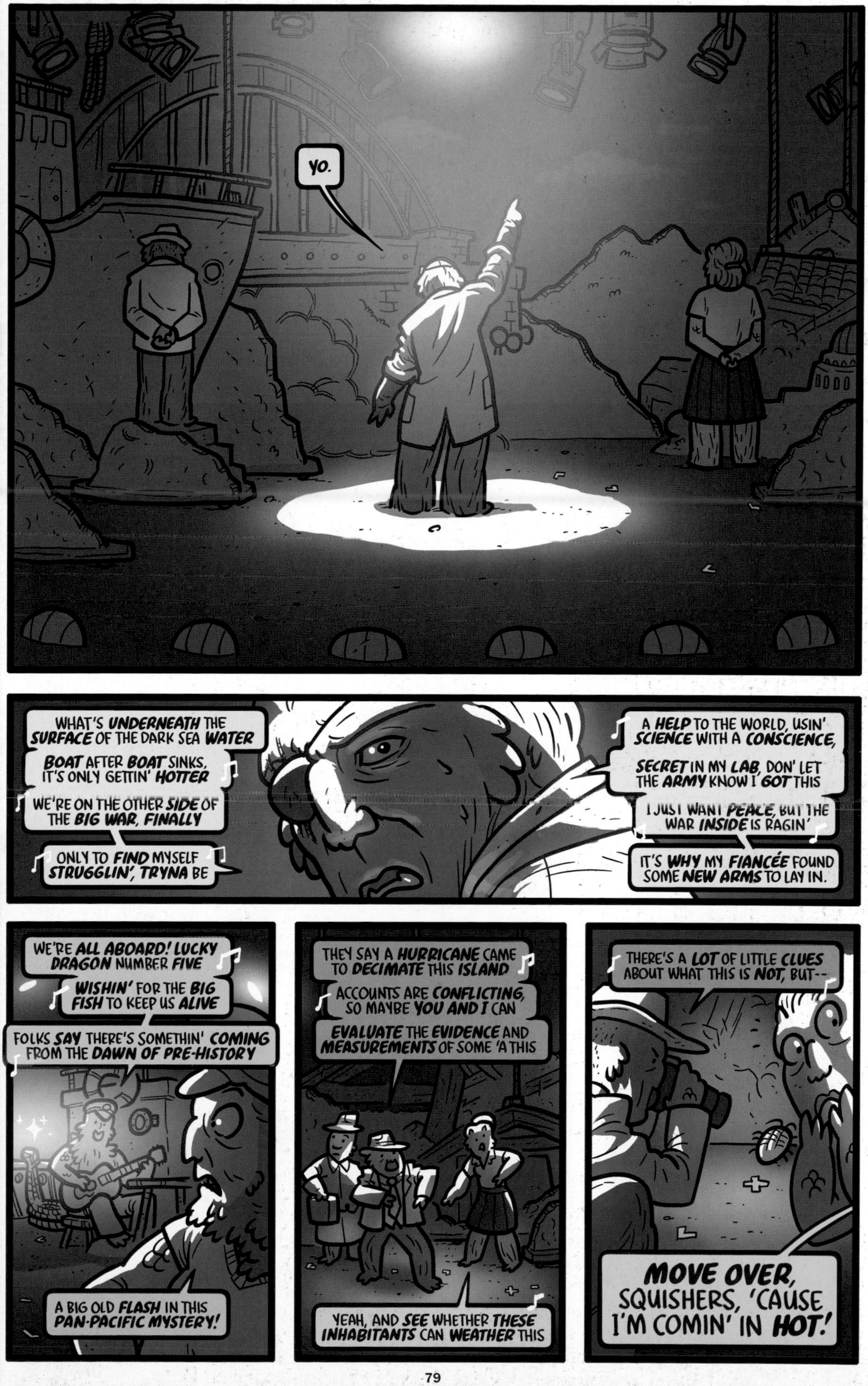
YO.
WHAT'S UNDERNEATH THE SURFACE OF THE DARK SEA WATER
BOAT AFTER BOAT SINKS, IT'S ONLY GETTIN' HOTTER
WE'RE ON THE OTHER SIDE OF THE BIG WAR, FINALLY
ONLY TO FIND MYSELF STRUGGLIN', TRYNA BE
A HELP TO THE WORLD, USIN' SCIENCE WITH A CONSCIENCE,
SECRET IN MY LAB, DON' LET THE ARMY KNOW I GOT THIS
I JUST WANT PEACE, BUT THE WAR INSIDE IS RAGIN'
IT'S WHY MY FIANCÉE FOUND SOME NEW ARMS TO LAY IN.
WE'RE ALL ABOARD! LUCKY DRAGON NUMBER FIVE
WISHIN' FOR THE BIG FISH TO KEEP US ALIVE
FOLKS SAY THERE'S SOMETHIN' COMING FROM THE DAWN OF PRE-HISTORY
A BIG OLD FLASH IN THIS PAN-PACIFIC MYSTERY!
THEY SAY A HURRICANE CAME TO DECIMATE THIS ISLAND
ACCOUNTS ARE CONFLICTING, SO MAYBE YOU AND I CAN
EVALUATE THE EVIDENCE AND MEASUREMENTS OF SOME 'A THIS
YEAH, AND SEE WHETHER THESE INHABITANTS CAN WEATHER THIS
THERE'S A LOT OF LITTLE CLUES ABOUT WHAT THIS IS NOT, BUT--
MOVE OVER, SQUISHERS, 'CAUSE I'M COMIN' IN HOT!

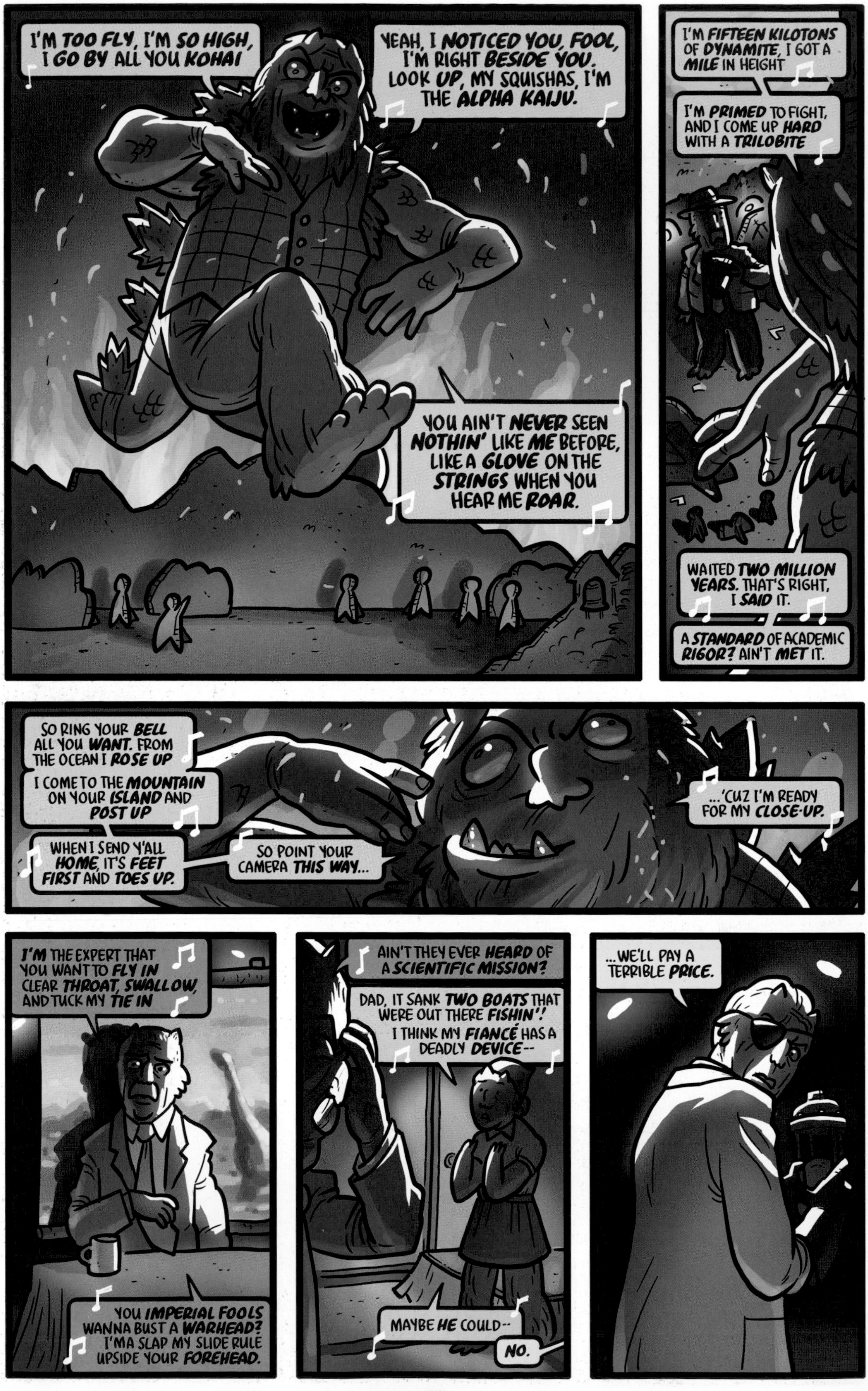
I'M TOO FLY, I'M SO HIGH, I GO BY ALL YOU KOHAI
YEAH, I NOTICED YOU, FOOL, I'M RIGHT BESIDE YOU. LOOK UP, MY SQUISHAS, I'M THE ALPHA KAIJU.
YOU AIN'T NEVER SEEN NOTHIN' LIKE ME BEFORE, LIKE A GLOVE ON THE STRINGS WHEN YOU HEAR ME ROAR.
I'M FIFTEEN KILOTONS OF DYNAMITE, I GOT A MILE IN HEIGHT
I'M PRIMED TO FIGHT, AND I COME UP HARD WITH A TRILOBITE
WAITED TWO MILLION YEARS. THAT'S RIGHT, I SAID IT.
A STANDARD OF ACADEMIC RIGOR? AIN'T MET IT.
SO RING YOUR BELL ALL YOU WANT. FROM THE OCEAN I ROSE UP
I COME TO THE MOUNTAIN ON YOUR ISLAND AND POST UP
WHEN I SEND Y'ALL HOME, IT'S FEET FIRST AND TOES UP.
SO POINT YOUR CAMERA THIS WAY...
...'CUZ I'M READY FOR MY CLOSE-UP.
I'M THE EXPERT THAT YOU WANT TO FLY IN
CLEAR THROAT, SWALLOW, AND TUCK MY TIE IN
YOU IMPERIAL FOOLS WANNA BUST A WARHEAD? I'MA SLAP MY SLIDE RULE UPSIDE YOUR FOREHEAD.
AIN'T THEY EVER HEARD OF A SCIENTIFIC MISSION?
DAD, IT SANK TWO BOATS THAT WERE OUT THERE FISHIN'!
I THINK MY FIANCÉ HAS A DEADLY DEVICE--
MAYBE HE COULD--
NO.
...WE'LL PAY A TERRIBLE PRICE.

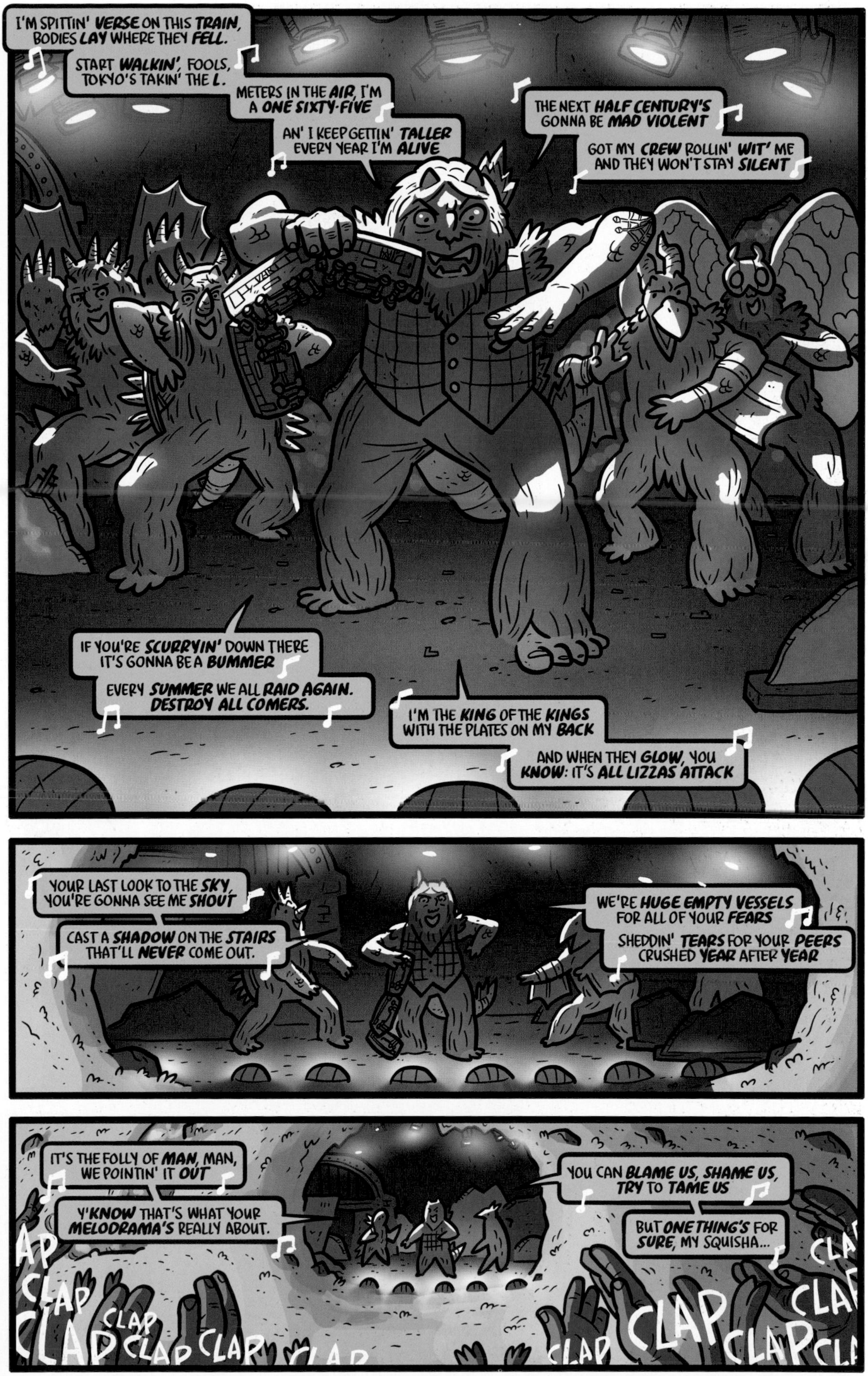
I'M SPITTIN' VERSE ON THIS TRAIN, BODIES LAY WHERE THEY FELL.
START WALKIN', FOOLS, TOKYO'S TAKIN' THE L.
METERS IN THE AIR, I'M A ONE SIXTY-FIVE
AN' I KEEP GETTIN' TALLER EVERY YEAR I'M ALIVE
THE NEXT HALF CENTURY'S GONNA BE MAD VIOLENT
GOT MY CREW ROLLIN' WIT' ME AND THEY WON'T STAY SILENT
IF YOU'RE SCURRYIN' DOWN THERE IT'S GONNA BE A BUMMER
EVERY SUMMER WE ALL RAID AGAIN. DESTROY ALL COMERS.
I'M THE KING OF THE KINGS WITH THE PLATES ON MY BACK
AND WHEN THEY GLOW, YOU KNOW: IT'S ALL LIZZAS ATTACK
YOUR LAST LOOK TO THE SKY, YOU'RE GONNA SEE ME SHOUT
CAST A SHADOW ON THE STAIRS THAT'LL NEVER COME OUT.
WE'RE HUGE EMPTY VESSELS FOR ALL OF YOUR FEARS
SHEDDIN' TEARS FOR YOUR PEERS CRUSHED YEAR AFTER YEAR
IT'S THE FOLLY OF MAN, MAN, WE POINTIN' IT OUT
Y'KNOW THAT'S WHAT YOUR MELODRAMA'S REALLY ABOUT.
YOU CAN BLAME US, SHAME US, TRY TO TAME US
BUT ONE THING'S FOR SURE, MY SQUISHA...
CLAP CLAP CLAP CLAP CLAP CLAP
CLAP CLAP CLAP CLAP CLAP

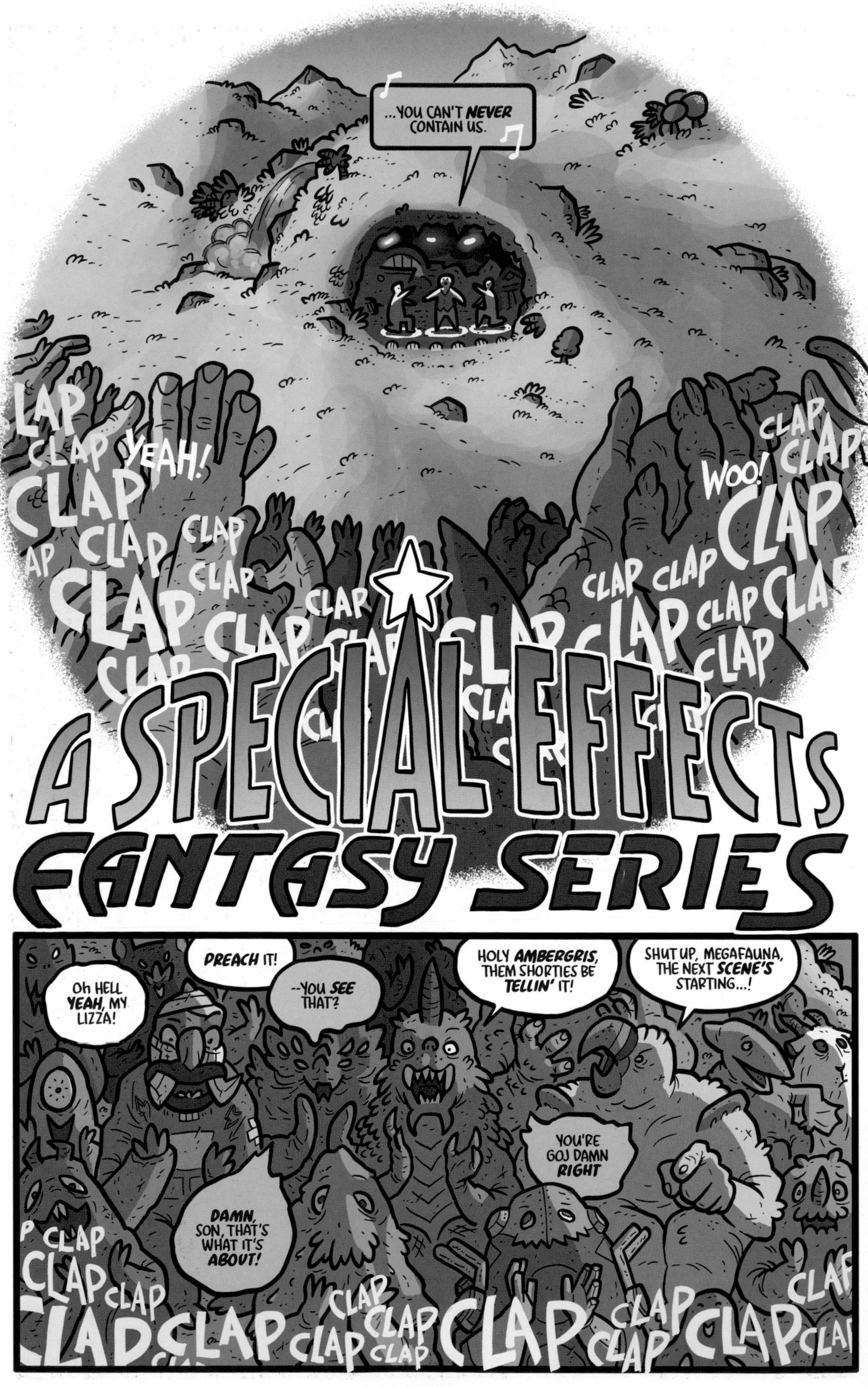

...YOU CAN'T NEVER CONTAIN US.
CLAP CLAP YEAH! CLAP CLAP CLAP CLAP CLAP CLAP CLAP CLAP
WOO! CLAP CLAP CLAP CLAP CLAP CLAP CLAP CLAP CLAP CLAP
A SPECIAL EFFECTS FANTASY SERIES
Oh HELL YEAH, MY LIZZA!
PREACH IT!
--YOU SEE THAT?
HOLY AMBERGRIS, THEM SHORTIES BE TELLIN' IT!
SHUT UP, MEGAFAUNA, THE NEXT SCENE'S STARTING...!
YOU'RE GOJ DAMN RIGHT
DAMN, SON, THAT'S WHAT IT'S ABOUT!
CLAP CLAP CLAP CLAP CLAP CLAP CLAP CLAP CLAP CLAP CLAP CLAP CLAP CLAP

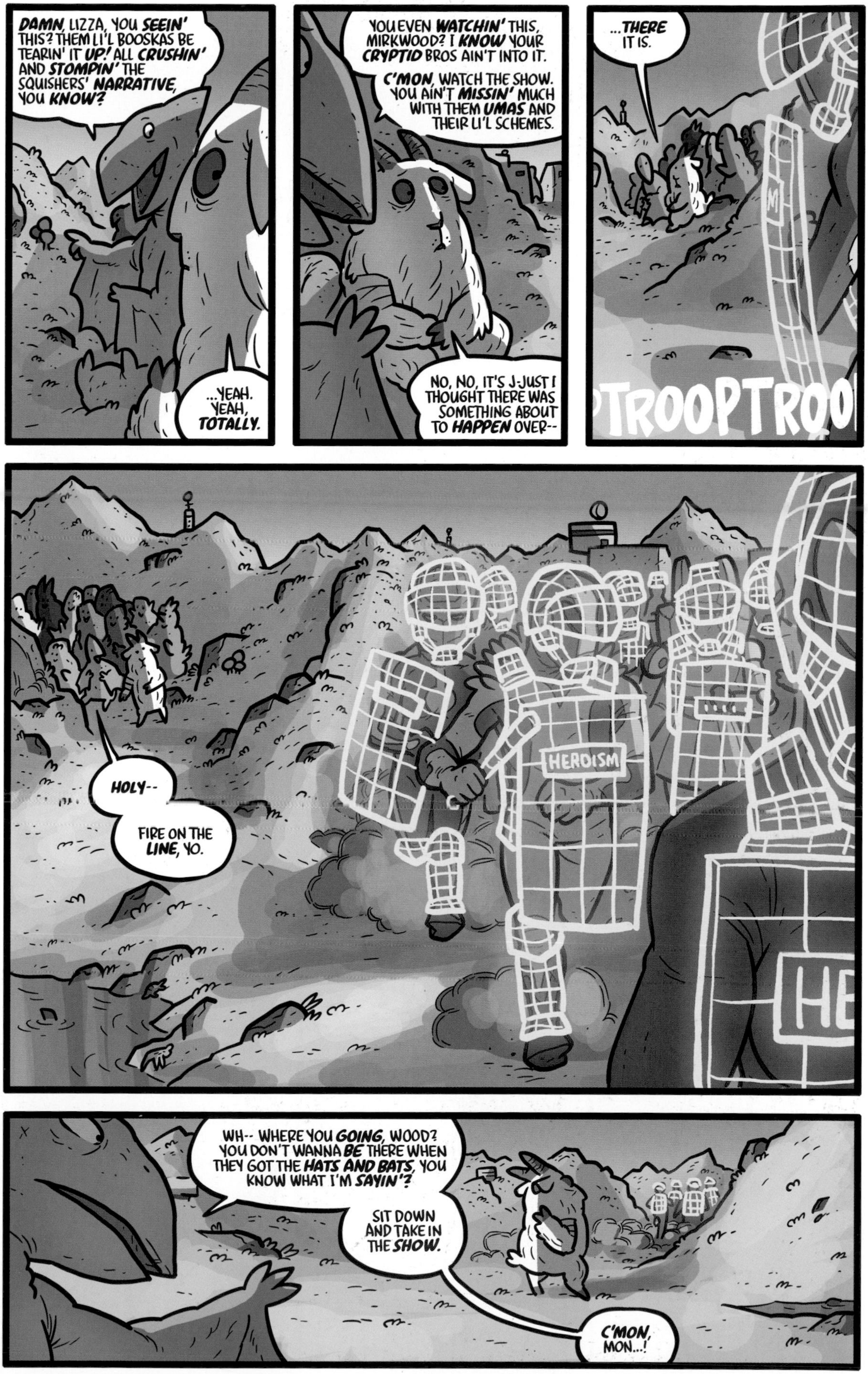

DAMN, LIZZA, YOU SEEIN' THIS? THEM LI'L BOOSKAS BE TEARIN' IT UP! ALL CRUSHIN' AND STOMPIN' THE SQUISHERS' NARRATIVE, YOU KNOW?
...YEAH. YEAH, TOTALLY.
YOU EVEN WATCHIN' THIS, MIRKWOOD? I KNOW YOUR CRYPTID BROS AIN'T INTO IT.
C'MON, WATCH THE SHOW. YOU AIN'T MISSIN' MUCH WITH THEM UMAS AND THEIR LI'L SCHEMES.
NO, NO, IT'S J-JUST I THOUGHT THERE WAS SOMETHING ABOUT TO HAPPEN OVER--
...THERE IT IS.
PTROOPTROO
HEROISM
HOLY--
FIRE ON THE LINE, YO.
HE
WH-- WHERE YOU GOING, WOOD? YOU DON'T WANNA BE THERE WHEN THEY GOT THE HATS AND BATS, YOU KNOW WHAT I'M SAYIN'?
SIT DOWN AND TAKE IN THE SHOW.
C'MON, MON...!

ALL RIGHT, PEOPLE. *TSU* BLOCK. CRATER *10*.

AFTER THIS *POINT*, NO *TALKING*. HE HEARS US *COMING* AND HE'S GONNA GET IN SOMEONE'S *HEAD*.

YOU DO *NOT* WANT THAT.

SOUNDS LIKE THE *LAST* COP THAT GAVE HIM AN *OPENING* WOUND UP *DEAD*.

GOT IT?

GOT IT.

LET'S *GO*.

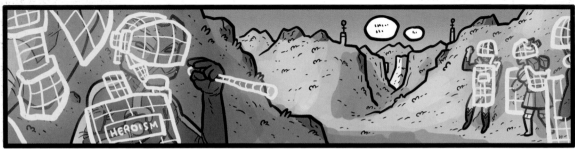

--DUE BACK *TODAY*. WORD *IS* HE'S GOT *PLANS*.

I KNOW HE'S *LOYAL*. WE DON'T HAVE TO WORRY ABOUT *THAT*. BUT IF HE GETS 'EM ALL RILED *UP*, THEN--

YEAH. *BIG* TIME. BUT I THINK WE CAN KEEP IT ON THE *DEEP* IF YOU TALK TO--

Oh, REDKING *AMBERG*--

KRAK

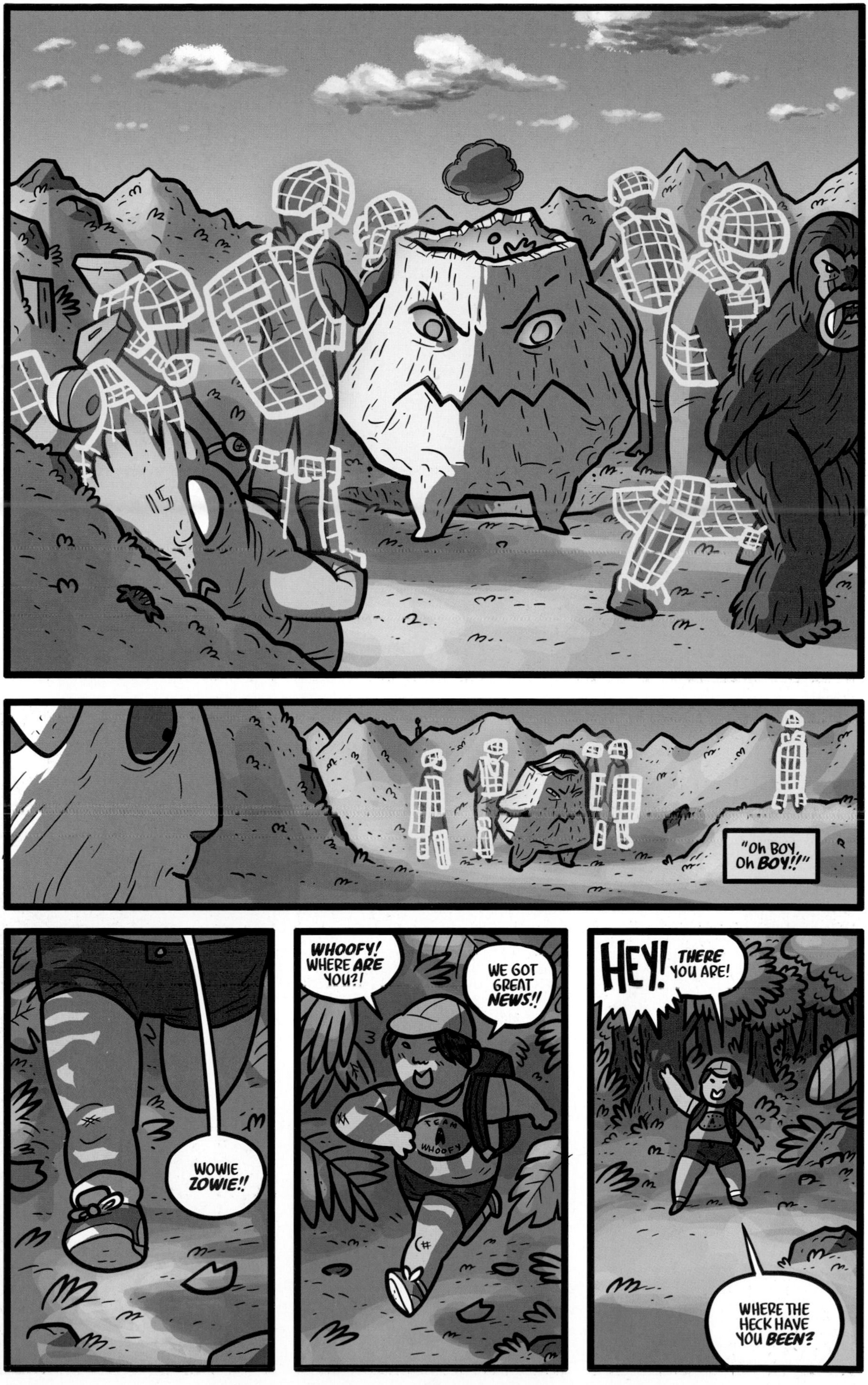
"Oh BOY, Oh BOY!!"
WOWIE ZOWIE!!
WHOOFY! WHERE ARE YOU?!
WE GOT GREAT NEWS!!
HEY!
THERE YOU ARE!
WHERE THE HECK HAVE YOU BEEN?

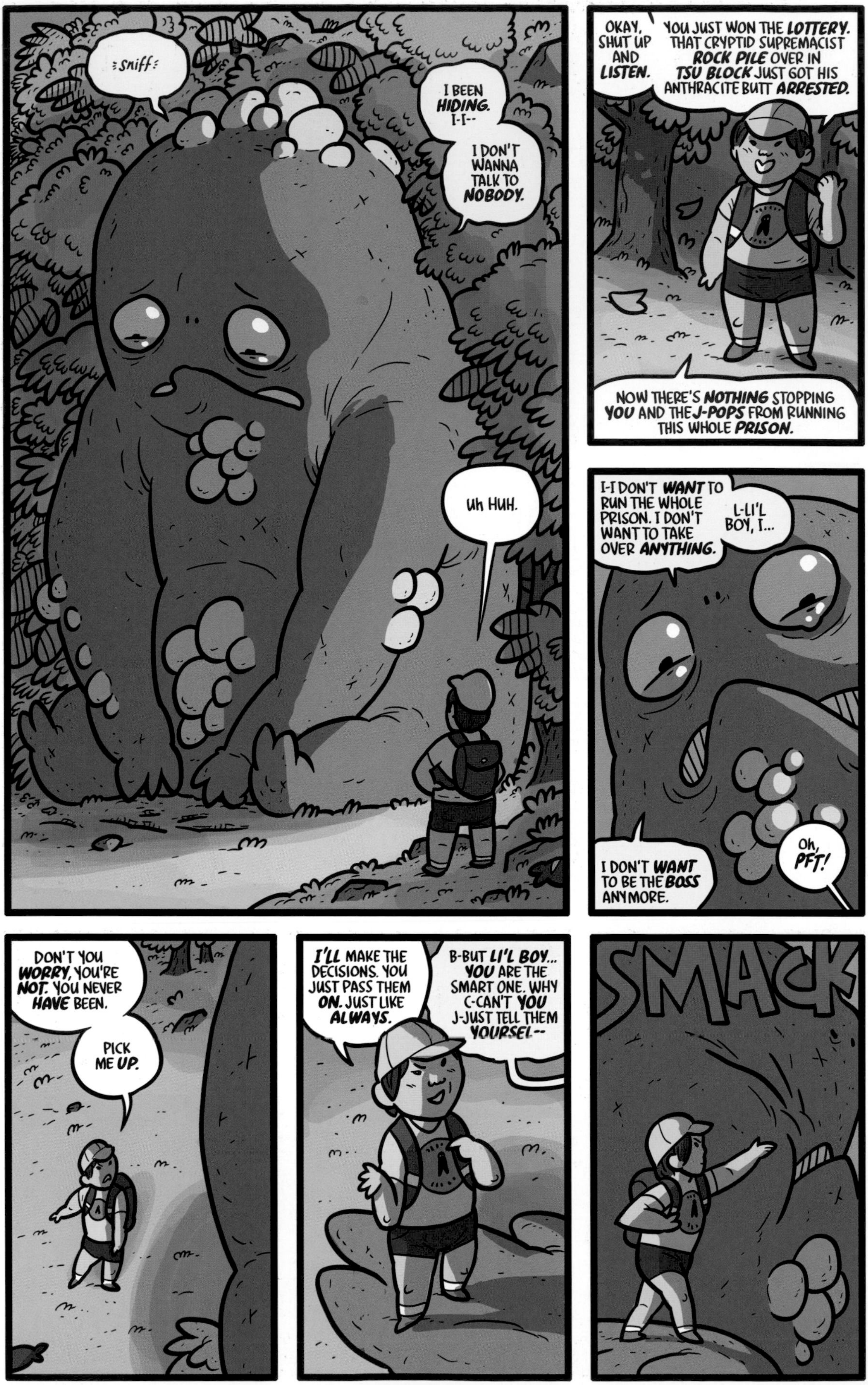
SNIFF
I BEEN HIDING. I-I--
I DON'T WANNA TALK TO NOBODY.
UH HUH.
OKAY, SHUT UP AND LISTEN.
YOU JUST WON THE LOTTERY. THAT CRYPTID SUPREMACIST ROCK PILE OVER IN TSU BLOCK JUST GOT HIS ANTHRACITE BUTT ARRESTED.
NOW THERE'S NOTHING STOPPING YOU AND THE J-POPS FROM RUNNING THIS WHOLE PRISON.
I-I DON'T WANT TO RUN THE WHOLE PRISON. I DON'T WANT TO TAKE OVER ANYTHING.
L-LI'L BOY, I...
I DON'T WANT TO BE THE BOSS ANYMORE.
OH, PFT!
DON'T YOU WORRY, YOU'RE NOT. YOU NEVER HAVE BEEN.
PICK ME UP.
I'LL MAKE THE DECISIONS. YOU JUST PASS THEM ON. JUST LIKE ALWAYS.
B-BUT LI'L BOY... YOU ARE THE SMART ONE. WHY C-CAN'T YOU J-JUST TELL THEM YOURSEL--
SMACK

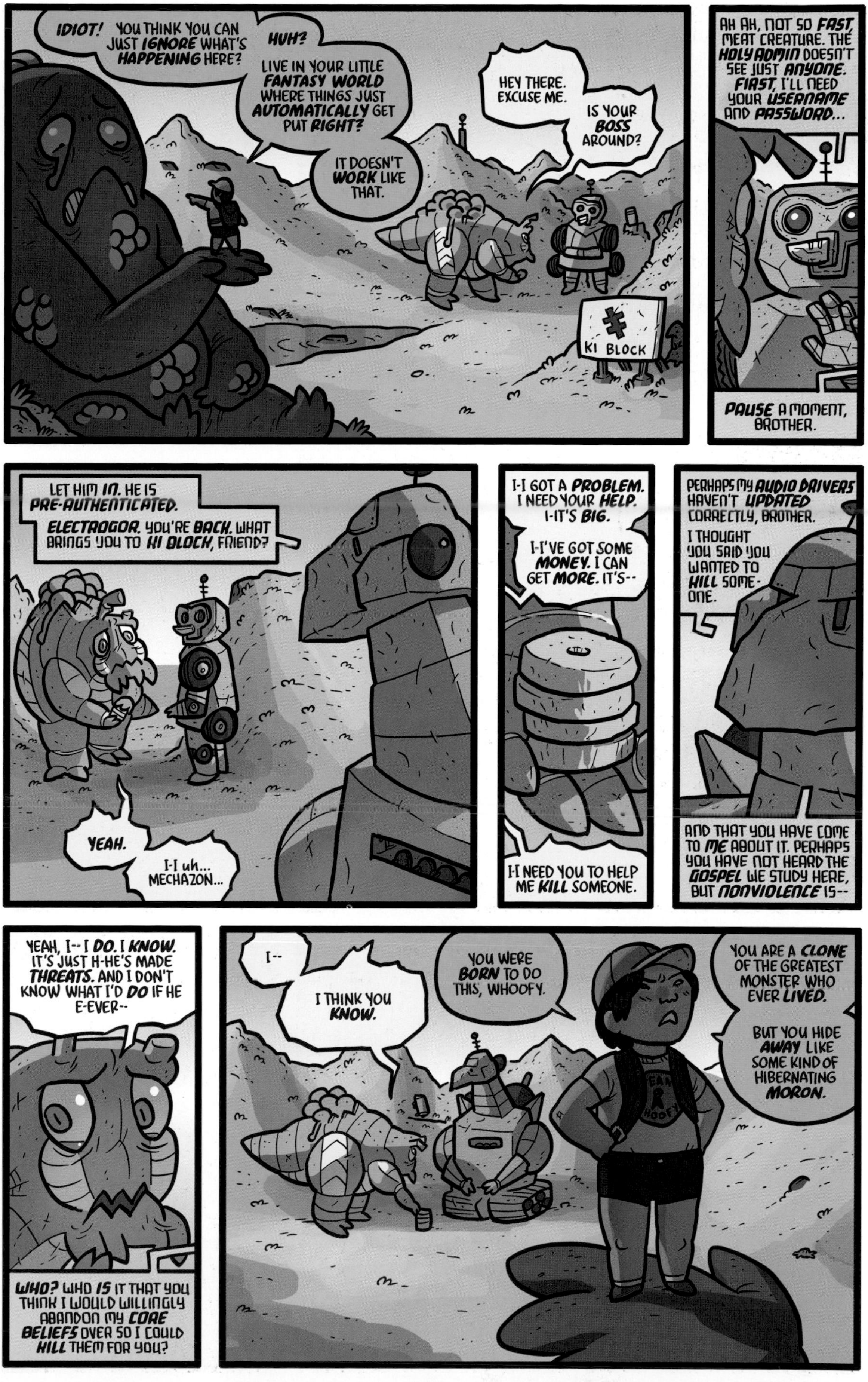
IDIOT! YOU THINK YOU CAN JUST IGNORE WHAT'S HAPPENING HERE?
HUH?
LIVE IN YOUR LITTLE FANTASY WORLD WHERE THINGS JUST AUTOMATICALLY GET PUT RIGHT?
IT DOESN'T WORK LIKE THAT.
HEY THERE. EXCUSE ME.
IS YOUR BOSS AROUND?
KI BLOCK
AH AH, NOT SO FAST, MEAT CREATURE. THE HOLY ADMIN DOESN'T SEE JUST ANYONE. FIRST, I'LL NEED YOUR USERNAME AND PASSWORD...
PAUSE A MOMENT, BROTHER.
LET HIM IN. HE IS PRE-AUTHENTICATED.
ELECTROGOR. YOU'RE BACK. WHAT BRINGS YOU TO KI BLOCK, FRIEND?
YEAH.
I-I uh... MECHAZON...
I-I GOT A PROBLEM. I NEED YOUR HELP. I-IT'S BIG.
I-I'VE GOT SOME MONEY. I CAN GET MORE. IT'S--
I-I NEED YOU TO HELP ME KILL SOMEONE.
PERHAPS MY AUDIO DRIVERS HAVEN'T UPDATED CORRECTLY, BROTHER.
I THOUGHT YOU SAID YOU WANTED TO KILL SOME-ONE.
AND THAT YOU HAVE COME TO ME ABOUT IT. PERHAPS YOU HAVE NOT HEARD THE GOSPEL WE STUDY HERE, BUT NONVIOLENCE IS--
YEAH, I-- I DO. I KNOW. IT'S JUST H-HE'S MADE THREATS. AND I DON'T KNOW WHAT I'D DO IF HE E-EVER--
WHO? WHO IS IT THAT YOU THINK I WOULD WILLINGLY ABANDON MY CORE BELIEFS OVER SO I COULD KILL THEM FOR YOU?
I--
I THINK YOU KNOW.
YOU WERE BORN TO DO THIS, WHOOFY.
YOU ARE A CLONE OF THE GREATEST MONSTER WHO EVER LIVED.
BUT YOU HIDE AWAY LIKE SOME KIND OF HIBERNATING MORON.

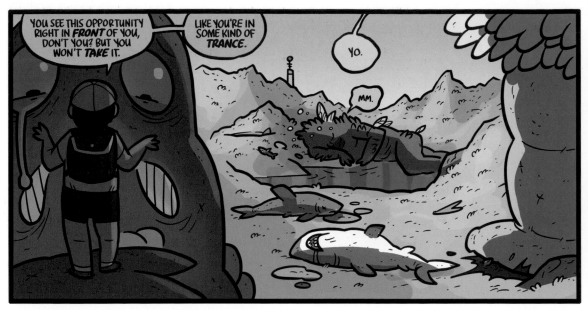

YOU SEE THIS OPPORTUNITY RIGHT IN *FRONT* OF YOU, DON'T YOU? BUT YOU WON'T *TAKE* IT.

LIKE YOU'RE IN SOME KIND OF *TRANCE*.

YO.

MM.

I'M HERE WITH YOUR *FIX*, JUNKIE.

FINEST *YELLOW-CAKE*. STRAIGHT FROM THE *MOON*.

LIKED THAT YESTERDAY, *DIDN'T* YA?

WELL, HERE'S *MORE*. BUT THE *COST* WENT UP.

I SAID *YO!*

SNXF?!

Z-ZONN? H-HEY, NO, M'*GOOD*. I'M OKAY.

UH HUH. I CAN *SEE* THAT.

KEEPIN' YOURSELF PRETTY *DOPED*.

DON'T EVEN GOT TIME TO FEED YOUR *SHARKS*.

SO I GOT ONE *QUESTION*.

THAP

WHY DO YOU THINK I *GAVE* YOU THE *SAMPLE*, MEGAFAUNA?!

SO YOU COULD GO AND TAKE YOUR BUSINESS ACROSS THE *MOUNTAIN RANGE* TO SOME *OTHER* PUSHER? *HUH?*

WHAT YOU *GAVE* ME-- S-SO *STRONG*, MON. I-I WAS *FIENDIN'*. I N-NEEDED IT. AN' *HE* COME BY AN'-- I-I JUST GAVE HIM TH-THE R-REST A' MY *MONEY*--

"*HE?*" WHO'S--

OH.

YEAH, I THINK I *KNOW*.

YOU CAN SEE WHERE *THIS* IS GOING.

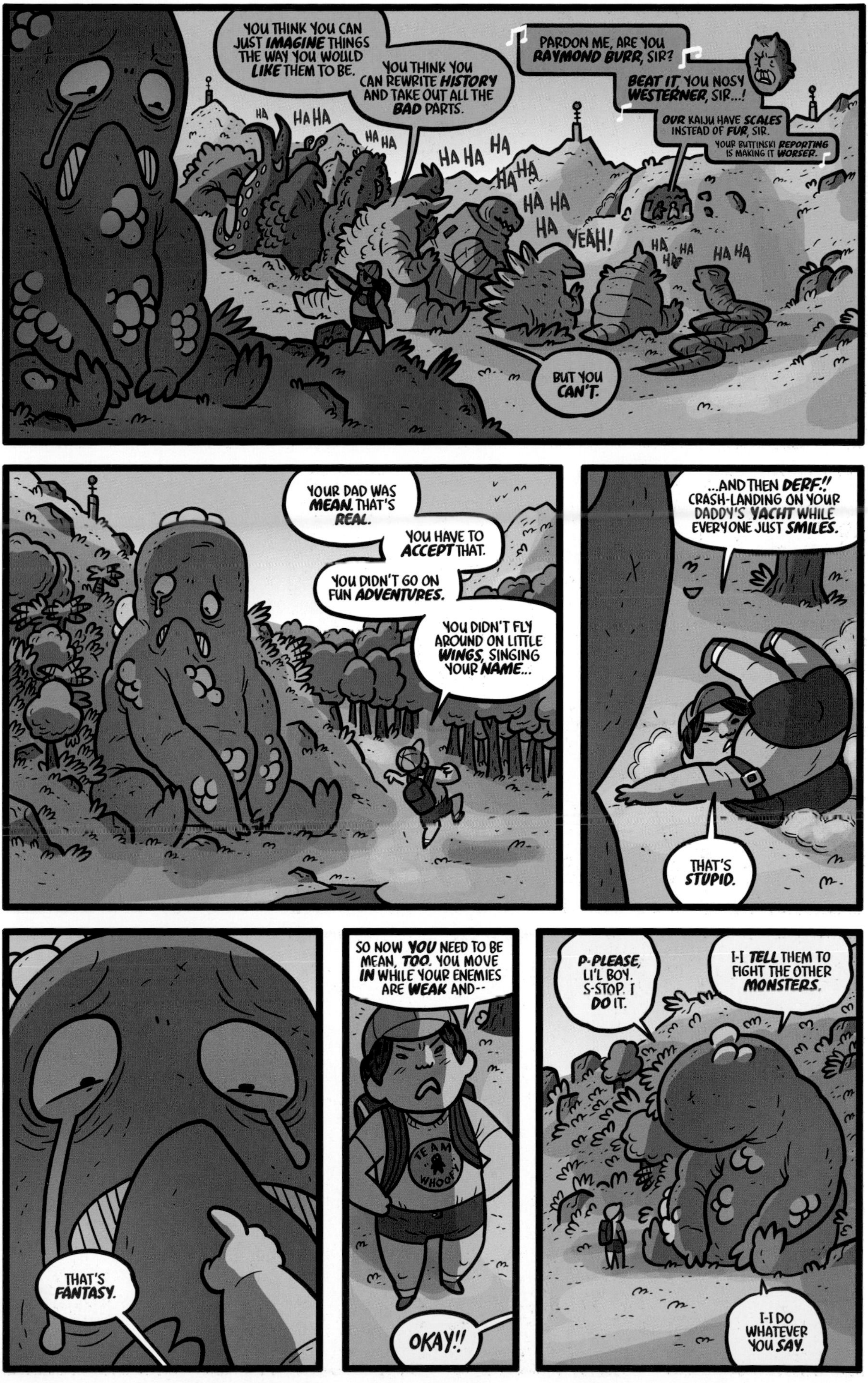
YOU THINK YOU CAN JUST IMAGINE THINGS THE WAY YOU WOULD LIKE THEM TO BE.
YOU THINK YOU CAN REWRITE HISTORY AND TAKE OUT ALL THE BAD PARTS.
HA HA HA HA HA HA HA HA HA HA HA HA HA HA HA
YEAH!
HA HA HA HA HA
PARDON ME, ARE YOU RAYMOND BURR, SIR?
BEAT IT, YOU NOSY WESTERNER, SIR...!
OUR KAIJU HAVE SCALES INSTEAD OF FUR, SIR.
YOUR BUTTINSKI REPORTING IS MAKING IT WORSER.
BUT YOU CAN'T.
YOUR DAD WAS MEAN. THAT'S REAL.
YOU HAVE TO ACCEPT THAT.
YOU DIDN'T GO ON FUN ADVENTURES.
YOU DIDN'T FLY AROUND ON LITTLE WINGS, SINGING YOUR NAME...
...AND THEN DERF!! CRASH-LANDING ON YOUR DADDY'S YACHT WHILE EVERYONE JUST SMILES.
THAT'S STUPID.
THAT'S FANTASY.
SO NOW YOU NEED TO BE MEAN, TOO. YOU MOVE IN WHILE YOUR ENEMIES ARE WEAK AND--
TEAM WHOOFY
OKAY!!
P-PLEASE, LI'L BOY. S-STOP. I DO IT.
I-I TELL THEM TO FIGHT THE OTHER MONSTERS.
I-I DO WHATEVER YOU SAY.

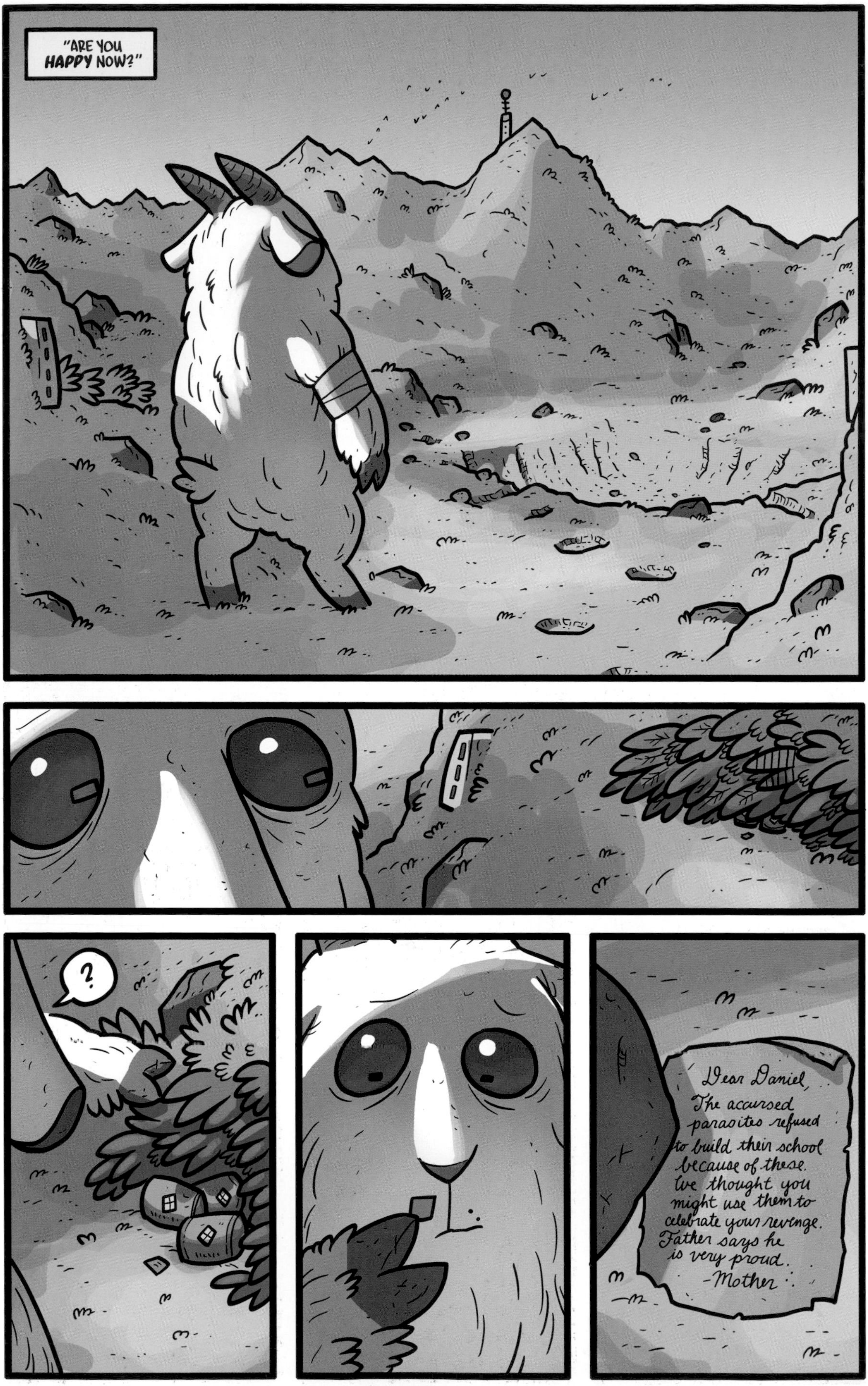
"ARE YOU HAPPY NOW?"
?
Dear Daniel,
The accursed parasites refused to build their school because of these.
We thought you might use them to celebrate your revenge.
Father says he is very proud.
-Mother

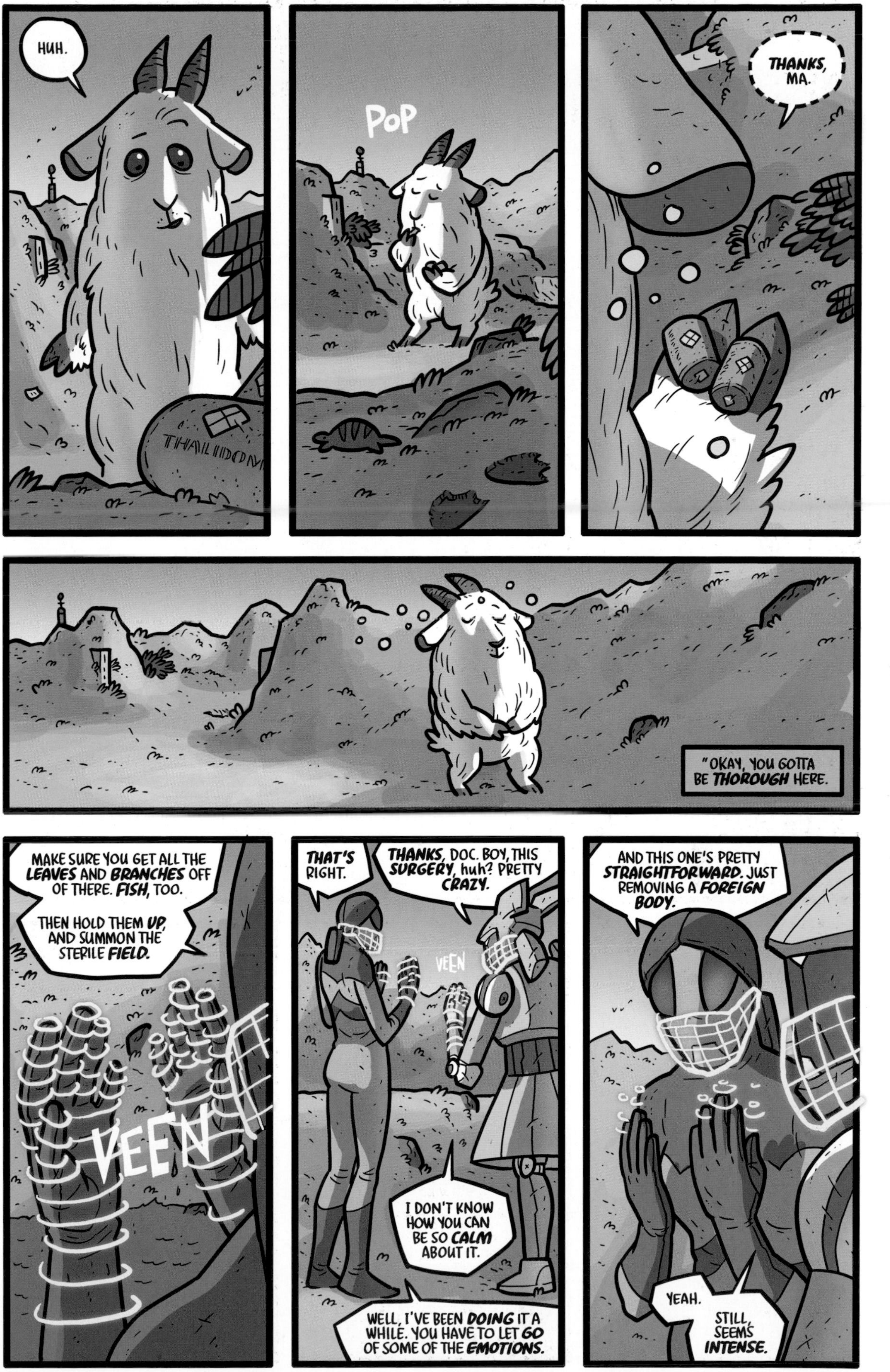
HUH.
THALIDOM
POP
THANKS, MA.
"OKAY, YOU GOTTA BE THOROUGH HERE.
MAKE SURE YOU GET ALL THE LEAVES AND BRANCHES OFF OF THERE. FISH, TOO.
THEN HOLD THEM UP, AND SUMMON THE STERILE FIELD.
VEEN
THAT'S RIGHT.
THANKS, DOC. BOY, THIS SURGERY, huh? PRETTY CRAZY.
VEEN
I DON'T KNOW HOW YOU CAN BE SO CALM ABOUT IT.
WELL, I'VE BEEN DOING IT A WHILE. YOU HAVE TO LET GO OF SOME OF THE EMOTIONS.
AND THIS ONE'S PRETTY STRAIGHTFORWARD. JUST REMOVING A FOREIGN BODY.
YEAH.
STILL, SEEMS INTENSE.

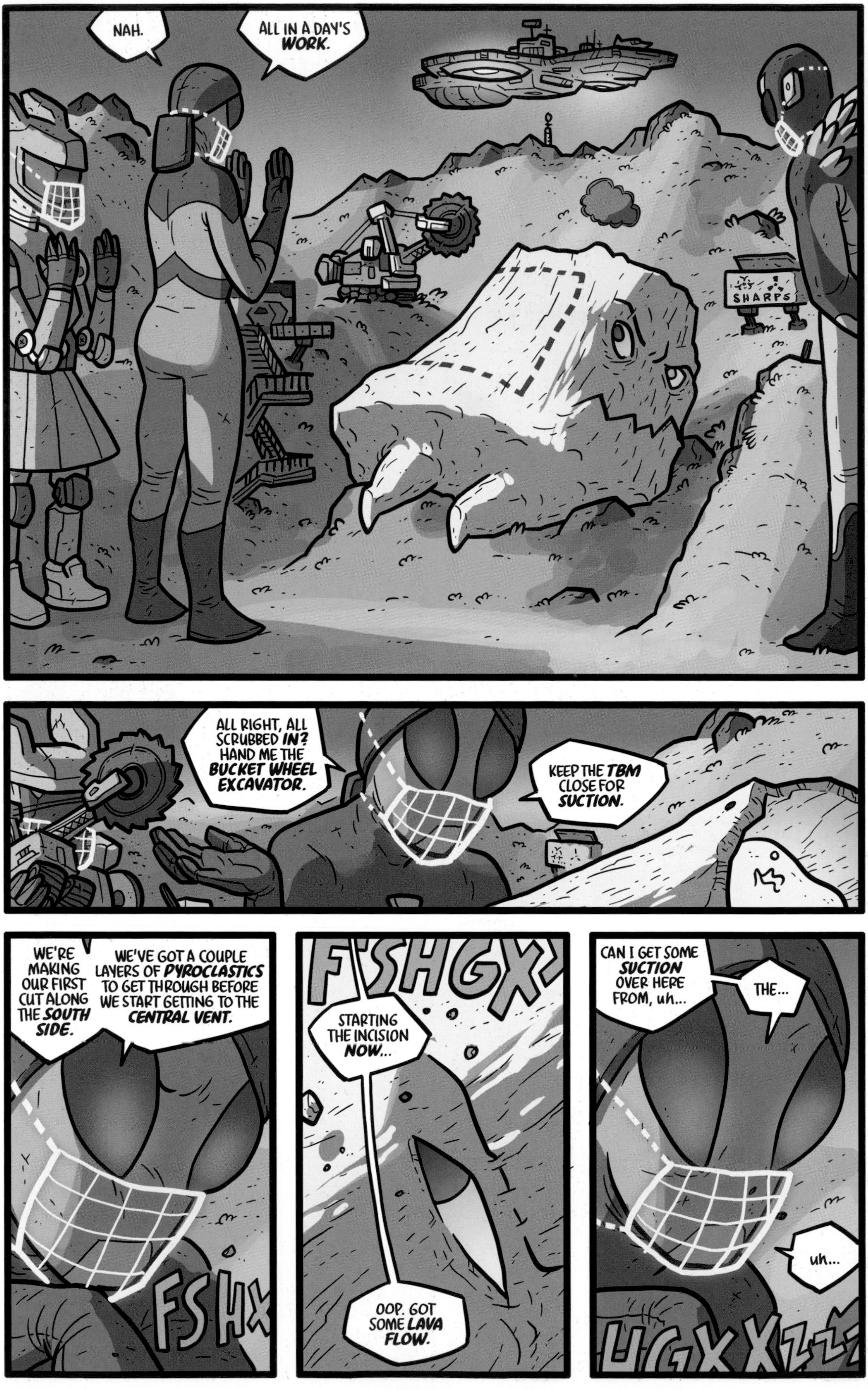
NAH.
ALL IN A DAY'S WORK.
SHARPS
ALL RIGHT, ALL SCRUBBED IN? HAND ME THE BUCKET WHEEL EXCAVATOR.
KEEP THE TBM CLOSE FOR SUCTION.
WE'RE MAKING OUR FIRST CUT ALONG THE SOUTH SIDE.
WE'VE GOT A COUPLE LAYERS OF PYROCLASTICS TO GET THROUGH BEFORE WE START GETTING TO THE CENTRAL VENT.
FSHX
FSHGX
STARTING THE INCISION NOW...
OOP. GOT SOME LAVA FLOW.
CAN I GET SOME SUCTION OVER HERE FROM, uh...
THE...
uh...
UGXXZZZ

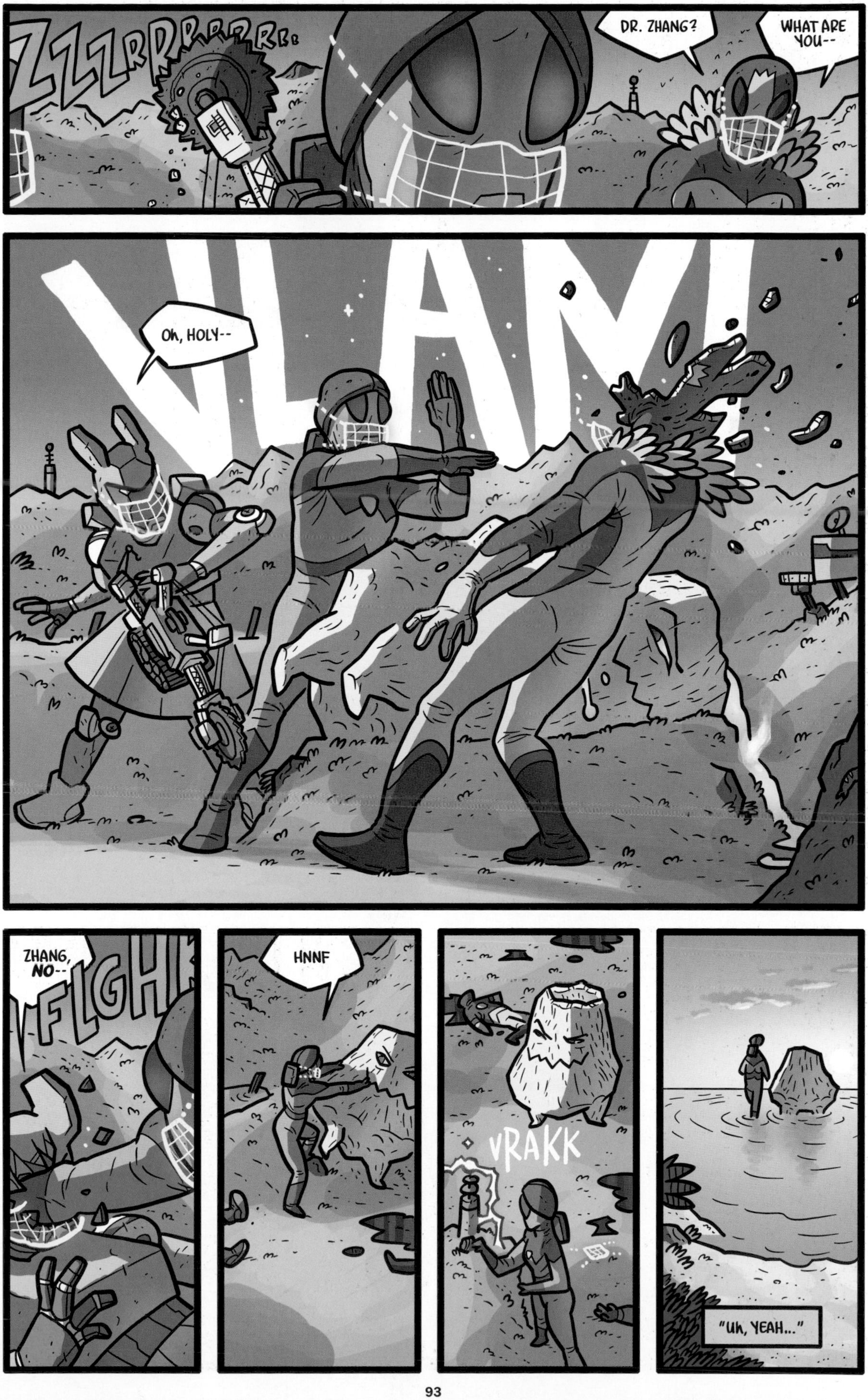
ZZZZRRRRRRRRR
DR. ZHANG?
WHAT ARE YOU--
VLAM!
Oh, HOLY--
ZHANG, NO--
FLGH
HNNF
VRAKK
"Uh, YEAH..."

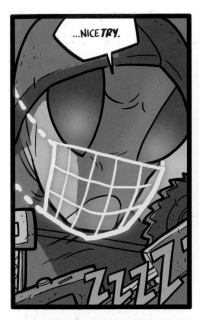

...NICE **TRY.**

ZZZZ

SHGHZZZH

Oh my **GOD.**

YOU--

SKLU

GLK

CHLP

YOU'RE GOING TO THE **CHAIR** FOR THIS.

WELL, THAT'S IT. WE'RE **DONE.**

HE'S GOIN' TO THE ORANGE **MILE,** AIN'T HE?

LO, THIS IS GONNA GET **UGLY,** MY BROTHERS. WE LOOKIN' AT THE **END** OF THE **CRYPTID BROTHERHOOD,** YOU **FEEL** ME?

YOU GONNA WANT TO BE **CAREFUL** HOW YOU FLAP THEM **SABERS,** WOOD...

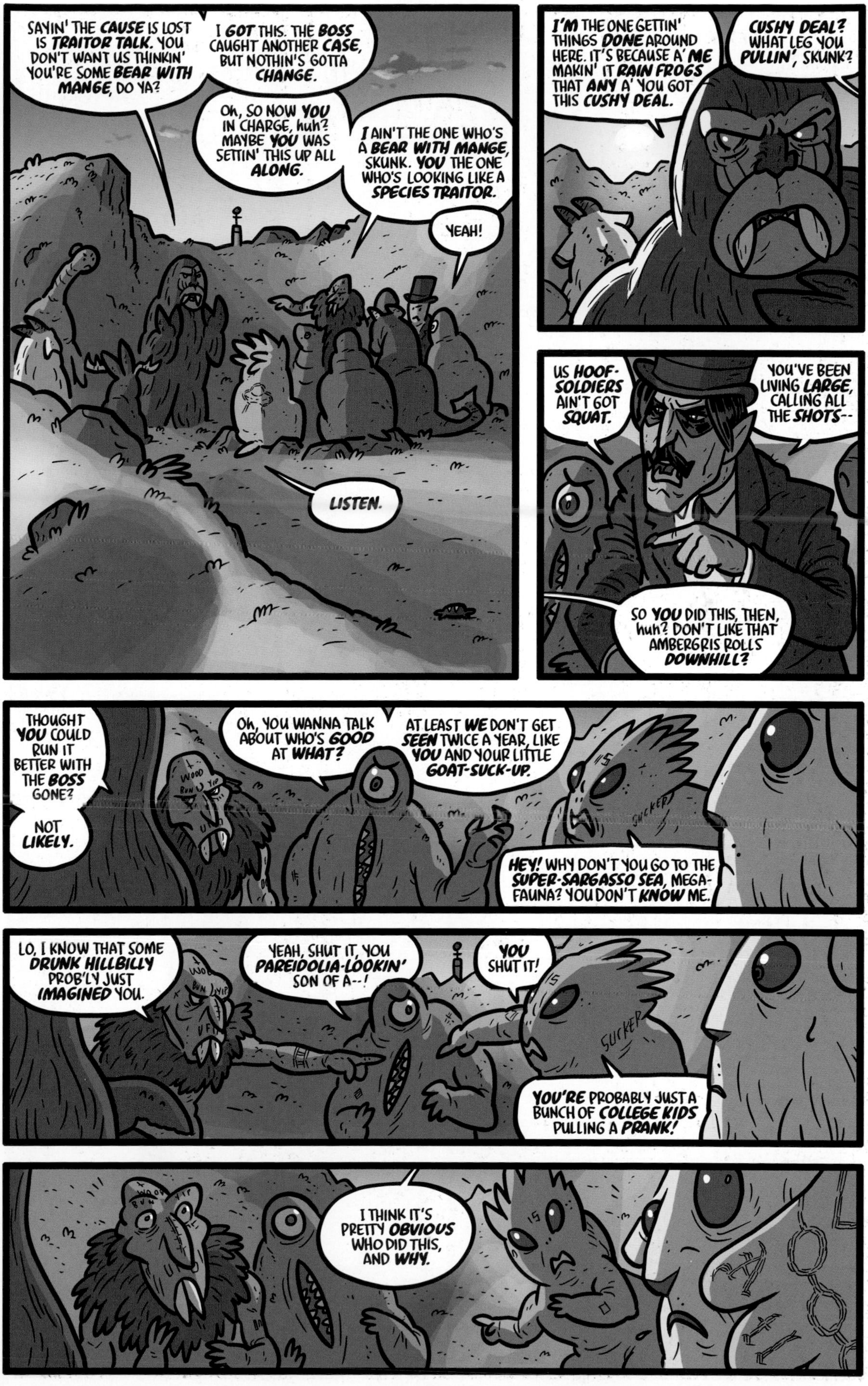
SAYIN' THE CAUSE IS LOST IS TRAITOR TALK. YOU DON'T WANT US THINKIN' YOU'RE SOME BEAR WITH MANGE, DO YA?
I GOT THIS. THE BOSS CAUGHT ANOTHER CASE, BUT NOTHIN'S GOTTA CHANGE.
Oh, SO NOW YOU IN CHARGE, huh? MAYBE YOU WAS SETTIN' THIS UP ALL ALONG.
I AIN'T THE ONE WHO'S A BEAR WITH MANGE, SKUNK. YOU THE ONE WHO'S LOOKING LIKE A SPECIES TRAITOR.
YEAH!
LISTEN.
I'M THE ONE GETTIN' THINGS DONE AROUND HERE. IT'S BECAUSE A' ME MAKIN' IT RAIN FROGS THAT ANY A' YOU GOT THIS CUSHY DEAL.
CUSHY DEAL? WHAT LEG YOU PULLIN', SKUNK?
US HOOF-SOLDIERS AIN'T GOT SQUAT.
YOU'VE BEEN LIVING LARGE, CALLING ALL THE SHOTS--
SO YOU DID THIS, THEN, huh? DON'T LIKE THAT AMBERGRIS ROLLS DOWNHILL?
THOUGHT YOU COULD RUN IT BETTER WITH THE BOSS GONE?
NOT LIKELY.
Oh, YOU WANNA TALK ABOUT WHO'S GOOD AT WHAT?
AT LEAST WE DON'T GET SEEN TWICE A YEAR, LIKE YOU AND YOUR LITTLE GOAT-SUCK-UP.
HEY! WHY DON'T YOU GO TO THE SUPER-SARGASSO SEA, MEGA-FAUNA? YOU DON'T KNOW ME.
LO, I KNOW THAT SOME DRUNK HILLBILLY PROB'LY JUST IMAGINED YOU.
YEAH, SHUT IT, YOU PAREIDOLIA-LOOKIN' SON OF A--!
YOU SHUT IT!
YOU'RE PROBABLY JUST A BUNCH OF COLLEGE KIDS PULLING A PRANK!
I THINK IT'S PRETTY OBVIOUS WHO DID THIS, AND WHY.

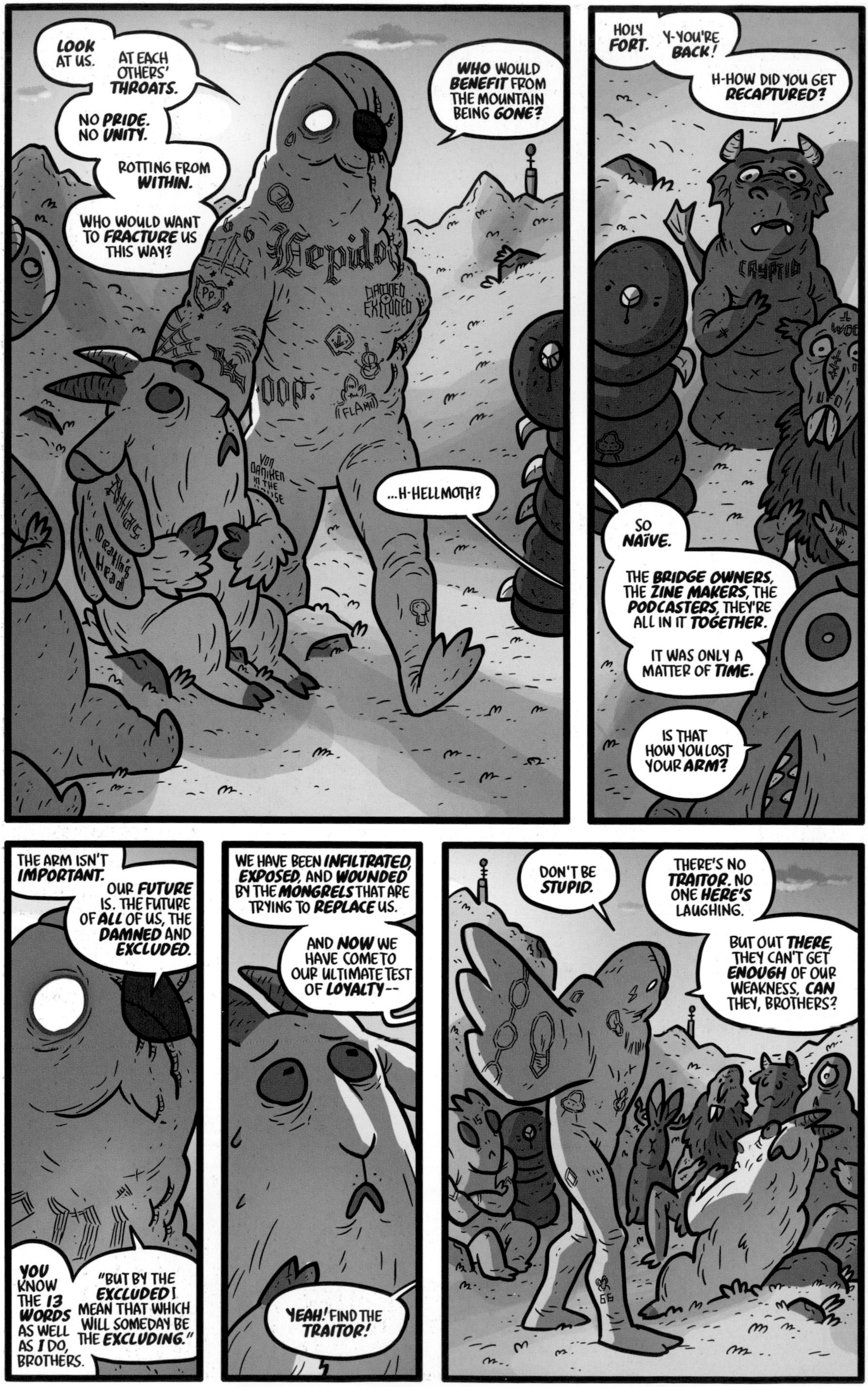
LOOK AT US.
AT EACH OTHERS' THROATS.
NO PRIDE. NO UNITY.
ROTTING FROM WITHIN.
WHO WOULD WANT TO FRACTURE US THIS WAY?
WHO WOULD BENEFIT FROM THE MOUNTAIN BEING GONE?
DAMNED EXCLUDED
...H-HELLMOTH?
HOLY FORT.
Y-YOU'RE BACK!
H-HOW DID YOU GET RECAPTURED?
CRYPTID
SO NAÏVE.
THE BRIDGE OWNERS, THE ZINE MAKERS, THE PODCASTERS, THEY'RE ALL IN IT TOGETHER.
IT WAS ONLY A MATTER OF TIME.
IS THAT HOW YOU LOST YOUR ARM?
THE ARM ISN'T IMPORTANT.
OUR FUTURE IS. THE FUTURE OF ALL OF US, THE DAMNED AND EXCLUDED.
YOU KNOW THE 13 WORDS AS WELL AS I DO, BROTHERS.
"BUT BY THE EXCLUDED I MEAN THAT WHICH WILL SOMEDAY BE THE EXCLUDING."
WE HAVE BEEN INFILTRATED, EXPOSED, AND WOUNDED BY THE MONGRELS THAT ARE TRYING TO REPLACE US.
AND NOW WE HAVE COME TO OUR ULTIMATE TEST OF LOYALTY--
YEAH! FIND THE TRAITOR!
DON'T BE STUPID.
THERE'S NO TRAITOR. NO ONE HERE'S LAUGHING.
BUT OUT THERE, THEY CAN'T GET ENOUGH OF OUR WEAKNESS, CAN THEY, BROTHERS?

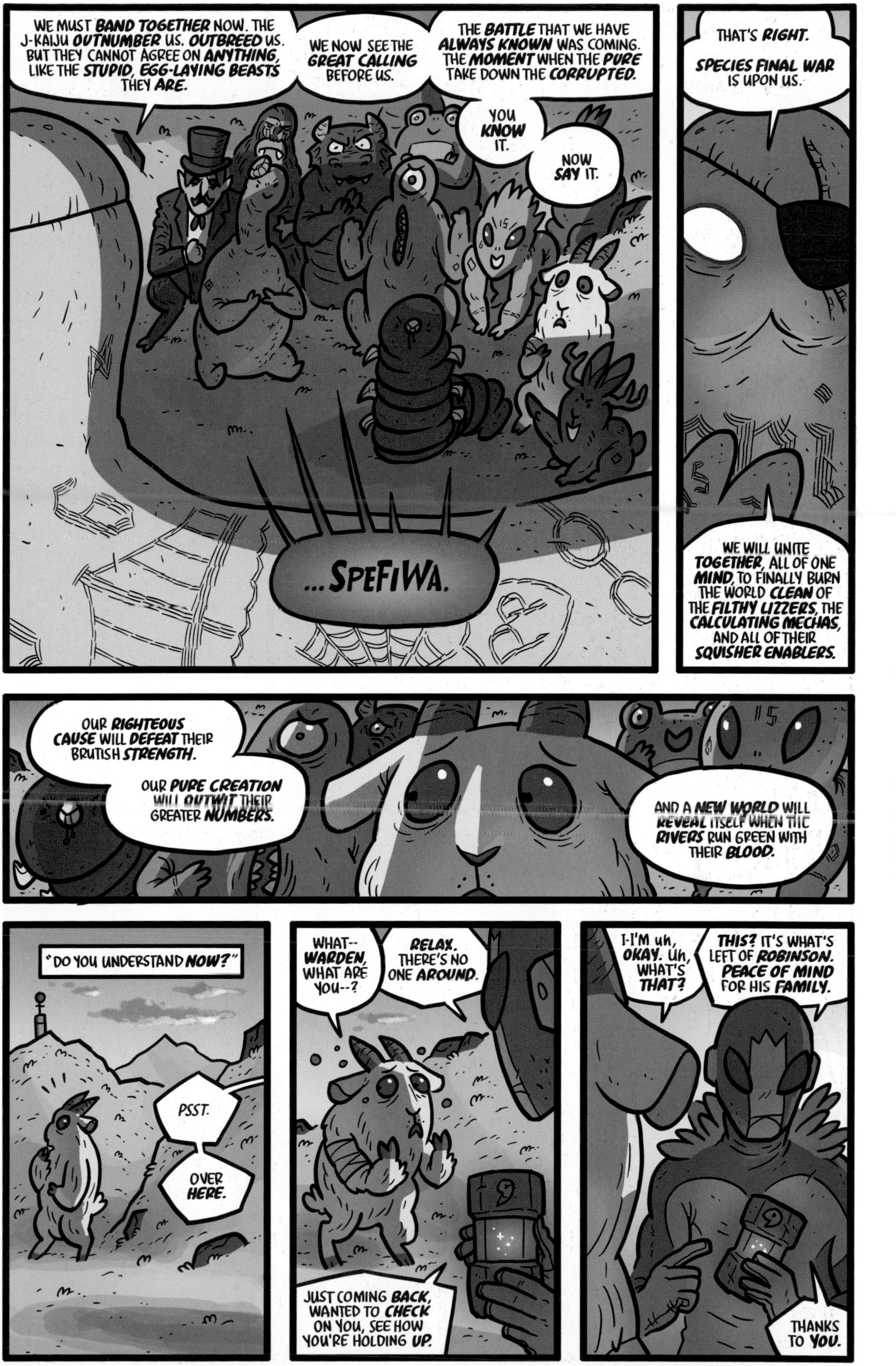
WE MUST BAND TOGETHER NOW. THE J-KAIJU OUTNUMBER US. OUTBREED US. BUT THEY CANNOT AGREE ON ANYTHING, LIKE THE STUPID, EGG-LAYING BEASTS THEY ARE.
WE NOW SEE THE GREAT CALLING BEFORE US.
THE BATTLE THAT WE HAVE ALWAYS KNOWN WAS COMING. THE MOMENT WHEN THE PURE TAKE DOWN THE CORRUPTED.
YOU KNOW IT.
NOW SAY IT.
...SPEFIWA.
THAT'S RIGHT.
SPECIES FINAL WAR IS UPON US.
WE WILL UNITE TOGETHER, ALL OF ONE MIND, TO FINALLY BURN THE WORLD CLEAN OF THE FILTHY LIZZERS, THE CALCULATING MECHAS, AND ALL OF THEIR SQUISHER ENABLERS.
OUR RIGHTEOUS CAUSE WILL DEFEAT THEIR BRUTISH STRENGTH.
OUR PURE CREATION WILL OUTWIT THEIR GREATER NUMBERS.
AND A NEW WORLD WILL REVEAL ITSELF WHEN THE RIVERS RUN GREEN WITH THEIR BLOOD.
"DO YOU UNDERSTAND NOW?"
PSST.
OVER HERE.
WHAT-- WARDEN, WHAT ARE YOU--?
RELAX. THERE'S NO ONE AROUND.
JUST COMING BACK, WANTED TO CHECK ON YOU, SEE HOW YOU'RE HOLDING UP.
I-I'M uh, OKAY. uh, WHAT'S THAT?
THIS? IT'S WHAT'S LEFT OF ROBINSON. PEACE OF MIND FOR HIS FAMILY.
THANKS TO YOU.

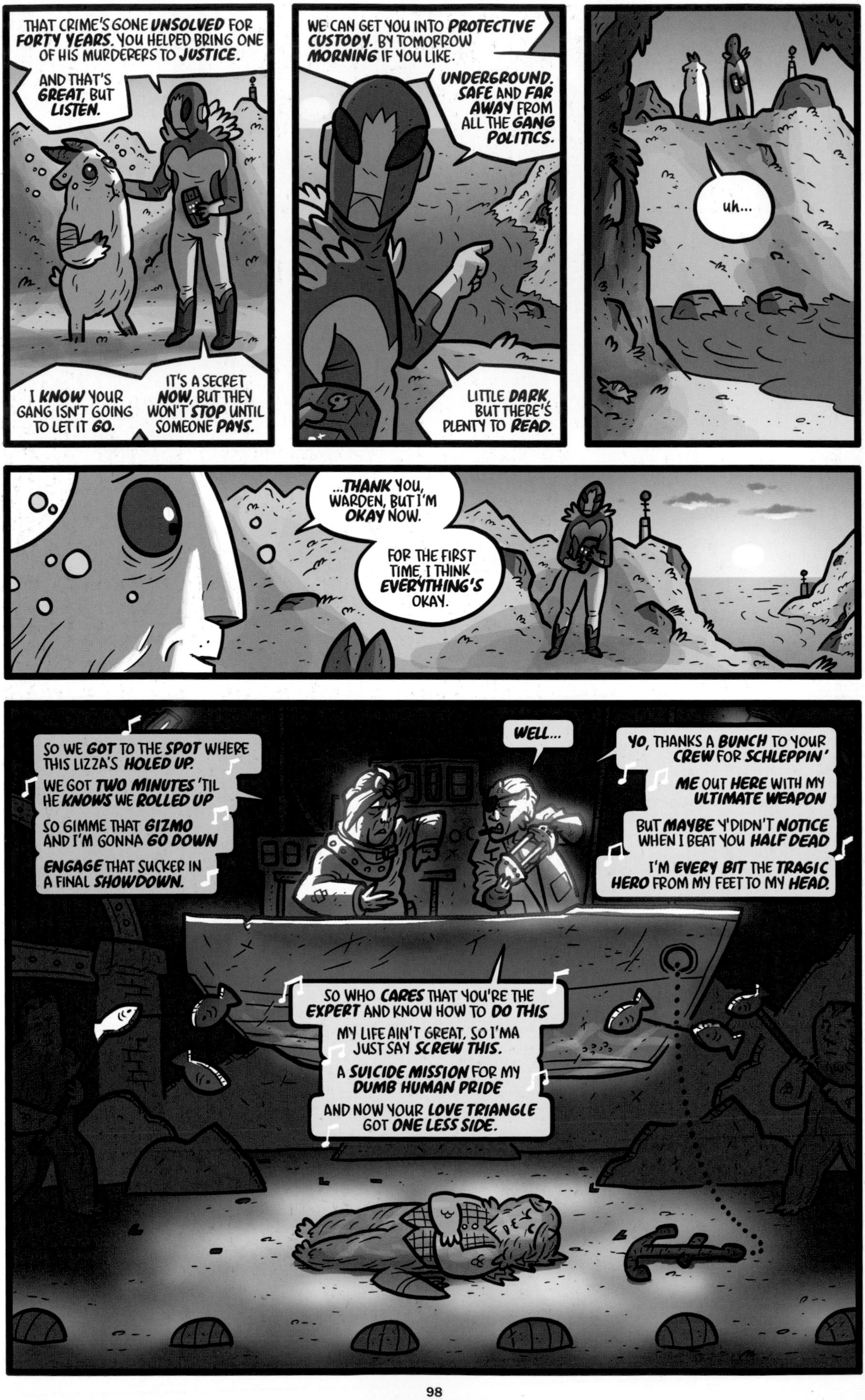
THAT CRIME'S GONE UNSOLVED FOR FORTY YEARS. YOU HELPED BRING ONE OF HIS MURDERERS TO JUSTICE.
AND THAT'S GREAT, BUT LISTEN.
I KNOW YOUR GANG ISN'T GOING TO LET IT GO.
IT'S A SECRET NOW, BUT THEY WON'T STOP UNTIL SOMEONE PAYS.
WE CAN GET YOU INTO PROTECTIVE CUSTODY. BY TOMORROW MORNING IF YOU LIKE.
UNDERGROUND. SAFE AND FAR AWAY FROM ALL THE GANG POLITICS.
LITTLE DARK, BUT THERE'S PLENTY TO READ.
uh...
...THANK YOU, WARDEN, BUT I'M OKAY NOW.
FOR THE FIRST TIME, I THINK EVERYTHING'S OKAY.
SO WE GOT TO THE SPOT WHERE THIS LIZZA'S HOLED UP.
WE GOT TWO MINUTES 'TIL HE KNOWS WE ROLLED UP
SO GIMME THAT GIZMO AND I'M GONNA GO DOWN
ENGAGE THAT SUCKER IN A FINAL SHOWDOWN.
WELL...
YO, THANKS A BUNCH TO YOUR CREW FOR SCHLEPPIN'
ME OUT HERE WITH MY ULTIMATE WEAPON
BUT MAYBE Y'DIDN'T NOTICE WHEN I BEAT YOU HALF DEAD
I'M EVERY BIT THE TRAGIC HERO FROM MY FEET TO MY HEAD.
SO WHO CARES THAT YOU'RE THE EXPERT AND KNOW HOW TO DO THIS
MY LIFE AIN'T GREAT, SO I'MA JUST SAY SCREW THIS.
A SUICIDE MISSION FOR MY DUMB HUMAN PRIDE
AND NOW YOUR LOVE TRIANGLE GOT ONE LESS SIDE.

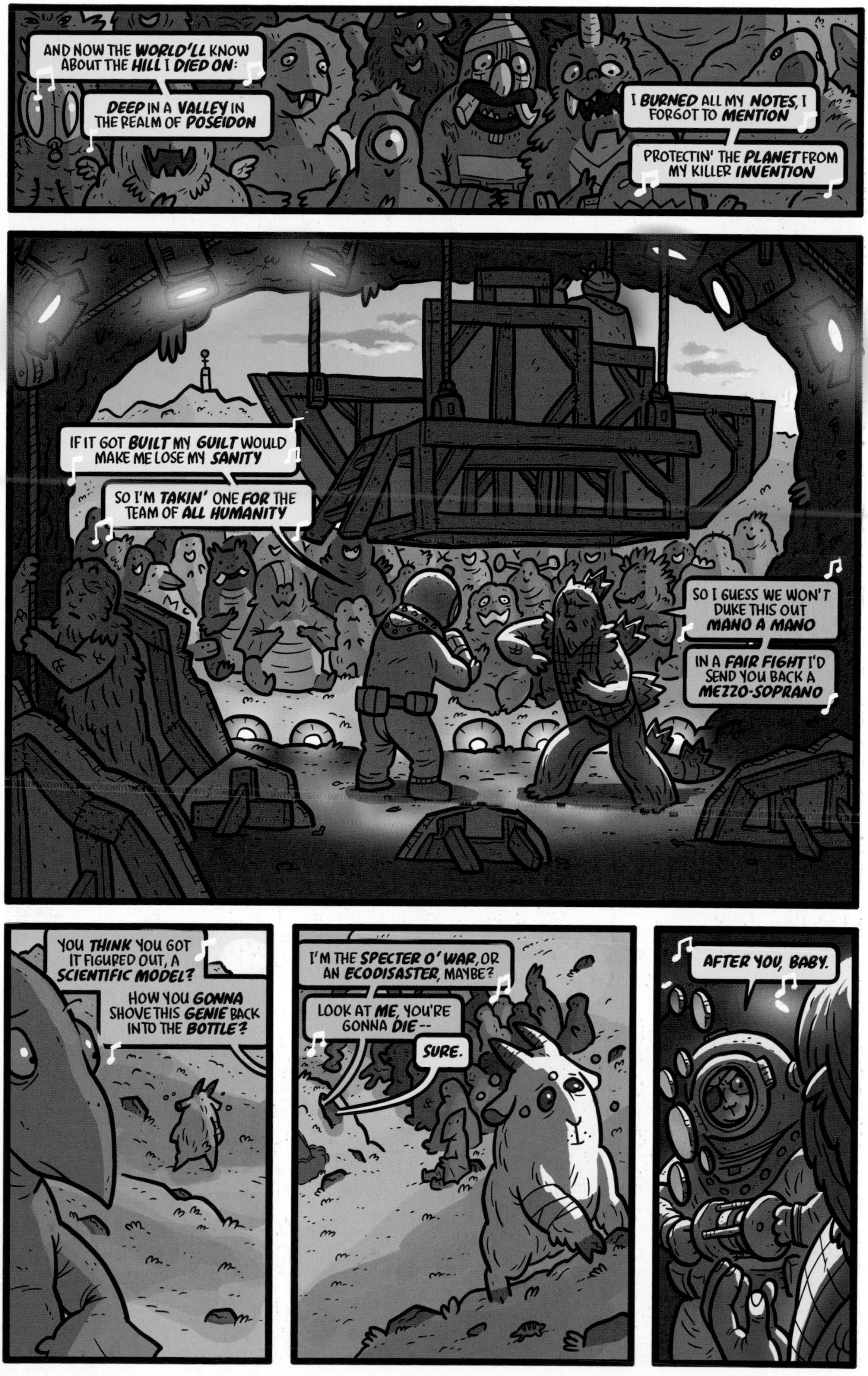
AND NOW THE WORLD'LL KNOW ABOUT THE HILL I DIED ON:
DEEP IN A VALLEY IN THE REALM OF POSEIDON
I BURNED ALL MY NOTES, I FORGOT TO MENTION
PROTECTIN' THE PLANET FROM MY KILLER INVENTION
IF IT GOT BUILT MY GUILT WOULD MAKE ME LOSE MY SANITY
SO I'M TAKIN' ONE FOR THE TEAM OF ALL HUMANITY
SO I GUESS WE WON'T DUKE THIS OUT MANO A MANO
IN A FAIR FIGHT I'D SEND YOU BACK A MEZZO-SOPRANO
YOU THINK YOU GOT IT FIGURED OUT, A SCIENTIFIC MODEL?
HOW YOU GONNA SHOVE THIS GENIE BACK INTO THE BOTTLE?
I'M THE SPECTER O' WAR, OR AN ECODISASTER, MAYBE?
LOOK AT ME, YOU'RE GONNA DIE--
SURE.
AFTER YOU, BABY.

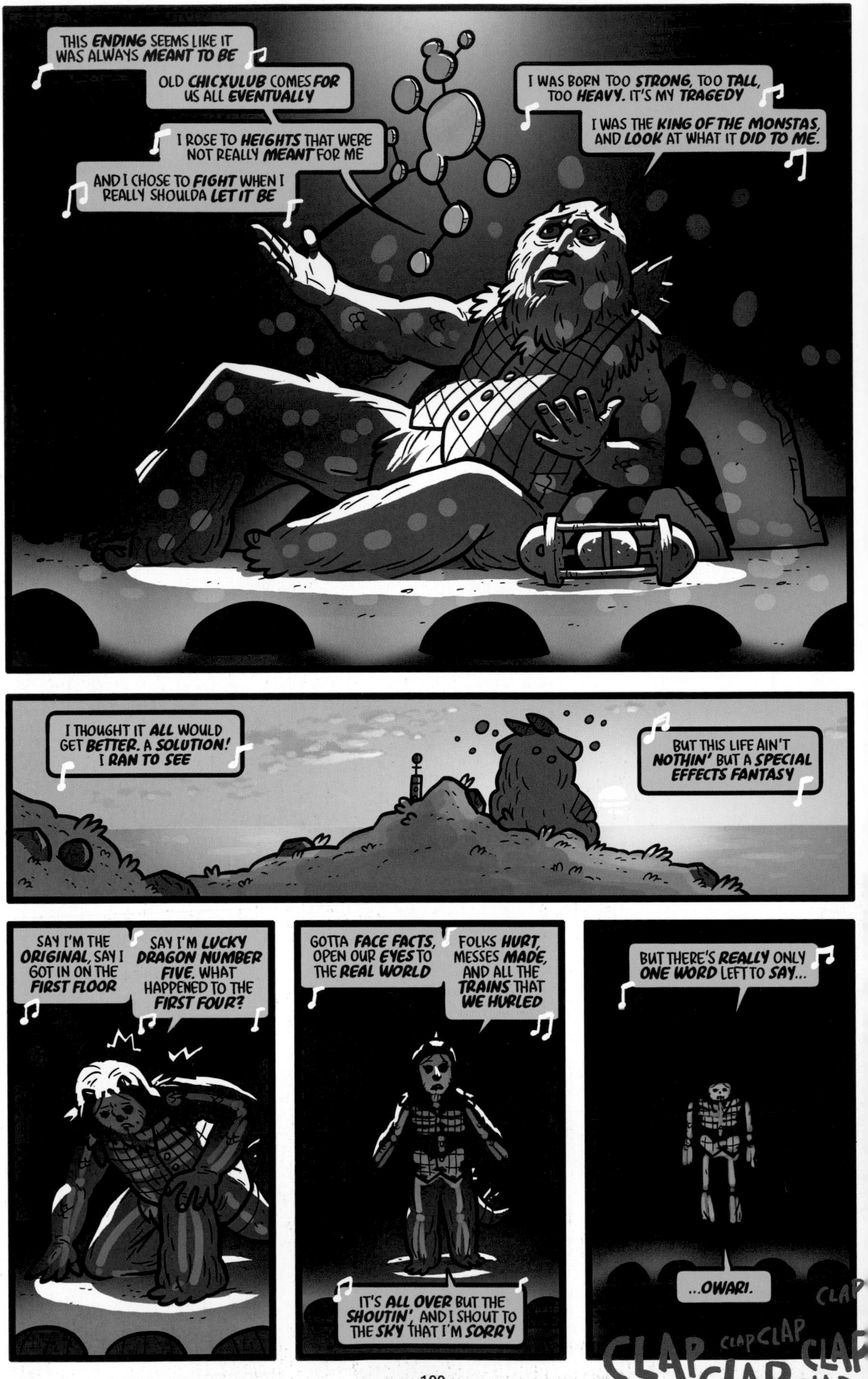
THIS ENDING SEEMS LIKE IT WAS ALWAYS MEANT TO BE
OLD CHICXULUB COMES FOR US ALL EVENTUALLY
I ROSE TO HEIGHTS THAT WERE NOT REALLY MEANT FOR ME
AND I CHOSE TO FIGHT WHEN I REALLY SHOULDA LET IT BE
I WAS BORN TOO STRONG, TOO TALL, TOO HEAVY. IT'S MY TRAGEDY
I WAS THE KING OF THE MONSTAS, AND LOOK AT WHAT IT DID TO ME.
I THOUGHT IT ALL WOULD GET BETTER. A SOLUTION! I RAN TO SEE
BUT THIS LIFE AIN'T NOTHIN' BUT A SPECIAL EFFECTS FANTASY
SAY I'M THE ORIGINAL, SAY I GOT IN ON THE FIRST FLOOR
SAY I'M LUCKY DRAGON NUMBER FIVE. WHAT HAPPENED TO THE FIRST FOUR?
GOTTA FACE FACTS, OPEN OUR EYES TO THE REAL WORLD
FOLKS HURT, MESSES MADE, AND ALL THE TRAINS THAT WE HURLED
IT'S ALL OVER BUT THE SHOUTIN', AND I SHOUT TO THE SKY THAT I'M SORRY
BUT THERE'S REALLY ONLY ONE WORD LEFT TO SAY...
...OWARI.
CLAP
CLAP CLAP CLAP
CLAP CLAP CLAP CLAP

EPISODE 5

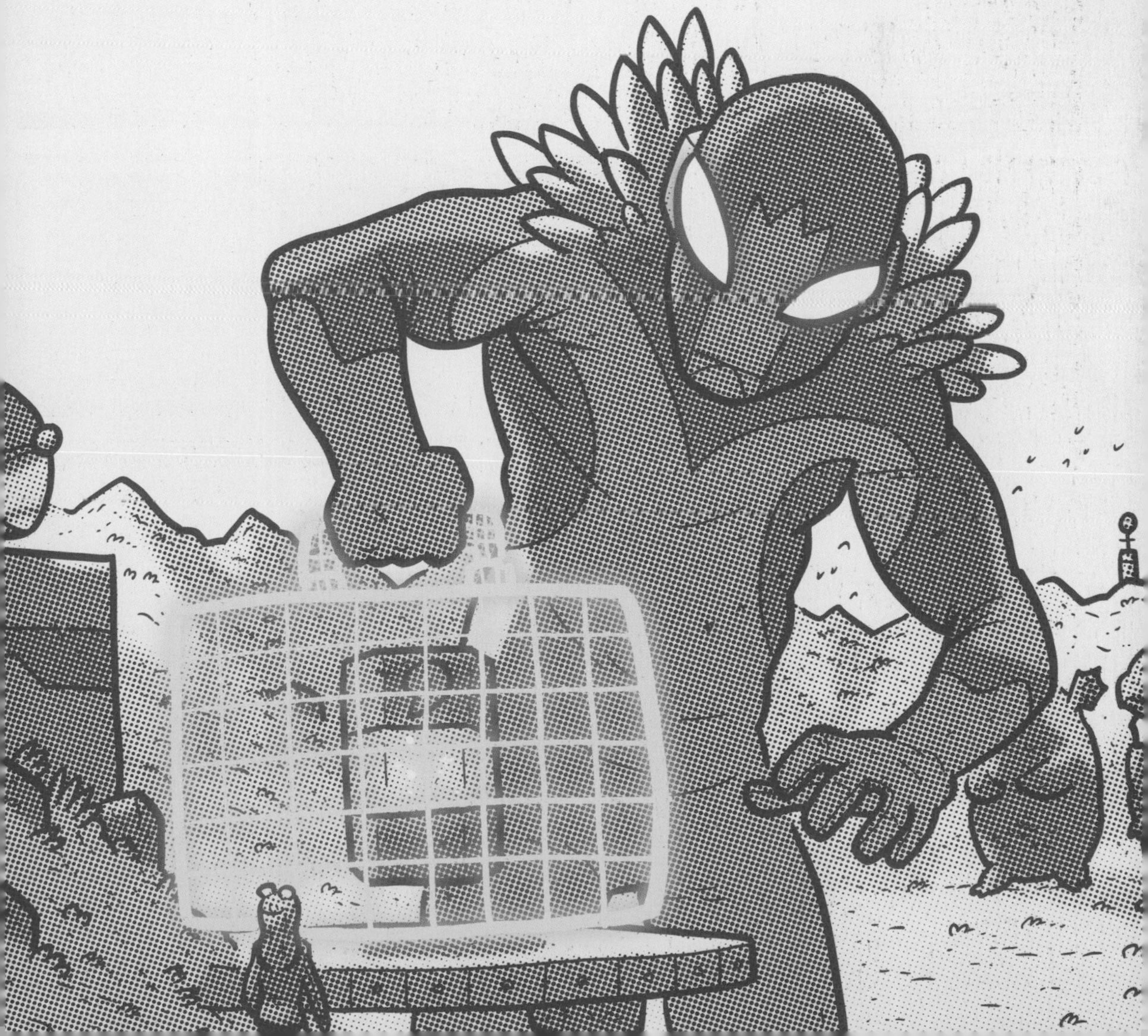

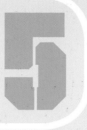

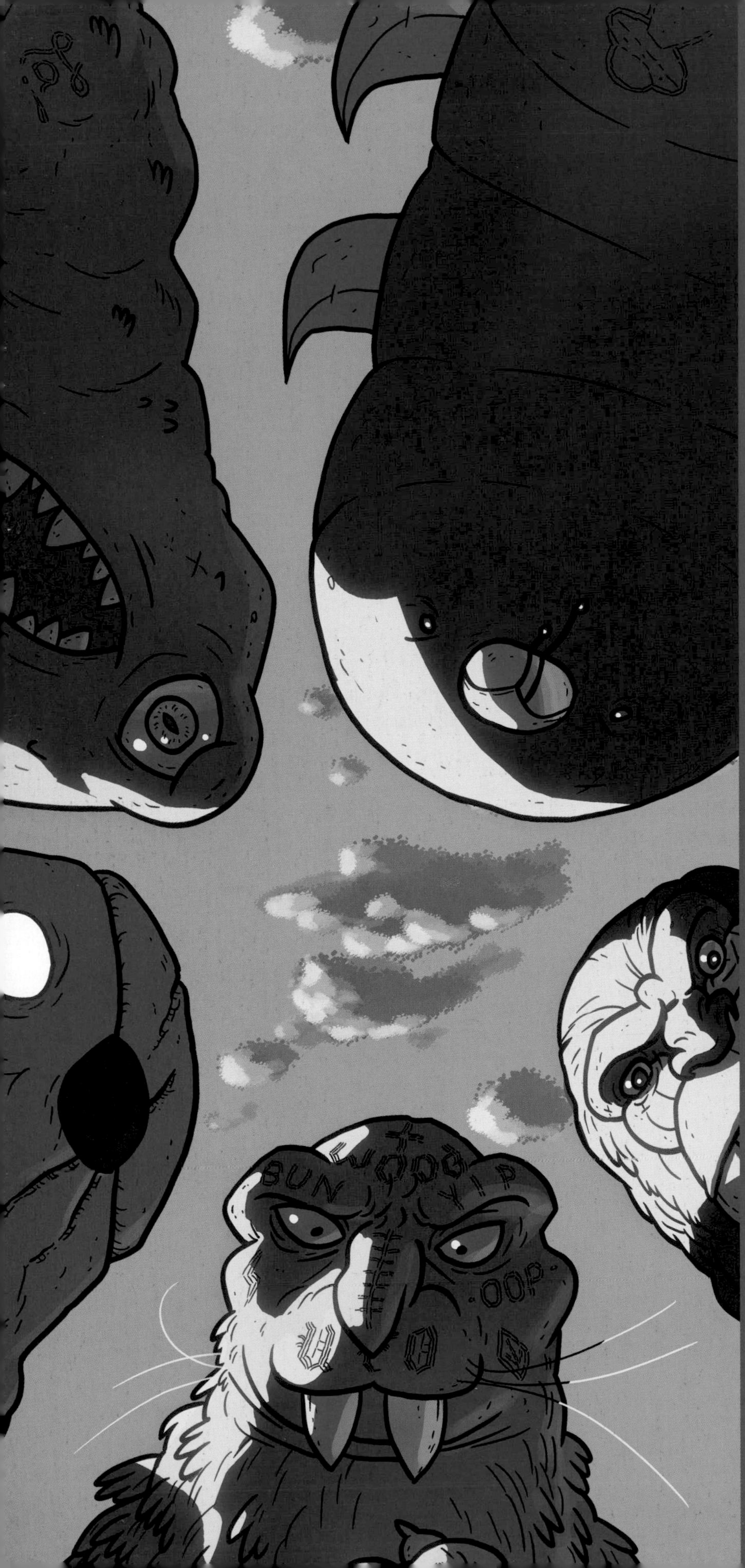
BUN
OOP

怪獣マックス

WHOOFY™

APE-WHALE™

MOUNTAIN™

SKUNK™

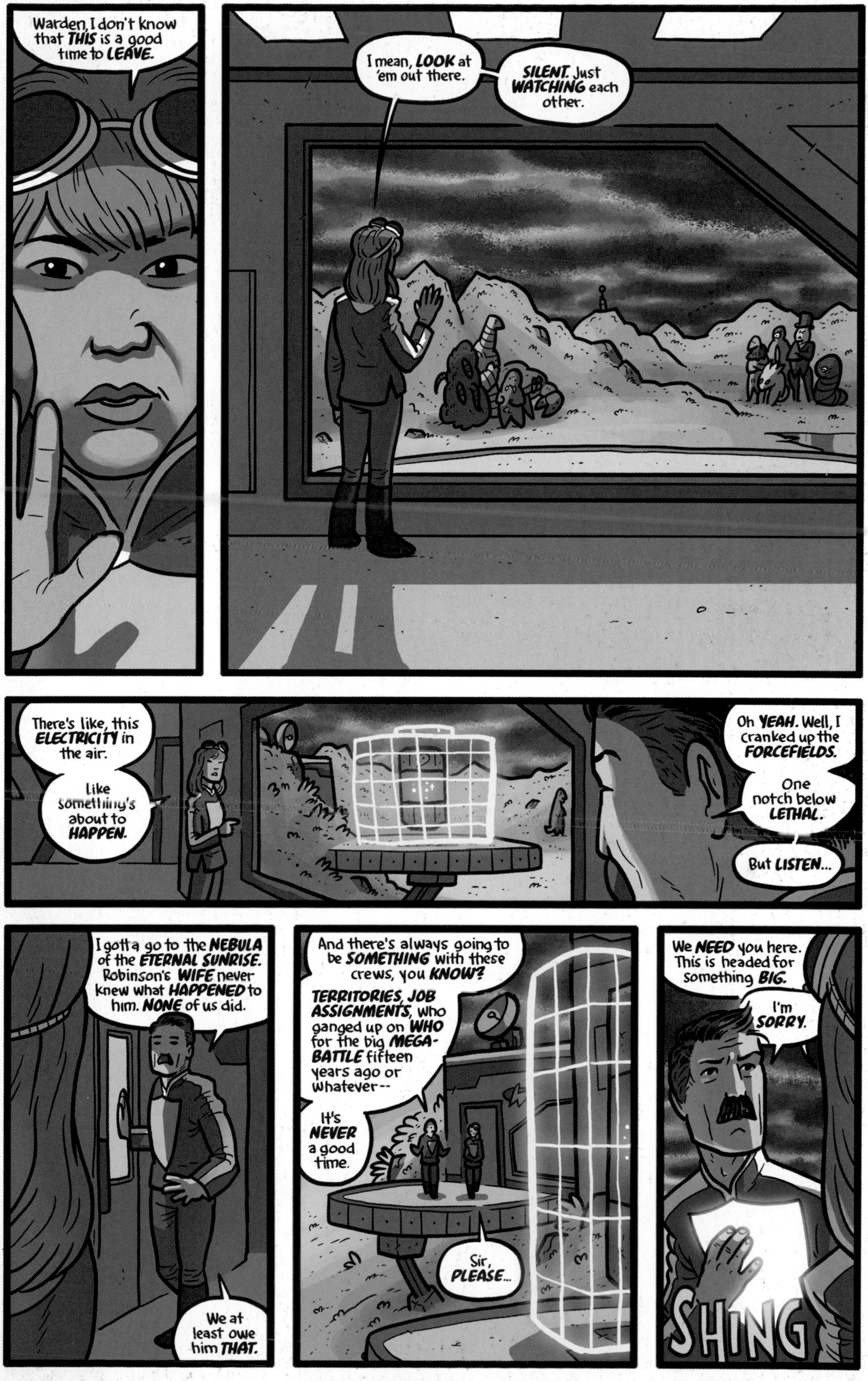
Warden, I don't know that THIS is a good time to LEAVE.
I mean, LOOK at 'em out there.
SILENT. Just WATCHING each other.
There's like, this ELECTRICITY in the air.
Like something's about to HAPPEN.
Oh YEAH. Well, I cranked up the FORCEFIELDS.
One notch below LETHAL.
But LISTEN...
I gotta go to the NEBULA of the ETERNAL SUNRISE. Robinson's WIFE never knew what HAPPENED to him. NONE of us did.
We at least owe him THAT.
And there's always going to be SOMETHING with these crews, you KNOW?
TERRITORIES, JOB ASSIGNMENTS, WHO ganged up on WHO for the big MEGA-BATTLE fifteen years ago or whatever--
It's NEVER a good time.
Sir, PLEASE...
We NEED you here. This is headed for something BIG.
I'm SORRY.
SHING

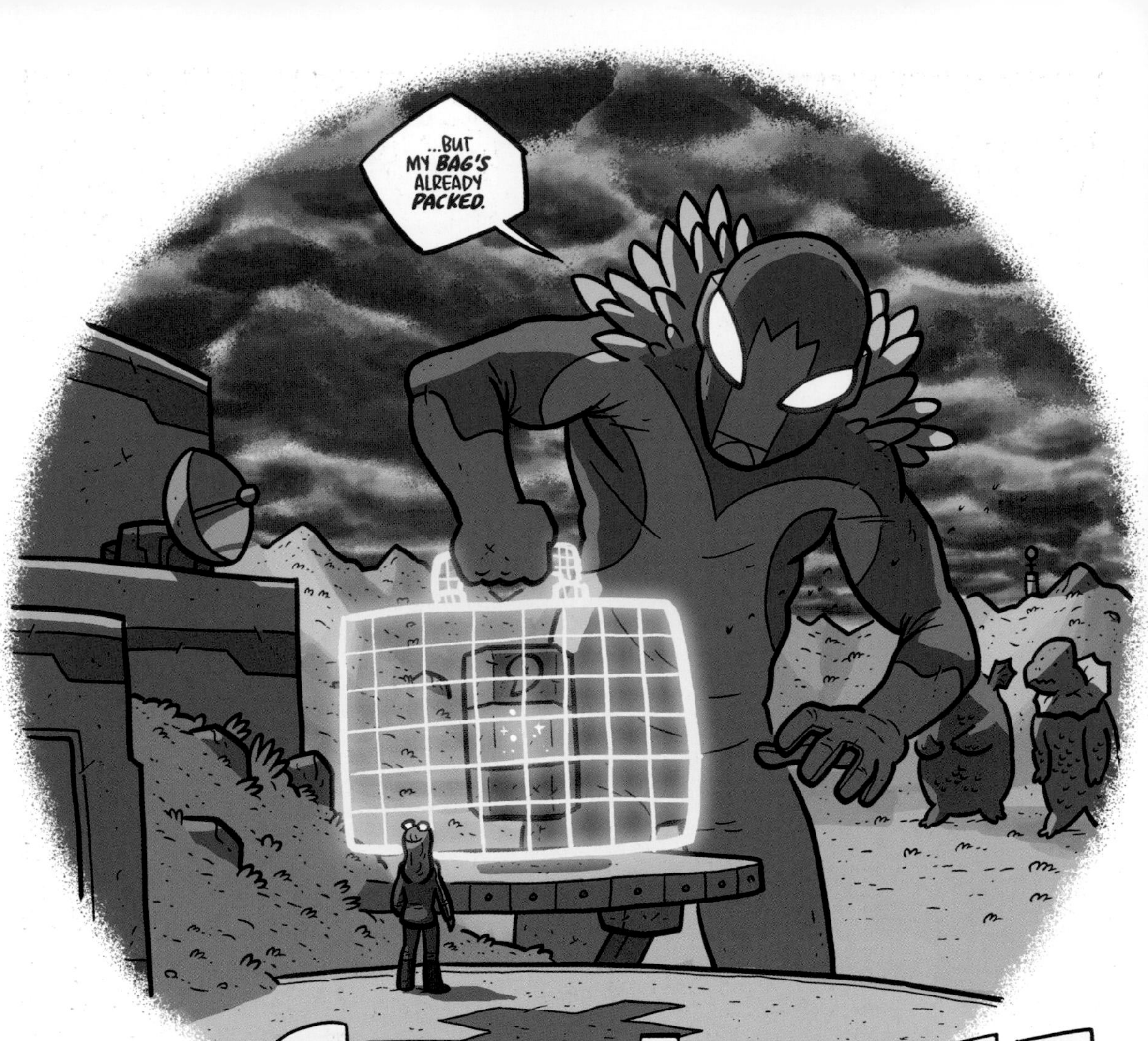
...BUT MY BAG'S ALREADY PACKED.

the STANDOFF

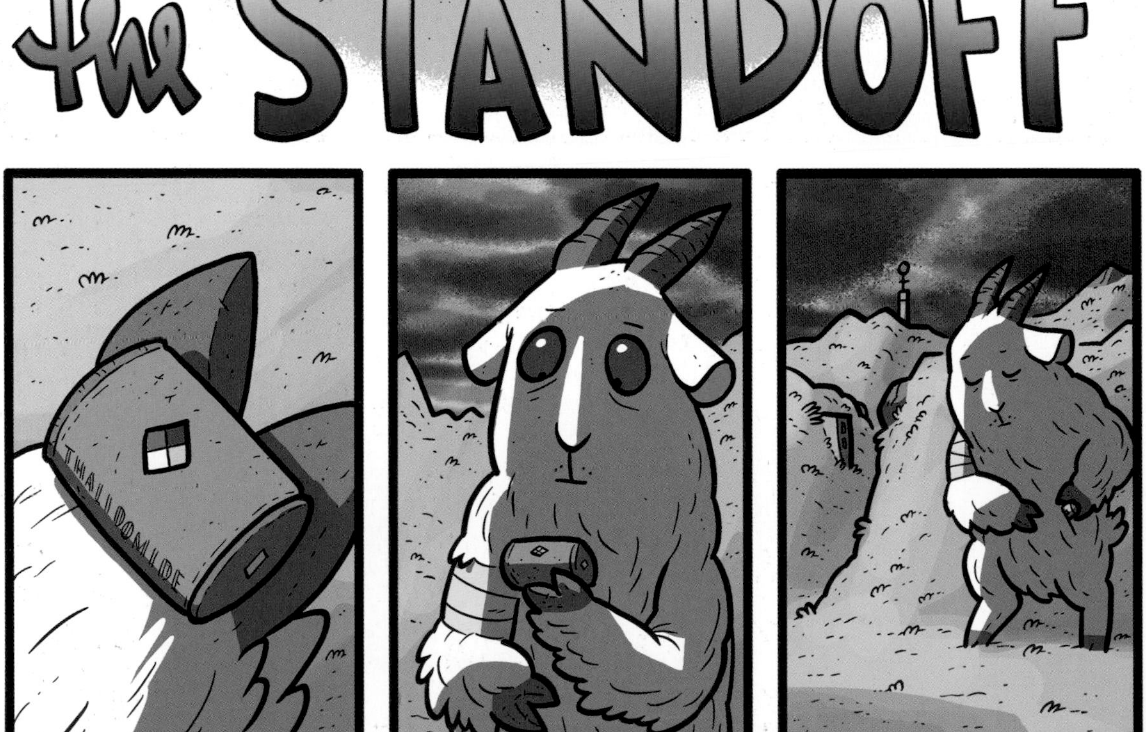

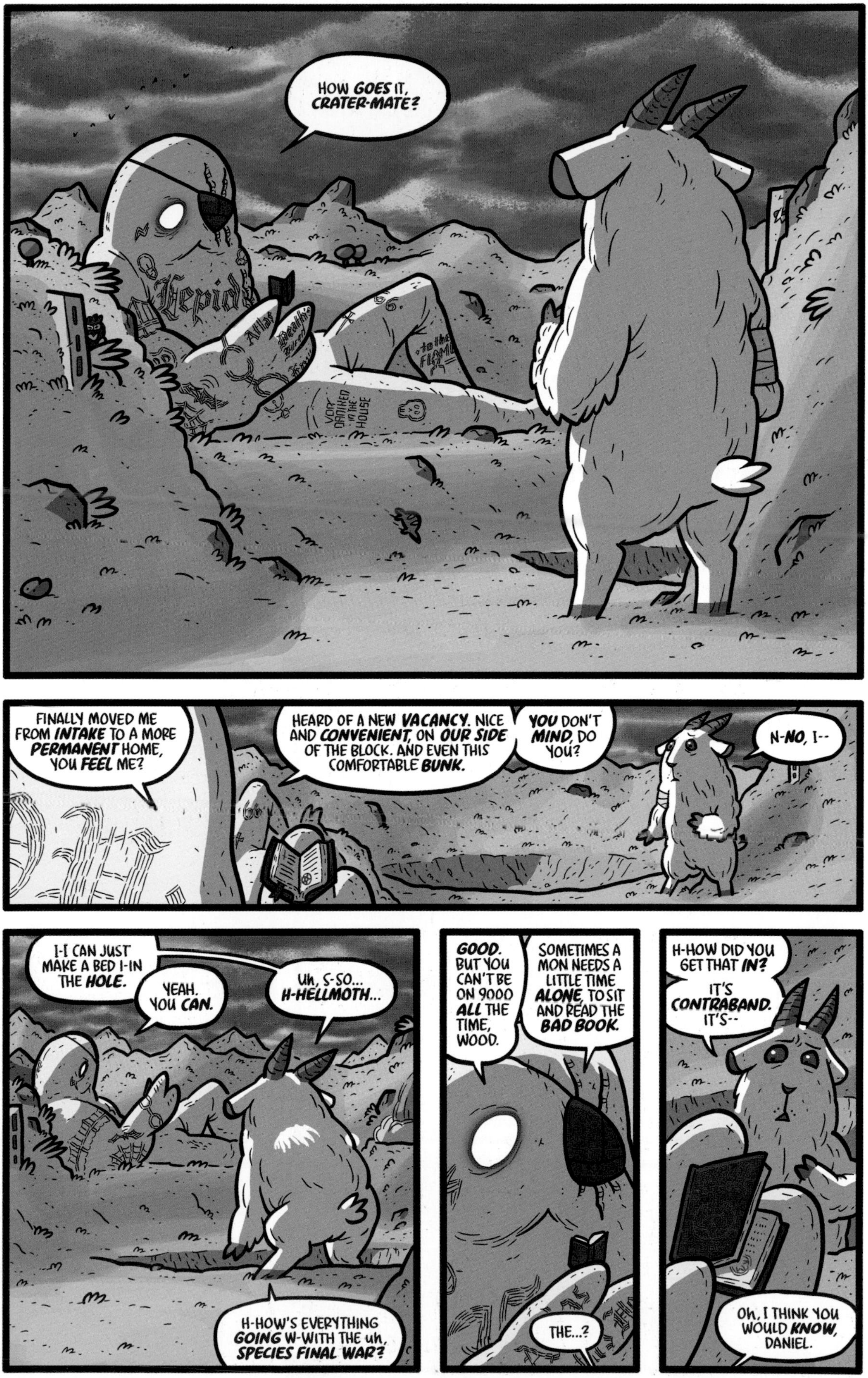
HOW GOES IT, CRATER-MATE?
FINALLY MOVED ME FROM INTAKE TO A MORE PERMANENT HOME, YOU FEEL ME?
HEARD OF A NEW VACANCY. NICE AND CONVENIENT, ON OUR SIDE OF THE BLOCK. AND EVEN THIS COMFORTABLE BUNK.
YOU DON'T MIND, DO YOU?
N-NO, I--
I-I CAN JUST MAKE A BED I-IN THE HOLE.
YEAH. YOU CAN.
Uh, S-SO... H-HELLMOTH...
H-HOW'S EVERYTHING GOING W-WITH THE uh, SPECIES FINAL WAR?
GOOD. BUT YOU CAN'T BE ON 9000 ALL THE TIME, WOOD.
SOMETIMES A MON NEEDS A LITTLE TIME ALONE, TO SIT AND READ THE BAD BOOK.
THE...?
H-HOW DID YOU GET THAT IN?
IT'S CONTRABAND. IT'S--
Oh, I THINK YOU WOULD KNOW, DANIEL.

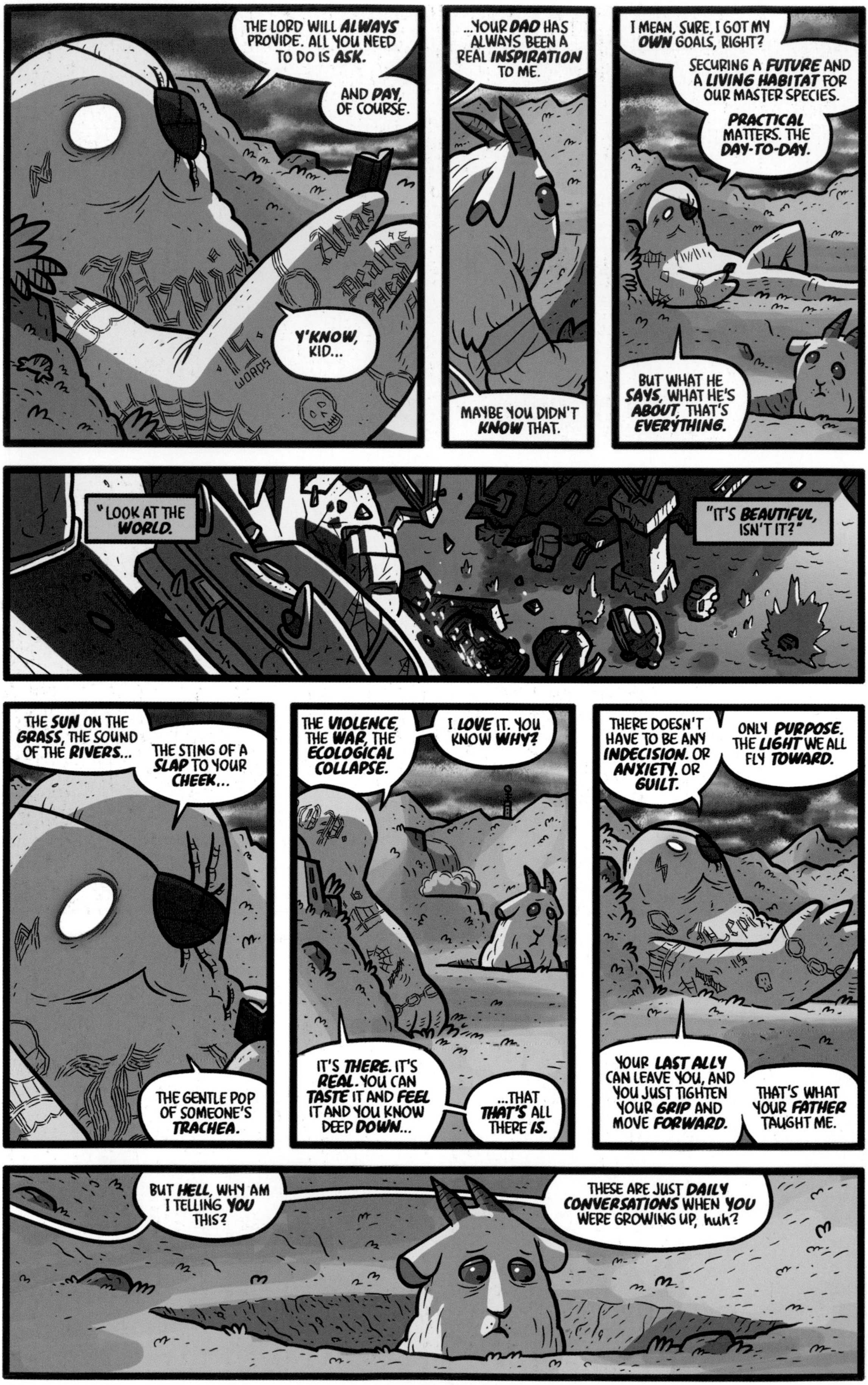
THE LORD WILL ALWAYS PROVIDE. ALL YOU NEED TO DO IS ASK.
AND PAY, OF COURSE.
Y'KNOW, KID...
...YOUR DAD HAS ALWAYS BEEN A REAL INSPIRATION TO ME.
MAYBE YOU DIDN'T KNOW THAT.
I MEAN, SURE, I GOT MY OWN GOALS, RIGHT?
SECURING A FUTURE AND A LIVING HABITAT FOR OUR MASTER SPECIES.
PRACTICAL MATTERS. THE DAY-TO-DAY.
BUT WHAT HE SAYS, WHAT HE'S ABOUT, THAT'S EVERYTHING.
"LOOK AT THE WORLD.
"IT'S BEAUTIFUL, ISN'T IT?"
THE SUN ON THE GRASS, THE SOUND OF THE RIVERS...
THE STING OF A SLAP TO YOUR CHEEK...
THE GENTLE POP OF SOMEONE'S TRACHEA.
THE VIOLENCE, THE WAR, THE ECOLOGICAL COLLAPSE.
I LOVE IT. YOU KNOW WHY?
IT'S THERE. IT'S REAL. YOU CAN TASTE IT AND FEEL IT AND YOU KNOW DEEP DOWN...
...THAT THAT'S ALL THERE IS.
THERE DOESN'T HAVE TO BE ANY INDECISION. OR ANXIETY. OR GUILT.
ONLY PURPOSE. THE LIGHT WE ALL FLY TOWARD.
YOUR LAST ALLY CAN LEAVE YOU, AND YOU JUST TIGHTEN YOUR GRIP AND MOVE FORWARD.
THAT'S WHAT YOUR FATHER TAUGHT ME.
BUT HELL, WHY AM I TELLING YOU THIS?
THESE ARE JUST DAILY CONVERSATIONS WHEN YOU WERE GROWING UP, huh?

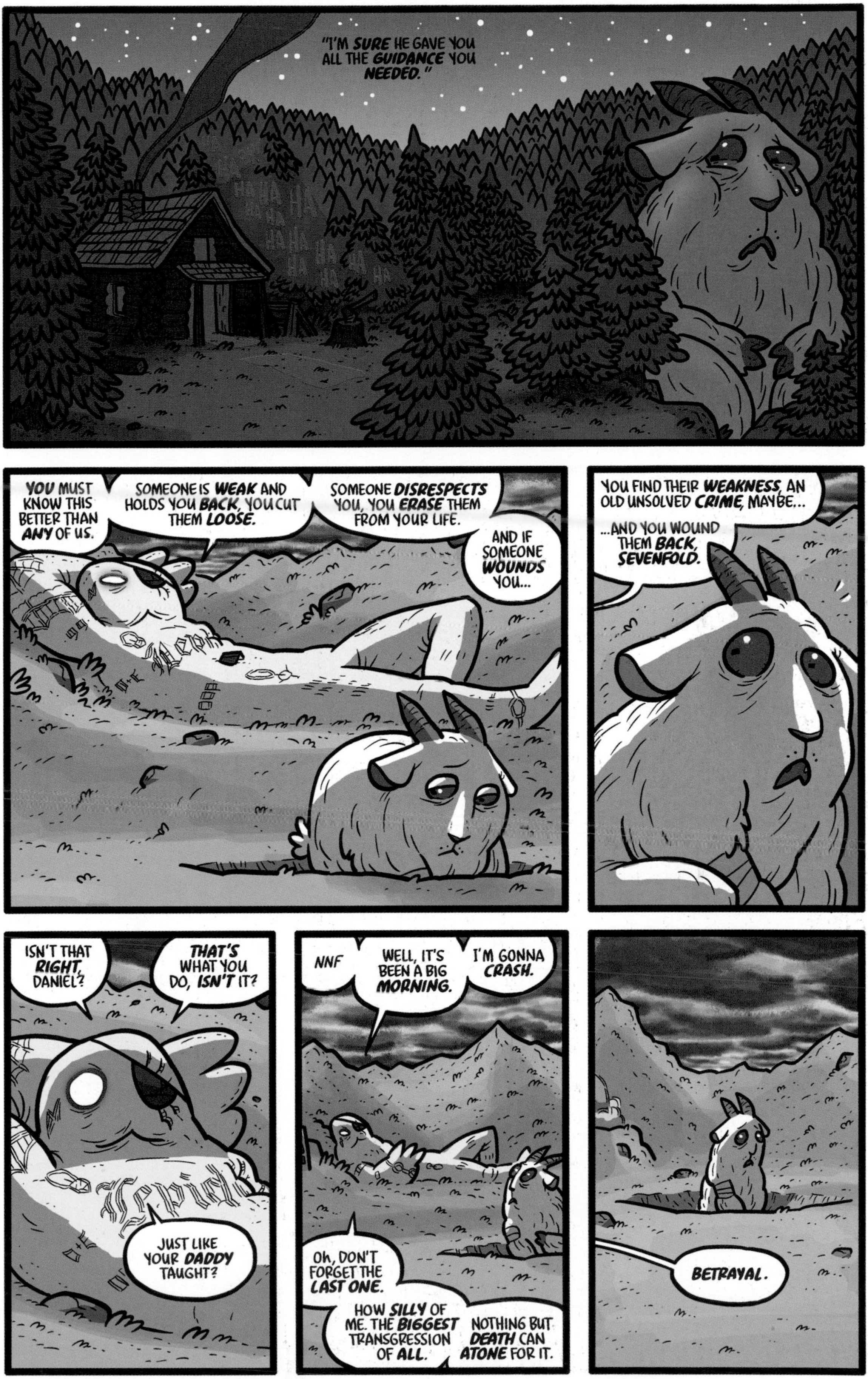
"I'M SURE HE GAVE YOU ALL THE GUIDANCE YOU NEEDED."
HA HA HA HA HA HA HA HA HA HA HA
YOU MUST KNOW THIS BETTER THAN ANY OF US.
SOMEONE IS WEAK AND HOLDS YOU BACK, YOU CUT THEM LOOSE.
SOMEONE DISRESPECTS YOU, YOU ERASE THEM FROM YOUR LIFE.
AND IF SOMEONE WOUNDS YOU...
YOU FIND THEIR WEAKNESS, AN OLD UNSOLVED CRIME, MAYBE...
...AND YOU WOUND THEM BACK, SEVENFOLD.
ISN'T THAT RIGHT, DANIEL?
THAT'S WHAT YOU DO, ISN'T IT?
JUST LIKE YOUR DADDY TAUGHT?
NNF
WELL, IT'S BEEN A BIG MORNING.
I'M GONNA CRASH.
Oh, DON'T FORGET THE LAST ONE.
HOW SILLY OF ME. THE BIGGEST TRANSGRESSION OF ALL.
NOTHING BUT DEATH CAN ATONE FOR IT.
BETRAYAL.

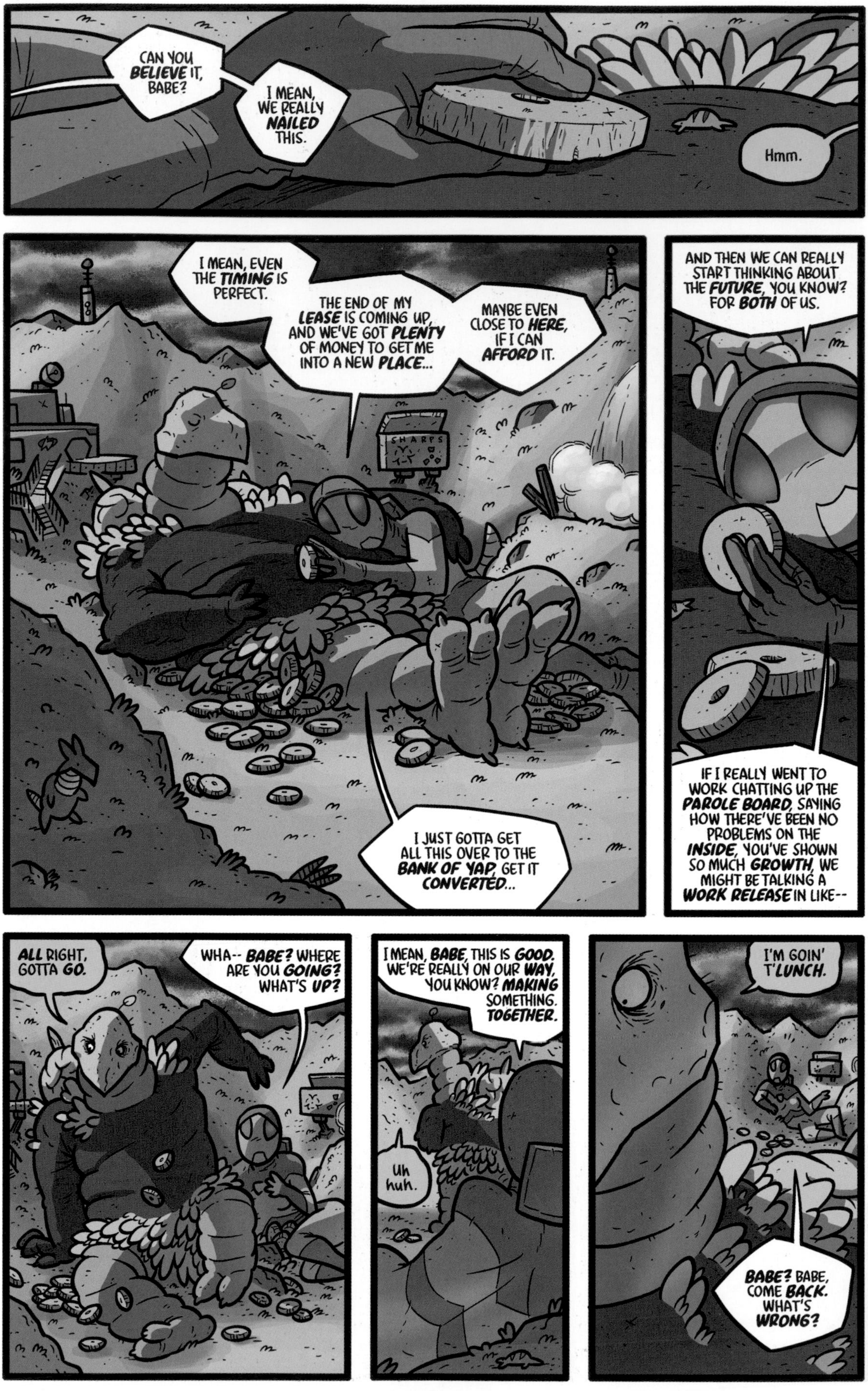
CAN YOU BELIEVE IT, BABE?
I MEAN, WE REALLY NAILED THIS.
Hmm.
I MEAN, EVEN THE TIMING IS PERFECT.
THE END OF MY LEASE IS COMING UP, AND WE'VE GOT PLENTY OF MONEY TO GET ME INTO A NEW PLACE...
MAYBE EVEN CLOSE TO HERE, IF I CAN AFFORD IT.
SHARPS
I JUST GOTTA GET ALL THIS OVER TO THE BANK OF YAP, GET IT CONVERTED...
AND THEN WE CAN REALLY START THINKING ABOUT THE FUTURE, YOU KNOW? FOR BOTH OF US.
IF I REALLY WENT TO WORK CHATTING UP THE PAROLE BOARD, SAYING HOW THERE'VE BEEN NO PROBLEMS ON THE INSIDE, YOU'VE SHOWN SO MUCH GROWTH, WE MIGHT BE TALKING A WORK RELEASE IN LIKE--
ALL RIGHT, GOTTA GO.
WHA-- BABE? WHERE ARE YOU GOING? WHAT'S UP?
I MEAN, BABE, THIS IS GOOD. WE'RE REALLY ON OUR WAY, YOU KNOW? MAKING SOMETHING. TOGETHER.
Uh huh.
I'M GOIN' T'LUNCH.
BABE? BABE, COME BACK. WHAT'S WRONG?

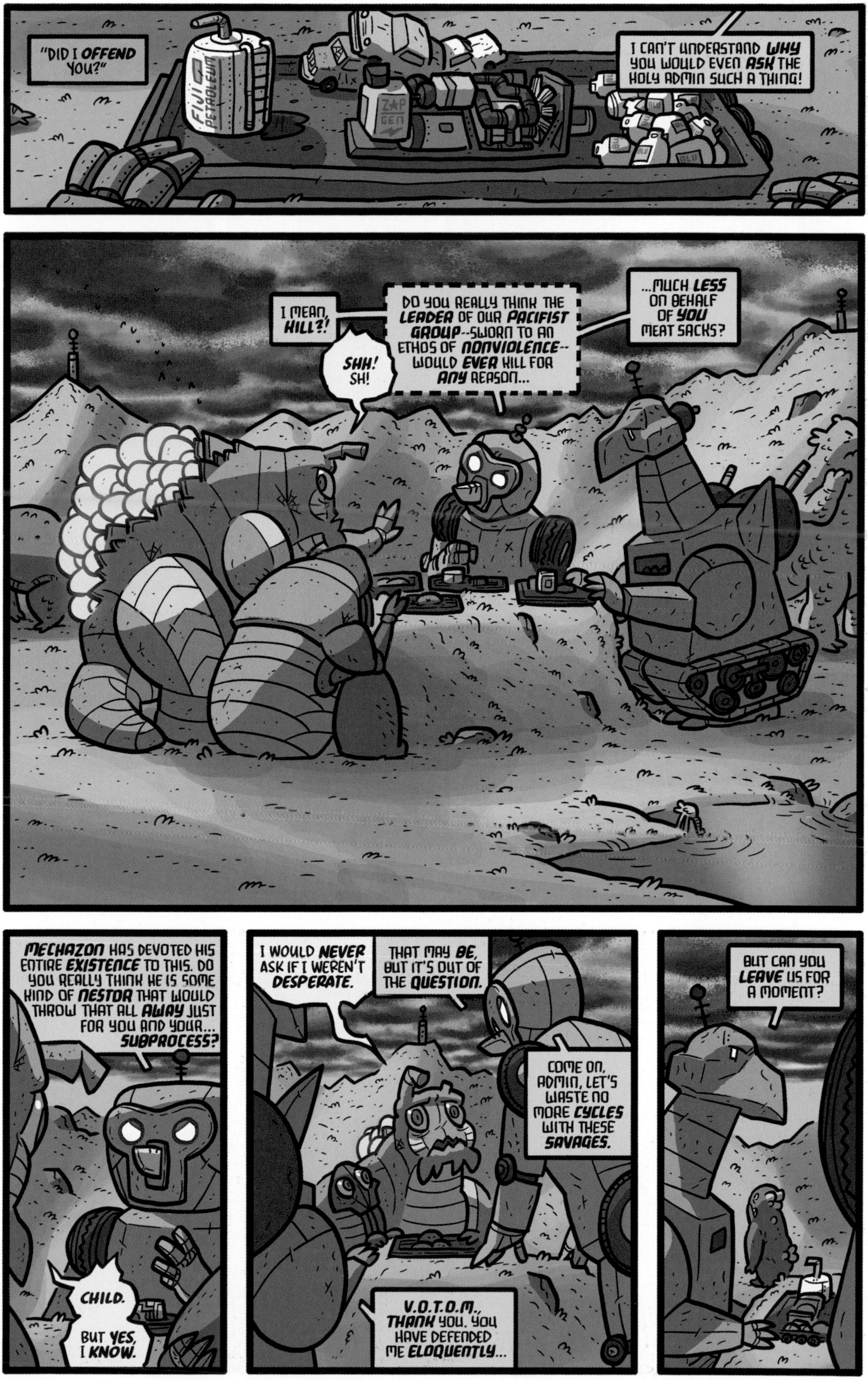

"DID I OFFEND YOU?"
I CAN'T UNDERSTAND WHY YOU WOULD EVEN ASK THE HOLY ADMIN SUCH A THING!
FIJI PETROLEUM
Z P GEN
BLU
I MEAN, KILL?!
DO YOU REALLY THINK THE LEADER OF OUR PACIFIST GROUP--SWORN TO AN ETHOS OF NONVIOLENCE--WOULD EVER KILL FOR ANY REASON...
SHH! SH!
...MUCH LESS ON BEHALF OF YOU MEAT SACKS?
MECHAZON HAS DEVOTED HIS ENTIRE EXISTENCE TO THIS. DO YOU REALLY THINK HE IS SOME KIND OF NESTOR THAT WOULD THROW THAT ALL AWAY JUST FOR YOU AND YOUR... SUBPROCESS?
CHILD.
BUT YES, I KNOW.
I WOULD NEVER ASK IF I WEREN'T DESPERATE.
THAT MAY BE, BUT IT'S OUT OF THE QUESTION.
COME ON, ADMIN, LET'S WASTE NO MORE CYCLES WITH THESE SAVAGES.
V.O.T.O.M., THANK YOU. YOU HAVE DEFENDED ME ELOQUENTLY...
BUT CAN YOU LEAVE US FOR A MOMENT?

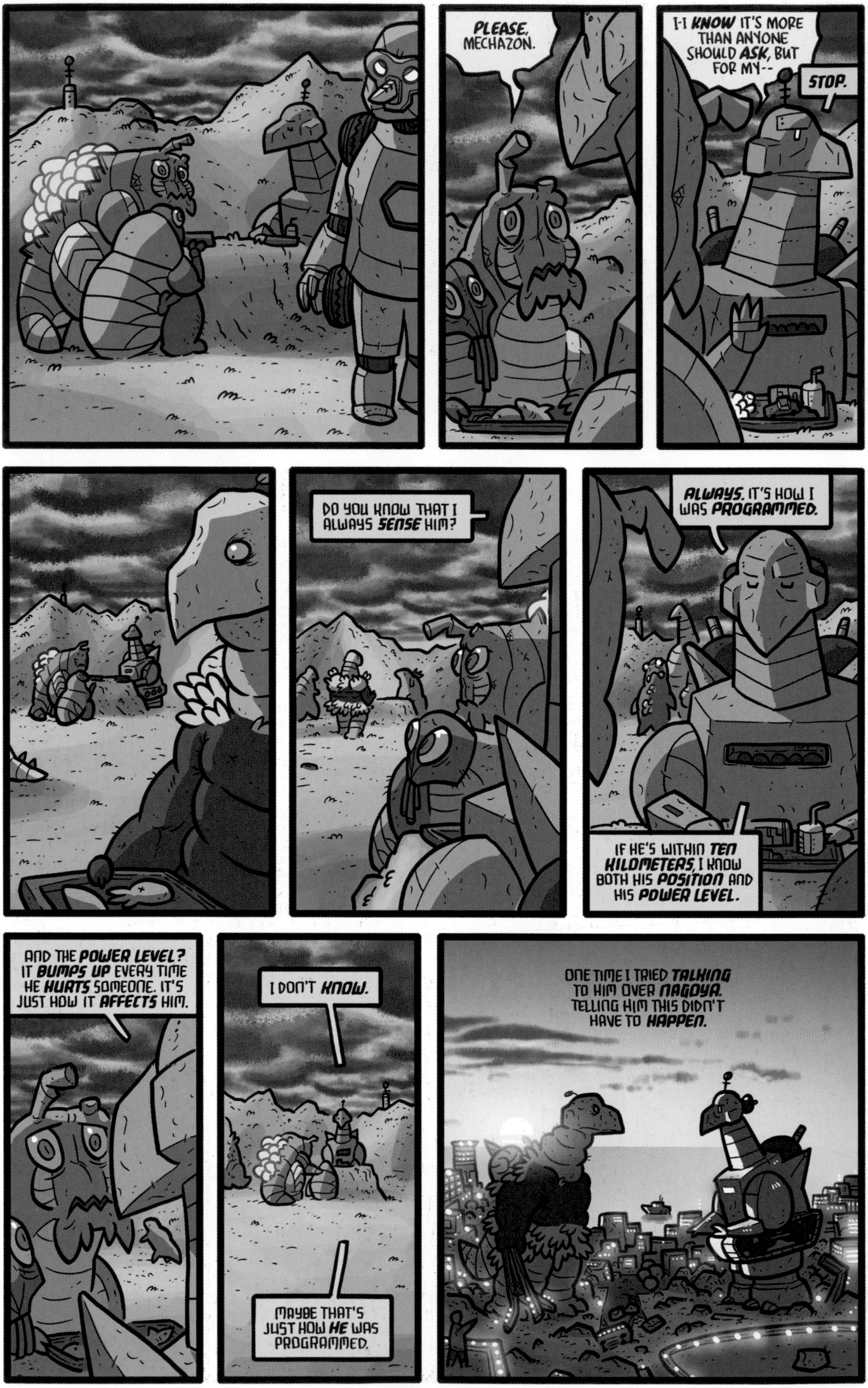
PLEASE, MECHAZON.
I-I KNOW IT'S MORE THAN ANYONE SHOULD ASK, BUT FOR MY--
STOP.
DO YOU KNOW THAT I ALWAYS SENSE HIM?
ALWAYS. IT'S HOW I WAS PROGRAMMED.
IF HE'S WITHIN TEN KILOMETERS, I KNOW BOTH HIS POSITION AND HIS POWER LEVEL.
AND THE POWER LEVEL? IT BUMPS UP EVERY TIME HE HURTS SOMEONE. IT'S JUST HOW IT AFFECTS HIM.
I DON'T KNOW.
MAYBE THAT'S JUST HOW HE WAS PROGRAMMED.
ONE TIME I TRIED TALKING TO HIM OVER NAGOYA. TELLING HIM THIS DIDN'T HAVE TO HAPPEN.

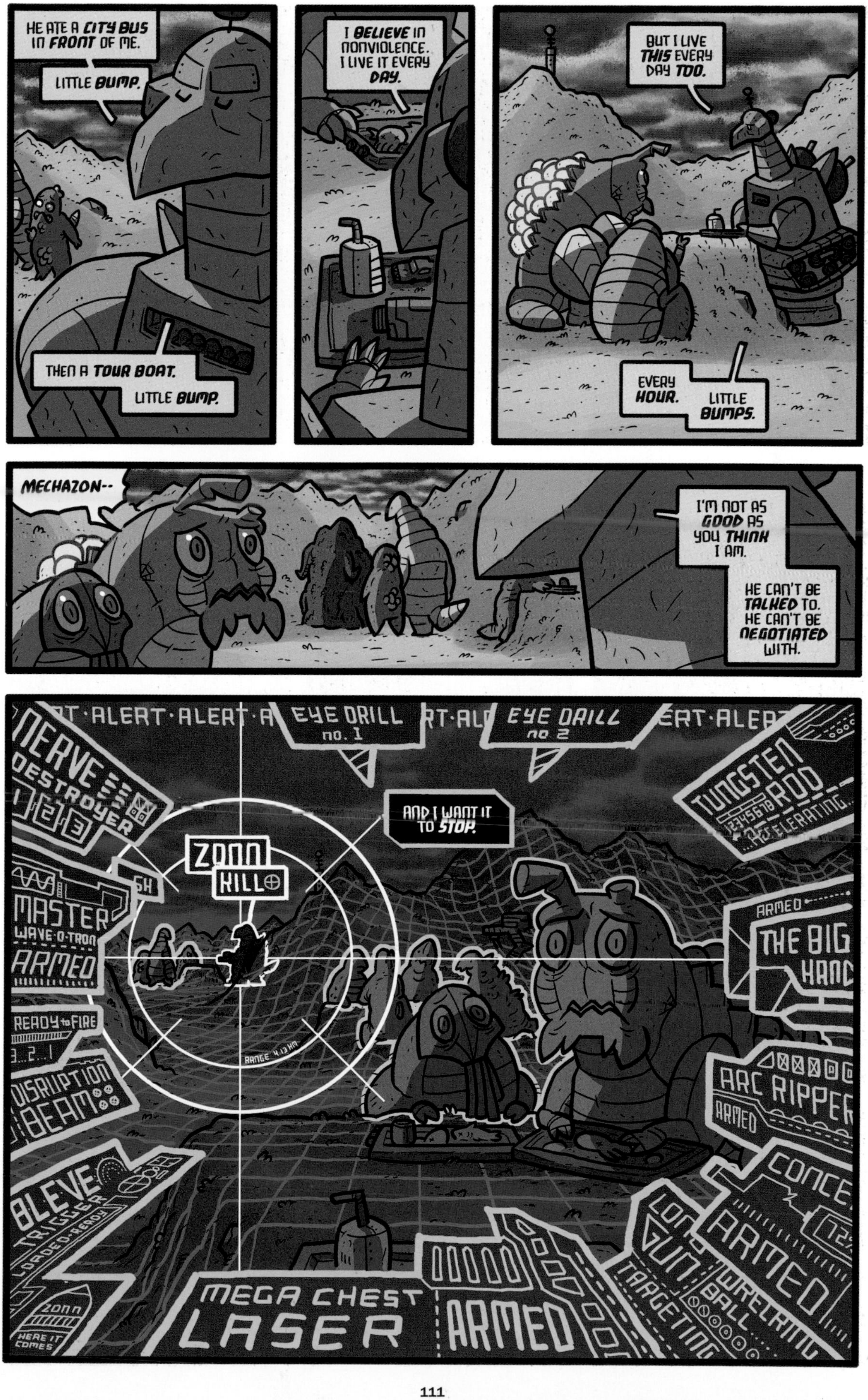
HE ATE A CITY BUS IN FRONT OF ME.
LITTLE BUMP.
THEN A TOUR BOAT.
LITTLE BUMP.
I BELIEVE IN NONVIOLENCE. I LIVE IT EVERY DAY.
BUT I LIVE THIS EVERY DAY TOO.
EVERY HOUR.
LITTLE BUMPS.
MECHAZON--
I'M NOT AS GOOD AS YOU THINK I AM.
HE CAN'T BE TALKED TO. HE CAN'T BE NEGOTIATED WITH.
ALERT · ALERT
EYE DRILL no. 1
EYE DRILL no 2
NERVE DESTROYER
1 2 3
TUNGSTEN ROD
ACCELERATING...
AND I WANT IT TO STOP.
ZONN
KILL
MASTER WAVE-O-TRON
ARMED
ARMED
THE BIG HAND
READY to FIRE
3...2...1
DISRUPTION BEAM
RANGE 4.13 KM
ARC RIPPER
ARMED
BLEVE TRIGGER
LOADED READY
ZONN
HERE IT COMES
MEGA CHEST LASER
ARMED
ARMED
WRECKING BALL
TARGETING

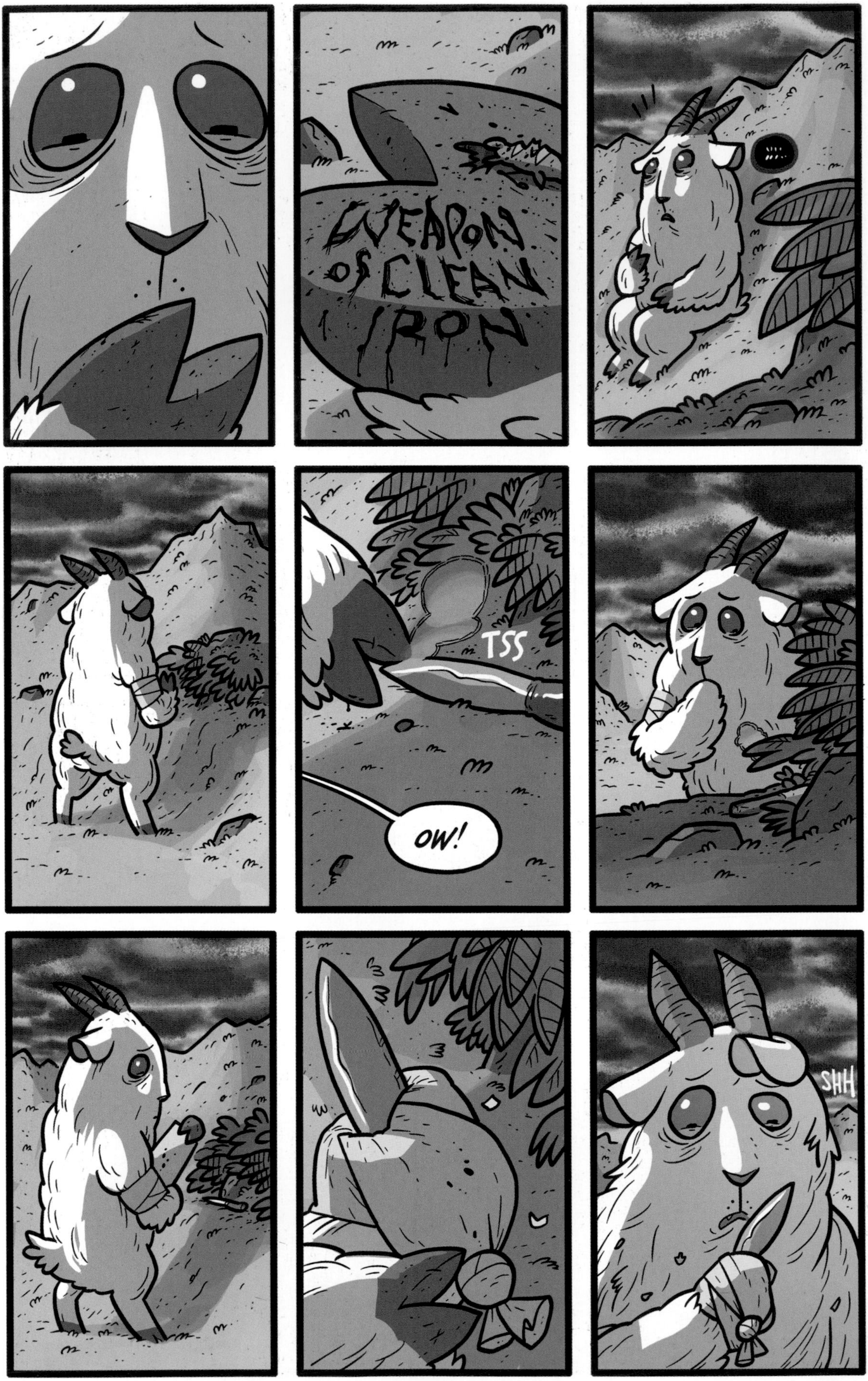
WEAPON OF CLEAN IRON
TSS
OW!
SHH

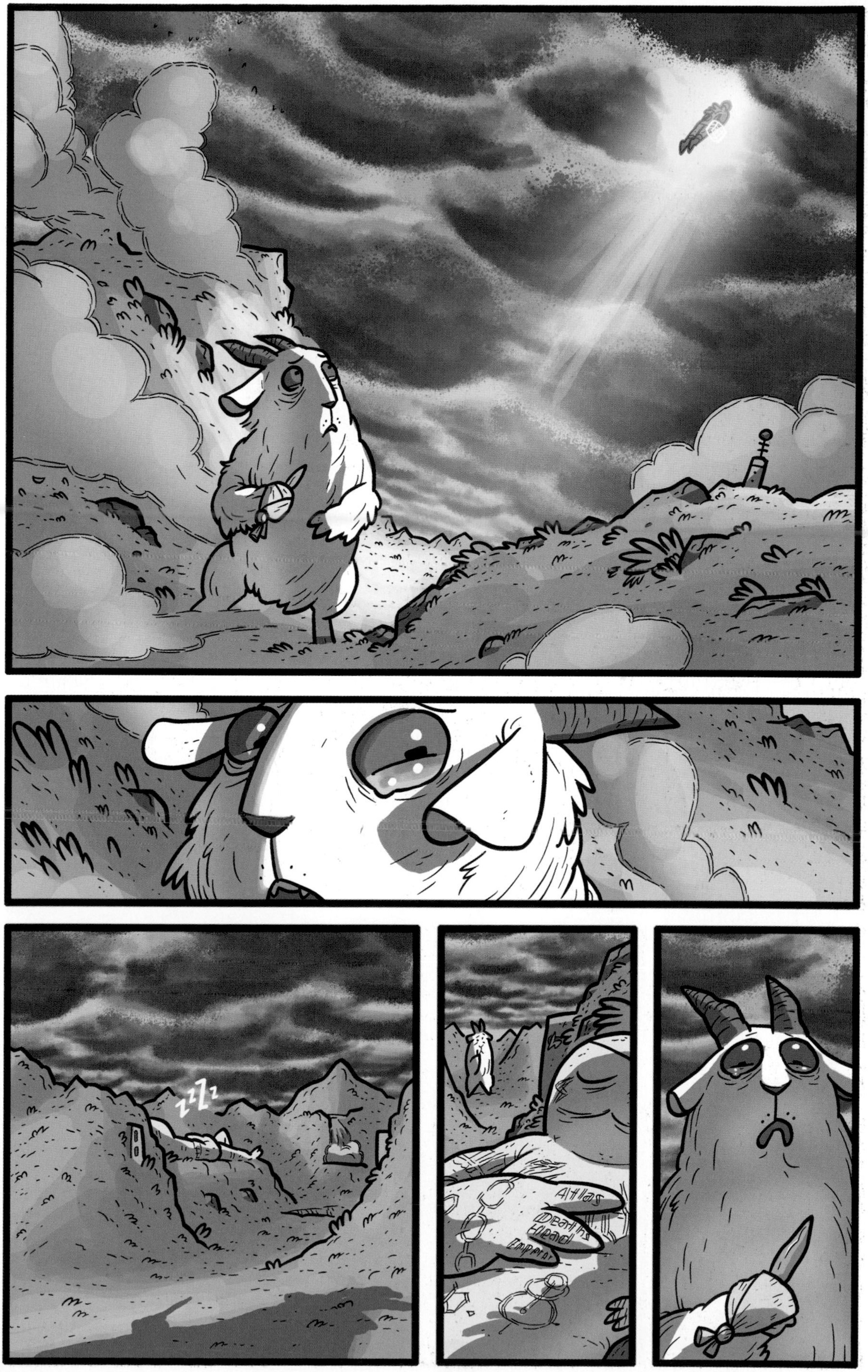
zzZz
Atlas
Deaths Head
Emperor

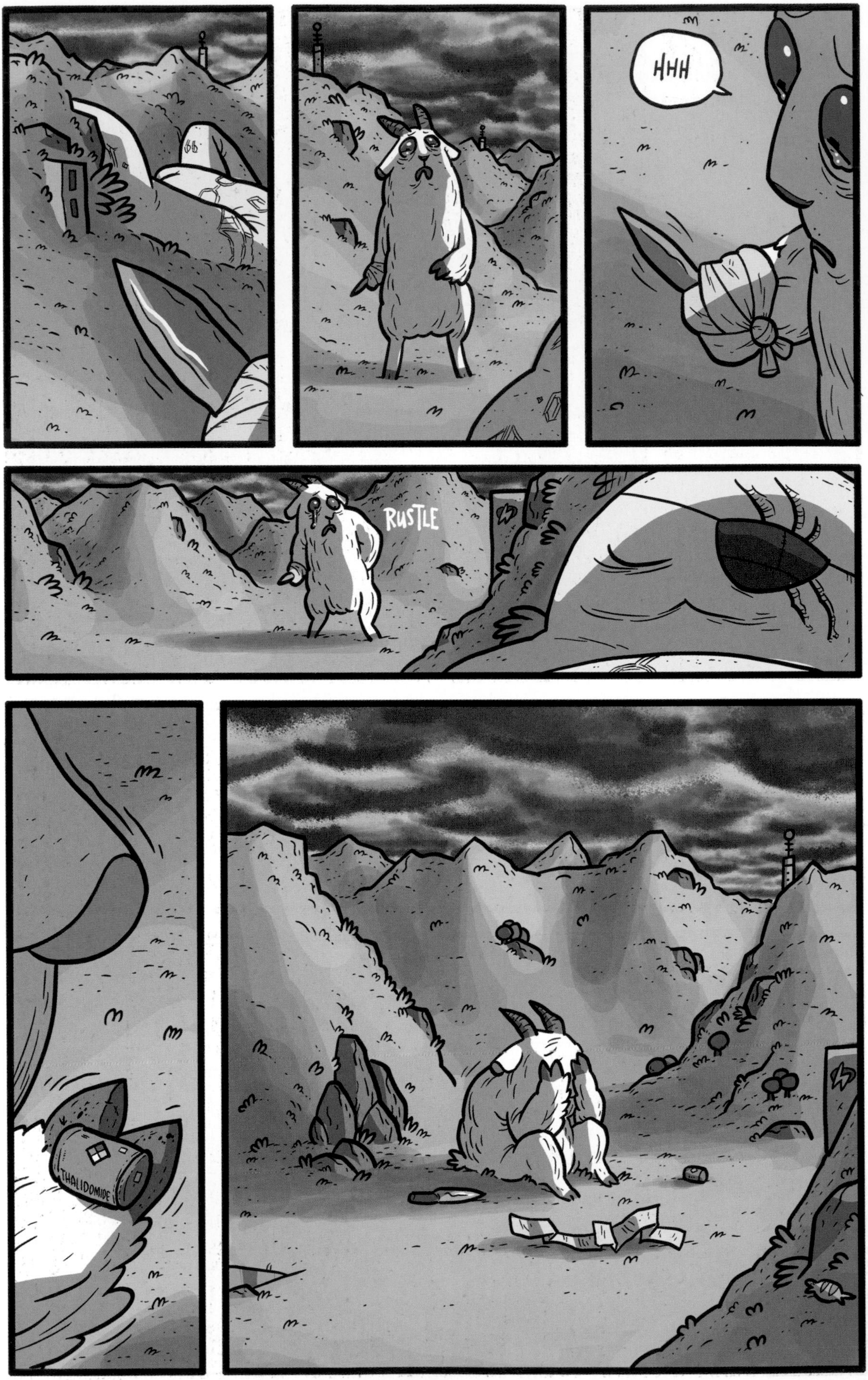
HHH
RUSTLE
THALIDOMIDE

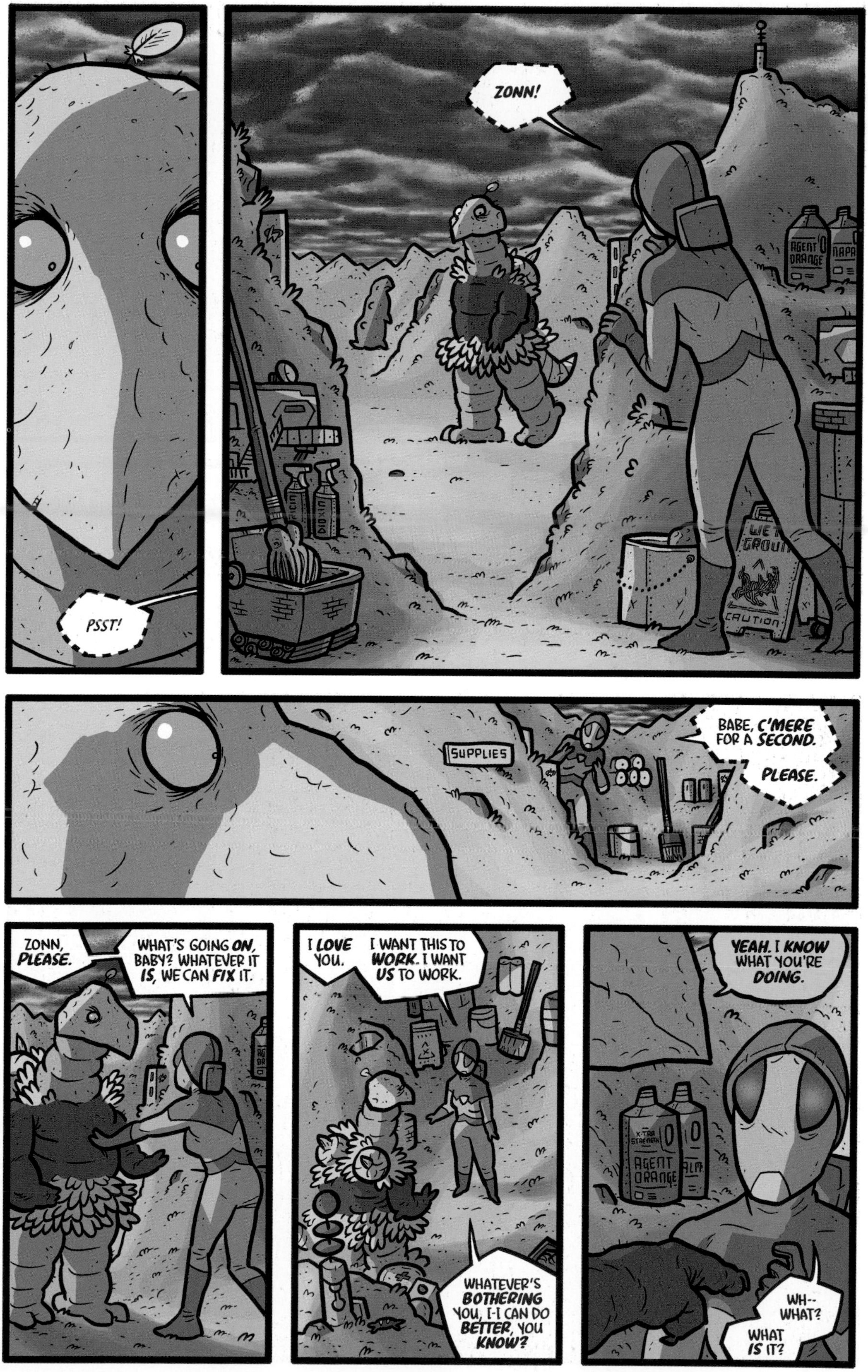

PSST!
ZONN!
AGENT ORANGE
NAPA
WET GROUN
CAUTION
SUPPLIES
BABE, C'MERE FOR A SECOND.
PLEASE.
ZONN, PLEASE.
WHAT'S GOING ON, BABY? WHATEVER IT IS, WE CAN FIX IT.
I LOVE YOU.
I WANT THIS TO WORK. I WANT US TO WORK.
WHATEVER'S BOTHERING YOU, I-I CAN DO BETTER, YOU KNOW?
YEAH. I KNOW WHAT YOU'RE DOING.
X-TRA STRENGTH
AGENT ORANGE
WH-- WHAT?
WHAT IS IT?

YEAH.

YOU THINK I CAN'T *SEE* THAT YOU WANT *OUT?*

OUT? NO, BABE, I--

CHANGING *APARTMENTS?* CAN'T LEAVE YOUR *MONEY* HERE? YOU WANT TO TAKE THIS GIG SOMEWHERE *ELSE,* DON'T YOU? YOU THINK I'M *WORTHLESS.*

WHAT? BABE, *WHAT* ARE YOU--

YOU *SAID* IT. "WORTHLESS." SOON AS I ANSWERED THE *PHONE.*

I...

COME ON, BABE, I WAS *S-STRESSED,* YOU KNOW?

TH-THERE WAS A LOT OF STUFF GOING *ON* THEN, AND...

YEAH. AND THEN YOU MAKE ME COME ALL THE WAY TO YOUR *REDKING INFIRMARY* TO GET THE *URANIUM.* I'M DOING ALL THE *WORK,* WHILE YOU CAN'T EVEN BRING THE STUFF *OVER* TO WHERE I AM--

BUT THAT'S WHERE *YOU* SAID YOU--

O-OKAY, THAT'S *OKAY,* I CAN PUT IT IN THE LAKE BY YOUR *CELL* IF YOU LIKE.

IT'S JUST A LITTLE *HARDER* TO-- BUT IT'S *FINE,* THAT'LL BE *FINE.*

I'LL DO IT HOWEVER YOU *WANT,* BABE.

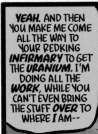

HMMH.

WELL.

JUST THAT *THEN* THERE'S THAT *SHRIMP-ASS MEGAFAUNA,* TOO, CUTTIN' INTO OUR *BUSINESS.*

SHRIMP-A...? Y-YOU MEAN... *ELECTROGOR?*

OH, BABE, DON'T *WORRY* ABOUT THAT WEAK *DAIEI-BRAND* URANIUM HE'S GOT.

IT HAS *NOTHING* ON THE STUFF WE GET FROM THE *MOON*...!

UH HUH. YOU *WOULD* DEFEND HIM, WITH THE WAY YOU *LOOK* AT HIM SOMETIMES...

WHAT--

BABE, *NO,* COME *ON,* ARE YOU *KIDDING* ME? THAT *CRYBABY* LITTLE *RARE-BEAST?*

I GOT HIM SENT TO THE *HOLE* FOR *TALKING* ABOUT YOU, *REMEMBER?*

YOU ARE THE *ONE,* BABY.

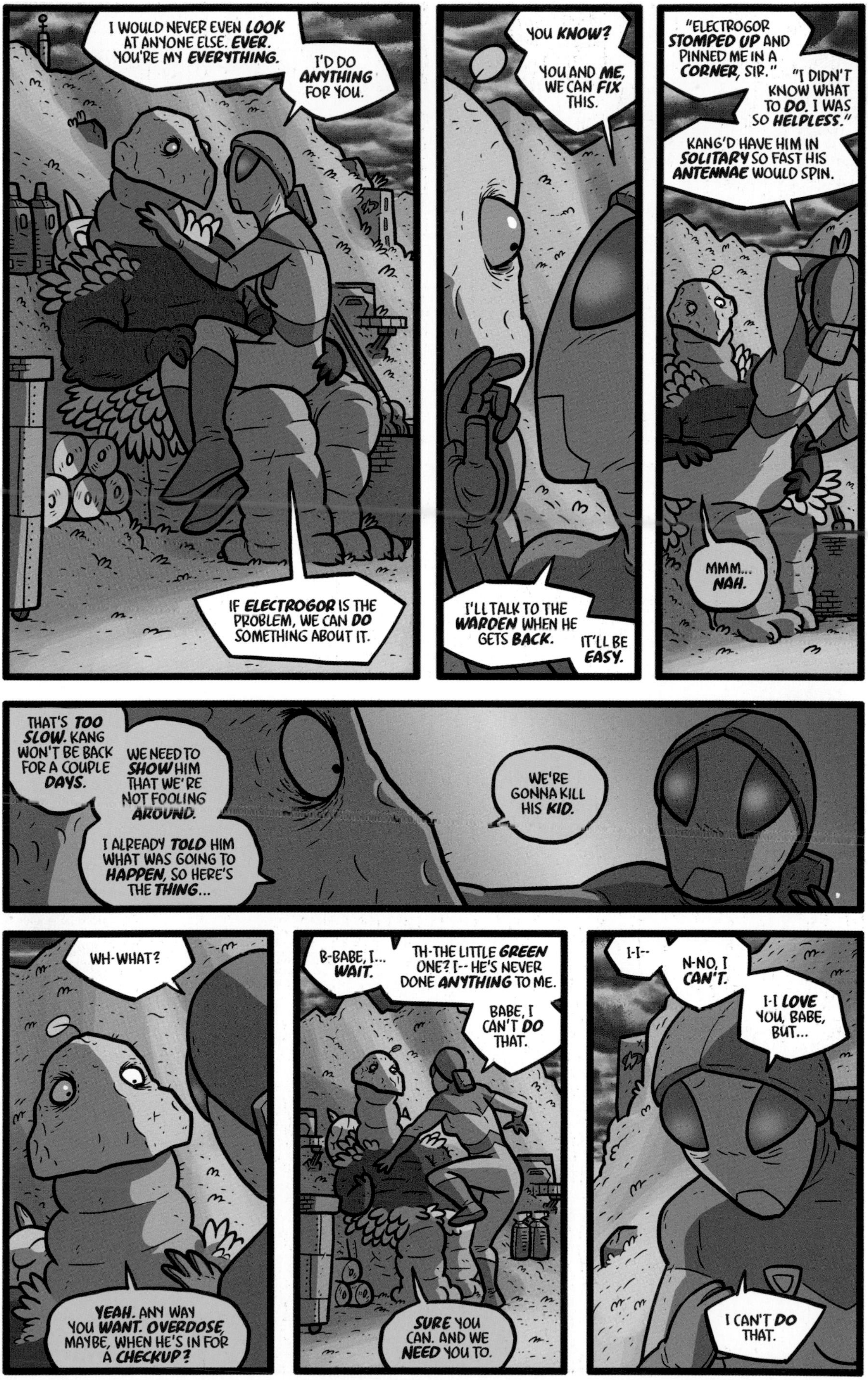
I WOULD NEVER EVEN LOOK AT ANYONE ELSE. EVER. YOU'RE MY EVERYTHING.
I'D DO ANYTHING FOR YOU.
IF ELECTROGOR IS THE PROBLEM, WE CAN DO SOMETHING ABOUT IT.
YOU KNOW?
YOU AND ME, WE CAN FIX THIS.
I'LL TALK TO THE WARDEN WHEN HE GETS BACK.
IT'LL BE EASY.
"ELECTROGOR STOMPED UP AND PINNED ME IN A CORNER, SIR."
"I DIDN'T KNOW WHAT TO DO. I WAS SO HELPLESS."
KANG'D HAVE HIM IN SOLITARY SO FAST HIS ANTENNAE WOULD SPIN.
MMM... NAH.
THAT'S TOO SLOW. KANG WON'T BE BACK FOR A COUPLE DAYS.
WE NEED TO SHOW HIM THAT WE'RE NOT FOOLING AROUND.
I ALREADY TOLD HIM WHAT WAS GOING TO HAPPEN, SO HERE'S THE THING...
WE'RE GONNA KILL HIS KID.
WH-WHAT?
YEAH. ANY WAY YOU WANT. OVERDOSE, MAYBE, WHEN HE'S IN FOR A CHECKUP?
B-BABE, I... WAIT.
TH-THE LITTLE GREEN ONE? I-- HE'S NEVER DONE ANYTHING TO ME.
BABE, I CAN'T DO THAT.
SURE YOU CAN. AND WE NEED YOU TO.
I-I--
N-NO, I CAN'T.
I-I LOVE YOU, BABE, BUT...
I CAN'T DO THAT.

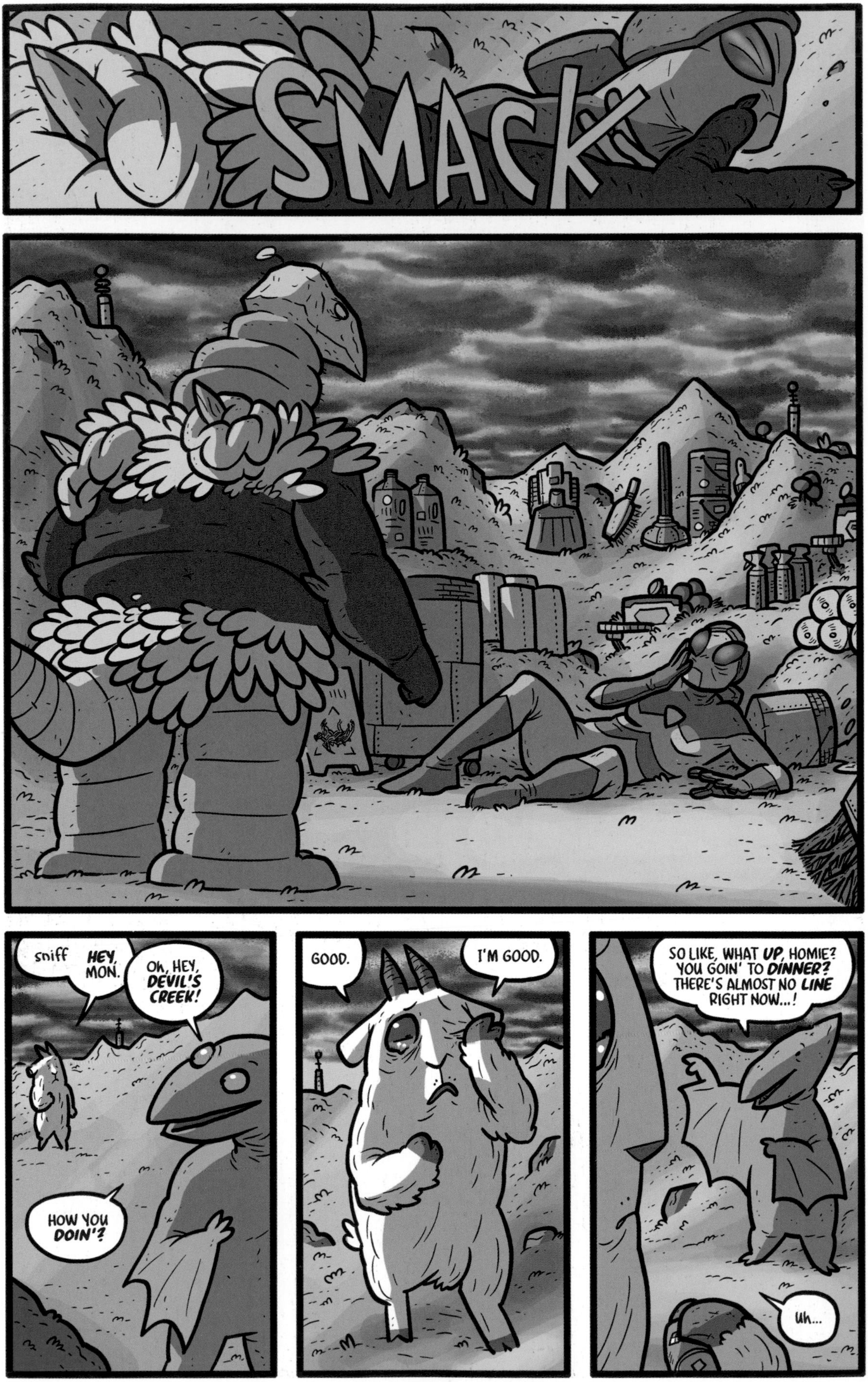
SMACK
sniff HEY, MON.
Oh, HEY, DEVIL'S CREEK!
HOW YOU DOIN'?
GOOD.
I'M GOOD.
SO LIKE, WHAT UP, HOMIE? YOU GOIN' TO DINNER? THERE'S ALMOST NO LINE RIGHT NOW...!
Uh...

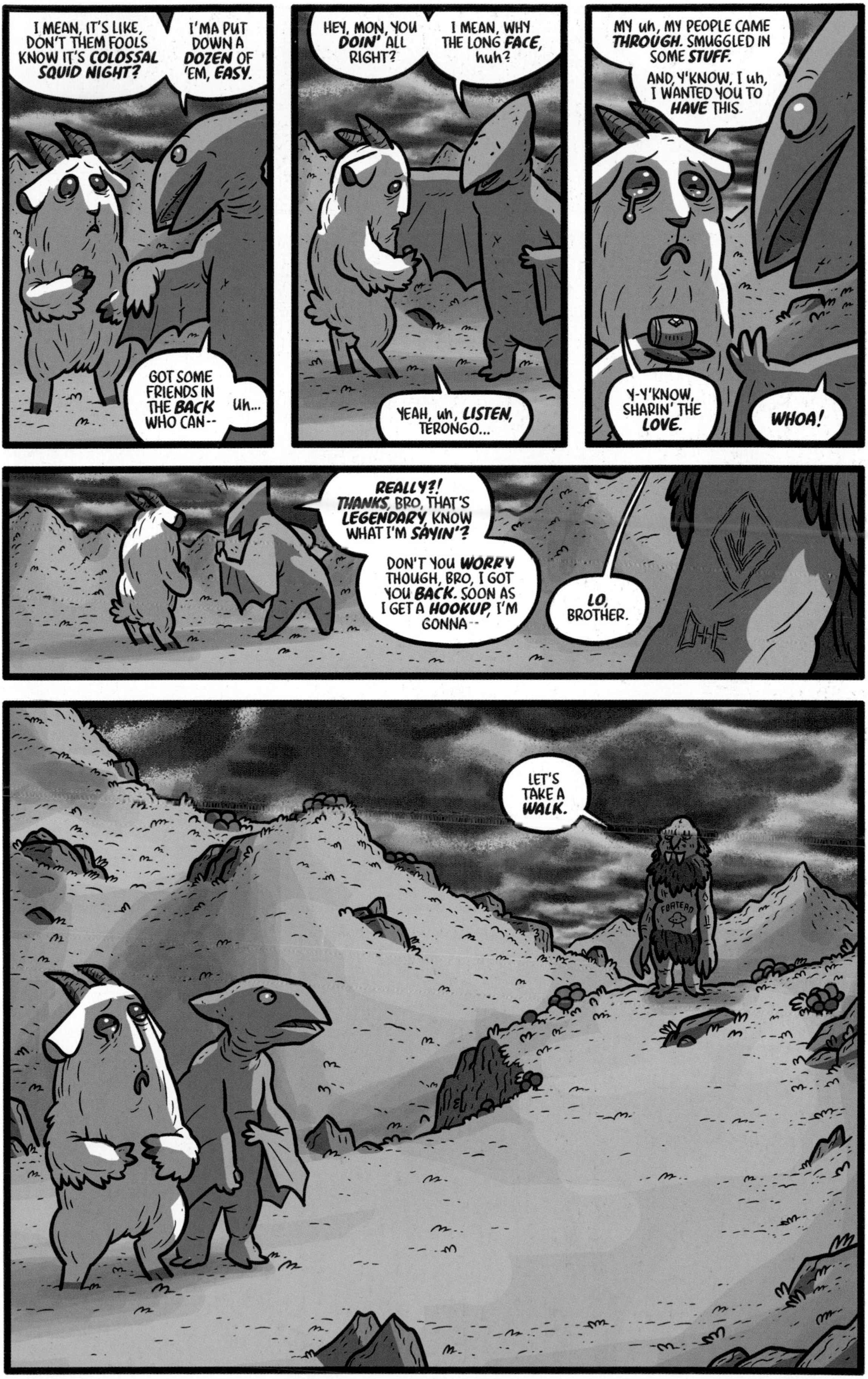
I MEAN, IT'S LIKE, DON'T THEM FOOLS KNOW IT'S COLOSSAL SQUID NIGHT?
I'MA PUT DOWN A DOZEN OF 'EM, EASY.
GOT SOME FRIENDS IN THE BACK WHO CAN--
uh...
HEY, MON, YOU DOIN' ALL RIGHT?
I MEAN, WHY THE LONG FACE, huh?
YEAH, uh, LISTEN, TERONGO...
MY uh, MY PEOPLE CAME THROUGH. SMUGGLED IN SOME STUFF.
AND, Y'KNOW, I uh, I WANTED YOU TO HAVE THIS.
Y-Y'KNOW, SHARIN' THE LOVE.
WHOA!
REALLY?! THANKS, BRO, THAT'S LEGENDARY, KNOW WHAT I'M SAYIN'?
DON'T YOU WORRY THOUGH, BRO, I GOT YOU BACK. SOON AS I GET A HOOKUP, I'M GONNA--
LO, BROTHER.
LET'S TAKE A WALK.

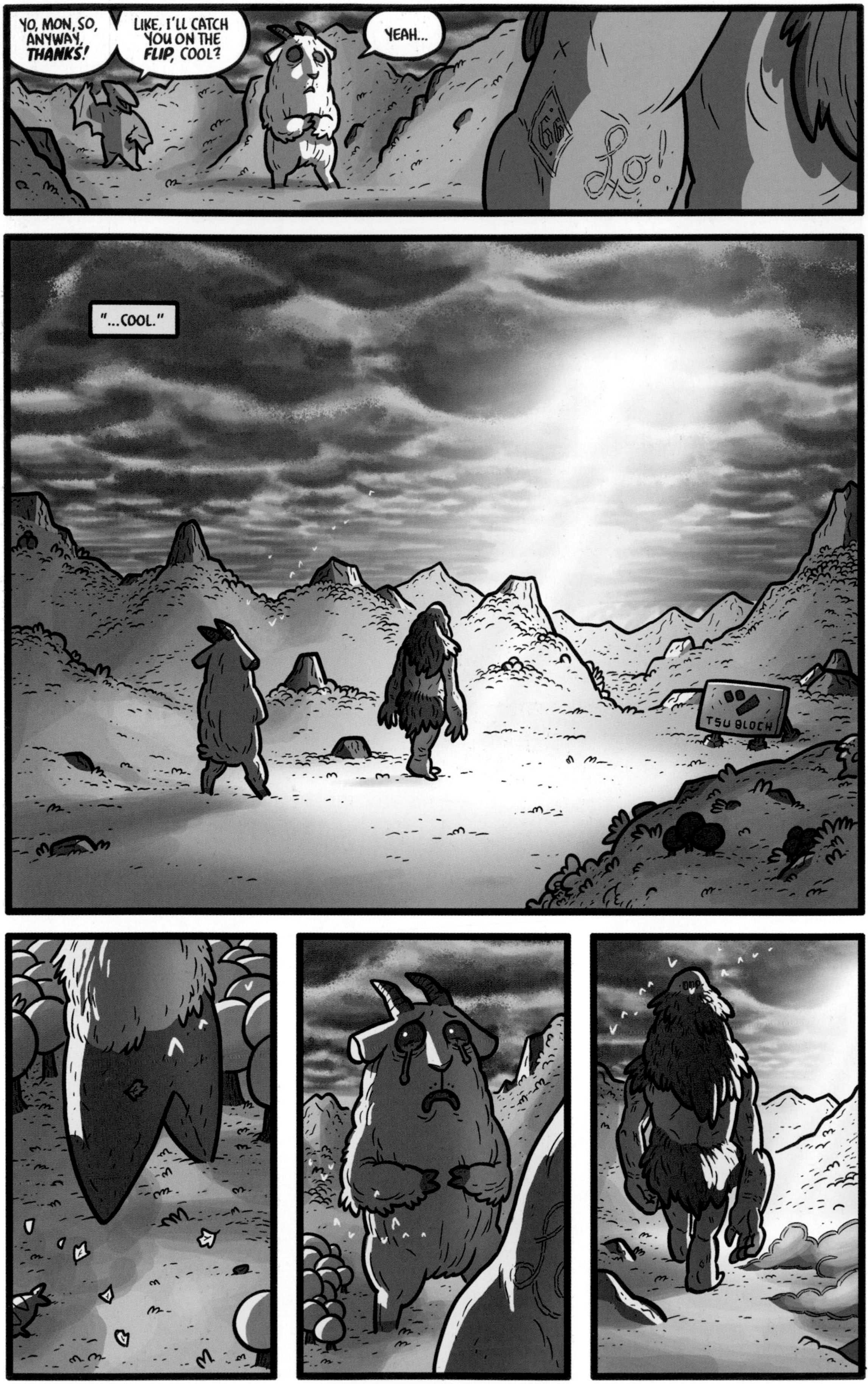
YO, MON, SO, ANYWAY, **THANKS!**
LIKE, I'LL CATCH YOU ON THE **FLIP**, COOL?
YEAH...
"...COOL."
TSU BLOCH

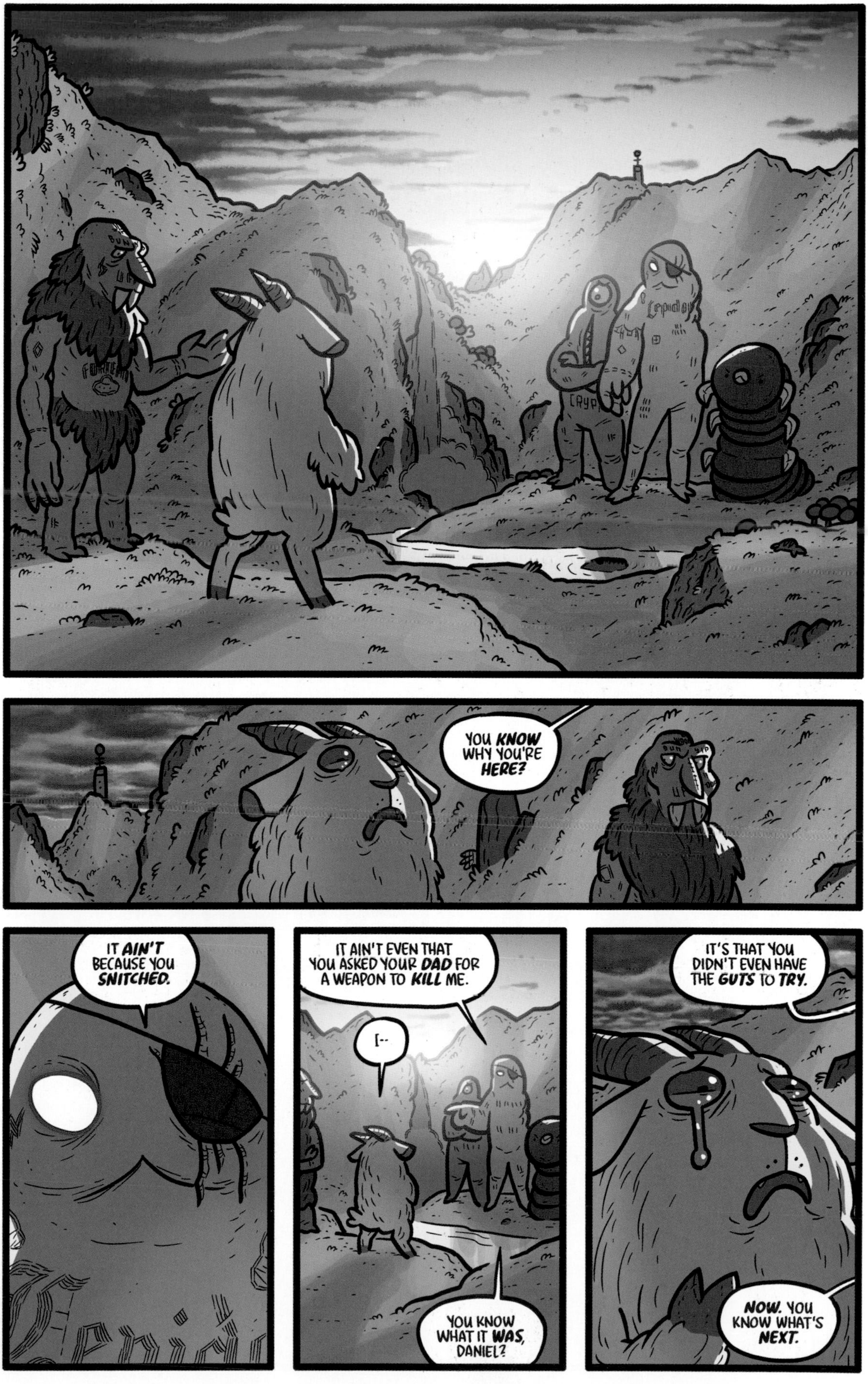

YOU KNOW WHY YOU'RE HERE?
IT AIN'T BECAUSE YOU SNITCHED.
IT AIN'T EVEN THAT YOU ASKED YOUR DAD FOR A WEAPON TO KILL ME.
[--
YOU KNOW WHAT IT WAS, DANIEL?
IT'S THAT YOU DIDN'T EVEN HAVE THE GUTS TO TRY.
NOW. YOU KNOW WHAT'S NEXT.

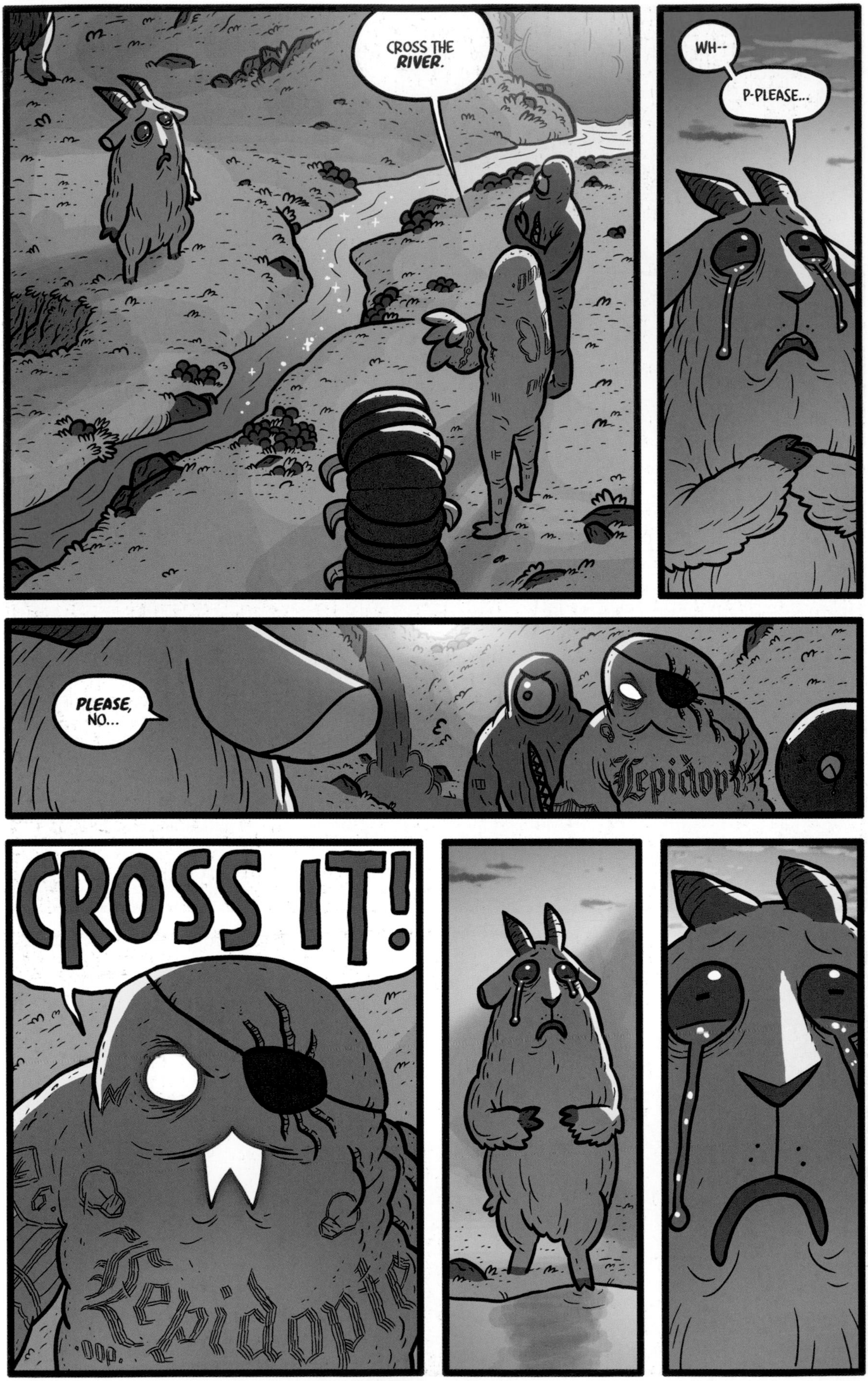
CROSS THE **RIVER**.
WH--
P-PLEASE...
PLEASE, NO...
CROSS IT!

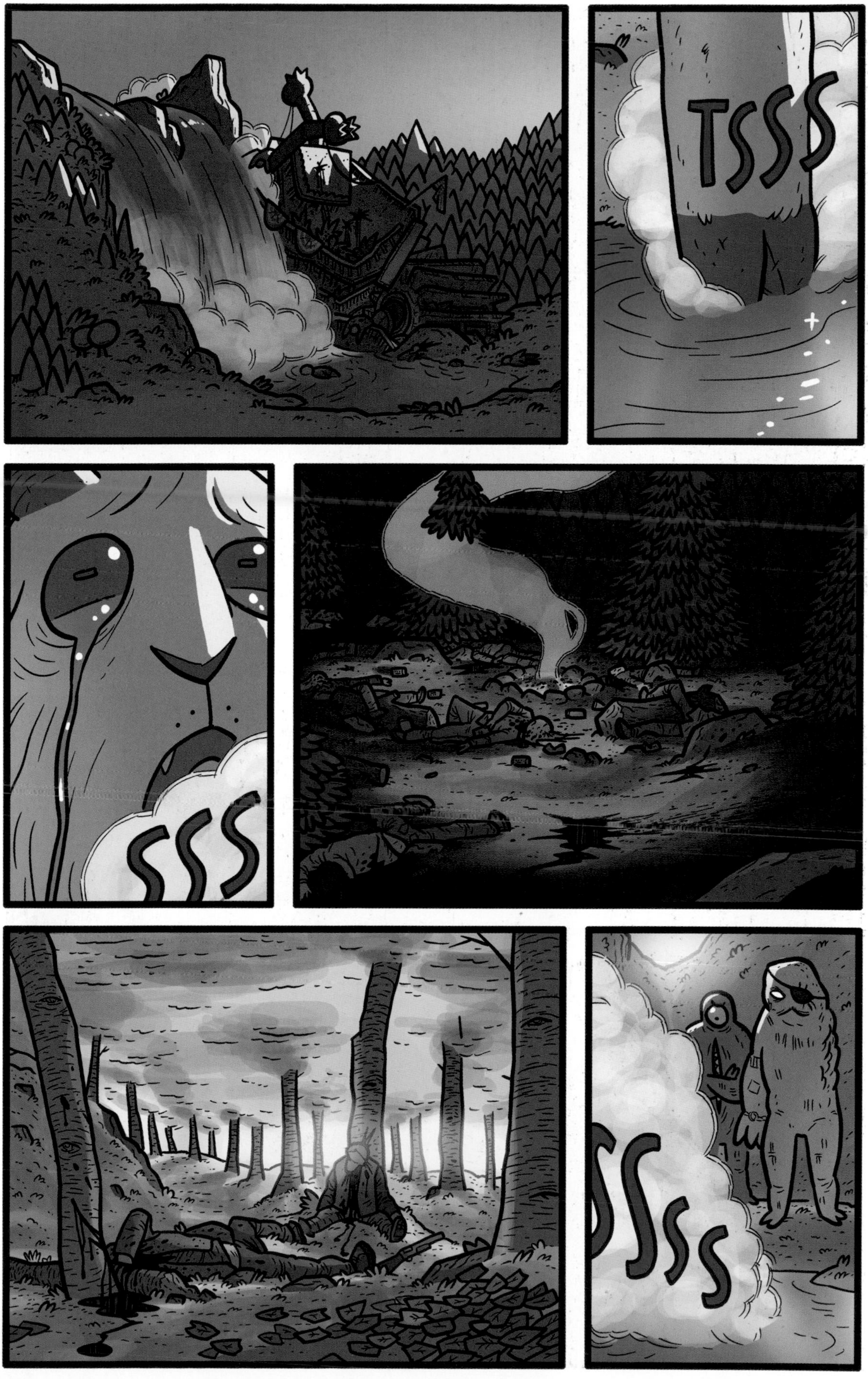
TSSS
SSS
SSSS

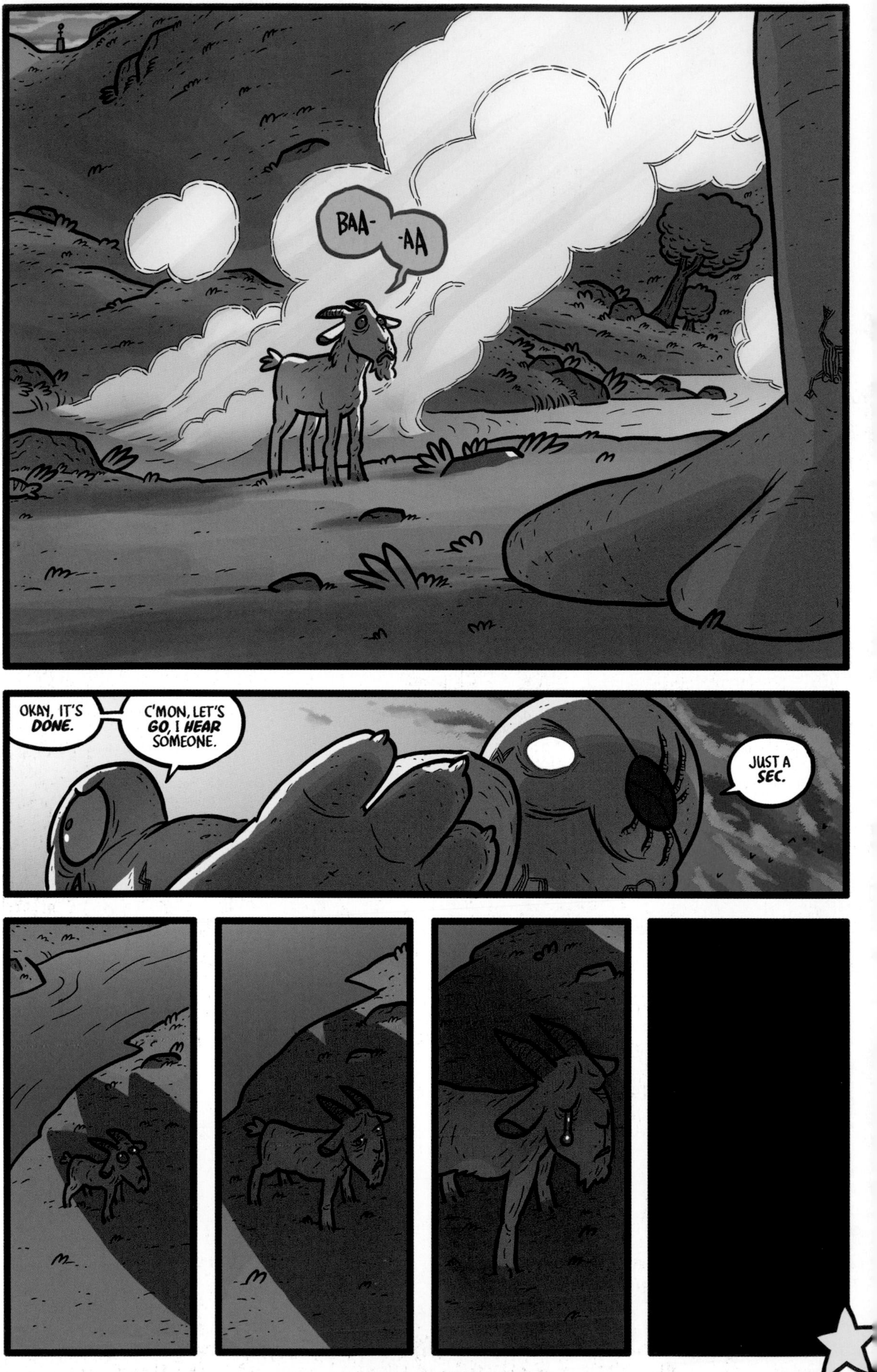
BAA-
-AA
OKAY, IT'S DONE.
C'MON, LET'S GO, I HEAR SOMEONE.
JUST A SEC.

EPISODE 6

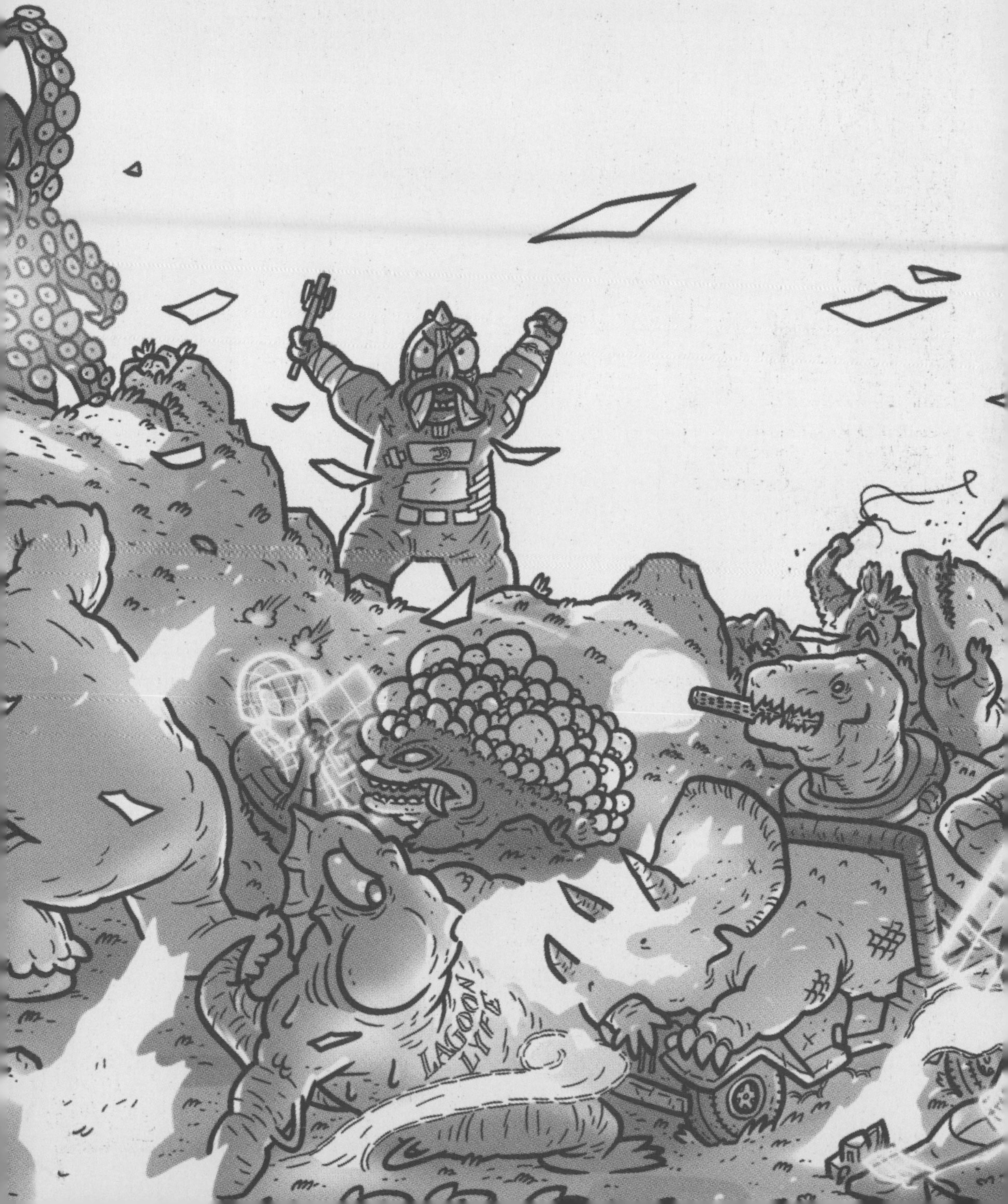
LAGOON LYFE

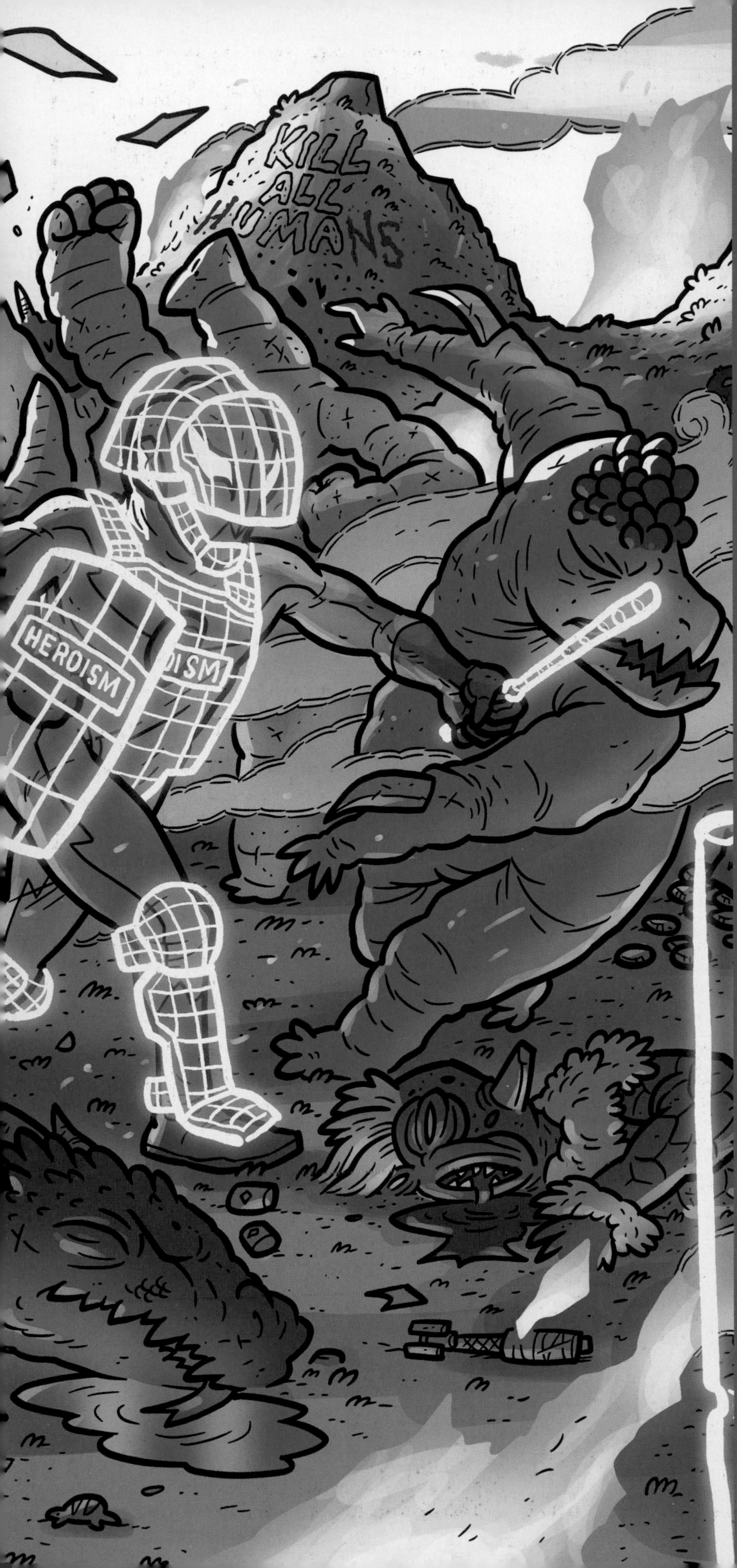
KILL ALL HUMANS
HEROISM
OISM

怪獣マックス

WHOOFY™

APE-WHALE™

MOUNTAIN™

SKUNK™

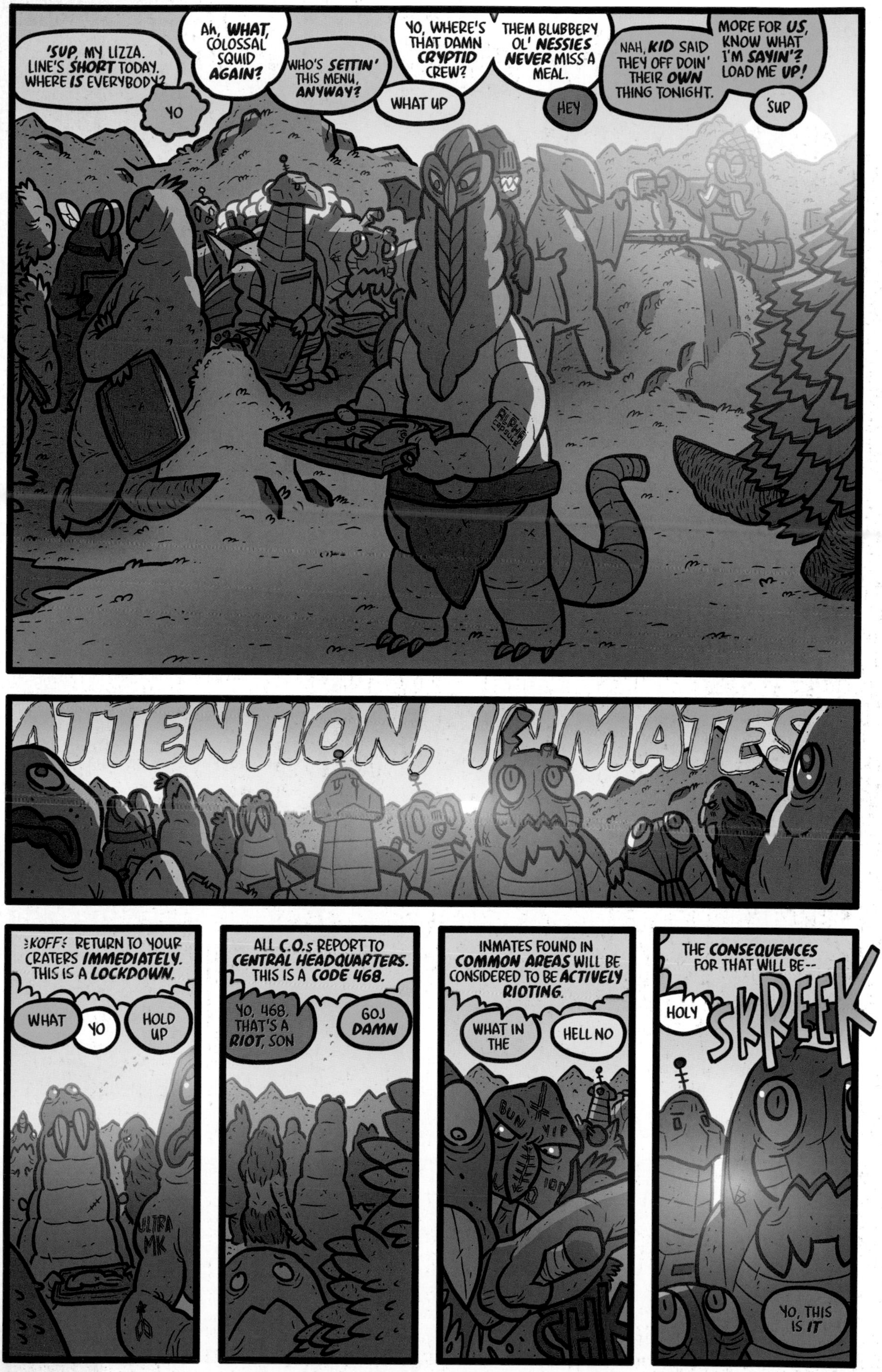
'SUP, MY LIZZA. LINE'S SHORT TODAY. WHERE IS EVERYBODY?
YO
Ah, WHAT, COLOSSAL SQUID AGAIN?
WHO'S SETTIN' THIS MENU, ANYWAY?
YO, WHERE'S THAT DAMN CRYPTID CREW?
WHAT UP
THEM BLUBBERY OL' NESSIES NEVER MISS A MEAL.
HEY
NAH, KID SAID THEY OFF DOIN' THEIR OWN THING TONIGHT.
MORE FOR US, KNOW WHAT I'M SAYIN'? LOAD ME UP!
'SUP
ALPHA CAPSULE
ATTENTION, INMATES
KOFF RETURN TO YOUR CRATERS IMMEDIATELY. THIS IS A LOCKDOWN.
WHAT
YO
HOLD UP
ULTRA MK
ALL C.O.s REPORT TO CENTRAL HEADQUARTERS. THIS IS A CODE 468.
YO, 468. THAT'S A RIOT, SON
GOJ DAMN
INMATES FOUND IN COMMON AREAS WILL BE CONSIDERED TO BE ACTIVELY RIOTING.
WHAT IN THE
HELL NO
CHK
THE CONSEQUENCES FOR THAT WILL BE--
HOLY
SKREEK
YO, THIS IS IT

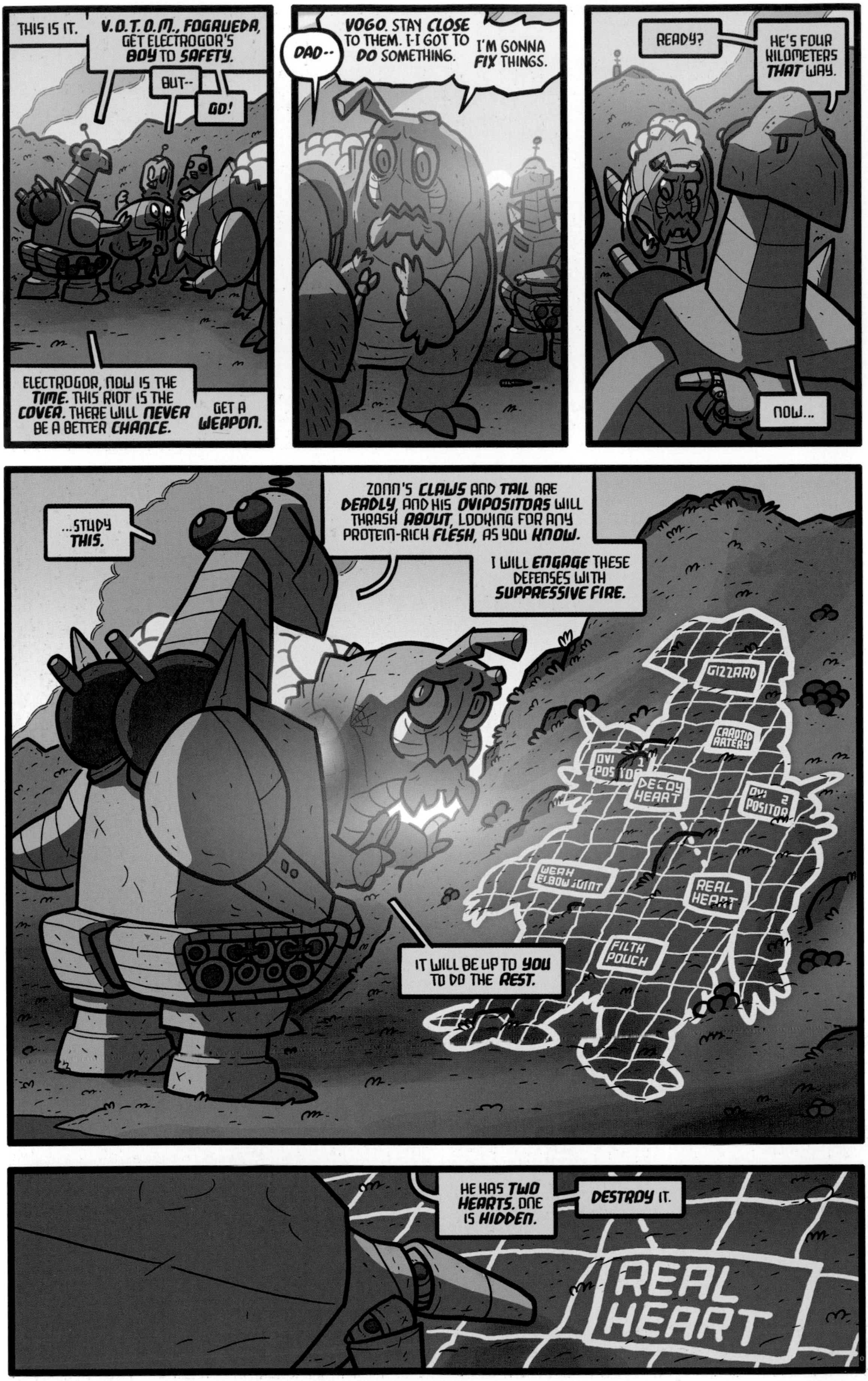

THIS IS IT.
V.O.T.O.M., FOGRUEDA, GET ELECTROGOR'S BOY TO SAFETY.
BUT--
GO!
ELECTROGOR, NOW IS THE TIME. THIS RIOT IS THE COVER. THERE WILL NEVER BE A BETTER CHANCE.
GET A WEAPON.
DAD--
VOGO. STAY CLOSE TO THEM. I-I GOT TO DO SOMETHING.
I'M GONNA FIX THINGS.
READY?
HE'S FOUR KILOMETERS THAT WAY.
NOW...
...STUDY THIS.
ZONN'S CLAWS AND TAIL ARE DEADLY, AND HIS OVIPOSITORS WILL THRASH ABOUT, LOOKING FOR ANY PROTEIN-RICH FLESH, AS YOU KNOW.
I WILL ENGAGE THESE DEFENSES WITH SUPPRESSIVE FIRE.
GIZZARD
CAROTID ARTERY
OVI POSITOR 1
DECOY HEART
OVI POSITOR 2
WEAK ELBOW JOINT
REAL HEART
FILTH POUCH
IT WILL BE UP TO YOU TO DO THE REST.
HE HAS TWO HEARTS. ONE IS HIDDEN.
DESTROY IT.
REAL HEART

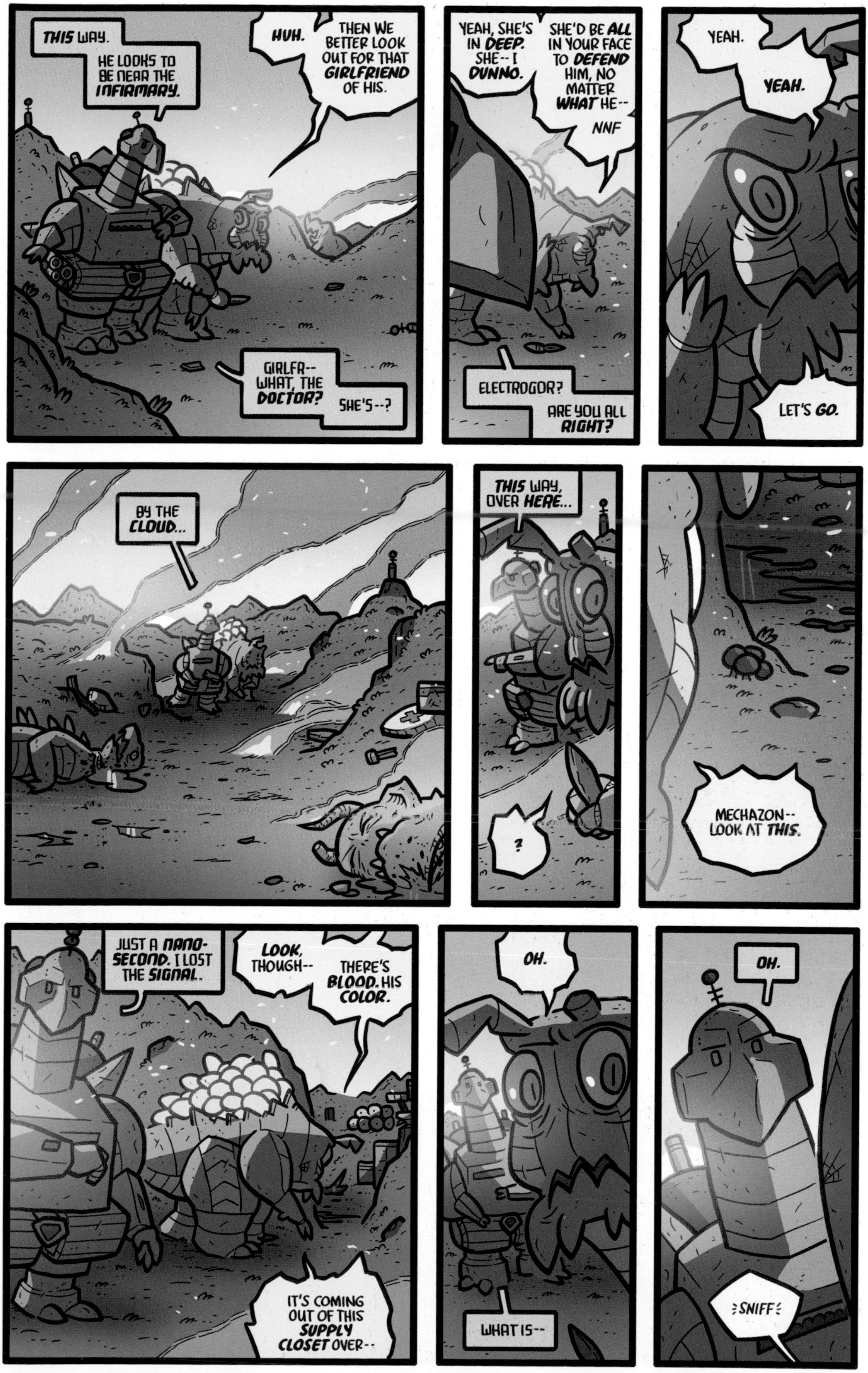
THIS WAY.
HE LOOKS TO BE NEAR THE INFIRMARY.
HUH.
THEN WE BETTER LOOK OUT FOR THAT GIRLFRIEND OF HIS.
GIRLFR-- WHAT, THE DOCTOR?
SHE'S--?
YEAH, SHE'S IN DEEP. SHE-- I DUNNO.
SHE'D BE ALL IN YOUR FACE TO DEFEND HIM, NO MATTER WHAT HE--
NNF
ELECTROGOR?
ARE YOU ALL RIGHT?
YEAH.
YEAH.
LET'S GO.
BY THE CLOUD...
THIS WAY, OVER HERE...
?
MECHAZON-- LOOK AT THIS.
JUST A NANO-SECOND. I LOST THE SIGNAL.
LOOK, THOUGH--
THERE'S BLOOD. HIS COLOR.
IT'S COMING OUT OF THIS SUPPLY CLOSET OVER--
OH.
WHAT IS--
OH.
SNIFF

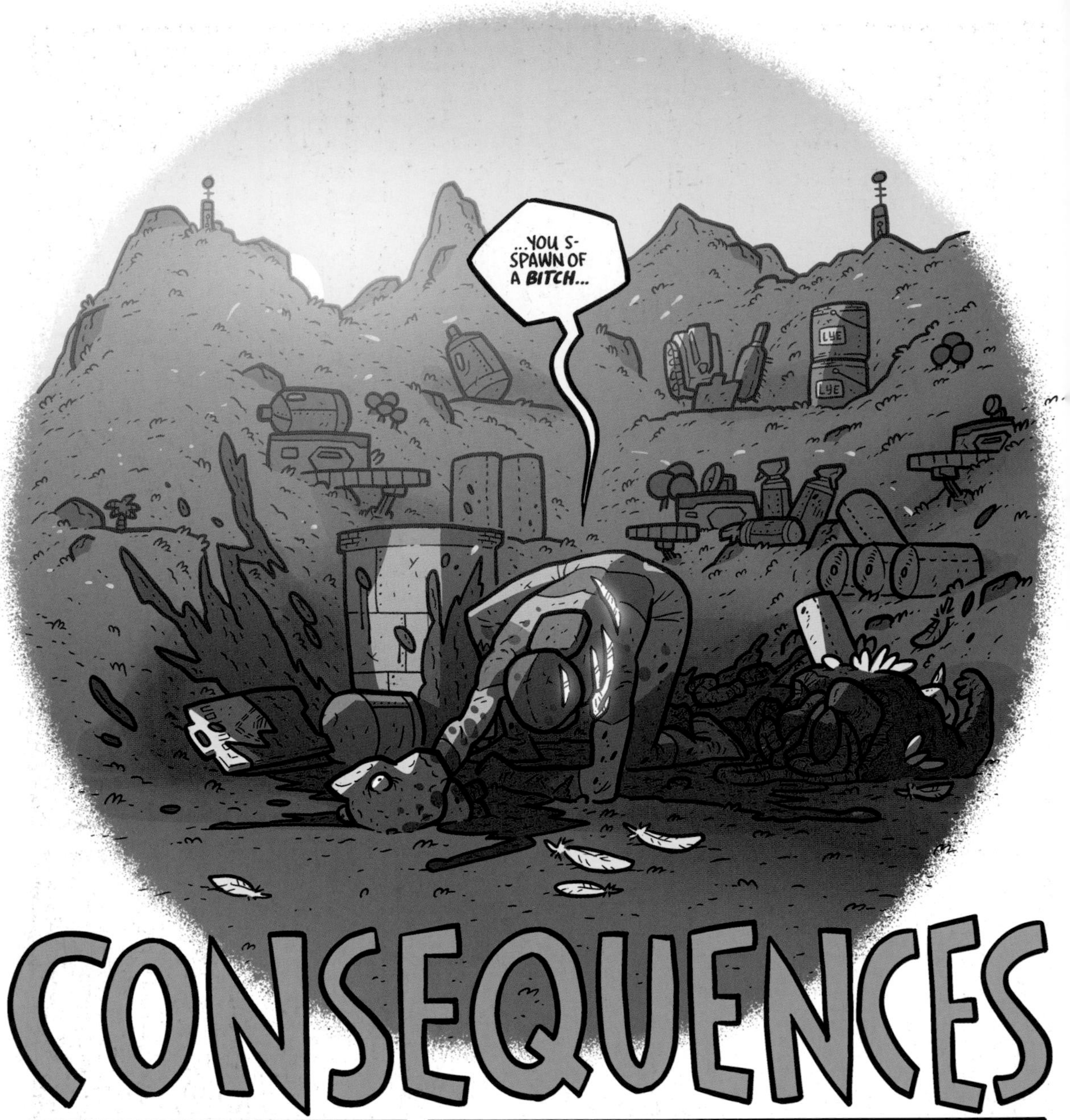
...YOU S-SPAWN OF A BITCH...

CONSEQUENCES

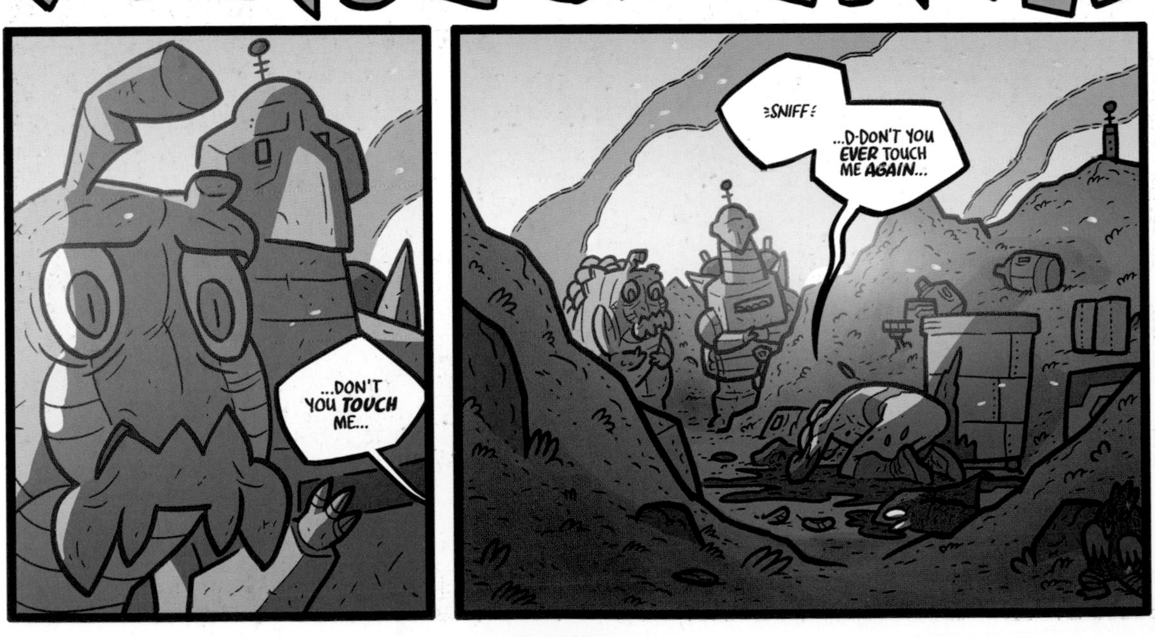
...DON'T YOU TOUCH ME...
SNIFF
...D-DON'T YOU EVER TOUCH ME AGAIN...

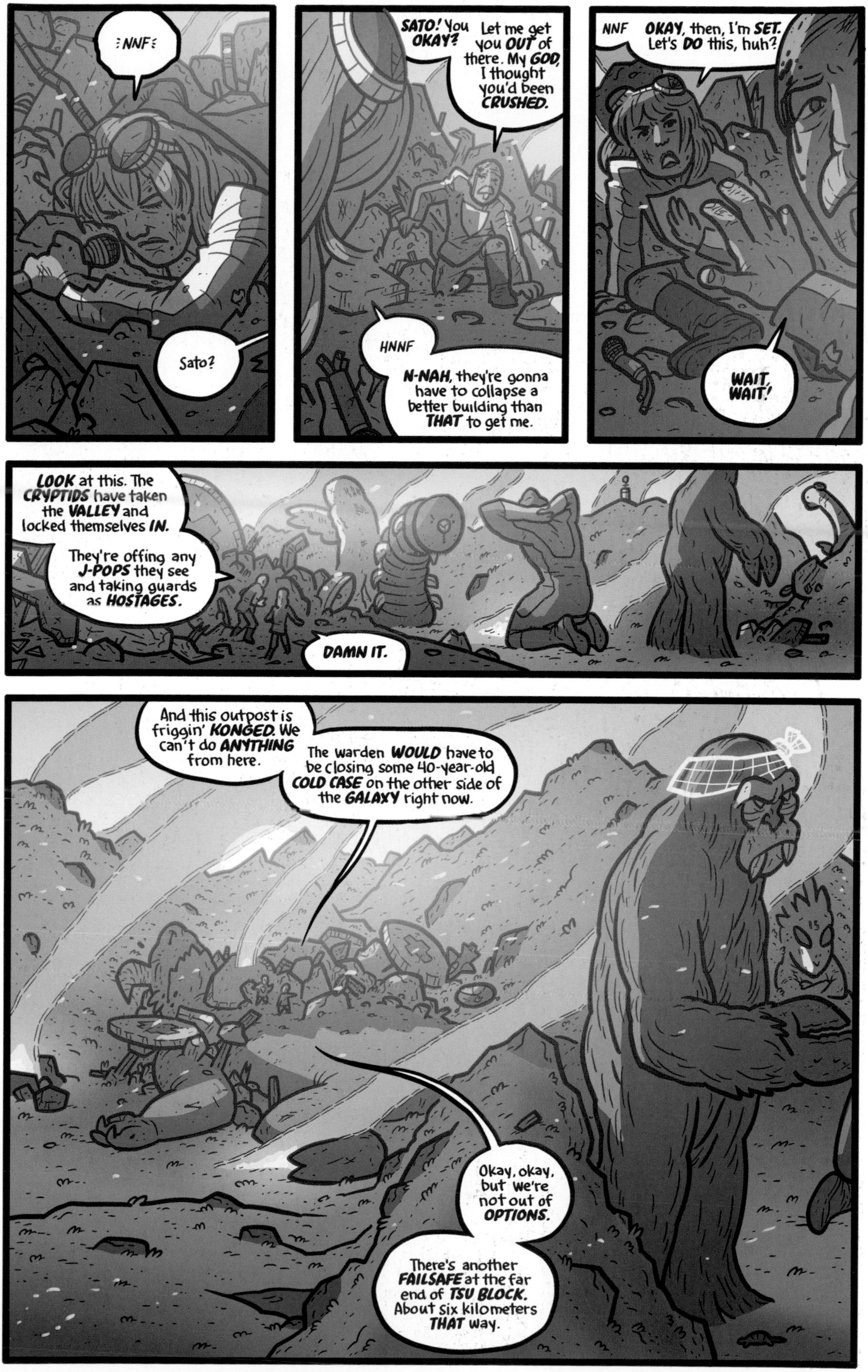
NNF
Sato?
SATO! You OKAY?
Let me get you OUT of there. My GOD, I thought you'd been CRUSHED.
HNNF
N-NAH, they're gonna have to collapse a better building than THAT to get me.
NNF
OKAY, then, I'm SET. Let's DO this, huh?
WAIT, WAIT!
LOOK at this. The CRYPTIDS have taken the VALLEY and locked themselves IN.
They're offing any J-POPS they see and taking guards as HOSTAGES.
DAMN IT.
And this outpost is friggin' KONGED. We can't do ANYTHING from here.
The warden WOULD have to be closing some 40-year-old COLD CASE on the other side of the GALAXY right now.
Okay, okay, but we're not out of OPTIONS.
There's another FAILSAFE at the far end of TSU BLOCK. About six kilometers THAT way.

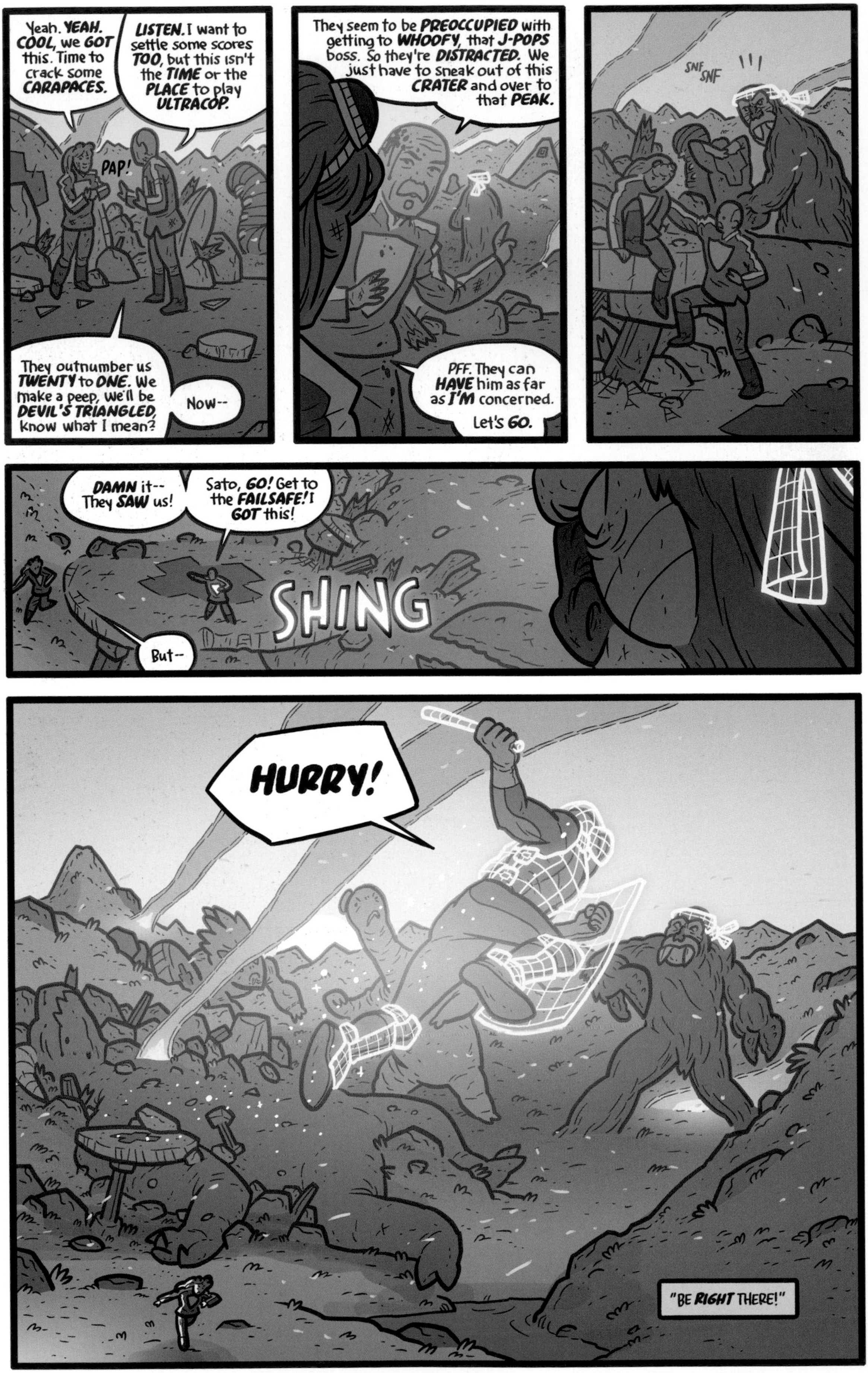
Yeah. YEAH. COOL, we GOT this. Time to crack some CARAPACES.
LISTEN. I want to settle some scores TOO, but this isn't the TIME or the PLACE to play ULTRACOP.
PAP!
They outnumber us TWENTY to ONE. We make a peep, we'll be DEVIL'S TRIANGLED, know what I mean?
Now--
They seem to be PREOCCUPIED with getting to WHOOFY, that J-POPS boss. So they're DISTRACTED. We just have to sneak out of this CRATER and over to that PEAK.
PFF. They can HAVE him as far as I'M concerned.
Let's GO.
SNF SNF
DAMN it-- They SAW us!
Sato, GO! Get to the FAILSAFE! I GOT this!
But--
SHING
HURRY!
"BE RIGHT THERE!"

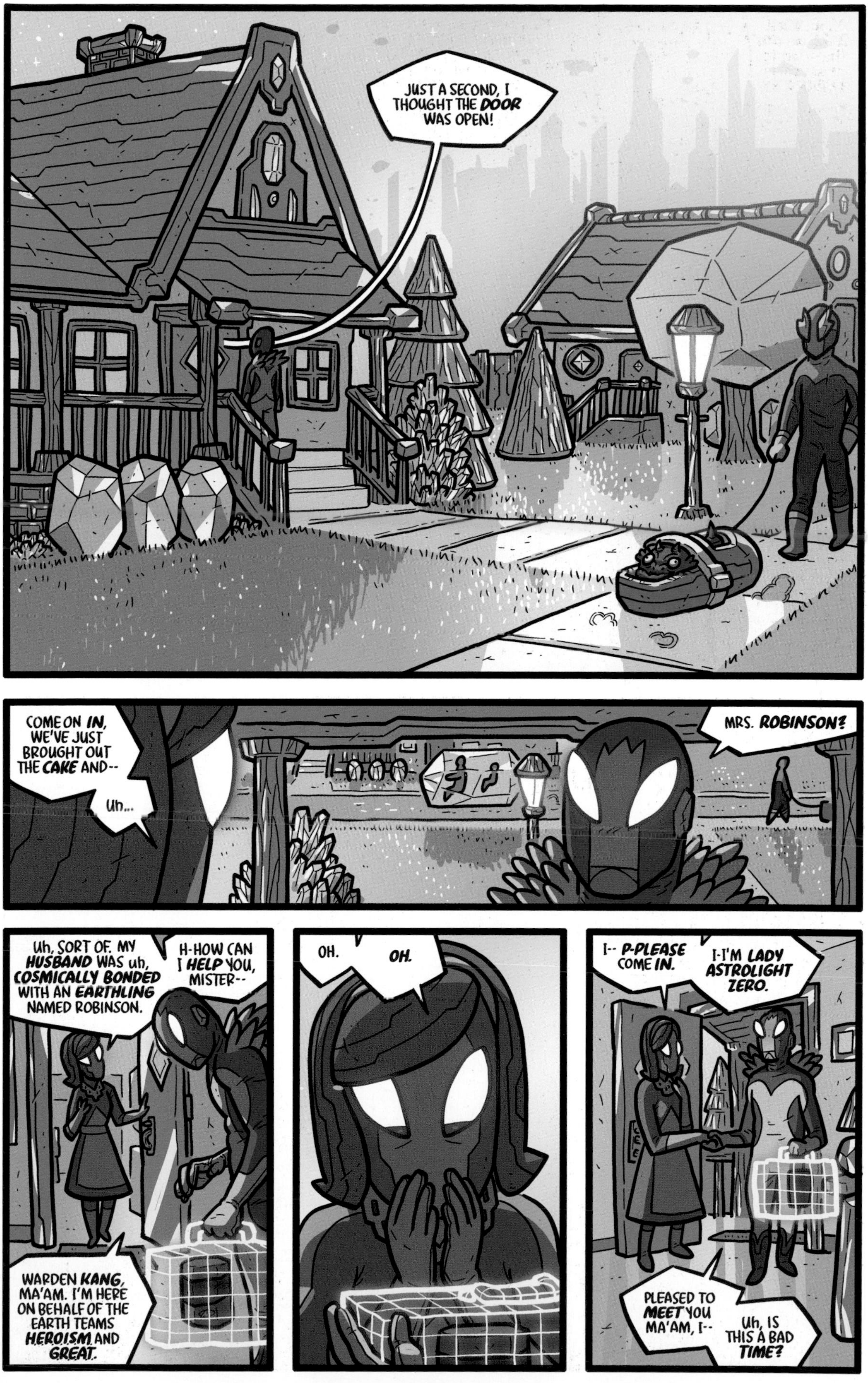
JUST A SECOND, I THOUGHT THE DOOR WAS OPEN!
COME ON IN, WE'VE JUST BROUGHT OUT THE CAKE AND--
Uh...
MRS. ROBINSON?
Uh, SORT OF. MY HUSBAND WAS uh, COSMICALLY BONDED WITH AN EARTHLING NAMED ROBINSON.
H-HOW CAN I HELP YOU, MISTER--
WARDEN KANG, MA'AM. I'M HERE ON BEHALF OF THE EARTH TEAMS HEROISM AND GREAT.
OH.
OH.
I-- P-PLEASE COME IN.
I-I'M LADY ASTROLIGHT ZERO.
PLEASED TO MEET YOU MA'AM, I--
Uh, IS THIS A BAD TIME?

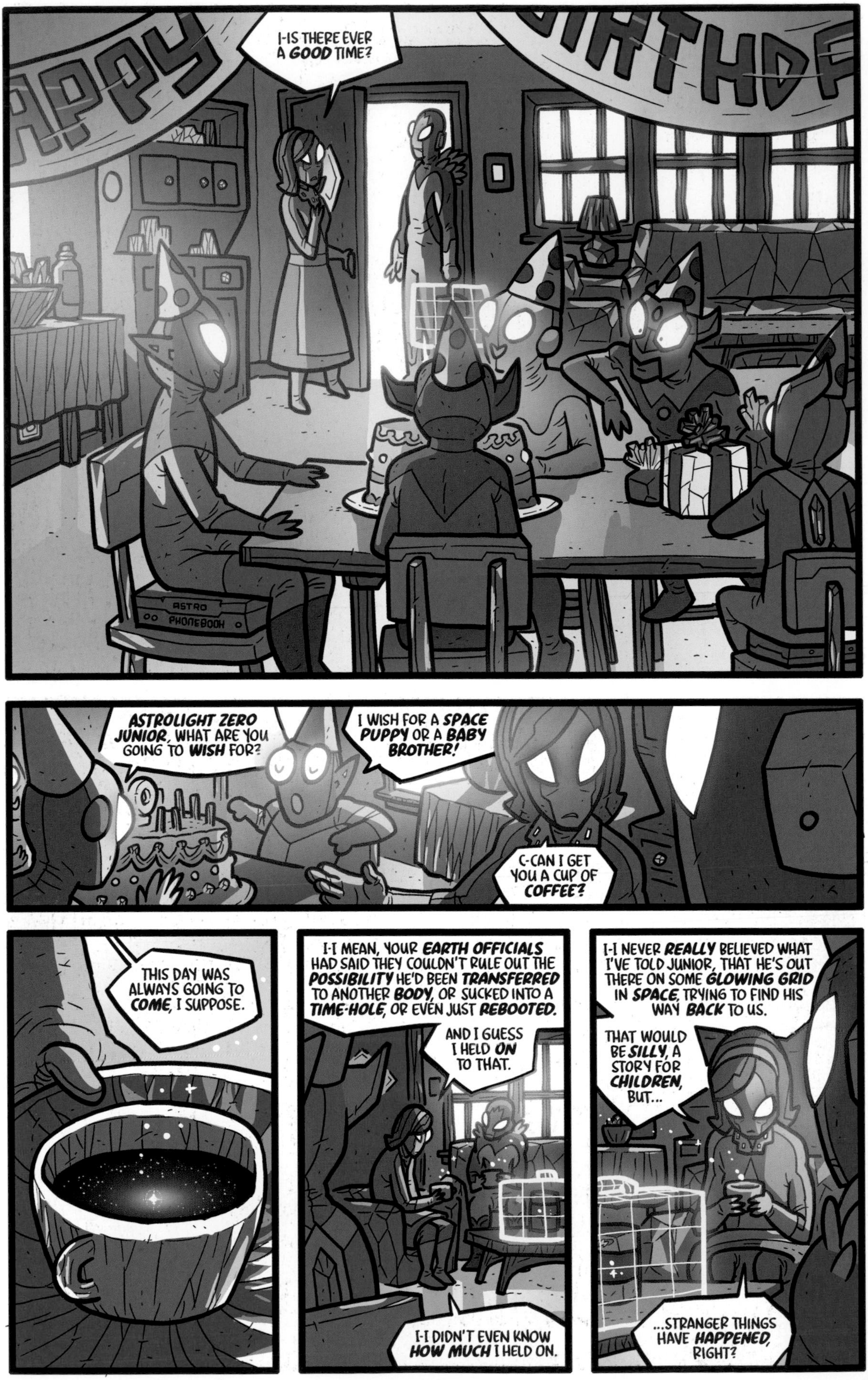
APPY
IRTHDA
I-IS THERE EVER A GOOD TIME?
ASTRO PHONEBOOK
ASTROLIGHT ZERO JUNIOR, WHAT ARE YOU GOING TO WISH FOR?
I WISH FOR A SPACE PUPPY OR A BABY BROTHER!
C-CAN I GET YOU A CUP OF COFFEE?
THIS DAY WAS ALWAYS GOING TO COME, I SUPPOSE.
I-I MEAN, YOUR EARTH OFFICIALS HAD SAID THEY COULDN'T RULE OUT THE POSSIBILITY HE'D BEEN TRANSFERRED TO ANOTHER BODY, OR SUCKED INTO A TIME-HOLE, OR EVEN JUST REBOOTED.
AND I GUESS I HELD ON TO THAT.
I-I DIDN'T EVEN KNOW HOW MUCH I HELD ON.
I-I NEVER REALLY BELIEVED WHAT I'VE TOLD JUNIOR, THAT HE'S OUT THERE ON SOME GLOWING GRID IN SPACE, TRYING TO FIND HIS WAY BACK TO US.
THAT WOULD BE SILLY, A STORY FOR CHILDREN, BUT...
...STRANGER THINGS HAVE HAPPENED, RIGHT?

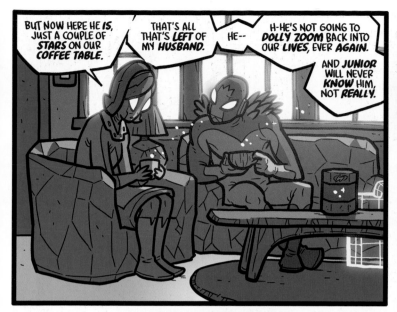

BUT NOW HERE HE *IS*, JUST A COUPLE OF *STARS* ON OUR *COFFEE TABLE*.

THAT'S ALL THAT'S *LEFT* OF MY *HUSBAND*.

HE--

H-HE'S NOT GOING TO *DOLLY ZOOM* BACK INTO OUR *LIVES*, EVER *AGAIN*.

AND *JUNIOR* WILL NEVER *KNOW* HIM, NOT *REALLY*.

I *WISH* I COULD BE MORE OF A *COMFORT* THAN TO SAY *THIS*:

YOUR *HUSBAND* DID ALL HE *COULD* TO MAKE THE WORLD *SAFER*.

HE DIED HOLDING THAT *THIN SILVER LINE* THAT KEEPS *HOPE* ALIVE.

AND I'M *SORRY* TO HAVE TAKEN YOUR HOPE *AWAY* TODAY.

BUT IF I'VE LEARNED *ANYTHING* LATELY, IT'S THAT THERE'S A TIME WHEN *HOPE* FOR SOMETHING THAT IS *GONE* JUST HURTS.

WE HAVE TO HIT *BOTTOM* TO MOVE ON.

WE HAVE TO PICK UP THE *PIECES*...

...CLICK THEM *TOGETHER*, ATTACH THEM TO OUR *BELTS*, AND *THEN* WE CAN START THE *HEALING PROCESS*.

HEY! LASER, OPEN MY PRESENT NOW!

I'M *WORKING* ON IT!

BECAUSE IT CAN TAKE A *VERY* LONG *TIME*.

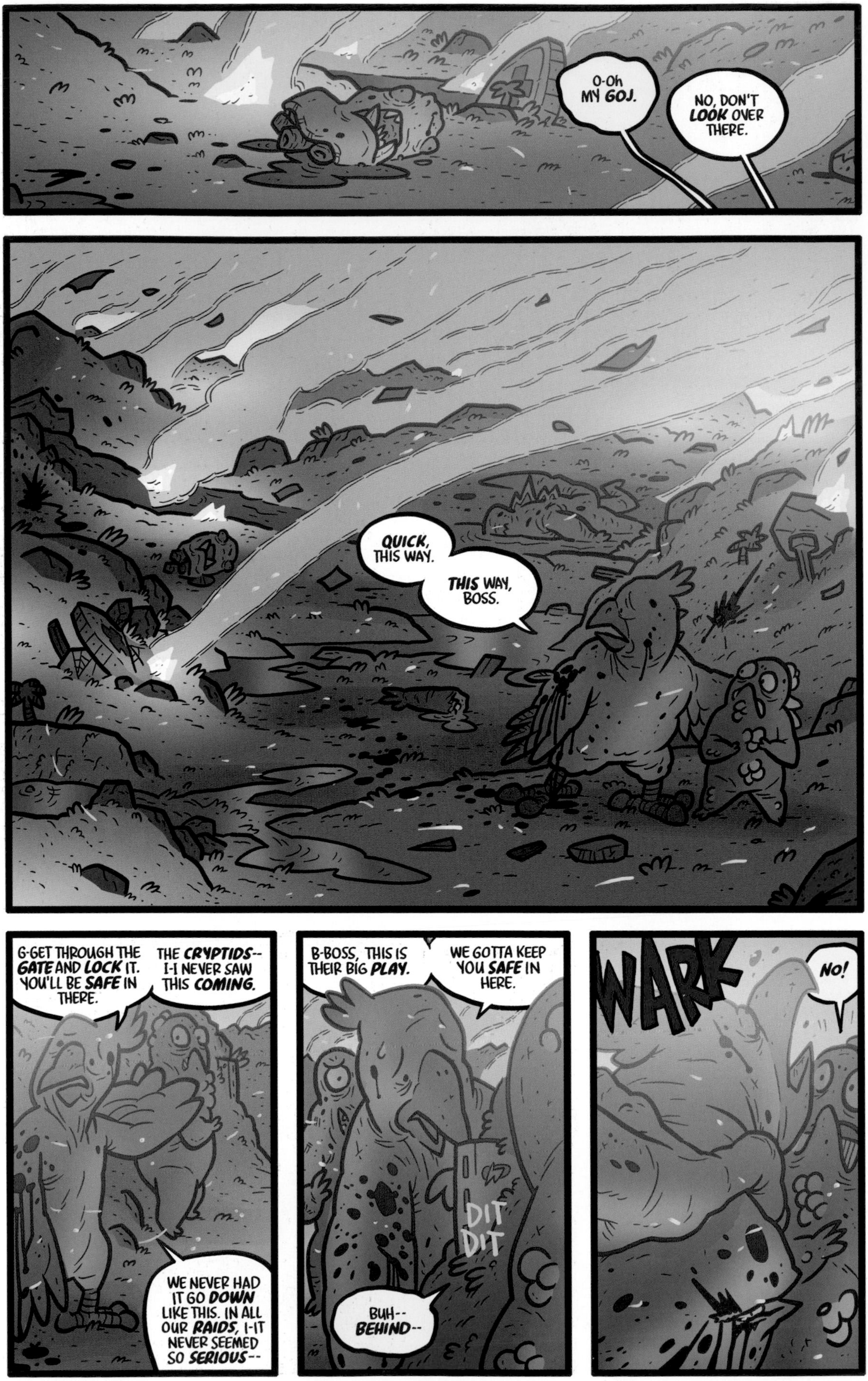
O-Oh MY GOJ.
NO, DON'T LOOK OVER THERE.
QUICK, THIS WAY.
THIS WAY, BOSS.
G-GET THROUGH THE GATE AND LOCK IT. YOU'LL BE SAFE IN THERE.
THE CRYPTIDS-- I-I NEVER SAW THIS COMING.
WE NEVER HAD IT GO DOWN LIKE THIS. IN ALL OUR RAIDS, I-IT NEVER SEEMED SO SERIOUS--
B-BOSS, THIS IS THEIR BIG PLAY.
WE GOTTA KEEP YOU SAFE IN HERE.
DIT DIT
BUH-- BEHIND--
WARK
NO!

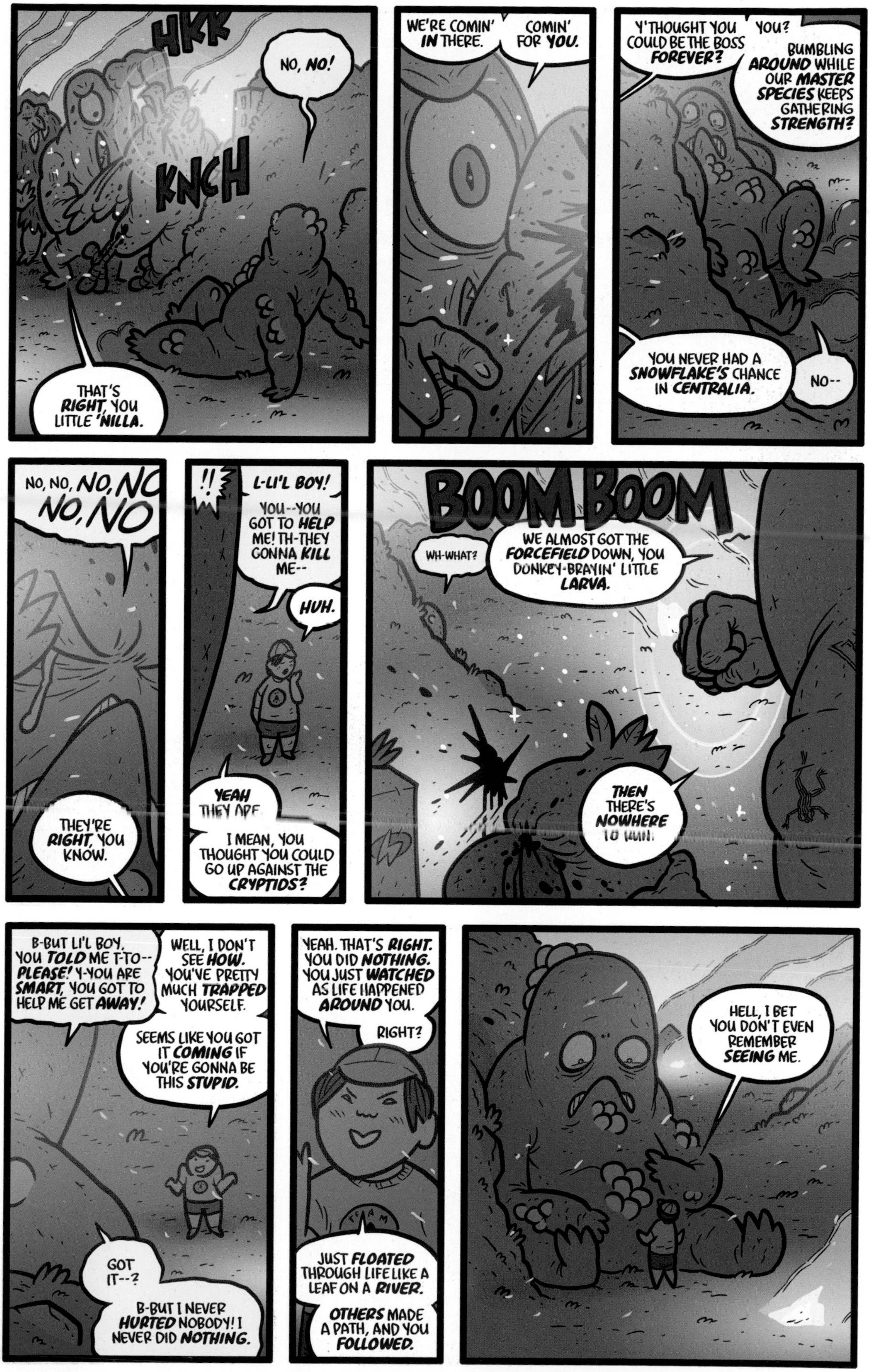
HKK
KNCH
NO, NO!
THAT'S RIGHT, YOU LITTLE 'NILLA.
WE'RE COMIN' IN THERE.
COMIN' FOR YOU.
Y'THOUGHT YOU COULD BE THE BOSS FOREVER?
YOU? BUMBLING AROUND WHILE OUR MASTER SPECIES KEEPS GATHERING STRENGTH?
YOU NEVER HAD A SNOWFLAKE'S CHANCE IN CENTRALIA.
NO--
NO, NO, NO, NO NO, NO
THEY'RE RIGHT, YOU KNOW.
!!
L-LI'L BOY!
YOU--YOU GOT TO HELP ME! TH-THEY GONNA KILL ME--
HUH.
YEAH
I MEAN, YOU THOUGHT YOU COULD GO UP AGAINST THE CRYPTIDS?
BOOM BOOM
WH-WHAT?
WE ALMOST GOT THE FORCEFIELD DOWN, YOU DONKEY-BRAYIN' LITTLE LARVA.
THEN THERE'S NOWHERE
B-BUT LI'L BOY, YOU TOLD ME T-TO-- PLEASE! Y-YOU ARE SMART, YOU GOT TO HELP ME GET AWAY!
WELL, I DON'T SEE HOW. YOU'VE PRETTY MUCH TRAPPED YOURSELF.
SEEMS LIKE YOU GOT IT COMING IF YOU'RE GONNA BE THIS STUPID.
GOT IT--?
B-BUT I NEVER HURTED NOBODY! I NEVER DID NOTHING.
YEAH. THAT'S RIGHT. YOU DID NOTHING. YOU JUST WATCHED AS LIFE HAPPENED AROUND YOU.
RIGHT?
JUST FLOATED THROUGH LIFE LIKE A LEAF ON A RIVER.
OTHERS MADE A PATH, AND YOU FOLLOWED.
HELL, I BET YOU DON'T EVEN REMEMBER SEEING ME.

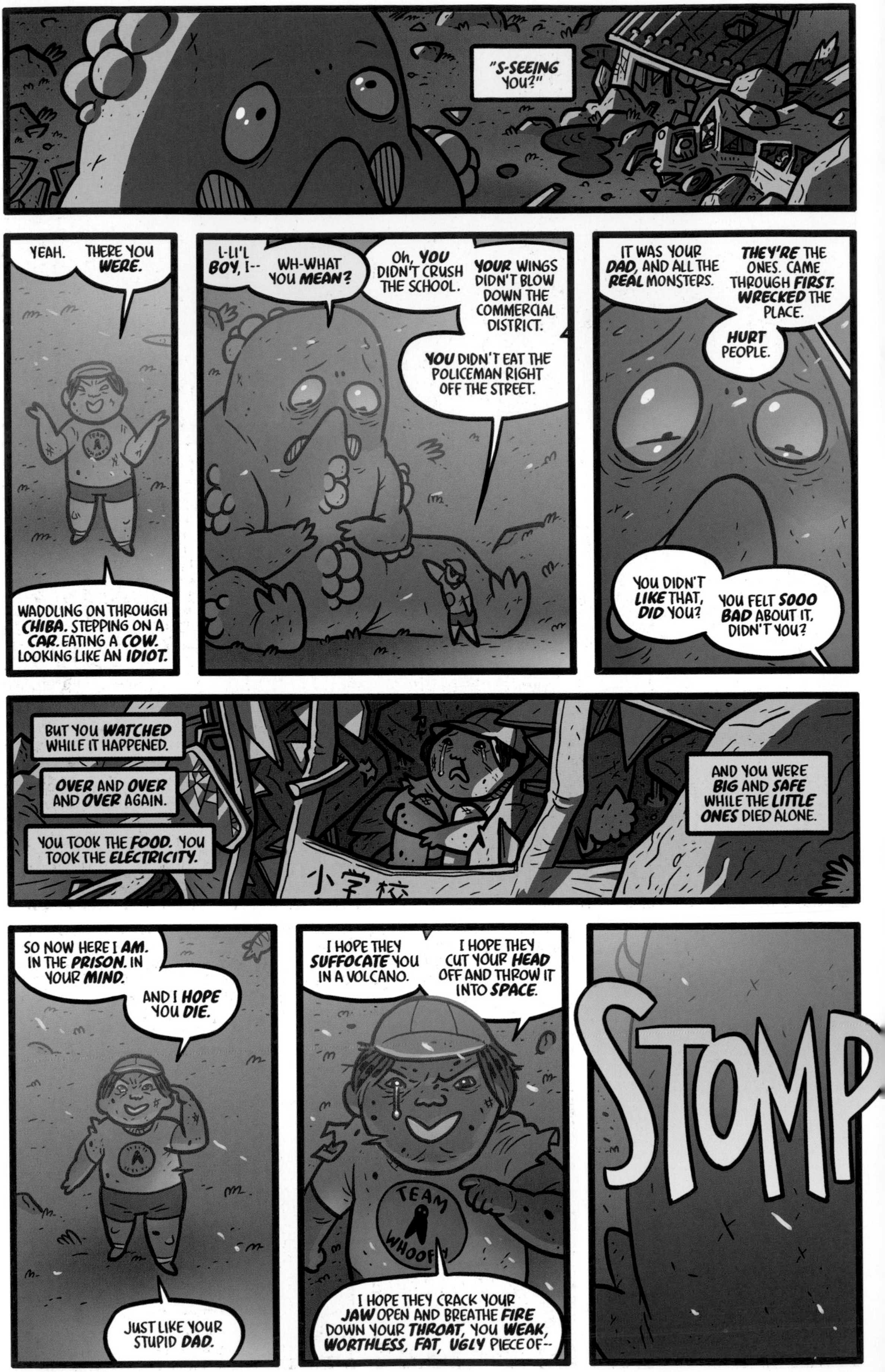
"S-SEEING YOU?"
YEAH. THERE YOU WERE.
WADDLING ON THROUGH CHIBA. STEPPING ON A CAR. EATING A COW. LOOKING LIKE AN IDIOT.
L-LI'L BOY, I--
WH-WHAT YOU MEAN?
Oh, YOU DIDN'T CRUSH THE SCHOOL.
YOUR WINGS DIDN'T BLOW DOWN THE COMMERCIAL DISTRICT.
YOU DIDN'T EAT THE POLICEMAN RIGHT OFF THE STREET.
IT WAS YOUR DAD, AND ALL THE REAL MONSTERS.
THEY'RE THE ONES. CAME THROUGH FIRST. WRECKED THE PLACE.
HURT PEOPLE.
YOU DIDN'T LIKE THAT, DID YOU?
YOU FELT SOOO BAD ABOUT IT, DIDN'T YOU?
BUT YOU WATCHED WHILE IT HAPPENED.
OVER AND OVER AND OVER AGAIN.
YOU TOOK THE FOOD. YOU TOOK THE ELECTRICITY.
小学校
AND YOU WERE BIG AND SAFE WHILE THE LITTLE ONES DIED ALONE.
SO NOW HERE I AM. IN THE PRISON. IN YOUR MIND.
AND I HOPE YOU DIE.
JUST LIKE YOUR STUPID DAD.
I HOPE THEY SUFFOCATE YOU IN A VOLCANO.
I HOPE THEY CUT YOUR HEAD OFF AND THROW IT INTO SPACE.
TEAM WHOOF
I HOPE THEY CRACK YOUR JAW OPEN AND BREATHE FIRE DOWN YOUR THROAT, YOU WEAK, WORTHLESS, FAT, UGLY PIECE OF--
STOMP

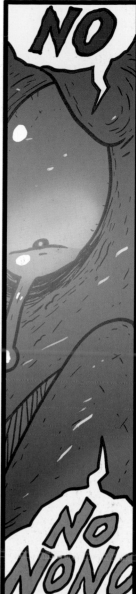

NO

NO NO NO

I-I NOT STUPID.

YOU ARE. YOU ARE!!

KTINK KZAAK

YEAH, WE'RE THROUGH.

NOW-- LOOK AT ME AND GET READY TO DIE YOU LITTLE--

uh...

?

YOU THINK YOU ARE S-SMART, huh?

L-LYING THERE IN YOUR GUTS ALL AROUND??

Y-Y-YOU'RE DEAD NOW!

AND I-I A MONSTER. I DONE IT.

139

I-I DON'T *CARE* ABOUT YOU, *LI'L BOY!*

I G-GONNA *EAT* YOU.

I *SH-SHOW* YOU I NOT WEAK. I SHOW YOU I A *REAL* MONSTER.

≡ GULP ≡

NOW *YOU.* YOU THINK I *WEAK?* YOU THINK I *STUPID?*

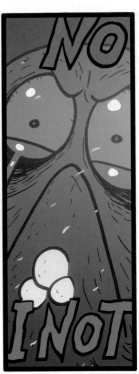

NO I NOT

TOOM

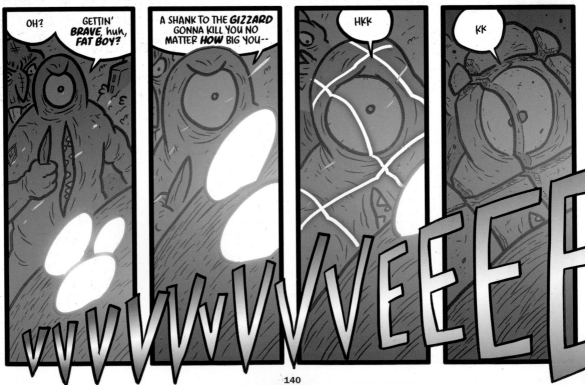

OH?

GETTIN' *BRAVE,* huh, *FAT BOY?*

A SHANK TO THE *GIZZARD* GONNA KILL YOU NO MATTER *HOW* BIG YOU--

HKK

KK

VVVVVVVVVEEEE

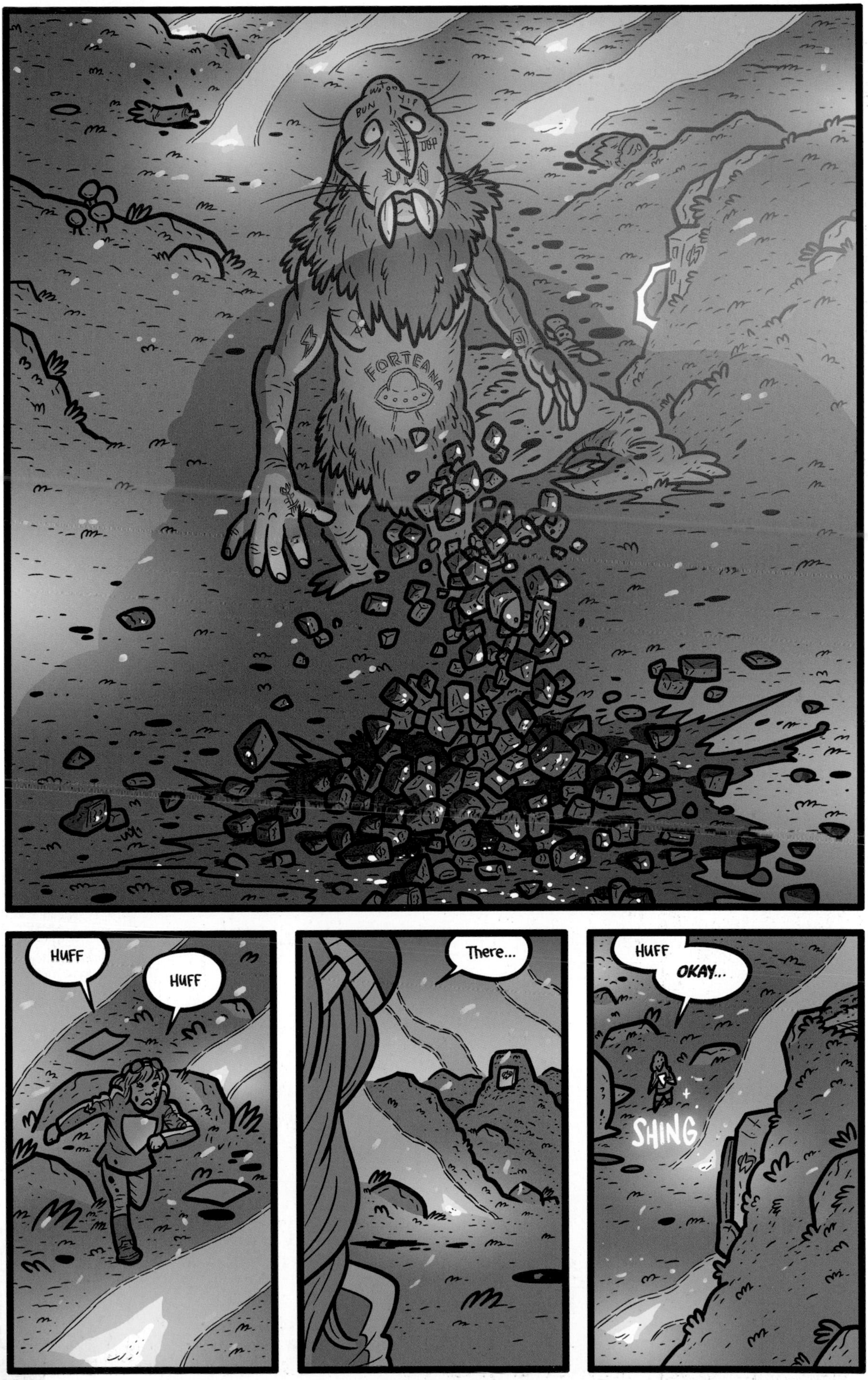
BUN
YIP
UFO
DSP
FORTEANA
HUFF
HUFF
There...
HUFF
OKAY...
SHING

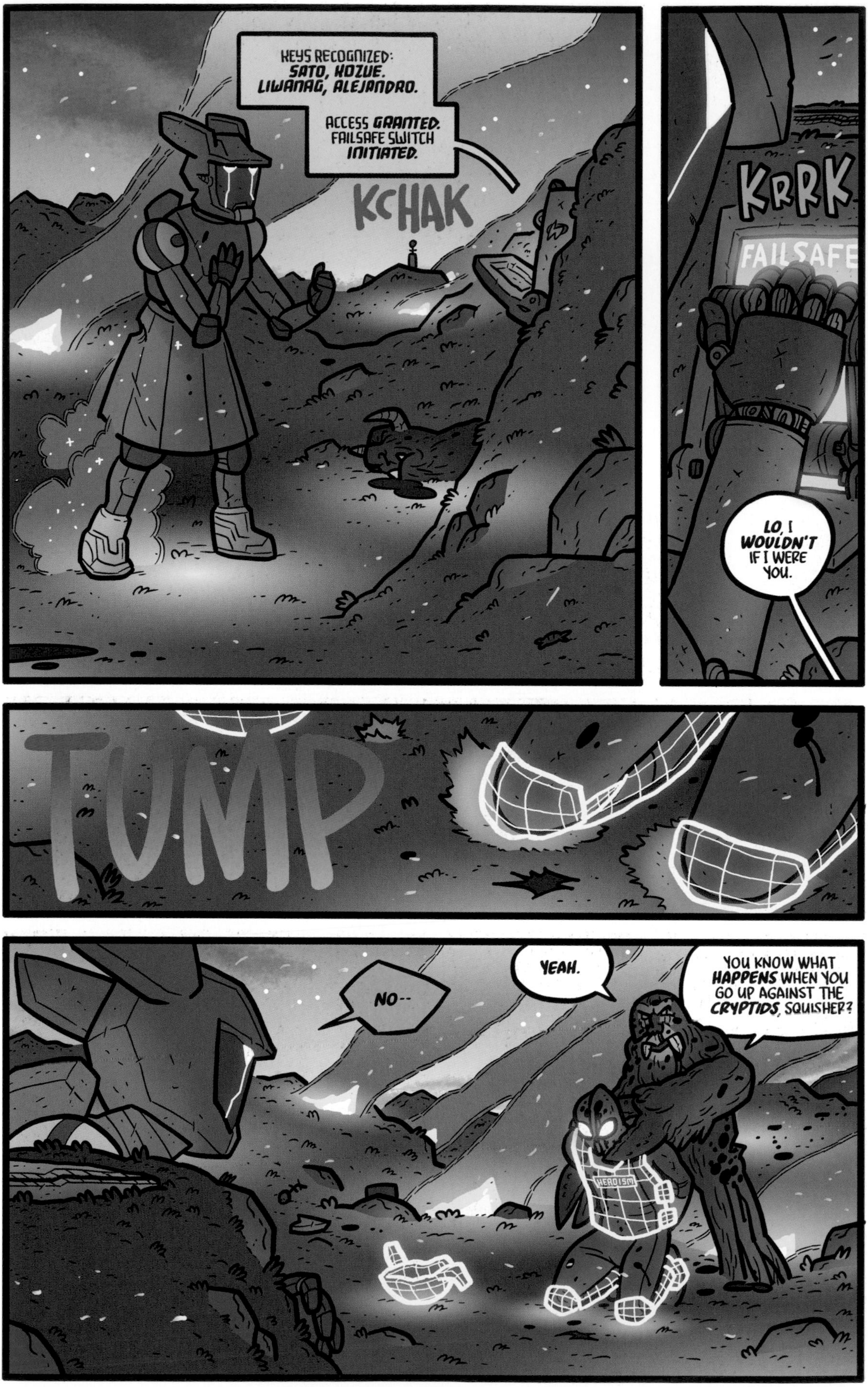
KEYS RECOGNIZED:
SATO, KOZUE.
LIWANAG, ALEJANDRO.
ACCESS GRANTED.
FAILSAFE SWITCH
INITIATED.
KCHAK
KRRK
FAILSAFE
LO, I WOULDN'T IF I WERE YOU.
TUMP
NO--
YEAH.
YOU KNOW WHAT HAPPENS WHEN YOU GO UP AGAINST THE CRYPTIDS, SQUISHER?
HEROISM

THIS.

NO

YEAH, PRETTY SOLDIER, THIS IS WHAT WAS PROMISED.

NO--

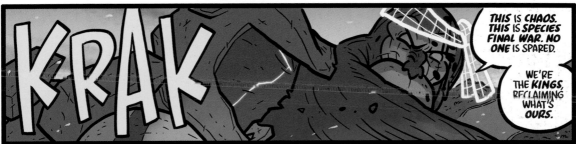

K'RAK

THIS IS CHAOS. THIS IS SPECIES FINAL WAR. NO ONE IS SPARED.

WE'RE THE KINGS, RECLAIMING WHAT'S OURS.

WE WAS NEVER THE BIGGEST GANG, BUT WE TOOK THIS PRISON. WE WIPIN' OUT THE LESSER SPECIES, AND WE MAKIN' YOU ALL PAY.

IT'S A LESSON YOU CAN TAKE TO YOUR COP GRAVE.

HKKK

THEM THAT'LL DO ANYTHING TO WIN?

YOU CAN'T NEVER STAND IN THEIR WAY.

NOW...

KKK

N--NN--

VLAM

143

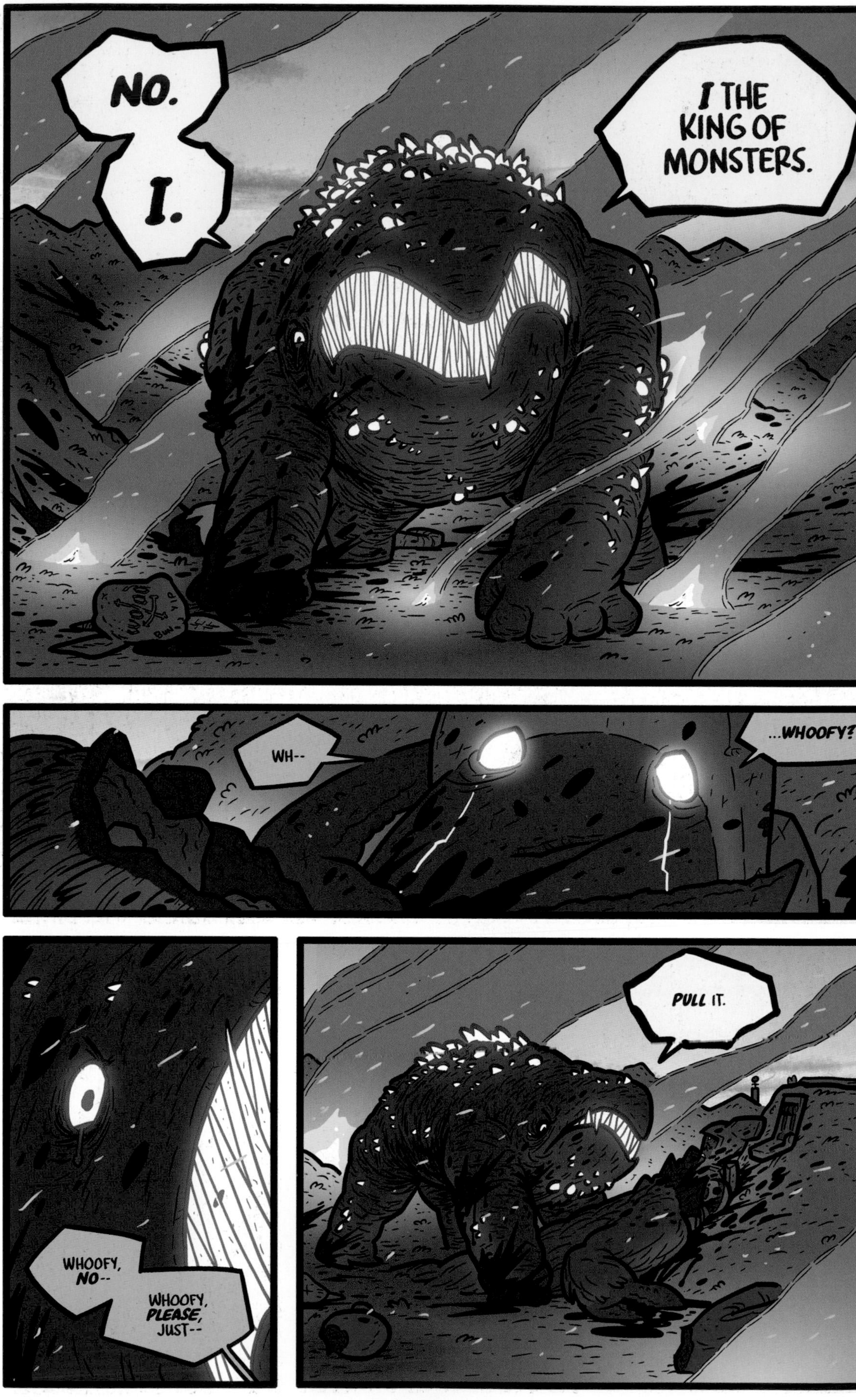
NO.
I.
I THE KING OF MONSTERS.
WH--
...WHOOFY?
WHOOFY, NO--
WHOOFY, PLEASE, JUST--
PULL IT.

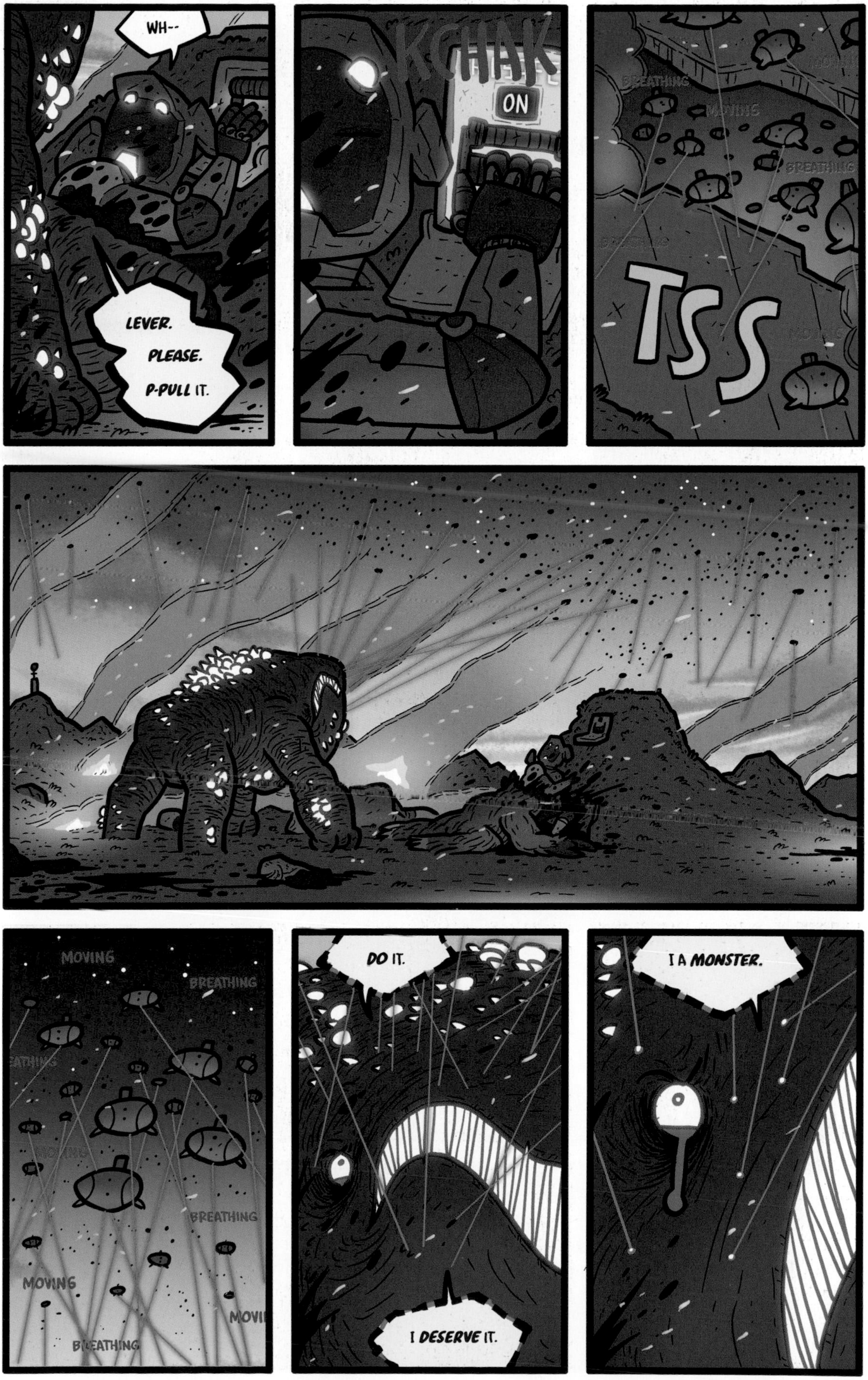
WH--
LEVER.
PLEASE.
P-PULL IT.
KCHAK
ON
BREATHING
MOVING
BREATHING
TSS
MOVING
BREATHING
BREATHING
MOVING
BREATHING
DO IT.
I DESERVE IT.
I A MONSTER.

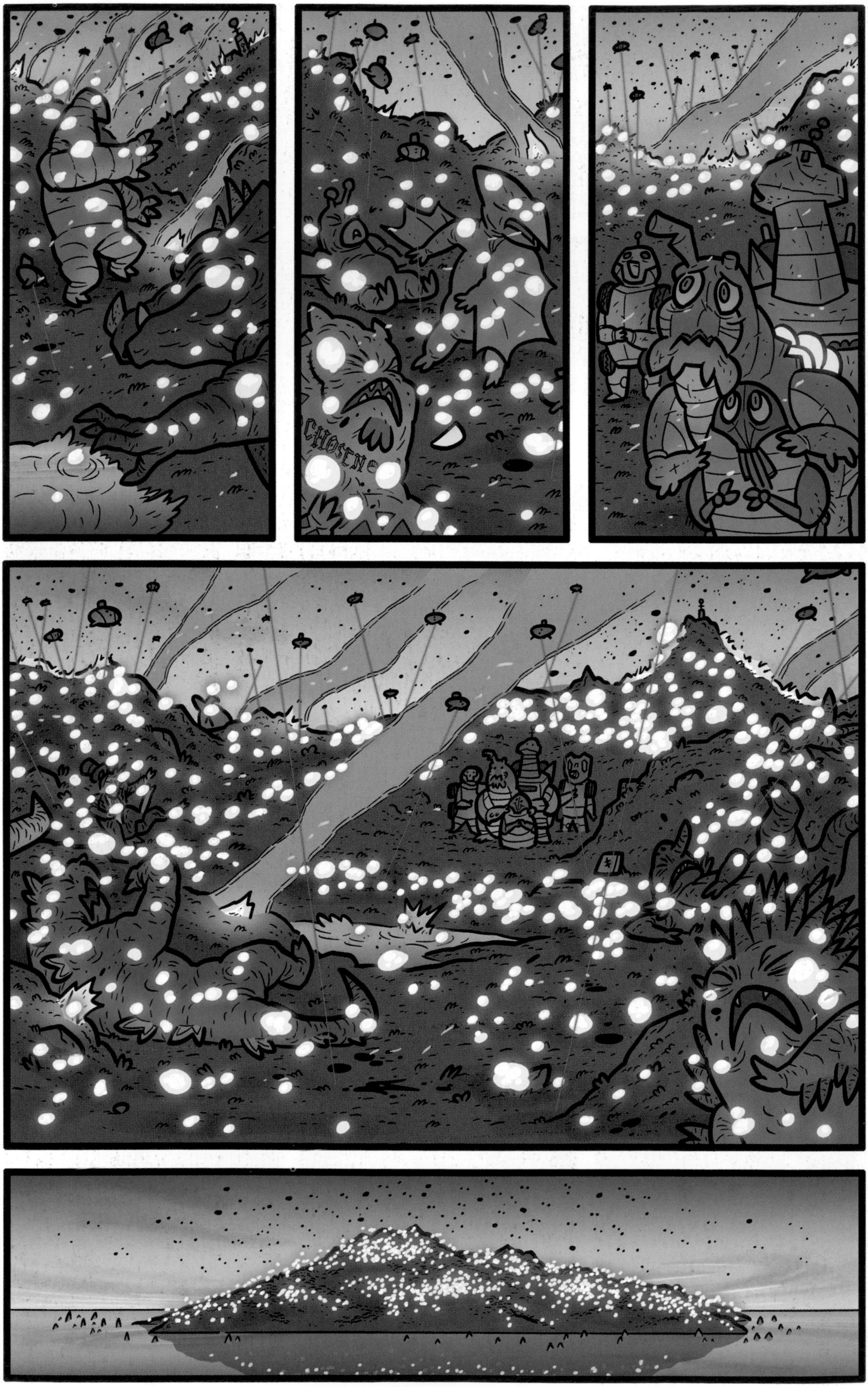
CHOSEN

H-HORLF

H-HELLO?

PLEASE, I-I'M *SICK*.

I-I NEED M-MY *MEDICINE*. I--

P-PLEASE, I-- WH-WHERE IS EVERYBODY?

HELLO INMATE, I AM TEAM H.E.R.O.I.S.M. ROBOT *HEIKO*.

THIS *LOCKDOWN* IS IN RESPONSE TO A *CLASS 4 RIOT*.

PBBBBBBB

KAIJUMAX IS BACK UNDER TEAM HEROISM *CONTROL*, AND WE WILL BE ADDRESSING *INMATE ISSUES* ACCORDING TO THEIR *SEVERITY* AND ORDER *LOGGED*. HERE IS A RECORDED *MESSAGE* FROM INTERIM CHIEF *SATO*:

You pieces of crap get *NOTHING*. I hope you like being in *LOCKDOWN*, because it's all you're gonna *KNOW* for a *LONG-ASS TIME*.

;PBB

THANK YOU AND PLEASE BE *PATIENT*.

WAIT! PLEASE!

WH-WHERE ARE YOU *GOING*??

PLEASE, S-SOMEBODY-- I'M SO *SICK*. I JUST N-NEED A *HIT*.

PBBPB BBBBPP

P-PLEASE. I'VE GOT *NOTHING*!

E-EVEN ALL MY *SHARKS* ARE GONE.

J-JUST NEED A...

..OVER HERE..

?

..OVER HERE..

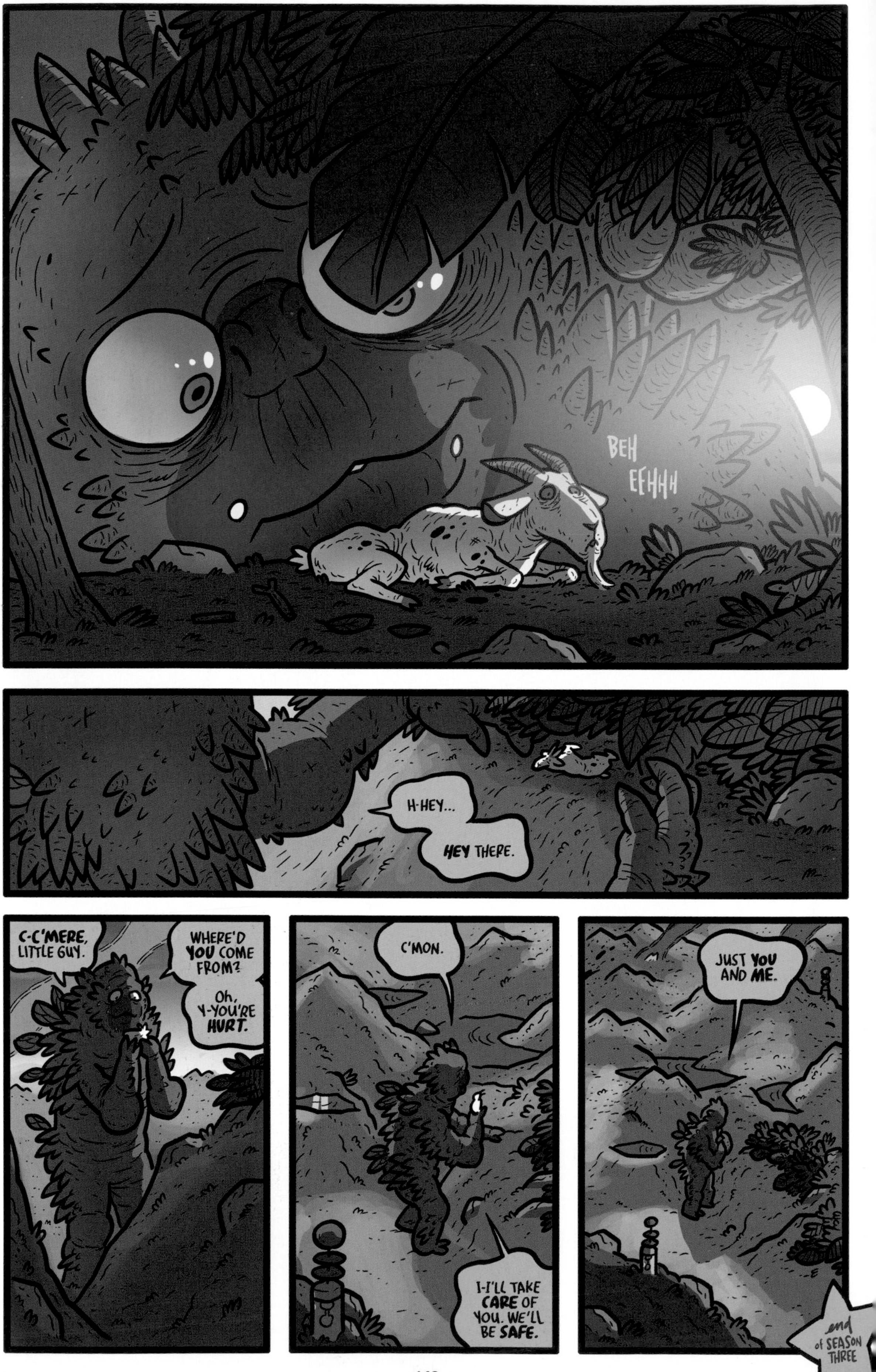
BEH EEHHH
H-HEY...
HEY THERE.
C-C'MERE, LITTLE GUY.
WHERE'D YOU COME FROM?
Oh, Y-YOU'RE HURT.
C'MON.
I-I'LL TAKE CARE OF YOU. WE'LL BE SAFE.
JUST YOU AND ME.
end of SEASON THREE

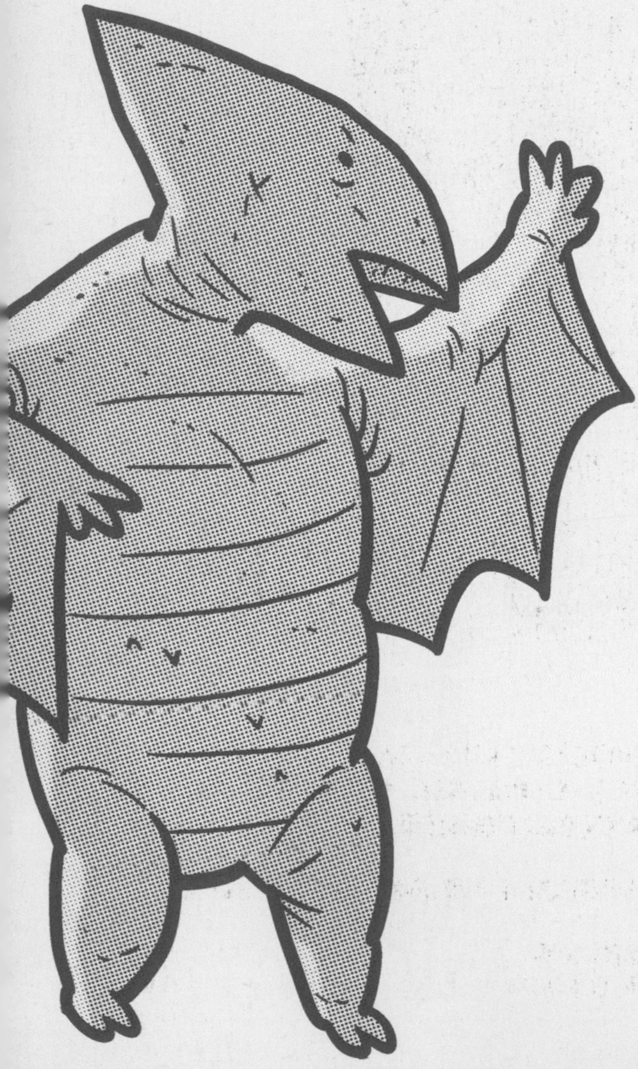

Published by Oni Press, Inc.
Joe Nozemack, founder & chief financial officer
James Lucas Jones, publisher
Charlie Chu, v.p. of creative & business development
Brad Rooks, director of operations
Rachel Reed, marketing manager
Melissa Meszaros, publicity manager
Troy Look, director of design & production
Hilary Thompson, senior graphic designer
Kate Z. Stone, junior graphic designer
Angie Knowles, digital prepress lead
Ari Yarwood, executive editor
Robin Herrera, senior editor
Desiree Wilson, associate editor
Alissa Sallah, administrative assistant
Jung Lee, logistics associate

onipress.com
facebook.com/onipress
twitter.com/onipress
onipress.tumblr.com
instagram.com/onipress

zandercannon.com / @zander_cannon

KAIJUMAX.COM

studiojfish.com / @studiojfish

This volume collects issues #1-6 of the Oni Press series *Kaijumax: Season Three.*

First edition: May 2018

ISBN 978-1-62010-494-1
eISBN 978-1-62010-495-8

KAIJUMAX SEASON THREE: KING OF THE MONSTAS, May 2018. Published by Oni Press, Inc. 1319 SE Martin Luther King Jr. Blvd., Suite 240, Portland, OR 97214.

PRINTED IN CHINA.

Library of Congress Control Number: 2017956255

1 3 5 7 9 10 8 6 4 2

SINCE 1993, *ZANDER CANNON* HAS WRITTEN AND DRAWN COMICS ABOUT GODS, ROBOTS, ASTRONAUTS, POLICE OFFICERS, PALEONTOLOGISTS, ALIENS, FENG SHUI MASTERS, SUPERHEROES, AND MONSTERS.

HE LIVES IN MINNESOTA WITH HIS STRONG WIFE JULIE AND ABOVE-AVERAGE SON JIN.

KAIJUMAX.COM
@ZANDER_CANNON